James Davidson

COURTESANS

&

FISHCAKES

THE CONSUMING PASSIONS OF
CLASSICAL ATHENS

FontanaPress

An Imprint of HarperCollinsPublishers

Fontana Press
An Imprint of HarperCollins*Publishers*
77–85 Fulham Palace Road,
Hammersmith, London W6 8JB

www.harpercollins.co.uk

Published by Fontana Press 1998
7 9 8

First published in Great Britain by
HarperCollins*Publishers* 1997

ISBN 0 00 686343 4

Set in Bembo by
Rowland Phototypesetting Ltd,
Bury St Edmunds, Suffolk

Printed and bound in Great Britain by
Clays Ltd, St Ives plc

COURTESANS AND FISHCAKES

JAMES DAVIDSON lectures in ancient history at the University of Warwick. He was previously Research Fellow of Trinity College, Oxford. *Courtesans and Fishcakes* is his first book.

from the reviews:

'James Davidson shows in this stylish, persuasive, scholarly book how classical Athens relished eating, drinking and copulating . . . It is a serious work, though always seasoned with wit, not only because it puts forward new ideas about big issues in social and cultural history, but also because it has a message for our times, a message unobtrusively but insistently registered.' OLIVER TAPLIN, *Observer*

'Commendably sceptical, *Courtesans and Fishcakes* is a significant contribution to Classical studies and marks an impressive debut. We will hear more from Mr Davidson.' CHRISTOPHER STACE, *Daily Telegraph*

' "Model democracy", or model for sensualists everywhere? Ancient Athens – or at least its ruling class – took pleasure very seriously, and this highly enjoyable study concentrates on the important things in life: food, drink and sex. There are fascinating details here about both prostitution and the hetaeras; some of Davidson's most amusing passages tell of the faux-respectable interpretations put, by prudish scholars, on frankly pornographic vase paintings and verses . . . For all its entertainment value, this is a serious contribution to classical studies.'
Independent on Sunday

'A splendid story . . . Davidson's canvas is vast.'
PETER JONES, *Sunday Telegraph*

'A relaxed interpretation of sensual life in the time of Pericles, Socrates and Plato. *Courtesans and Fishcakes* is about sex, food and drink and the part all three played in developing Athenian identity. Where others have found exploitation and outrage, Davidson is more likely to have found fun. He spars with Foucault and Freud, biographers and bishops, with open glee.' PETER STOTHARD, *The Times*

'James Davidson with skill teases out deeper meanings from ancient literature to provide an absorbing look at society and politics in the world's first democracy. If classical history had been like this at school I might have tasted its joys long before now . . . This book is itself a feast.'
DAVID STAFFORD, *Scotland on Sunday*

'It is fashionable for classicists to lament the passing of their light. They have largely themselves to blame. Obsessed with arid language they continued to sell their vision of eternal oranges and sunshine in a land where people ate apples and it rained a lot. So we lost sight of a world that was vibrantly alive. Books like *Courtesans and Fishcakes* are doing much to turn the tide . . . Davidson does well with his rich material. He has a fine eye for semantics. It is delightful to learn that the language of purest thought has 33 terms for abusing a tax collector – and 52 for praising a king. *Courtesans and Fishcakes* [is full of] good academic work, an excellent reinterpretation. But above all, Davidson brings ancient Athens unforgettably to life.'
ROSS LECKIE, *The Oldie*

'A worldly study of ancient Hellenic appetites concentrating on eating, drinking, sex and politics – but mostly sex. Whether interpreting erotic images on vases, taking us room by room through a 5th century BC brothel, or explaining the various declensions of Athenian prostitutes, Davidson uses accessible yet scholarly prose.'
ANDREW ROBERTS, *Mail on Sunday*

'Excellent, promising, written with biting clarity . . . to my delight, he blows Nietzsche full of holes and blasts Foucault out of the water. We will watch what he undertakes next with the expectation of delight.'
PETER LEVI, *Spectator*

'There's much fascinating information on the relationships in Ancient Greece between men, women, and boys.'
WILLIAM LEITH, *Observer*, Summer Reading

'The motto of the ancient Athenians was "nothing in excess", but they still knew how to enjoy themselves. James Davidson's survey of their eating, drinking and sexual habits reveals a more inventively hedonistic society than previous studies of the period. While conspicuous consumption was taboo in the age of Socrates and Plato, the Athenians still drank vast amounts of wine, adopted a myriad of sexual positions and were as keen on exotic fish dishes as any Nineties foodie.'   *The Week*

'enjoyable . . . a splendid debut'   *Oxford Mail*

'Eating, drinking and sex were the abiding passions of Classical Athens, but have so far been treated as no more than pleasures indulged in by the wealthy. Now James Davidson puts these pleasures in the context of society and politics and comes up with some startling conclusions. If you thought you knew all about the ancient Greeks, be prepared for some surprises.'
Northern Echo

For
D. A. D. and G. H. D.

Contents

Acknowledgements

THIS BOOK HAS BEEN WRITTEN over a period of seven years and has incurred a correspondingly large number of debts. Thanks are owed in the first place to the supervisor of the thesis on which it is based, Oswyn Murray, for his generosity, encouragement, and patience. Daniel Ogden has been a collaborator and a friend for twenty years now, and assisted me at many points in the course of the book's development, providing references and commentary both flattering and acerbic, for which I am grateful. Thanks are also due to the British Academy, St Hugh's College, Oxford, which subsidised the initial stages of research, and to the President and Fellows of Trinity College, Oxford who elected me to a Junior Research Fellowship in 1992, providing time and a spectacular backdrop for my investigations to mature. Emma Dench at Birkbeck College helped to keep me in 1995 and my colleagues at Warwick University have been indulgent while I finished the last leg. Some of the material to be found here has been presented in various papers at various conferences, seminars and job interviews, provoking various responses. Thanks to all those who made comments on each occasion and in those cases where the paper was published, to the respective editors and readers too.

Simon Price, Peter Derow and Roger Brock helped me with my doctoral dissertation. Rosalind Thomas and Robin Lane Fox examined the results. Richard Billows and William Harris at Columbia gave me my academic training. Robin Osborne and Christiane Sourvinou-Inwood encouraged and supported me throughout my time in Oxford. Sitta von Reden first put me on to the importance of the Gift. John Sturrock at the *London Review of Books* and Stuart Proffitt and Philip Gwyn Jones at HarperCollins have tried indirectly and directly to improve my prose and clarity of thinking. Many others have made their own work or time available during the book's preparation, including the late David Lewis, Peter Brown, Catharine Edwards, John Wilkins, François Lissarrague, Shaen Catherwood, Jonathan Walters, Ewen Bowie, Peter Wilson, Nicholas Purcell, Richard Canning, David Harvey, Duncan Kennedy, Uttara Natarajan, Leslie Kurke and Peter

ACKNOWLEDGEMENTS

Garnsey. I would like to take this opportunity to thank them all for their generosity and interest. Most acknowledgements finish by absolving those named from any complicity in the author's errors. Some of those acknowledged here, however, will be reading work that flies in the teeth of their recommendations. This is a symptom of my obduracy rather than scorn.

A debt of a quite different order is owed to my partner Alberto Perez Cedillo and to my parents, to whom I dedicate this book with much love.

List of Illustrations

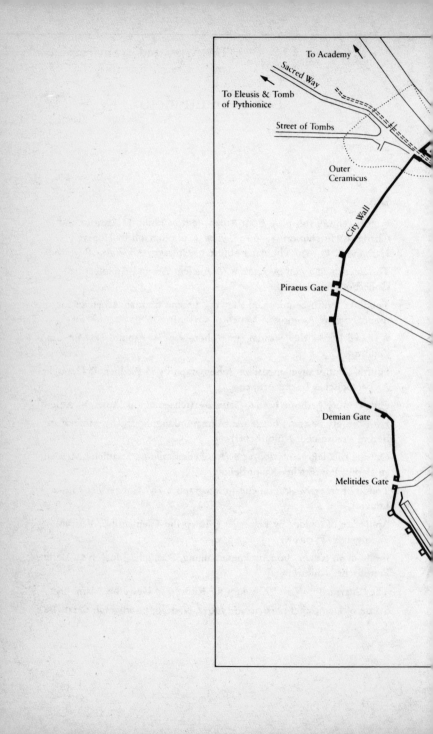

To Academy

Sacred Way

To Eleusis & Tomb
of Pythionice

Street of Tombs

Outer
Ceramicus

City Wall

Piraeus Gate

Demian Gate

Melitides Gate

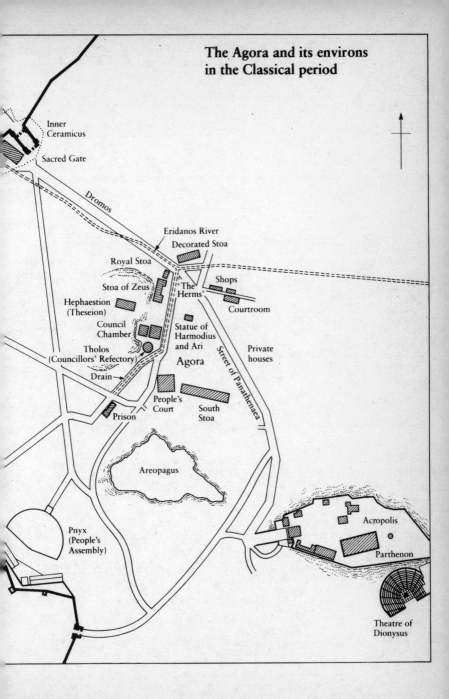

The Agora and its environs in the Classical period

Inner Ceramicus

Sacred Gate

Dromos

Eridanos River

Decorated Stoa

Royal Stoa

Shops

Stoa of Zeus

The Herms

Hephaestion (Theseion)

Courtroom

Council Chamber

Statue of Harmodius and Ari

Tholos (Councillors' Refectory)

Agora

Private houses

Drain

People's Court

South Stoa

Street of Panathenaea

Prison

Areopagus

Acropolis

Pnyx (People's Assembly)

Parthenon

Theatre of Dionysus

Introduction

IN THE COLLECTION of the Vatican Museums is a mosaic signed by one Heraclitus. Across a white background is an even scattering of debris: a wish-bone, a claw, some fruit, various discarded limbs of sea-creatures, the remains of a fish. It is a copy of a famous mosaic by the artist Sosos of Pergamum, called the *Unswept Hall*. Sosos, whom the Roman antiquarian Pliny called 'the most renowned' of all mosaicists, worked in the first half of the second century BCE. He specialized in illusionistic works, trying to turn the unpromising medium of coloured tiles into something lifelike and real. His most famous and remarkable work depicted doves drinking from a birdbath. You could even see their reflections on the surface of the water, says Pliny. A copy was discovered at Hadrian's villa at Tivoli. It is indeed a fine example of what ancient artists were capable of, achieving a very real sense of the basin's three-dimensional form and burnished metallic sheen. What is so remarkable, however, about the *Unswept Hall*, is not its illusionistic ambition, but its objective humility. It is a floor that depicts a floor, closing the gap between art and life. This is most obvious, perhaps, with the white tiles, which have a perfect identity with the white tiles of an unswept floor. More honest than the sipping doves, on one level it really is what it claims to be; it is a trick-floor, impossible to clean.

But the floor is not really the subject at all. The true theme is an unseen banquet, as we can tell from the strewn litter. And this feast still seems to be going on. There was a pause in Greek banquets between the eating part and the drinking part of the meal, when tables were cleared, floors swept, hands washed and perfumes splashed. Sosos' banquet has not quite reached that stage. Moreover, some of the debris casts rather strange shadows as if it is hovering half a millimetre above the ground, as if it has a little way still to fall.

The subject of this book is similar to Sosos' – not the ancient banquet exactly, but the pleasures of the flesh that were indulged there: eating and drinking and sex. These are the consuming passions, three varieties of bodily gratification to which the whole human race, according to Plato, was susceptible from birth. Aristotle described them as animal cravings: hunger, thirst and lust, base and servile urges with their true foundation, contrary to appearances, in the sense of touch. This accounts for the gourmand, he says, who prayed for the throat of a crane so he could enjoy his food for the longest time, as it travelled slowly down. More exactly, this book is about the pleasures of the flesh in classical Athens, because although not all the material I have used falls inside the classical period (479–323 BCE – Before the Common Era) and a little of it is not even pure Athenian, it is Athens and the Athenian democracy that provide the context.

Its material is the scraps that have fallen from the tables of ancient literature, snatches of conversation, anecdotes abruptly curtailed and stories that seem to make no sense: an explorer comes across a savage tribe on the shores of the Persian Gulf who live off bread made from fish and 'fishcakes' for special occasions; the philosopher Socrates visits a beautiful woman who lives in luxury with no visible means of support and refers obliquely to 'her friends'; the guests at a drinking-party imagine they are at sea and throw furniture out of the windows to prevent their boat from capsizing; a politician makes a speech about towers and walls and finds himself accused of prostitution; a tyrant finds a lost ring inside a magnificent fish and thinks he recognizes the work of the gods, but when he tells the King of Egypt he immediately breaks off their friendship; the general Alcibiades drinks wine without water, countless statues of Hermes are vandalized in the night and Athens loses the Peloponnesian War.

One particular table has provided especially rich pickings, Athenaeus' *Dinner-sophists* or *Banquet of Scholars*, composed at the turn of the second century of the Common Era (CE), a long work in the form of a dialogue in the tradition of Plato's *Symposium*. Instead of discussing the meaning of life or the nature of love, however, Athenaeus' guests talk only of the banquet itself, of different kinds of food and wine, of famous courtesans and boastful chefs, of cups and riddles, of a league-table of luxurious nations. They are hardly interested in their own period, concentrating on the world before the Romans arrived, particularly the world of classical Athens which had succumbed to an army of Macedonians five hundred years before. Most importantly, the guests are astonishing pedants, bolstering the most trivial comments with a formidable array of quotations from ancient literature, literature which has now almost entirely disappeared.

Very few scholars are interested in Athenaeus himself and his pernickety banquet, but the scraps from his table provide a unique resource for historians of pleasure. Ancient historians often find themselves relying on only one author for matters of the greatest importance. Thanks to Athenaeus, however, those who wish to know what the Greeks thought of crustaceans, or of various courtesans, or of the proper way to drink wine, can draw on a huge number of authors and a wide range of genres. Of course Athenaeus has his own clear predilections and his selection must not be seen as a representative cross-section of Athenian culture or Athenian literature in general. He draws especially on the comic poets and it is Attic comedy, produced each year at festivals of Dionysus, that provides the basis for much of what we know of Athenian life. Unlike the tragedies which gave up on the present early in the classical period, comedy was very much about the contemporary world and contemporary issues. It often named contemporary politicians and public figures or featured them in its plots, resorting to the world of myths and heroes only in order to parody tragic rivals or to set up incongruous juxtapositions between then and now.

Comedy is not the only source, however, for Athenian pleasures. We also have a large number of speeches covering the period from the late fifth century to the late fourth in the corpus of the 'Attic Orators', the top ten classical rhetoricians, selected by later critics as suitable models for emulation and preservation – plus a few others who managed to slip incognito through the canon's net. Most of these speeches are forensic, attacking enemies in the law-courts or trying to provide a feasible defence. Some are deliberative, speeches on public policy delivered in the Assembly. A few are epideictic, demonstration pieces, designed to show off the speaker's skill. Because of their context they present a very different perspective on pleasure from the festive comedies, emphasizing the dangers that appetite presents to the household and the city and to fellow-citizens; not their own appetites of course, but those of their enemies.

Apart from these sources, there are a large number of miscellaneous works preserved in Athenaeus or independently; treatises and pamphlets on various themes, including one very famous manual of sex and seduction by Philaenis, a classical Kama Sutra, of which, sadly, only the barest scraps survive. There are also a large number of anecdotal works by the likes of Lynceus of Samos and Machon, who collected the witticisms of courtesans and put them in verse. Chief among these anecdotal works, perhaps, is Xenophon's *Memoirs*, in which the philosopher Socrates discourses on various issues of everyday life, advising the author against kissing a handsome boy, and engaging the mysterious beauty, Theodote, in conversation.

It might be thought that such an interesting subject, fundamental as well as sensational, with such a wealth of material to work with, must have been thoroughly investigated long ago, but this is far from being the case. Even now there is considerable resistance to an area of ancient studies which is seen as no more than light relief between papers on more important topics. It is true that this kind of antiquarian/philological research into customs and lifestyles has a rather longer pedigree than other branches of ancient history. Isaac Casaubon, whose notes on Athenaeus first appeared in 1600, can still be useful to modern researchers. On the other hand, since the beginning of the twentieth century, and especially since the Second World War, there has been an astonishing decline in interest in the subject among professional historians. In part their attention has been absorbed by archaeology and inscriptions, which often have a more straightforward relationship to the 'Real World' than fantastical authors such as Aristophanes or unreliable gossips such as Lynceus, and which often carry with them the kudos of new discoveries. Material objects, documents and 'solid facts' carry a kind of mystical objectivity for many historians, constituting what some refer to as the 'meat and potatoes' part of history. In fact, some historians are so distrustful of airy-fairy texts and soufflés like Athenaeus, they would rather not use them at all, trusting only to silent stones, ground-plans and artefacts when conducting their research – as well as large doses of their own (objective) intuition. Ancient history, however, is not so rich in resources that it can afford to ignore any of them. A neglected or misused text is as much a lost artefact as something buried several feet underground.

While scholarly attention has been distracted elsewhere, some extraordinary gaps have been allowed to open up in our knowledge of ancient culture and society. The lack of work on Greek heterosexuality and (until recently and outside France) ancient food are particularly striking. I can only think that prostitutes and courtesans are not considered worthy of women's history or that they have been overlooked in the belief that Greek homosexuality was more significant or important. Even at the end of this research I am left not with a sense of satisfaction that the material is exhausted, but with the realization that much is still preliminary and an anxiety about how much remains to be done. Anyone with time on their hands and a desire to make a substantial contribution to human knowledge will find few more promising areas of investigation than Greek bring-your-own 'contribution-dinners', Attic cakes, the 'second' dessert table, the consumption of game, gambling, perfumes, flower wreaths, hairstyles, horse-racing, pet birds and all the various entertainments of the symposium, including slapstick, stand-up comedy and acrobatics. The only necessary qualification would be a willingness to take these subjects seriously (not too seriously), since they are worth much more than a superficial survey. With the comic fragments recently edited and judiciously annotated by Rudolf Kassel and Colin Austin, there is no longer any excuse.

I mention the general neglect of this area of ancient studies in part to correct a common and rather bizarre misapprehension that sex and other indulgences have received more than their fair share of scholarly attention in recent years and to crave the reader's indulgence for my notes. It has occasionally been necessary to spend time and space establishing some very basic facts which have to be argued for and supported with citations from ancient texts, before going on to the more interesting task of drawing out their implications, suggesting solutions and putting them in context, the main role of the second half of the book. However, those who get impatient with the spade-work can comfort themselves with the thought that they are at the cutting edge of this soft subject.

To be fair, one problem with this kind of research has always been that the evidence is rather slippery and difficult to handle. Historians of the ancient world prefer to work with honest-seeming, authorita-tive sources, such as Thucydides or Polybius who seem to have done their homework properly. Greek comedy, on the other hand, though it was clearly dealing with the real world, was far from straightfor-wardly realistic, as anyone will know who has attended a performance of one of Aristophanes' plays. This means we have to approach comic fragments with caution to see whether they are referring to an everyday situation or some fantastic scenario. If a comic poet talks of a law to stop fishmongers drenching their fish with water to make them look fresher than they really are, do we imagine there really was a law at Athens to that effect, or rather that a law has been passed in the play because of some imaginary crisis (the Clouds boycotting Athens, Zeus on strike, or the goddess Truth taking over the city)? On the other hand, it is often in the most extravagant images that the most powerful insights into Athenian society are found. Aristophanes' *Ecclesiazusae*, for instance, a satire on women seizing power, opens with the ringleader addressing a lamp, the trusty confidante of women's secrets and witness to their adulteries, whose silence alone they trust. Few would consider Athenian women ever seriously con-templated a revolution or that they ever spoke to their lamps. Nor is it likely that they were engaged in endless bouts of sex with forbidden lovers. On the other hand, the address to the lamp throws light on various aspects of Athenian life and culture that can be confirmed from elsewhere: that the sexes were often segregated, that men looked on women as rather mysterious creatures, that the segregation carried an erotic charge, that women had to be extremely careful if they broke the sexual rules, that sexual insubordination and political insubordination could be linked in the imagination and on stage.

Speeches too have their pitfalls. Standards of proof were rather low in Athenian courts and truth was not necessarily placed at a premium. Modern scholars are extremely doubtful that the events are as the orators describe. They suspect orators of inventing laws, lying about their opponents' families and status, lying about their age. One prosecutor positively boasts that he has no evidence for his accusations apart from rumour, whose testimony he praises to the skies. On the other hand, we know that the defendant against whom rumour testified was convicted and although the orators are unreliable witnesses of what went on in Athens, they are excellent witnesses of what was thought convincing. We may not really believe that a man could 'spend an entire estate on affairs with boys' or that the largest fortune in Greece could evaporate because of expensive parties and women, but the Athenians certainly did believe these things and that is interesting in itself.

It will be clear from this that ultimately the subject of this book is not so much the pleasures of the flesh themselves, but what the Greeks, and especially the Athenians, said about them, the way they represented them, the consequences they ascribed to them, the way they thought they worked. Instead of looking at the ancient sources as windows on a world, we can see them as artefacts of that world in their own right. We know that the *Unswept Hall* is not an accurate representation of the floor of a banquet. The randomly scattered rubbish is in fact not random at all, but evenly spaced, and contains a bit of everything without the repetitions and haphazard accumulations we would expect. But even though the picture is 'wrong', it might tell us a lot about the importance of banquets in the ancient world, the nature of realism, the notion of extravagance, of randomness; the artist's 'error' might even give insights into why the lottery was made the linchpin of Athenian democracy. If, to take another example, a particular poet describes a courtesan as whorish, greedy and deceitful, it is rather difficult to decide now whether his assessment was accurate. On the other hand, we know for sure that it is very good evidence for the way courtesans were represented on stage. Alexander the Great may or may not have died from taking a massive swig of wine, but many Greeks said he did, and their ideas about the effects of wine are what concern us.

This kind of investigation is known as the study of discourse, a term popularized by the French philosopher and historian Michel

Foucault. Discourse is more or less the same thing as 'attitudes', if we allow that term its full balletic implications of posturing and plurality. In Greece, above all, where the sophists had made praising gnats, playing devil's advocate and arguing black was white a national sport, it would be dangerous to take our sources as good evidence even for their own views, but what is interesting about Foucault's work is the realization that misrepresentations are just as interesting as representations, and even more useful, when you can identify them, are outrageous lies.

Critias, for instance, a right-wing philosopher and a leader in the oppressive regime imposed on Athens after its defeat in the Peloponnesian War, is almost certainly lying when he says the Spartans drank only water from their mug-like cups. If this was no more than a personal idiosyncrasy we could not draw any broader conclusions, but his little lie is part of a pattern we find in other authors who spend time and effort defending Spartan institutions, their effeminate long hair, their fancy cloaks dyed Tyrian purple. A whole host of other sources, moreover, seem to contradict Critias directly, representing Spartan cups as the kind of cups used for the most degenerate kind of drinking: strong wine, greedy swigs, drinking solely to get drunk as quickly as possible. Critias is clearly participating in a debate defending the Spartan reputation for asceticism in the face of the quite different reputation acquired in Athens by their cups.

These debates over Sparta and over the right way to drink, carried on by many different authors over a long period of time, are like super-discourses, a kind of generalized conversation carried on within Athenian culture, of which Critias' extraordinary defence of Spartan cups is merely a particular exemplar. These ideal and repetitive debates are, for some cultural historians, the real object of historical investigation, and individual texts mere instances.

Historians not only use texts as windows, sometimes they assume that is their purpose too, as if the Greeks wanted to give us a view on the ancient world, to let posterity see what they were like, as if the real audience is not the audience sitting in the law-courts or the theatre, but us. Very occasionally, this view is fair enough. Thucydides wanted to put down the most accurate record of the war he lived through and intended his history to be a 'possession for all time' which includes us, even though he may not have been thinking quite so far ahead. People produce images and texts for all kinds of reasons, for beauty, for art itself, to make a living, to commemorate, to amuse, to create an atmosphere, as therapy and so on. It seems fair to say, however, that in Critias' case it is the debate about Sparta that causes him to put pen to paper. He is intervening in a controversy. He is a propagandist, a pamphleteer. The debate, the problematization of Sparta, or of Spartan cups, comes first. The texts are symptoms of that controversy. This way of looking at our sources leads to some strange conclusions: the more people talk about something, the more contentious that subject was, the less of a consensus there was about it. Far from reflecting the way the Greeks normally spoke, texts are often arguing uphill, insisting on a point of view that few of their contemporaries would share. The text is produced to change minds. By the same argument, the most obvious and unquestioned things may never make it into texts at all. We hear very little, for instance, of how the Greeks ate their food, because it involved a set of banal practices that no one considered worthy of remark. In the case of appetites, we hear much more about dangerous activities than about everyday consumption.

Often, then, what looks like the most promising evidence, addressing a question directly, turns out to be the least trustworthy. When an orator stops in mid-speech to tell his audience the difference between wives, concubines and courtesans, we should be immediately on our guard. When a philosopher provides us with a useful definition of what a gourmand really is, we should resist the temptation to copy it into our dictionaries. Foucault himself seems to have forgotten this useful principle in his own study of sexuality, which is overwhelmingly dependent on philosophical and prescriptive texts which set out to tell him the answers. He seems to have thought that even if these sources were unreliable witnesses of what went on, they were good representatives of Greek concerns with sexuality. They were not. Foucault's study of Greek sexuality has very little on women at all and gives the impression the Greeks were much more interested in boys. Any examination of comic fragments, vase-paintings and Attic oratory, however, shows this impression is quite false, a Platonic mirage. Philosophers are often useful, devoting more space to pleasure and working towards a deeper analysis, but they feature rather less in this book than in other studies of Greek attitudes and when they do appear, some context is sought to measure the angle and spin on what these tricksters are saying.

The shift from using texts as windows to using texts as artefacts in their own right has rescued the study of ancient pleasure from endless arguments about reliability and the 'rhetorical topos' or cliché. Private life has by its nature fewer witnesses than battles and political debates and there are fewer checks on lies and misrepresentations. The discourse of private life on the other hand is eminently public. Much of our evidence comes from central areas of debate, the theatres and law-courts, from the hill of the Pnyx itself where the Athenian Assembly met. The audiences it was supposed to amuse and persuade were numbered in their thousands. Moreover, in this context, statements gain meaning instead of losing it when they are found repeated elsewhere by other authors. Instead of dismissing such things as mere commonplaces that mean nothing apart from the speaker's hostility, admiration or contempt, we can put them together, making connections, working out their mechanisms, illuminating patterns of debate. We can even construct little narratives of pleasure with their own implied beginnings and their own augured ends. We can try to see if our author is relating a casual consensus or casually trying to defend a sticky wicket and, thanks to Athenaeus, the conclusions we draw about what Athenians talked about and wrote about will be more reliable, since the statements have come from many different authors and have been exposed to a wide audience. We know next to nothing about Plato's audience, by contrast, and he may be, and sometimes clearly is, a testament only to his own (very interesting) self.

We can, however, sometimes go too far with discourse and start fetishizing it as a new reality. Foucault and his followers often run into trouble on three counts especially. Although he is interested in ancient debates and not some single 'ancient view', the debate is often conceived too narrowly and rigidly. What the Greeks said about pleasure is much messier and much more varied than what you would expect from Foucault. Secondly, on the basis of this narrow and rigid idea of discourse, human history has been divided into discrete ages (often making sense only in France) or *epistemes* separated by world-shattering intellectual revolutions that open up great chasms in time. Each of these *epistemes* is viewed as a crystal that must be shattered before a new *episteme* is crystallized again in a quite new age. Originally the theory was applied only to the category of knowledge and used to account for a culture's peculiar blind-spots and fantasies. In his later work on sexuality, however, and in the work of his followers, it was applied more generally. Greek civilization, according to this interpretation, is an irretrievably alien culture, constituting a separate sealed world with its own peculiar possibilities for experience. Finally, in fetishizing a culture's representations of the world in this way, Foucault and his followers sometimes seem to forget about the world itself, which is still waving through the window, as if what a culture says is, is, on some important level, as if the Greeks walked around in a virtual reality they had constructed for themselves from discourse.

One very popular theory about the Greeks, for instance, showing the influence of Freud and de Beauvoir as well as Foucault, claims that the Greeks divided the world up into two parts, Them and Us. Us being the adult male citizens who wrote all the texts, Them being the others or Other, slaves, women, barbarians and so on who didn't. Foucault unfortunately incorporated this Manichaean view into his history of sexuality. With Us cast as the penetrators, Them the penetrated. This absurd oversimplification predictably produces very banal self-fulfilling results. That slaves are like women, that women are like slaves, that slaves have automatically lost their phalluses, and are all always metaphorically penetrated by their masters, that everything is whatever the adult male citizen says it is. While it is true that the Greeks often talked about the world in binary terms as polarized extremes, this was simply a way of talking and thinking about things (and not the only way), while the terms of the opposition might change all the time. Sometimes they talk about Greeks versus Persians, sometimes about Persians versus Scythians, and the representation of what the Persians are will be transformed accordingly. Likewise, sometimes they talk about women in terms of an opposition between common prostitutes and wives. In the next sentence, however, the terms of the polarity might have changed. The distinction is now between flute-girls and courtesans, or concubines and hetaeras. This Black and White way of arguing does not reflect a Manichaean view of the world.

There are two main dangers in approaching the Greeks. The first is to think of them as our cousins and to interpret everything in our own terms. We are entering a very different world, very strange and very foreign, a world inconceivably long ago, centuries before Christ or Christianity, a century or so before the first Chinese emperor's model army, a world indeed without our centuries, or weeks or minutes or markings of time. And yet these Greeks will sometimes seem very familiar, very lively, warm and affable. Occasionally we might even get their jokes. We must be careful, however, that we are not being deceived by false friends. Often what seems most familiar, most obvious, most easy to understand is in fact the most peculiar thing of all. On the other hand, we must resist the temptation to push the Greeks further into outer space than is necessary. They are not our cousins, but neither are they our opposites. They are just different, just trying to be themselves.

PART I

FEASTS

I

EATING

THERE WAS A BANQUET and people were talking and, as so often
in accounts of banquets at this period, Socrates was there. The topic was
language: the origin of words and their true meanings, their relationships
with other words. In particular, according to Xenophon, who describes
the scene in his *Memoirs of Socrates*, they were talking about the labels
applied to people according to their behaviour.[1] This was not in itself an
uninteresting subject, but failed nevertheless to absorb Socrates' complete attention. What distracted him was the table-manners of another
guest, a young man who was taking no part in the discussion, too much
engrossed in the food in front of him. Something about the way the
boy was eating fascinated Socrates. He decided to shift the debate in a
new direction: 'And can we say, my friends,' he began, 'for what kind
of behaviour a man is called an *opsophagos*?'

FISH

If Plutarch had been present (and Plutarch would have given anything
to be present had five centuries not intervened) the question might
have been a non-starter. For Plutarch is quite categorical: 'and in
fact, we don't say that those, like Hercules, who love beef are
opsophagoi. . . nor those who, like Plato, love figs, or, like Arcesilaus,
grapes, but those who peel back their ears for the market-bell and
spring up on each occasion around the fish-mongers.'[2] An *opsophagos*,
according to this ancient authority at any rate, was someone with a
distinct predilection for fish.

'But if you go to the prosperous land of Ambracia and happen to see the boar-fish, buy it! Even if it costs its weight in gold, don't leave without it, lest the dread vengeance of the deathless ones breathe down on you; for this fish is the flower of nectar.' The Greeks were fond of fish. Fondness, on second thoughts, is rather too moderate a word for such a passion. What the literature of pleasure manifests, time and time again, is something rather more intense, a craving, a maddening addiction, an indecent obsession. The flavour of this yearning is easily sampled in the work of Archestratus of Gela in Sicily, from whom the eulogy of the boar-fish is taken. Another passage from the same work advises readers on what to do if they come across a Rhodian dog-fish (*émissole*?): 'It could mean your death, but if they won't sell it to you, take it by force . . . afterwards you can submit patiently to your fate.'[3] Archestratus acquired a certain amount of notoriety for his mock-heroic hexameters rhapsodizing food, but his work, variously known as *Gastronomy*, *Dinnerology* or *The Life of Luxury*, was by no means untypical of the discourse of gourmandise. What should be noted is not so much the extravagance of the language used to describe the fish, as the fact that in a work about the pleasures of eating in general, reference is made to almost nothing else. The Greeks, to be sure, recognized as delicacies some foods which had nothing to do with the sea: some birds and other game (especially thrushes and hares), various sausages and offal (sow's womb was particularly revered), some Lydian meat stews and various kinds of cake, but these were exceptions. The edible creatures of the sea seem to have established a dominance over the realm of fine food in classical Greece that scarcely fell short of a monopoly.

It is hard to say who it was who first put the marine into cuisine. The invention of the sumptuous 'modern' style of cookery was usually traced back to the Sicilians or their neighbours across the straits, the people of Sybaris on the instep of Southern Italy. The latter were defeated by their neighbours in 510 and their city was razed to the ground, but stories of their fabulous riches were still being told at Athenian dinner-parties one hundred years later. One historian recorded a Sybaritic law that gave inventors of new dishes a year's copyright (perhaps, says one modern commentator, the earliest patent known). Moreover, he claimed there was a special dispensation that eel-sellers and eel-fishers should pay no tax. In about 572, Smindyrides, distinguished even among the Sybarites for his decadence, had made a great impression when he came over to mainland Greece to seek the hand of the daughter of Cleisthenes the ruler of Sicyon near Corinth. Fearing that the motherland might not be up to his standards, he brought with him one thousand attendants, consisting of fishermen, cooks and fowlers.[4]

Fish also seems to have been very prominent in the culinary culture of Sicily. According to one source they called the sea itself 'sweet' because they so enjoyed the food that came out of it. Athenaeus tells us of a fish-loving painter from Cyzicus, Androcydes, who painted the sweet fare of these sweet waters in enthusiastic and luxurious detail when depicting a scene of the multiheaded monster Scylla in the early fourth century; we should, perhaps, view the numerous ancient mosaics of marine life with the same perspective we now bring to Dutch flower-paintings, not as cerebral studies in realism, but as loving reproductions of desirable and expensive commodities. The comic poet Epicharmus, who worked in Syracuse, the island's greatest and richest city, at the beginning of the fifth century, seems to have been preoccupied with sea-food, judging from the surviving fragments, although later writers were not always sure what he was referring to: 'According to Nicander another kind of crab, the colybdaena, is mentioned by Epicharmus ... under the name "sea-phallus". Heracleides of Syracuse, however, in his *Art of Cookery* claims that what Epicharmus is referring to is, in fact, a shrimp.' In one play, *Earth and Sea*, Epicharmus seems to have included a debate between farmers and fishermen, arguing over which element produced the best fare.

Sicily also produced the first cookbooks. Among the earliest of these treatises was one by Mithaecus of Sicily, a famous chef mentioned by Plato and described by one writer as the Pheidias of the kitchen. His fragments are very few, but do nothing to contradict the impression that fish already predominated by this time: 'Mithaecus mentions wrasse'; Mithaecus advises, 'Cut off the head of the ribbon fish. Wash it and cut into slices. Pour cheese and oil over it' – one of the earliest surviving published recipes.[5]

No cookery books or treatises on gastronomy survive from Athens, and the Athenians' own contribution to the history of gourmandize was confined to their cakes, but Attic comedy, especially the so-called Middle and New Comedy of the fourth and early third centuries, provides plenty of evidence that the preoccupations of the gourmands of Sicily and Southern Italy were fully shared by the citizens of this, the largest and richest classical city. Anyone who picks up a collection of fragments of fourth-century comedy is likely to be struck immediately by the large number of references to the consumption of fish. Characters regularly turn aside to enunciate long and metrically elaborate shopping-lists for fish, menus of fish and recipes for fish-dishes, with the ingredients and method of preparation graphically described. One comic chef, for example, in Philemon's *Soldier*, describes a simple recipe in the following rodomontade:

> For a yearning stole up on me to go forth and tell the world, and not only the world but the heavens too, how I prepared the dish — By Athena, how sweet it is to get it right every time — What a fish it was I had tender before me! What a dish I made of it! Not drugged senseless with cheeses, nor window-boxed with dandifying herbs, it emerged from the oven as naked as the day it was born. So tender, so soft was the fire I invested in the cooking of it. You wouldn't believe the result. It was just like when a chicken gets hold of something bigger than she can swallow and runs around in a circle, unable to let it out of her sight, determined to get it down, while the other chickens chase after her. It was just the same: the first man among them to discover the delights of the dish leapt up and fled taking the platter with him for a lap of the circuit, the others hot on his heels. I allowed myself a shriek of joy, as some snatched at something, some snatched at everything and others snatched at nothing at all. And yet I had merely taken into my care some mud-eating river-fish. If I had got hold of something more exceptional, a 'little grey' from Attica, say, or a boar-fish from [Amphilochian] Argos, or from dear old Sicyon the fish that Poseidon carries to the gods in heaven, a conger-eel, then everyone would have attained to a state of divinity. I have discovered the secret of eternal life; men already dead I make to walk again, once they but smell it in their nostrils.

Outside comedy, references to fish-consumption are somewhat fewer in number, but often present even more direct and striking testimony to the citizens' obsessions. Demosthenes notes in disgust that when Philocrates betrayed his city to the Macedonians for the price of a bribe he spent his ill-gotten gains on whores and fish. Aeschines attacking his opponent Timarchus with the aim of depriving him of his rights as a citizen recalls the many occasions he was seen hanging around the fish-stall with his 'friend' Hegesander.[6]

The Greeks were not so blinded by love as to ignore the responsibilities of connoisseurship. Within the exalted ranks of the piscifauna, distinct hierarchies were recognized, if not always with universal agreement. The preserved fish or *tarichos*, for instance, was generally looked down on and the phrase 'cheaper than salt-fish' is used by Aristophanes to mean 'ten a penny'. Certain varieties did have their supporters; tuna bottled at the right season in steaks or chunks received much praise, and Archestratus had some nice things to say about salted mackerel. Euthydemus, a writer on diet of the Hellenistic period, even wrote a treatise on the subject although the encomium of salt-fish, which he ascribed to Hesiod and quoted in support of his cause, was strongly suspected of being a forgery.[7]

Among the fresh fish, the bottom rung was occupied by various small species and immature specimens, not always easily translatable into the taxonomies of modern biology. A fragment of Timocles' comedy, *Epichairekakos* (*He Who Enjoys Other Men's Difficulties*), follows the gate-crasher known as Lark in the, for him, rather novel exercise of shopping. He comes to the eels, the tuna, the electric rays, the crayfish, and asks the price of each in turn. They are all far beyond the range of the four bronze coins he is carrying. Finally realizing he is outclassed he scuttles off in the direction of the *membradas*, the anchovies or sprats. Another parasite in Alexis' *Principal Dancer* complains of the hard work involved in cadging an invitation to a fancy dinner; he would prefer to share a plate of sprats with someone who can talk in plain Attic. Other passages confirm that in Athens, at least, these little fish were considered food fit only for beggars, freedmen, and peasants who didn't know any better, attitudes that the sprats-seller in Aristophanes' *Wasps* attacks vigorously, accusing those who disdain her wares of elitism.[8]

At the other end of the scale we find the great delicacies, among them the tuna, the sea-perch or grouper, the conger-eel, grey mullet, red mullet, gilt-head, sea-bass, an unidentified creature known as the 'grey-fish', or *glaukos*, and the crustacean known as the *karabos*, a heavy-handed crayfish lying somewhere along the line between langouste and langoustine. Certain parts were especially prized: of the tuna, the belly and the 'keys' taken from the shoulder or neck area, and of sea bass, grey-fish and conger-eels, the head. Towering effortlessly above all challengers, however, the undisputed master of the fishmonger's stall was the eel. Archestratus thought the best were those caught opposite the straits of Messina:

> There you have the advantage over all the rest of us mortals, citizen of Messina, as you put such fare to your lips. The eels of the Strymon river, on the other hand, and those of lake Copais have a formidable reputation for excellence thanks to their large size and wondrous girth. All in all I think the eel rules over everything else at the feast and commands the field of pleasure, despite being the only fish with no backbone.

It was widely believed that the Egyptians offered the eel worship, handing more than one comic author the opportunity for resonant cultural comparisons: 'I would never be able to make an alliance with you; there is no common ground for our manners and customs to share, and great differences to separate them. You bow down before the cow, I sacrifice her to the gods. The eel you consider the greatest divinity, and we the very greatest dish.' Another thought the Egyptians had got it just about right: 'They say the Egyptians are clever, not least because they recognize that the eel is equal to the gods; in fact she has a much higher value than gods, since to gain access to them we just have to pray, whereas to get within sniffing distance of eels we have to pay at least a dozen drachmas, maybe more, so absolutely sacred a creature is she.'[9]

Reading these fragments we can get some idea of the extraordinary power their passion for fish exercised over the Athenians. Fish are treated as quite irresistible, lusted after with a desire that comes close to a sexual one. The strength of this Athenian appetite is demonstrated most graphically by passages in which fish are involved in a literal or metaphorical seduction. Anaxandrides' play *Odysseus*, for instance, contains the following eulogy of the fisherman's art:

> What other craft gets youthful lips burning, gets their fingers fumbling, has their lungs gasping for air, in their haste to swallow? And isn't it only when it's well-supplied with fish that the agora brings about liaisons? For what mortal gets a dinner-date if all he finds for sale when he gets to the counter are fish-fingers, crow-fish, or a picarel? And when it comes to seducing a real beauty, with what magic words, with what chat-up lines would you overcome his defences if you take away the fisherman's art? For his is the craft that conquers with stargazy pie's overwhelming eyes, that draws up lunch's (arsenal?) to undermine the defences corporal(?), his, the expertise that gets the free-loader to recline, unable to decline to pay his way.

The anecdotalist Lynceus of Samos even suggested, a little mischievously, that it was for the sake of a fish from Rhodes (the famous dogfish, of course) that the Athenian hero Theseus yielded his favours to Tlepolemus, the island's mythical founding father. In a later period there is evidence that the influence exercised by fish in the processes of seduction was thought to reveal some occult power. Apuleius, author of the *Golden Ass*, had to defend himself from a charge of casting a love-spell over his rich and aged wife with the magical assistance of fish purchased in the market. There is little evidence for this supernatural connection in the classical period, although because of her triple-sounding name, the red-mullet, or *trigle*, was associated with the triple-faced patron of witches and guardian of road junctions, Hecate. On the other hand, fish are sometimes found used as love-gifts in Attic vase-painting. One depicts a young man and his attendant approaching a hetaera spinning wool, with gifts of an octopus and two birds. Another vase, once in Leningrad, now lost, had a boy seated and wrapped in a cloak being offered a hoop and a large fish by a winged Cupid.[10]

It is not just their tastiness that connects fish to seduction, but also the way they look. The two sisters popularly known as the 'anchovies' mentioned in a speech of Hyperides were apparently so named because of their 'pale complexions, slender figures and large eyes'.

And so, by way of a startling metaphorical transition from appetizement to seduction, fish come to be represented themselves as coquettish flirts and paramours. The conflation of images is found fully developed in a fragment of Diphilus' comedy *The Merchant*. The speaker complains about the high price asked for the fish: 'nevertheless, if one of them ever smiled at me, I would pay, albeit with a groan, all that the fishmonger asked of me.' This representation, which sounds so extraordinary to our ears, of fish as seductive bodies comparable in some way to the beautiful boys and hetaeras they helped to seduce, is what lies behind the common trope in which the eel, typically 'appareled' in beet (perhaps, most feasibly, beet-leaves), is compared to a nubile woman or a gorgeous goddess. When Dicaeopolis, the hero of Aristophanes' *Acharnians*, learns that the Boeotian smuggler has fifty 'Copaic maidens' in his sack, he goes into raptures: 'O my sweetest, my long-awaited desire.' In the *Peace*, someone imagines the reaction of Melanthius, a certain fish-loving tragedian, arriving at the fish-stalls too late for the eels: 'Woe is me, woe is me,' he cries, launching into a spoof soliloquy excerpted from a climactic scene of his own *Medea*, 'bereaved of my darling in beet-bed confined.' It could be suggested that such extraordinary metaphors are only to be expected in comic discourse, with its fondness for startling and jarring images, but the practice of comparing women to mouth-watering fish and fish to women seems to have been rather more general in Athenian society. Apart from the anchovy sisters mentioned above, we find flute-girls and hetaeras given nicknames like 'Sand-smelt', 'Red Mullet' and 'Cuttlefish', a practice exploited to full comic effect by the poet Antiphanes in his play *She Goes Fishing*, where he plays on this double-meaning of the names of fish, so that it is hard to know at any one time whether he is satirizing his victims for their love of fish or for their excessive devotion to hetaeras and boys.[11]

Fish seduces and conquers. It functions like the forces of persuasion, or the allure of a hetaera, or the magical power of charms. Comic authors made use of this notion of piscine irresistibility to create spoof imprecations and oaths. In Aristophanes' *Knights* the Sausage-seller curses the Paphlagonian (a thinly disguised caricature of the demagogue Cleon), his rival for the favours of old Demos (i.e. the people), in the following terms:

> I will not make threats, but I do offer the following prayer: May your sizzling skillet of squid be standing by. And may you be about to make a speech on the Milesian business and turn a talent in bribes if you get the job done. And may you hurry to get the calamary down in time for going to the Assembly. And may the man come for you before you have time to eat. And, in your eagerness to get the talent, may you choke to death with your mouth full.

In his *Acharnians* a similar malediction is invoked against a rival playwright; this time the longed-for squid is pictured sailing slowly and tantalizingly towards the accursed and putting ashore on the table beside him only to be snatched away at the last minute by a dog. Antiphanes even uses the irresistibility of fish to a fish-lover in an oath: 'I'd as soon give up my purpose as Callimedon would give up the head of a grey-fish', says one character in resolute defiance. It is perhaps not surprising that the Stoic Chrysippus, writing in the following century, preferred to refer to such people as *opsomanes* instead of *opsophagos*, meaning 'fish-mad', and comparing the man so afflicted to the *gunaikomanes*, mad about girls.[12]

THE FISH MISSING FROM HOMER

Historians are sometimes criticized for taking in earnest what their sources clearly meant in joke. Others are accused of deliberately exaggerating, without explaining, a period's idiosyncrasies in order to exoticize a culture for the reader's amusement. Any study of the phenomenon of ancient fish-madness is in danger of committing both these errors at the same time. These writers are being ironic. The extraordinary celebrations of fish penned by Archestratus or put by Aristophanes into the mouth of Melanthius are manifestly tongue-in-cheek. Demosthenes was sending up Philocrates and his treacherous purchases, Aristophanes was sending up the tragic fish-lover, and Archestratus, with his epic hexameters and mock epithets, was sending up himself. Any amusement we might feel at the ancients' excitement at the prospect of fish for dinner is forestalled by the irony and bathos which is already a distinctive feature of the Greek evidence. It's almost as if they catch the amused eye of posterity in the rear-view mirror and play to it, as if they know how peculiar they are going to look to future generations.

It is true that the Greeks considered self-knowledge one of the very highest virtues, but that kind of foresight was beyond even them. So why is fish as strange and amusing for them as it is for us? This is more than a marginal question. Their ironic tone holds a clue to unravelling the mystery of fish-madness. What made fish funny for the Greeks goes some way towards explaining what made them so good to eat.

The first thing to notice is that fish never found its way into the rituals that surrounded the consumption of beef, mutton and pork. With one or two exceptions, fish was not considered a suitable animal for sacrifice. The origins of this exclusion are open to debate. Some believe it was because Greek sacrifice was essentially a blood sacrifice, or a sacrifice of large animals that must be eaten communally. The tuna, one of the few fish that could be sacrificed (to Poseidon, of course) is noted both for its exceptional bloodiness, and for the fact that these large fish are usually trapped and killed in large numbers, providing a single huge catch for the community to consume. Others emphasize that the Greeks sacrificed only domestic animals, and that fish are to be counted among the animals of the chase, wild game that could be killed willy-nilly, outside the symbolic rigours of formal sacrifice. However, the rationale behind the exclusion does not really concern us. What is important is that the omission of fish helped to construct an opposition between the meat of pigs, sheep and cattle, all of which had to be sacrificed before it could be eaten, and fish, which was quite free of such structures, an item for private, secular consumption, as and when desired. In an important sense, fish-consumption was simply not taken as seriously as other kinds of carnivorousness.

Fish were also absent from another important scene, noted by a character in a comedy of Eubulus: 'Where has Homer ever spoken of any Achaean eating fish?' Fish were not present at the banquets of the *Iliad*, something the fish-mad Greeks of the classical period were not slow to pick up on. A contemporary of Eubulus, the philosopher Plato, thought the missing fish very significant. In a discussion of the regime appropriate for the warrior athletes of his *Republic* he takes Homer as his reference:

'You know that when his heroes are campaigning he doesn't give them fish to feast on, even though they are by the sea in the Hellespont, nor boiled meat either. Instead he gives them only roasted meat, which is the kind most easily available to soldiers, for it's easier nearly everywhere to use fire alone than to carry pots and pans . . . [The philosopher goes on to make other connections:] Nor, I believe, does Homer mention sauces anywhere. Indeed, aren't even the other athletes aware that if one's body is to be kept in good condition, one must abstain from all such things?'

'Yes and they do well to be aware of it and to abstain from them.'

'If you think that,' Socrates continues, 'then it seems you don't approve of Syracusan cuisine, or Sicilian-style dishes.'

'I do not.'

'Then you also object to Corinthian girls for men who are to be in good physical condition . . . and Attic pastries . . . I believe that we would be right to compare this diet . . . to the kinds of lyric odes and songs that are composed in all sorts of modes and rhythms.'[13]

The modern banquet with its cakes and hetaeras is contrasted with the heroic feasts of the *Iliad*. The conspicuous absence of fish from these antique scenes and from sacrifice as well is perhaps connected, inasmuch as the sacrificial rituals of the classical period were often self-consciously based on the Homeric model. Put together, the structures of exclusion carve out a space for fish as something peculiarly secular and distinctively, decadently 'modern'.

It is this absence of heroic gravity that produces the bathetic humour and mock epic irony of the classical period. The caricature and self-parody which seems to infect descriptions of fish-lovers and fish-loving has an eye not on our future, but on their past, looking back across the gap that yawns between the Homeric age and the classical present. The eulogies of fish in epic language and hexameter rhythms, which are such a feature of Middle Comedy and writers such as Archestratus and Matro, get their sense of *bathos* from a clash of tone between the heroic form and the fishy content.[14] The very names of fish were unheroic and their presence in these inappropriate contexts was unavoidably ironic. The effect must have been in some respects like a recitation of modern brand-names, Daz and Persil, for instance, or Weetabix and Coca-Cola in the language and rhythms of Shakespeare. In particular, comic poets seem to have kept in mind the juxtaposition of comedy and tragedy in the dramatic festivals, the one placed firmly in the modern world, the other confining itself to the age of myth. It is no coincidence, perhaps, that fourth-century comedy is characterized both by its spoofs of mythological tales and its preoccupation with fish. By parodying tragic forms, by setting up a heroic context and then infiltrating it with incongruous and anachronistic images from the modern city, comic poets gave resonance to their representation of the present, a greater consciousness of being contemporary. It is not too much to say that fish in these comedies and parodies contributes significantly to one of the earliest manifestations of the idea of the modern, the contemporary, in Western intellectual history, an appropriate achievement perhaps for a food that in hot countries scarcely lasts a day.

The rule that excludes fish from sacrificial offerings to the gods is often transgressed for comic effect in a very similar way. One play has a chef whose conger-eel is described as cooked fit for the gods, the poet fully aware that no deity was likely to get near such a delicacy. Another talks of 'the belly-piece of a tunny, or the head of a sea-bass, or a conger-eel, or cuttle-fishes, which I fancy not even the gods despise.' These passages exalt the fish they refer to, but also denaturalize sacrifice, reinventing the gods as gourmands and connoisseurs in the modern style. An early play of Menander's discusses the consequences of exclusion quite explicitly:

Well then, our fortunes correspond, don't they, to the sacrifices we are prepared to perform? At any rate, for the gods, on the one hand, I bring an offering of a little sheep I was happy to pay ten drachmas for. For flute-girls, however, and perfume and girls who play the harp, for wines of Mende and Thasos, for eels, cheese and honey, the cost scarcely falls short of a talent; you see, you get out what you put in, and that means ten drachmas' worth of benefit for the sheep, if, that is, the sacrifice is auspicious, and you set off against the girls and

> wine and everything, a talent's worth of damages . . . At any rate if I
> were a god, I would never have allowed anyone to put the entrails on
> the altar unless he sacrificed the eel at the same time.

Here the eel represents 'real' food, some fish for pleasure's sake, instead of a wretched and perfunctory sheep for ritual's sake. Forget all of that smoking essence of cow and goat, the gods would much rather tuck into a plate of sea-food.[15]

The fact that fish was not sacrificed had more than symbolic repercussions. Ritual made a very real difference to the way animals were made into food. A crucial element in the sacrifice was the sharing out of the victim among the participants. The division had to be conspicuously fair, and to this end, after the animal had been disembowelled, and the gods and the priest had received their prerogatives, the animal was simply divided into portions of more or less equal size. This marks a substantial divergence from the way animals are butchered today, with very careful differentiation of the cuts according to relative tenderness, sliced along or against the grain. In terms of quality, therefore, the ancient portions of meat were both uneven and unequal, some mostly fat and bone, some largely fillet and rump, and had to be distributed among the sacrificing community by drawing lots to ensure everyone at least got an equal chance at a good piece. It seems probable that, as in many Middle Eastern cultures, all beef, pork and mutton available was the product of this ritualized process. Even the meat sold in the market, it seems, had been cut from animals that had been killed ritually. As a student of ancient butchery puts it: 'The perpetuation of a method of butchering that maintained a careless disregard for the animal's different joints meant for the eventual purchaser the possibility of making only one choice, meat (*to kreas*), or offal: we never get to see in our sources people presenting themselves at the market and asking for a gigot or a cutlet.'[16] The ideology of sacrifice, therefore, and the isometric butchery which resulted, meant that the very form these animals assumed as items of food was dominated by their positioning within symbolic ritual, a positioning that tended to exclude concerns of taste or tenderness in favour of a theatre of participation, where equality took precedence over quality. Fish, on the other hand, along with game and offal, fell outside the rituals of sharing. It was free to be appreciated according to the excellence of its own flavours. Pleasure alone sorted out the most highly regarded species, the finest specimens, the most succulent parts, selected on their own terms according to the *opsophagos*' taste. With other meat protected from gourmandise by religious rituals, it was the taxonomy, the biology and the body of fish that became subject to the exacting discourse of connoisseurship. Other meat had to be shared out. Fish you were free to fall in love with, grabbing the best bits for yourself. Here in this very small section of the Athenian economy in the fifth and fourth centuries BCE, we have what looks like a fully-fledged system of consumer objects.

In the Hellenistic period some Homeric scholars, the so-called 'separators', noted that although fish were indeed off the menu at the *Iliad*'s banquets, there were some occasions when they were eaten in the *Odyssey*. This seemed decisive proof that the two epics had different authors. Against this view, the scholar Aristarchus observed that, though he may have banned fishing and fish-eating from Troy, the author of the *Iliad* was not unaware of the existence of fishermen, or of the technologies of fishing, and used the imagery of angling and trawling in similes and metaphors.[17] This meant on the one hand that the two poems could indeed have a single author and, on the other hand, that there must be some reason other than ignorance for the exclusion of fishing from the *Iliad*, namely that the poet wanted to avoid *to mikroprepes*, what was demeaning – the same reason he remained silent about vegetables.

But in that case how to explain the fact that fishing and fish-eating did occur in the *Odyssey*? This, argued Aristarchus, was only to be found in exceptional circumstances, when the heroes were suffering from extreme hunger, for instance. The episode when Odysseus and his companions disembark on the island where the Sun-god kept his cattle, having just survived the ordeal of Scylla and Charybdis, provided just such circumstances: 'all the food in the ship was gone and they were forced instead to go roaming in search of prey, using bent hooks to catch fish and birds, anything that might come to hand, because hunger gnawed their bellies.' From passages such as these it seems clear that in the Homeric world, as in medieval and early modern Europe, fish could be considered a poor man's food, a food for Lent and Friday fasting.[18] It was clearly not fitting for heroes of the calibre of Achilles and Diomedes to be seen eating such poor fare, unless the poet wanted to show them pushed to extremes of deprivation. Greeks of later generations, however, whose view of fish was, as we have seen, much more exalted, misunderstood the significance and saw the absence in quite different terms. Athenaeus, for instance, thought Homer was protecting his heroes not from the diet of paupers, but from luxury: the poet is silent about the eating of vegetables, fish and birds because that is a mark of gourmandise [*lichneia*].'

When Plato discusses the absence of fish in Homer, therefore, he probably gets it quite wrong, placing the omission in the context of the exclusion of hetaeras, fancy cakes and Sicilian cuisine, the decadent and debilitating accoutrements of the classical dinner-party. In fact, we could say that fish would have been rather an appropriate source of protein for the inhabitants of the simple proto-city outlined by Socrates, a providential food, as in the *Odyssey*, found in rivers and along shorelines to go with the collard greens and acorns he allows them. Between Homer and Plato a huge shift had occurred in perceptions of what a diet of fish represented. It had shifted from the country to the city, from something scavenged to something bought.

The feasts of the Homeric world take place in an economy without money, an economy based on the exchange of gifts and its attendant systems of patronage. Sacrifice is also decidedly part of this giving economy, and sacrificial meat is often conceived as a gift of the city or of the private citizen on whose behalf the sacrifice is made, a gift designed to extract favours from the gods, and to unite the participants in the act of eating together. Reciprocity meant an obligation to sacrifice, which few could ignore. Even the Pythagoreans, who were famous for their vegetarianism, felt the need to participate in sacrifice occasionally to avoid a charge of disrespect. Eating meat was a religious duty, and ultimately indispensable. Fish on the other hand was an extra, something that could not be justified on grounds other than a sheer love of pleasure. Ancient vegetarians in this respect display a striking contrast with their modern counterparts who are often more ready to eat fish than any other animal. In both cases it is perhaps the relative bloodlessness of the piscifauna that is the deciding factor.[19]

Meat did find its way occasionally from the altar to the market but it is only represented there on very rare occasions. Its potential as a consumer item was heavily limited, as we have seen, by the isometric techniques of butchery demanded by ritual. Fish, on the other hand, is the quintessential commodity. The agora is its element. It is even on occasion compared to money. The silver that comes to Athens from its allies is described in one image of Aristophanes as a shoal of tuna spied swimming from far out at sea. In comedies, jokes are made comparing fish-scales with the small change that Athenians carried in their mouths. As a corollary, fishermen, who are often represented as stereotypes of extreme poverty in the ancient world, are, with a few exceptions, quite invisible in the Athenian discourse of fish-madness, victims of the extraordinary fetishization of their products. Instead the focus is consistently and repetitively on the market-place and on the processes of buying and selling. A particular feature of this concern is the caricaturing of greedy fishmongers, often foreigners, and their attempts to trick the citizen-consumer. A typical example is from Antiphanes' play the *Pro-Theban*: 'Is it not strange, that if someone happens to be selling fish recently deceased, he addresses us with a devilish scowl and knotted brow, but if they are quite past their sell-by date, he laughs and jokes? It should be the other way round. In the first case the seller should laugh, and in the second go to the devil.' Another fragment from Xenarchus' *Porphura* (*Mauve* or *The Purple-fish*) includes a character praising fishmongers as more imaginative even than poets when it comes to inventing ways to get round a (probably fictional) law:

For since they are no longer at liberty to anoint their wares with water (this is forbidden by the law), one of these chaps, not exactly loved by the gods, when he saw his fish dehydrating, quite deliberately started a fair old scrap among the traders. Punches were thrown and one seemed to have mortally wounded him. Down he goes, gasping what seems to be his last gasp, lying prone amongst his fish. Someone shouts 'Water! Water! Straightaway, another of his fellow-traders grabs a jug and empties it, missing him almost completely, but managing to drench the fish. You would say they had just been caught.

Such were the perils of shopping that the early Hellenistic writer Lynceus of Samos actually wrote a treatise on how to do it properly, addressed to one of his friends who was a market failure. He advises taking along a copy of Archestratus to intimidate the traders:

> One thing you will find useful, when standing at the fish-stalls face to face with the unblinking ones, the unyielding-on-price ones, is abuse. Call Archestratus to the stand, the author of the *Life of Luxury*, or another one of the poets and read out a line, 'the shore-hugging striped bream is an awful fish, worthy ever of nought' and try the line 'bonito buy when autumn wanes', but now alas 'tis spring, and in summer 'the grey-mullet is wonderful when winter has arrived', and many other lines of that sort. For you will scare off shoppers by the score and many passersby, and in so doing you will force him to accept a price you think is right.[20]

The fishmongers in question belonged to a characteristically urban environment of crafty charlatans and tricksy merchants, for one consequence of the placing of fish in a trade-economy was that it came to be seen as part of the world of the city. If fish do ever make an appearance in the countryside they seem almost exotic, as a fragment from a satire on peasants makes clear:

> 'You, Pistus, will take some money and do some shopping for me.'
>   'Not me, I never mastered the art of shopping.'
>   'Well then, Philumenus, what's your favourite fish?'
>   'I like them all.'
>   'Go through them one by one, which fish would you like to taste?'
>   'Well, once a fishmonger came to the country, and he had sprats with him and little red-mullets, and by Zeus he was popular with all of us!'
>   'So, now you would like some of them?'
>   'Yes, and if there is any other small one; for it is my opinion that all those large fishes are man-eaters.'

The notion of the fish-ignorant countryside goes back at least as far as Aristophanes who in one fragment describes a city-dweller who decides to move out to the country so that he can 'have chaffinches and thrushes to eat instead of hanging around for little fishies from the market, two days old, overpriced and tortured at the hands of a lawless fishmonger'.[21] Eating fish, and knowing which ones to prefer, is not only an indication of modernity and secularity, it is also a mark of urbanity.

The ancient passion for fish, then, can be explained largely in terms of what it was not, in terms of its positioning within a series of intersecting contrasts that set it against other types of food. Eating fish was free of a prehistory commemorated in festival banquets, or Homer's epics, or Platonic recollections of the primitive condition. It was not a serious or venerable activity. Fish were not slaughtered or distributed in a ritualized symbolic context. Fish stood outside the theatre of sacrifice and outside official banquets. It had no public role or responsibilities, free to play itself, the quintessential modern commodity fully fetishized for the private consumer, a food whose value could be gauged only according to desirability and demand, the object of constant assessment according to species and specimen, and the subject of an exquisite discourse, argued over and haggled for in comedies and dinner-parties, in markets and treatises.

A DANGEROUS SUPPLEMENT

So far so good. We have answered Socrates' question. Thanks to Plutarch we know what an *opsophagos* is and we can see why philosophers might get upset about it. An *opsophagos* was a fish-lover. Fish-lovers were mad about fish and philosophers thought them decadent. Unfortunately, Plutarch was not at the banquet and the question is not as simple as that. In Xenophon's discussion a number of possibilities are canvassed for the meaning of *opsophagia* but fish-eating is not one of them. But if the vice of the *opsophagos* is not fish-philia, what is it?

We need, perhaps, to go back to basics. The noun and its verb, *opsophagein*, first make an appearance in Greek literature towards the end of the fifth century in the poetry of Aristophanes. During his battle with bad-mannered Badlogic in the *Clouds*, for instance, old-fashioned Betterargument claims *opsophagein* is one of those bad habits the Athenians of former times prohibited, along with giggling, fidgeting and snatching celery from one's elders. In another of Xenophon's anecdotes, Socrates comes across someone thrashing an attendant. When he asks what the man has done to deserve such punishment his master replies it is for being 'an *opsophagos* to an extreme degree'. It seems clear the word is made up of two elements, *opson* and *phagein*. *Phagein* means eating. It does seem clear, then, that an *opsophagos* is a man with some kind of reprehensible eating-habit. *Opson* too should be quite transparent in meaning. Whereas we normally talk of nourishment as comprising two elements, food and drink, the Greeks could distinguish three, a feat achieved by dividing the solid part of sustenance into two distinct halves: the staple and what you eat on the staple, *sitos* and *opson*. The staple was usually bread made from wheat or some other grain. *Opson* represented almost everything else. This tripartite division of diet: staple, relish and drink, or bread, *opson* and wine, occurs in numerous passages in ancient literature from Homer onwards, whenever the Greeks discussed sustenance as a medical, economic or moral question. The most famous example perhaps is Thucydides' story of how the Great King rewarded Themistocles for going over to the Persian side by granting him the revenues of three rich cities to meet his needs, 'Magnesia for his bread . . . Lampsacus for his wine and Myus for his *opson*'.[22]

An *opsophagos*, then, straightforwardly enough, is an *opson*-eater, a relish-eater, 'an eater of non-farinaceous food'. This appellation, however, is not quite as transparent as it appears. To begin with, it seems to distinguish nobody, for of course man cannot be expected to live by bread alone . . . But perhaps at this point we should rejoin the dinner-party and let Socrates continue in his own words:

'[A]ll men, of course, eat *opson* on their bread when it is available; but they have not yet, I think, been labelled *opson-eaters* for doing so.'

'No, certainly not,' said one of those present.

'What, then, if someone eats the *opson* itself, without the staple, not as part of an athletic regime, but for the sake of pleasure, does he seem to be an *opsophagos* or not?'

'If not, it's hard to say who would be,' replied the other.

And someone else said, 'What about the man who eats a large amount of *opson* on a bit of staple?'

'He too seems to me to deserve the epithet,' said Socrates.

By this time the ears of the young man whose eating habits have been under such close scrutiny start to burn. He surreptitiously takes a piece of bread. Socrates notices this complaisant gesture and, not being a man to let things lie, calls on the boy's neighbours to watch he does not use the bread as a mere garnish, 'to see whether he treats the *sitos* as *opson*, or the *opson* as *sitos*'.

The three elements of diet were carefully differentiated in practice. Eating and drinking, for a start, were formally quite separate activities; dinner was concluded, the tables sided, and the floor swept, before the symposium, the liquid part of the meal, could begin. Staples and *opson* were not to be so drastically divided, but there are a number of indications that a strict code of dining protocols incorporated this fundamental division too into the structure of eating. The practice of eating with fingers appears to our Western manners as an absence rather than a difference of manners. However, contrary to the popular image of medieval banqueters with greasy faces tearing with abandon at the flesh of animals, societies which use their hands to eat have very strict rules governing not only which hands may be used for what, but also which parts of the hand, which fingers, and even which parts of fingers. Eating by hand was such a natural and habitual part of ancient life that it is rarely referred to in the sources, but there are enough indications to show that the Greeks were not less rigorous in their manners than other hand-to-mouth cultures. Plutarch, for instance, notes intriguingly that children are taught to use one finger to take preserved fish, but two for fresh. Such table-manners seem to have been the principal method of keeping the two elements of food separate at mealtimes. Margaret Visser inferred from their habit of reclining on the left elbow that the Greeks and Romans, like the ancient Chinese, kept their left hands away from food altogether. In fact, it seems, their table-manners were closer to those of the Abbasids, their successors on the southern side of the Aegean, who allowed the left hand to touch bread alone, reserving the right for communal dishes, and for bringing food to the mouth, a perfectly practicable arrangement even while in the Greek reclining position (which was not an everyday practice anyway). Thus *sitos* was taken with the left hand, *opson* with the right. Plutarch describes how children were castigated if they used their hands the wrong way round. This practice throws light on two passages from the classical period. Xenophon, for instance, describes how Cyrus' tent was organized with the *opson*-chefs on the right and the bakers on the left and a satirical attack on the gourmand Callimedon suggests erecting a statue of him in the agora with a roasted crayfish in his right hand as if to eat it.[23] Perhaps there were, as in many modern societies, toilet habits which complement these eating habits, helping to complete a system based on ideas of a clean hand, which can be used to dip into communal dishes and a dirty hand which one keeps to oneself. The *opson/sitos* separation depends perhaps on an even more important differentiation between food and excrement.

On the one hand so unremarkable and unremarked a feature of daily life that it could almost have escaped the notice of posterity, this distinction seems a classic case of a habit which inscribes ideology into practice. A particular set of beliefs about the world can become more rather than less powerful through being unspoken, aspiring to the rank of habit rather than ideology, and a status beyond language, questioning and argument in the cultural unconscious. In place of articulation, value and meaning can be assigned by means of carefully modulated differences between symbolically charged zones and directions. In a city like Athens, contrasted spaces, such as the women's quarters and the men's room, or private interiors and public streets, were symbolically charged. In the case of food, value could be read into the orientations of personal geography: left and right, bottom and top, staple and *opson*.[24] *Opson* is not a material object, and not really an idea. It is, above all, a space.

This space turns out to be somewhat ambivalent. It has a well-established position in the diet and yet seems somehow superfluous, merely decorative. In this it bears more than a passing resemblance to what Derrida identified as a persistent source of anxiety in Western philosophy, an addition which seems to complete something and yet to be extraneous, threatening all the time to forget its negligible subordinate role and take over what it is supposed merely to complete or embellish. Following Rousseau, he labelled this ambiguous addition the 'dangerous supplement', a phrase that seems to describe *opson*, the dietary supplement, rather accurately. Numerous passages seem to treat *opson* as an essential; it is what the right hand reaches out for to complement the bread in the left; it is one of the three pillars of existence, listed in numerous ancient writings on diet. It crops up in accounts of daily expenditure along with other essentials such as barley and wood. It is a prerequisite of allowances and salaries.[25] On the other hand it can be considered a mere dietary accessory, whose only purpose is to make the real sustaining part of diet, the staple, more palatable. This treatment of *opson* as the merest garnish is also found early on in the annals of Greek literature, in a passage well known to the Socratic circle and cited by both Plato and Xenophon: a scene from *Iliad* 11.630 in which the poet describes Nestor's servant preparing a drink in a magnificent cup of heroic proportions to which is added a piece of onion as *opson*. The habitual differentiation at meal-times of left and right, bottom and top is easily translated into more ideological contrasts: substance and decoration, necessity and excess, truth and façade.

The other two elements of diet could be fixed and controlled without difficulty. Bread could be substituted for *sitos*, and water or wine for *potos*, but there was no such simple solution to the space of *opson*, which remained intrinsically awkward to pin down, a space for dietary variety. Philosophers in particular were deeply suspicious about a part of sustenance which represented an opportunity for innovation and extravagance, as Plato makes clear in a section of dialogue from the *Republic*. Socrates is fantasizing about early society in a pristine state of nature: 'They will produce *sitos* and wine and clothes and shoes. They will live off barley-meal or wheat-meal, laid out on rushes or fresh leaves and they will feast magnificently with their children around them, recumbent on couches of myrtle and bryony, drinking wine, festooned with garlands and singing hymns to the gods, in enjoyment of each others' company.' After this little excursus on an ancient idyll, Glaucon interrupts, to point out the obvious omission: 'You're making these people dine without *opson*.'

'You're quite right', says Socrates disingenuously, 'I forgot that they will have *opson* too,' going on to list the most desultory things he can think of: salt, oil and cheese and whatever vegetable matter can be gathered from the fields: acorns, for example. Glaucon is outraged and adds the rather sinister comment that Socrates has been talking as if he were fattening up a city of pigs. He demands 'What is normal', including '*opsa* that modern men have'. Socrates counters that Glaucon, in that case, is talking not simply of a city, but of a luxurious city, a city with couches and tables and all the other articles of furniture, he continues contemptuously, '*opsa*, of course, as well as perfumes, aromatic fumigations, hetaeras and cakes, in all their various varieties'.[26]

Plato was a famously careful writer. After his death a tablet was found among his possessions with the first eight words of the *Republic* written out in different arrangements. Socrates' carelessness here is extremely well calculated and it illustrates perfectly the problem with *opson*. It already has a well-established position in the traditions of Greek diet and cannot ultimately be dislodged, but this omission puts it firmly in its negligible place. It is something to be ignored, elided or forgotten, something of no importance. When forced to address the oversight, Socrates tries to fix *opson* in a state of nature; he fills the dietary space with the most perfunctory edibles, whatever is ready to hand, requiring the bare minimum of preparation. *Opson* receives a similar kind of limitation, a progressive annihilation, even, in Xenophon's *Cyropedia*, an idealistic and ascetic vision of the ancestral Persians. In the old system of education, we are told, boys up to sixteen or seventeen lived off bread as *sitos*, water from a river to supply them with liquid, and *cardamon* (a type of cress) as *opson*. The slightly older boys, whom Xenophon calls the ephebes, went hunting with one day's ration of bread, and nothing at all in the way of *opson* but what they managed to catch in the field. *Opson* has at this point become no more than an opportunity. According to Xenophon, however, Socrates went even further and ate just sufficient food 'so that desire for *sitos* was its *opson*', appetite the best sauce.[27]

The philosophers' efforts to neglect, elide or reduce *opson* to the status of a vacuum are evidence of a profound nervousness about the whole category. The dangerous supplement threatens to divert eating away from sustenance and into pleasure, and even to usurp the place of bread as the bedrock of existence. It is this anxiety that explains why Socrates is so disturbed by the young man's table manners at the banquet with which we began. By taking no bread or only a little, the *opsophagos* threatens to invert the dietary hierarchy and allow simple sustenance to be diverted into pleasure. The error of the *opsophagos* lies not in eating *opson*, as everyone else does, but in living off it.

ST JOHN THE FISHMONGER?

One version of the vice of *opsophagia*, then, relates to carefully balancing the elements of diet to keep staples staple and everything else decorative. Plutarch's version on the other hand more straightforwardly says *opsophagia* is love of fish. How can these two rather different versions be reconciled? Whom do we trust to translate for us, Plutarch the eminent antiquarian or Xenophon, a reliable witness, surely, of the language of his own time?

To resolve this dispute we need to take another detour, to another controversy and another part of the ancient world, the sea of Galilee in the reign of the emperor Tiberius. An unlucky night is at last drawing to a close, revealing on the water's surface a boat, with plenty of fishermen aboard but no fish. In the breaking light a figure can be made out on shore. He asks if they have caught anything. They answer that they have not. He advises them to cast the net on the right-hand side of the boat. They follow his instructions and find their nets full, so full in fact that they cannot bring the catch on board and have to tow it ashore. When they reach the land, they find that the stranger has already started cooking a breakfast of bread and fish. They daren't ask him who he is because they now know it must be the risen Christ.

This is the tale of the miraculous draught of fishes, as told by John. The story itself occurs with slight variations in Luke as well and raises many points of interest for Bible scholars and theologians. What concerns us here, however, is not theology but philology. John uses two different words for fish, first, as we would expect, *ichthus* (which by the logic of the acronym – *Iesous CHristos THeou Uios Soter* [Jesus Christ, Son of God, Saviour] – made fish a secret sign of Christian credence in the first centuries after Christ and a symbol of Christian pride in our own), but when the fish are brought to be eaten John uses a different word, *opsarion*, a word which occurs five times in John and nowhere else in the New Testament. This idiosyncrasy of vocabulary has led to some bold conclusions about the author. For John A. T. Robinson, Bishop of Woolwich, the word properly referred to cooked fish and was proof that the evangelist, usually considered the latest of the gospel-writers, was on the contrary the earliest, a witness of the things he described, being none other than John the son of Zebedee, one of the twelve disciples, a fisherman and trader in fish. Only a professional, Robinson implies, would bother with such trade distinctions.

A. N. Wilson, in a more recent biography of Jesus, took this observation as proof that new things can still be discovered in the text of the Bible. He clarified the Bishop's rather allusive argument by suggesting that by 'cooked fish' this professional fishmonger was referring to something like a bloater or smoked fish.[28] Disappointingly, however, there is nothing technical about John's vocabulary. 'The feeding of the five thousand' is not about to become 'the miracle of the kippers'. *Opson* together with its diminutive *opsarion* were by this period perfectly commonplace words for fish, not smoked, and not necessarily cooked, but certainly in dire danger of being, since they corresponded to *ichthus* as pork does to pig, referring to fish as food. In fact it is from *opsarion*, and not *ichthus*, that the modern Greeks get their own word for fish, *psari*. This explains why Plutarch thought an *opsophagos* was simply a fish-lover. It proves nothing about the identity or profession of his near contemporary St John other than his fluency in the currencies of Greek, the *lingua franca* of the Eastern Roman Empire.[29]

That one word could mean 'anything we eat with bread' and also simply 'fish as food' caused misunderstandings among generations of Greek readers down the centuries, of which the disagreement between Plutarch and Xenophon over *opsophagia* is only one example. The historian Diodorus of Sicily, a contemporary of Julius Caesar, read Thucydides' description of the three cities, representing the three pillars of diet, granted by the Great King to Themistocles for going over to the Persian side, but understood something rather different. After commenting on the productivity of Lampsacene vineyards and the fecundity of the wheat-fields of Magnesia he couldn't resist adding an explanatory footnote to the choice of the city of Myus for his *opson*: 'it has a sea well-stocked with fish', although the city was by that time many stades inland.

It is clear, then, that *opson* could mean simply 'sea-food' already by the first century BCE. The question which exercised ancient students of the language was how much earlier than this the usage first appeared, and in particular whether it counted as good classical Attic Greek. To push it back a couple of centuries seems straightforward. Some modern scholars have argued convincingly that Plutarch took his definition from Hegesander of Delphi, a Hellenistic source of the second century BCE, and some Egyptian papyri attest the use in the third century, but are there any earlier passages where *opson* means fish? Are there any classical authors in the fourth or even the fifth centuries who use *opson* like John the Evangelist? Never with greater urgency was this important question addressed than during the rise of Atticism in the reign of Hadrian and his Antonine successors.[30]

In the second century CE educated men from all over the Roman Empire were growing philosophical beards and trying to write, to speak, even, the kind of Greek thought to have been used in classical Athens five or six hundred years earlier. At this time there was prestige and money to be made out of being a man of letters. An imperial chair of rhetoric was set up at Athens and rival grammarians and lexicographers from every province fought for the right to sit on it by discharging eulogies at the royal family and recriminations against each other. In this climate Atticism became a burning issue and rival camps sprang up of extremists and moderates. While this often bitter pedantry may not be to our taste, it was not without benefit to posterity, and a large number of the fragments on which this book is based survive simply because someone writing centuries later cited them as evidence for the classical purity of his vocabulary. Needless to say, thanks to its complex and confusing history, *opson* and its derivatives became something of a *cause célèbre* in the Atticist debate.

Pollux of Naucratis, a moderate, was said to be of limited talent as a speech-maker but blessed with a mellifluous delivery which seduced the emperor Commodus' ear and won him the professorship at Athens some time after 178 CE. His *Onomasticon*, or *Book of Words*, which survives in an abridged and interpolated form, was a collection of Attic vocabularies grouped by topic, including thirty-three terms with which to abuse a tax-collector, and fifty-two terms useful in praising a king. When he came to list words to do with the fish-trade he didn't let himself fret about it too much: 'fishmongers, fish-selling, fish, fishies, *opson*.' His critic and rival for the emperor's favour, Phrynichus 'the Arab', a scholar whose standards of Attic purity were so high that even some of the classical authors failed to make the grade, was contemptuous of such laxity. He wrote his own lexicon of Attic in thirty-seven books: '*not* fish,' he says in a gloss on *opsarion*, 'although people today use it like that.' Athenaeus, like Pollux, was from Naucratis. His *Banquet of Scholars* was composed *c.* 200 CE and takes the form of a dinner attended by certain luminaries of the period, including the physician Galen and the jurist Ulpian of Tyre. The banqueters alternate between consuming food and talking about it, managing also to fit in learned disquisitions on sex, decadence and crockery. This discourse in turn is interrupted by a meta-discourse which comments on the conversation and on the appropriateness of the words in which it is conducted, all carefully supported with the citation of classical authorities. The diners make great efforts to talk in the most authentic Greek possible and jump on one another with a vicious pedantic energy if they think they have spotted something too modern. Inevitably, the subject of *opsarion* crops up: 'A huge fish was then served in a salty vinegar sauce, and someone said that all fish [*opsarion*] was at its tastiest if served in this way. At this Ulpian, who likes to collect thorny questions, frowned and said, ". . . I can think of none of the authors 'at source' using *opsarion*." Now most people told him to mind his own business and carried on dining,' says Athenaeus. However, one member of the company, a character known as Myrtilus of Thessaly, rises to the bait and proceeds to catalogue the use of *opsarion* as fish in various Attic comedies of the fifth century and later, including Pherecrates' *Deserters*, Philemon's *Treasure*, and Anaxilas' *Hyacinthus the Whoremonger*.

Myrtilus' appeal to actual usage should have been enough to answer the question once and for all. But unfortunately the problem could not be resolved by a survey of classical texts, because the answers they gave were not consistent. To be put against the comic poets cited by Myrtilus, for instance, were Xenophon, and above all mighty Plato, a prince among prosateurs and the greatest authority for the strict Atticists. Although he wrote later than some of the authorities cited by Athenaeus, he seems to have been completely unaware that *opson*, not to speak of its numerous derivatives, could mean fish. What accounts for such a discrepancy in the vocabulary of these classical contemporaries? How is it that a usage which was bandied about quite happily in the theatres never made it into the groves of the Academy? One solution is provided by examining the influence of etymology on Greek ideas about language. Another, by examining Plato's attitude to fish.

From an early period the Greeks manifested a great interest in language in general and etymology in particular. This concern with where words came from was not simply a casual preoccupation with the history of language. Etymology, which comes from *etymos* 'truth', was believed to give access to a word's authentic meaning. Modern lexicographers are profoundly suspicious of this approach: 'Etymology may be valuable in its own right,' writes Sidney Landau, 'but it tells us little about current meaning and is in fact often misleading.'[31] Nevertheless, an interest in where words come from retains a powerful hold on our collective imagination and in newspaper columns, classrooms and dinner-parties a careless speaker will often be upbraided for an error of usage, by being reminded of its derivation.[32] 'Such a view of etymology', notes the critic Derek Attridge, 'implies the belief that the earlier a meaning the better, which must depend on a diagnosis of cultural decline . . . or a faith in a lost Golden Age of lexical purity and precision.'[33] Nowadays, etymological folk are content to trace words back as far as Latin and Greek, leaving this lexical *age d'or* no more than an inference. In antiquity, however, the putative original and pure state of language was the subject of a certain amount of speculation. Herodotus records the famous experiment of the pharaoh Psamtik to discover the oldest language by isolating two babies from human communication at birth and listening for the first sound to emerge spontaneously from their mouths. That utterance, it turned out, was *bekos*, which meant nothing in Egyptian, but was a word for bread in Phrygian, which was thus awarded the distinction of first language. Cratylus in Plato's dialogue of that name postulates a single prehistoric inventor of language, who assigned signifiers not arbitrarily but with superhuman insight into the *true nature* of things. Socrates in the same dialogue imagines language having its roots in nature and the body. According to this theory *anthrōpos* (man) was derived from man's characteristic upright posture, *ho anathrōn ha opōpen* ('the one who has seen what he has seen, by looking up'). Chrysippus the Stoic went even further in search of the natural origins of language and claimed that in pronouncing the word for self, *ego*, the lip and chin pointed to the speaker, thus bringing word and meaning into immediate and intimate identity in a single original articulate gesture.[34]

But this golden age, where signifier and signified enjoyed so perfectly honest a relationship, so pristine a unity of purpose, was not to last. A hero's offspring may fall far short of his father's heroism, notes Socrates in the *Cratylus*, but he will still be entitled to inherit his name. Under the influence of the etymological fallacy the history of words is no longer a neutral recording of changes in usage, noting diachronic differences without ascribing differential value, but instead a genealogical narrative, a story of strays wandering further and further away from the garden of Eden, deviants whose distance from original and true meaning is measurable in terms of dilution, distortion and error. This makes of writing much more than a straightforward medium of communication. An ideological element creeps in. Texts can be used not merely as a means to communicate most efficiently according to the most generally accepted contemporary understanding, but as a restorative of language, leading words back to their roots, closer to their original authenticity, to their 'proper' prelapsarian truth.

The researches of Wilhelm Schulze and Friedrich Bechtel at the turn of the century suggested that the most plausible origin of *opson* was from a word like *psōmos* meaning a 'mouthful' or a 'bite' plus a prothetic *o*, indicating 'with'. The most recent etymological dictionaries, considering even this a little reckless, give its derivation as 'obscure' and '*nicht sicher erklärt*'.[35] In antiquity, however, philologists were less circumspect and confidently traced *opson* back to words relating to cooking, especially from *hepso*, 'boil', a derivation which was widely accepted until the end of the nineteenth century, and which still survives as the 'proper' meaning in some modern dictionaries (thus drawing A. N. Wilson and Bishop Robinson off the track of the Miraculous Draught of Fishes). For the earliest explicit statement of this etymology we are indebted once more to Athenaeus, but it looks as if it was already known to Plato in the classical period. Apart from the circumstantial evidence of his own usage – in his work *opson* most often refers to a cooked dish – he draws attention to this etymology in the discussion of the diet of primitive civilization. Socrates, we remember, has just been reprimanded for 'forgetting' to give his ancient citizens any *opson*. He retorts that 'they will indeed have *opson*': cheese and onions, olives and vegetables, 'such things as there are in the countryside for boiling, they will boil' (*hepsēmata*, *hepsēsontai*). With this bizarre terminology, Plato is pointing to a true meaning for *opson* as 'something boiled' at the time of the misty golden age of language formation.[36]

If it was the ordinary fate of words to slip their moorings and wander casually into error, what happened to *opson* must have seemed the very pinnacle of luxurious degeneration. There have been many theories in recent times to explain how *opson* came to mean 'fish', but the simplest as well as the most convincing account was provided by Isaac Casaubon's notes on Athenaeus, published in 1600. He suggested it was short for *opson thalattion* (sea-food), a more obviously comestible term than *ichthus*, and also more inclusive, appropriate for those delicacies of the deep like crustaceans and molluscs whose inclusion in the category of fish was sometimes considered problematic. Ancient scholars, however, seem to have been quite unaware of this neat process of linguistic shift. Instead, the coinage was presented as a triumph comparable to Homer's triumph in the canons of literature: 'Though there are many poets, it is only one of them, the foremost, whom we call "the poet"; and so, though there are many *opsa*, it is fish which has won the exclusive title "*opson*" . . . because it has triumphed over all others in excellence,' as Plutarch puts it.[37]

Plato himself, along with many other philosophers, was far from sharing this opinion, and seems on the contrary to have disapproved strongly of his contemporaries' taste for *poissonerie*. This is implicit in the *Republic* where he carefully elides sea-food from the golden age feast and where, in the discussion of the fish missing from Homer, he connects the eating of fish with perfume and hetaeras and all the degenerate paraphernalia of the modern banquet. In addition, at least two Hellenistic authors knew of a story in which the philosopher reproached another member of the Socratic circle, Aristippus, for his fish-consumption. According to Hegesander's version, 'Plato objected to him returning from a shopping-spree with a large number of fish, but Aristippus answered that he had bought them for only two obols. Plato said he himself would have bought them at that price, to which Aristippus replied "Well, then, in that case, my dear Plato, you must realize that it is not I who am an *opsophagos*, but you who are a cheapskate." '[38]

For such ascetics, the use of *opson* to mean fish took on a rather different meaning. It was not so much a triumph as a naturalization of vice, a perversion of language as morally objectionable as when we use 'drink' – 'I need a drink' – 'No! A real drink!' – as a reference to alcohol or 'smoke' for 'smoke cannabis'. To assume that when someone mentioned *opson* they were referring to some kind of sea-food, the finest and most expensive of delicacies, must have seemed to Plato, who thought about these things, a quite enervated assumption. After having carefully removed fish from the category of *opson* when discussing golden age diet he was not going to allow it into his semantic field.[39] Morality and usage were too closely connected. Ancient authors have long been suspected of being unreliable witnesses of the world they affect to describe. In some cases they are not better witnesses of the language they affect to describe it in.

The definition of *opsophagia* that Xenophon puts into the mouth of Socrates can now be seen for what it really is: not a straightforward discussion of meaning, but an attempt to impose one particular meaning and one particular method of finding meaning to the exclusion of others. It is extraordinary that in a discussion of the vice of *opsophagia*, fish, which had long before become the *opsophagos*' favourite food (no matter how he was defined), is never mentioned. Just afterwards the memorialist records another remark of Socrates: 'In the Attic dialect,' he used to say, 'they call sumptuous banqueting "having a bite to eat."'[40] Xenophon was not about to make the same mistake.

Socrates' apparently idle question, directed obliquely at the young man he was trying to embarrass and redirected by Xenophon at us, has stimulated a whole range of answers down the centuries in the work of Plato, Plutarch, Athenaeus, Phrynichus 'the Arab', Pollux the lexicographer, and modern classicists such as Casaubon, Passow, Kalitsunakis and Liddell Scott and Jones. They do not agree with one another and the question cannot be described as settled even today. It seems a very dry debate, terribly pedantic and rather hard-going, exactly what a reader fears perhaps when she opens a book on classical Athens. Worst of all, it may seem irrelevant. Most people in classical Athens would have recognized the vice of *opsophagia* when they witnessed it, though the accused might have denied the charge or someone else might have disputed what exactly it was in this kind of eating that made the epithet applicable. In many cases there was nothing to debate about: 'Another fish, proud of its great size, has Glaucus brought to these parts,' says a character in Axionicus' play *The Euripides Fanatic*, 'some bread for *opsophagoi*.' A big word, perhaps *opsophagein* meant different things to different groups of people, especially perhaps to different levels of society. Words do not have fixed and unitary meanings and it distorts one's understanding of a text to treat them as if they do. If this is true today, it must have been even more true of classical Athens. In a world that was still free of the tyranny of dictionaries and public education systems, the meaning of words would have been generally quite slippery and quite difficult to tie down.[41]

I do not intend to devote too much space in the rest of this book, trying the reader's patience with this kind of philology, but far from being dead or dry or irrelevant, this debate over words gives access to the very heart of Greek desires. Just as psychoanalysts can discover the key to traumas in a slip of the tongue, the fish conspicuously missing from the texts of Xenophon and Plato testify to the real danger that lay in appetites. Ancient texts do more than inform us about ancient desires. They do more than provide us with samples of the ancient discourse of desires. Ancient desire itself is in the text, repressed perhaps, but still present. In their hesitations and omissions our authors reveal a struggle in the very composition of their prose, an ongoing battle with dangerous passions that threaten all the time to consume them and their readers.

II

DRINKING

CHARLES BAUDELAIRE DID not much like Brillat-Savarin's *Physiologie du Goût*. Above all he objected to the brief entry for wine: 'Noah the patriarch is regarded as the inventor of wine; it is a liqueur made from the fruit of the vine.' If a man from the moon or a further planet, the poet notes sarcastically, were to land on Earth in need of some refreshment and turned to Brillat-Savarin, how could he fail to find all he needed to know '*de tous les vins, de leurs différentes qualités, de leurs inconvénients, de leur puissance sur l'estomac et sur le cerveau*'. He offers as compensation his own gushing celebration of the properties of wine, an anecdote about a Spaniard and a prosopopoeia of the spirit of wine itself. As Roland Barthes pointed out in his introduction to the 1975 edition of the *Physiologie*, Baudelaire's sarcasm reveals a fundamental conflict of views about the nature of wine: 'For Baudelaire, wine is remembering and forgetting, joy and melancholy; it enables the subject to be transported outside himself . . . it is a path of deviance; in short, a drug.'

For Brillat-Savarin, on the other hand:

Wine is not at all a conductor of ecstasy. The reason for this is clear: wine is a part of food, and food, for BS, is itself essentially convivial, therefore wine cannot derive from a solitary protocol. One drinks while one eats and one always eats with others; a narrow sociality oversees the pleasure of food . . . Conversation (with others) is the law, as it were, which guards culinary pleasure against all psychotic risk and keeps the gourmand within a 'sane' rationality: by speaking – by chatting – while eating, the person at the table confirms his ego and is protected from any subjective flight by the image-repertoire of discourse. Wine holds no privilege for BS: like food and with it,

36

wine lightly amplifies the body (makes it 'brilliant') but does not mute it. It is an anti-drug.[1]

Alcohol has long been famous for its ability to make men voluble. In the last two hundred years in particular, occupying an optimal position on the scale of vices intermediate between what is too banal to notice and what is too terrible to speak of, it has become a division of knowledge in its own right, the stimulus for a vast array of investigation, categorization and legislation, public debate and academic study. From the pamphlets of the Temperance Movement to the self-help groups of the late twentieth century, by way of Prohibition, the perceived dangers of alcohol have put drinkers under the close watch of churches, doctors, satirists, the police and sociologists, not to speak of the most unforgiving gaze of all, the careful invigilation by drinkers of themselves, of their own habits and desire for a drink.

The residue of this fascination has provided rich pickings for modern social historians who can study without ideological fervour the drinking practices of the last century carefully catalogued by fervent teetotallers, but the tenor of this discourse has made prevalent some rather universalizing and totalizing notions, which have had the effect of pushing the study of drinking beyond the bounds of history. The broad range of intoxicating liquors known to man are viewed as manifestations of a single drug, alcohol, in various disguises. The wide experience of enjoying these beverages and the manifold forms of consuming them are viewed as manifestations of a monotonous pathology of intoxication and addiction, as ethyl first ensnares and then takes over the body.

This view which is still pervasive in modern society has been challenged recently by anthropologists. They have found it difficult to apply categories such as 'alcoholic' and conditions like 'alcoholism' to the drinking practices of other societies and have tended to group liquors under the rubric of commensality (the fellowship of the table), with food and other non-intoxicating beverages, stressing the drinker's relationship with other drinkers rather than with his drink, emphasizing *companionship*, that breaking of the bread together, which is such a quaint feature of Oxford and Cambridge colleges, the

Inns of Court and mass. Some have gone so far as to suggest that problem-drinking is a purely Western phenomenon that could be remedied through socialization.[2]

It is not difficult to see that the general outline of the debate between anthropologists and alcoholists is anticipated already by Baudelaire's differences with Brillat-Savarin. For the poet and the alcoholist drink is an essence, a drug. What concerns them is the alien state of being within one's own private intoxication. For the gourmand and the anthropologist drink is merely another part of food. What is important is the context in which it is consumed, the rituals of drinking, the community of drinkers. One could argue, at the risk of oversimplification, that the root of the controversy lies in a modern Western prejudice against solitary drinking, a pervasive feeling that alcohol's effects are moderated or at least rendered negligible by the presence of other drinkers, that alcoholism reveals its true form in the period before the pubs are open and after they have closed, when the drinker is left alone with his drink. This special anxiety about opening a bottle for oneself seems misplaced. Many dangerous and persistent drinkers reach their state of intoxication in company although the violence that accompanies their inebriation may appear only at home. Nevertheless, for many it is the quiet spinster caught swigging amontillado in the morning rather than rowdy behaviour at the bar that crystallizes most clearly the image of the alcoholic.

Both the alcoholist approach and the anthropological have been employed in recent studies of wine-consumption in antiquity. While some have concentrated their efforts on looking for ancient evidence of ethyl-addiction and the problem behaviour modern sociologists associate with problem drinking, others have adopted the anthropologists' lens, through which an apparently commonplace practice like drinking wine is transformed into something rich and strange. The familiar intoxicating liquid is a distraction. It has no importance in and of itself but only as the catalyst of peculiar cultural practices, as the sticky glue of distinctive social relationships.

The Greeks' own vinous discourse was rich. By accident as well as by design an enormous proportion of surviving Greek painting of the sixth and early fifth centuries BCE comes from vases made for drinking, whose decorative imagery more often than not echoes their function. At about the same time a drinking literature was flourishing in the form of sympotic poetry performed at drinking-parties on the subject of women, boys, wine and pleasure. Belonging to a rather later period and much closer in appearance to branches of the modern discourse there were medical texts, although few modern doctors would repeat the advice of Athens' most illustrious fourth-century physician, Mnesitheus, who considered heavy drinking beneficial. A number of ancient philosophers, including Aristotle and Theophrastus, produced treatises *On Drunkenness* although none of them unfortunately survives intact. Something of their style and concerns may be intimated in the series of questions and answers about the physiological aspects of intoxication, collected as book three of the Aristotelian *Problemata*. Wine even infiltrated history and politics. One historian in particular, Theopompus of Chios, seems to have had a keen nose for the scent of alcohol on the breath of tyrants and statesmen. A large portion of his surviving fragments, ascribed to a large number of different books of his histories of Greece and of Philip, allude to the drinking habits of princes and nations. Athenaeus even says of Theopompus that he 'compiled a list of drink-lovers and drunks'.[3] To add to this are occasional allusions in the orators to watering-holes of low repute and disapproved-of drinking practices. Demosthenes, for instance, notoriously, was teetotal. Perhaps the most important source for Athenian drinking in the classical period, however, is Attic comedy, which in all periods managed to place drunks on stage and enact the preparations for drinking-parties. This was nothing less than appropriate given that the plays were performed under the tutelage of Dionysus, the god of wine himself.

This ancient discourse falls readily within the boundaries set by the two sides of the modern controversy, turning from drink to the community of drinkers and back again to drink, enabling us to escape in the first place some of Baudelaire's most trenchant criticisms and present a brief survey '*de tous les vins, de leurs différentes qualités. . .*'

WINE

The vine was familiar all over mainland Greece and in those coastal enclaves from Catalonia to the Crimea that the Greeks colonized. In fact, wine-drinking was considered nothing less than a symbol of Greek cultural identity. It was a mark of their barbarism that the barbarians drank beer. If they did know of wine, and the Greeks acknowledged that other cultures were not totally ignorant of it, they misused it. The wine itself, in the raw and undiluted form rarely tasted by the Greeks, was often sweet and thanks to hot weather and low yields probably towards the upper end of the scale of potency at 15–16 per cent as opposed to the 12.5 per cent which is normal today. It usually had bits of grape and vine debris floating in it and needed to be sieved before being mixed or poured out. This will have made red wines correspondingly dark in colour and somewhat tannic. The scent of ancient wine was said to have a powerful effect on wine-lovers and was often compared to the scent of flowers. Some other aromas may have been unfamiliar to the modern nose. For a start, the wine absorbed the taste of the container in which it had been carried or stored; not the oak that lends to modern wines their characteristic vanilla flavours, but pitch or resin used to seal amphoras and, on occasion, the sheep and goats that provided the raw material for wine-skins. Other items were sometimes added at various points in the process of manufacturing and preparation including salt water, aromatic herbs, perfume and in one case honey and dough. Aristotle in a fragment of his treatise *On Drunkenness* mentions drinking wine from a 'Rhodes jar' which was prepared with an infusion of myrrh and rushes. Apparently when heated the vessel lessened the intoxicating power of the liquid inside.

According to Mnesitheus, three colours of wine were differentiated, 'black', 'white' and *kirrhos*, or amber. The white and amber wines could be either sweet or dry, the 'black' could also be made 'medium'. The Hippocratic treatise *On Diet* categorizes wines also as 'fragrant' or 'odourless', 'slender' or 'fat', and 'strong' or 'weaker'. Theophrastus says wines were sometimes blended.[4]

The Greeks, unlike the Romans after them, seem to have had no appreciation of particular vintages, but certainly recognized the value of ageing, something which amazed antiquarians as late as the early eighteenth century, when wines usually deteriorated quickly. This misunderstanding seems to be a simple consequence of the fact that in the early Middle Ages readily sealable clay amphoras fell out of favour to be replaced by less air-tight receptacles. The age of wine was a matter of some importance to connoisseurs, inspiring the gourmand Archestratus to heights of purple poetastery that make modern connoisseurs look prosaic:

> Then, when you have drawn a full measure for Zeus Saviour, you must drink an old wine, bearing on its shoulders a head hoary indeed, a wine whose wet curls are crowned with white flowers, a wine begat of wave-girdled Lesbos. And Bybline, the wine that hails from holy Phoenicia, I recommend, though I do not place it in the same rank as the other. For if you were not previously on intimate terms and it catches your taste-buds unaware, it will seem more fragrant than the Lesbian, and it does retain its bouquet for a prodigious length of time, but when you come to drink it you will find it inferior by far, while in your estimation the Lesbian will soar, worthy not merely of wine's prerogatives but of ambrosia's. Some swagger-chattering gas-bags may scoff that Phoenician was ever the sweetest of wines but to them I pay no heed ... The wine of Thasos too makes noble drinking, provided it be old with the fair seasons of many years.

Wine's ability to age well drew some unfavourable comparisons with the human species. A character in a play of Eubulus, for instance, remarks on how the hetaeras esteem old wine, but not old men. A fragment of Cratinus conjures up a more sophisticated deployment of the human lifetime analogy. He talks of 'Mendaean wine coming of age' (*hēbōnta*, literally 'in bloom' or 'pubescent'), thereby bringing to mind modern maturity charts of the 'life' of a wine divided into periods of maturation: 'Ready', 'Peak', 'Tiring', 'Decline'.[5]

The vast bulk of the wine consumed was undistinguished local produce from the harvest of small unspecialized holdings. This was what the Athenians called *trikotylos*, or 'litre wine' (literally, three half-pints) because, according to the lexicographer Hesychius, you could get three half-pint measures of it for only an obol. Some, however, was of a much higher quality imported from areas famous for their wines and grown on large estates. These wines are often found listed along with other fine foods in comedy, although the top rank contains rather fewer specimens than the number of fishes, for instance, at the poets' command, rarely amounting to more than three or four at a time. Membership of this elite is not always consistent, but the wines of Thasos, Chios and Mende, a city in the Chalcidice, are the most prominent for most of the classical period. These are joined by the wines of Lesbos which are occasionally found in lists as early as the fifth century BCE, although Pliny has the impression that their reputation dated only from the end of the fourth. Characters in the plays discourse freely on the peculiar qualities of each wine, its characteristic colour and scent, its sweetness, as in this speech of Dionysus from a play of Hermippus: 'With . . . Mendaean wine the gods themselves wet their soft beds. And then there is Magnesian, generous, sweet and smooth, and Thasian upon whose surface skates the perfume of apples; this I judge by far the best of all the wines, except for blameless, painless Chian.'[6]

The fine wines of the classical period have left traces of their popularity not only in the remnants of ancient literature, but also in fragments of amphoras, dug up around the Athenian Agora and elsewhere. Each of the great wine-exporting cities packaged its wine in distinctive and more or less uniformly-shaped vases, which can be differentiated by archaeologists. The Chians even used their amphora as an identifying symbol on their coinage. This confirms what the comic fragments suggest, that these city wines were specific products, with recognizable characteristics. Some cities specialized in producing only one kind of wine, others produced more. Chian wine, for instance, came in three types, *austēros* (dry), *glukazōn* (sweet), and one called *autokratos* in between the two. The individuality of these wines can be explained as the result of the natural prevalence of particular varieties of vine and certain traditional methods specific to a region. It is not a coincidence that the sources of these distinctive wines are, without exception, isolated agricultural economies, literally in the case of islands like Thasos and Chios, or, like Mende, surrounded by barbarians. It is significant, in this respect, that Lesbian wine takes its name from the island itself, the geographical entity, rather than from the cities, the political entities, Mitylene, Eresus and Methymna, that divided the territory between them. Some very occasional references indicate ancient recognition of that rather less tangible quality of *terroir*, the magical influence of specific plots of land. The best Chian wine apparently came from an area in the north-west of the island, and was known as Ariusian. We also hear of a wine called Bibline which, *contra* Archestratus, probably came not from Phoenician Byblos, but from an area in Thrace opposite the north-western part of Thasos, and which probably belonged to the territory of one of the cities in the area, perhaps to Thasos itself.[7]

Thasos also provides, in contrast, the best evidence for highly organized viticulture carried out on a large scale, the haphazard blessings of sound traditional methods and good soil supplemented with legislation. A series of inscriptions from the island reveal that political intervention in the wine trade could be intense and far-reaching. The overall concern of the laws seems to be for quality, a consideration which benefited not only the Thasian consumers of Thasian wine, but the exporters too, whose success depended on maintaining the island's reputation for high standards.[8]

THE SYMPOSIUM

The most formal context for the consumption of wine in the Greek world was the drinking-party or symposium, a highly ritualized occasion and an important crucible for the forging of friendships, alliances and community in ancient Greece, an almost perfect example in fact of the anthropologists' commensal model of drinking in which socializing is paramount. Its practices can be pieced together from a number of accounts. The space in which it took place was the 'men's room', the *andrōn*, a small room with a slightly raised floor on all sides, which makes it one of the most easily identified spaces in the archaeology of the Greek house. This ledge provided a platform for the couches, which usually numbered seven, sometimes eleven, and occasionally as many as fifteen. Each couch could take two people, reclining on their left sides. The arrangement was more or less a squared circle but the seating was not for that reason undifferentiated. The circle of drinkers was broken by the door, which meant that there was a first position and a last and places for host, guests, symposiarchs, honoured guests and gate-crashers. Wine, song and conversation went around the room from 'left to right', that is, probably, anti-clockwise. The arrangement was less a static circle of equality than a dynamic series of circulations, evolving in time as well as in space, with the potential for uncoiling into long journeys, expeditions, voyages.[9] Within the little *andrōn* the drinkers could travel long distances.

The symposium occupied a space perfectly commensurate with the walls. The atmosphere was correspondingly intense and intimate. 'Nothing takes place behind the drinkers; the whole visual space is constructed to make sightlines converge and to ensure reciprocity.'[10] The sympotic space conspired with the effect of the alcohol to create a sense of entering a separate reality. The managers of modern nightclubs and casinos make sure there are no windows or clocks to remind their clientele of the time-zone outside. In the symposium a similar severing of ties to the extramural world was effected with a repertoire of images and discourse peculiar to itself, reflecting the symposium and reflections of the symposium *en abîme*. In the men's room they would recline and drink from cups decorated with images of men reclining and drinking from decorated cups; they would recite sympotic poetry and tell anecdotes about other drinking-parties in other times and other places. They never need stray from the sympotic themes of love and sex, pleasure and drinking. In fact, it could be said that the symposium for the period of its duration, symbolically constituted the world.

A bizarre story told by Timaeus of Taormina illustrates graphically the sense of separation between the world within and the world without the drinking-party:

In Agrigentum there is a house called 'the trireme' for the following reason. Some young men were getting drunk in it, and became feverish with intoxication, off their heads to such an extent that they supposed they were in a trireme, sailing through a dangerous tempest; they became so befuddled as to throw all the furniture and fittings out of the house as though at sea, thinking that the pilot had told them to lighten the ship because of the storm. A great many people, meanwhile, were gathering at the scene and started to carry off the discarded property, but even then the youths did not pause from their lunacy. On the following day the generals turned up at the house, and charges were brought against them. Still sea-sick, they answered to the officials' questioning that in their anxiety over the storm they had been compelled to jettison their superfluous cargo by throwing it into the sea.

The story belongs to a rich Greek tradition of marine metaphors for the sympotic community.[11] The high sea represents the boundlessness of wine, the obliteration of points of reference. The metaphor is captured with characteristic economy inside a cup of the archaic painter Exekias. He shows Dionysus, relaxed and triumphant on a boat decked out with bunches of grapes and the irrepressible branches of a vine, having turned the tables on his pirate abductors who swim around the vessel transformed into fishes. Normally the interior decoration of a kylix is reserved for a small central tondo, but here the red-painted sea has burst the banks of its confinement and laps the edges of the cup in vine-like exuberance, just as the drinking-party washes against the walls of the *andrōn*. On the boundless sea of wine the company floats free from the boundaries of reality and off into the deep. It is not surprising that in another context, among the Etruscans of Italy, the symposium was associated with the rituals of death.

The solid section of the dinner was concluded by the removal of tables. The floor was swept of the shells and bones that had accumulated during the feast and water was passed around for the guests to wash their hands. The guests were sometimes garlanded with flowers at this point and anointed with perfumed oils. The symposium itself began with a libation of unmixed wine for the *Agathos Daimōn*, the 'Good divinity', accompanied by paeans sung to the god. This was the only occasion on which a taste of undiluted wine was permitted and reflects the atmosphere of danger that permeated the evening's carousal. The banqueters were embarking on a dangerous voyage. According to the historian Philochorus, the ritual toast of unmixed

wine was instituted along with the other drinking customs by
Amphictyon, a legendary king of Athens, as a 'demonstration of the
power of the good god. Moreover, they had to repeat over this cup
the name of Zeus the Saviour as a warning and reminder to drinkers
that only when they drank in this way [i.e. mixing the wine with
water] would they be safe and sound.' The libation was made out
of a special cup called a *metaniptron*, which was passed around among
the guests. By election, or by some other means, a symposiarch was
selected to preside over the mixing and the toasts.[12]

It was a peculiar custom of the Greeks, not shared by other ancient
wine-drinking cultures, to add water to their wine. The two were
blended in a large mixing-bowl known as the krater. The water
could be cold or warm, and snow was sometimes used to chill the
unmixed wine in a psykter (wine-cooler), or even allowed to melt
directly into the bowl. According to Theophrastus, in his own time
it was fashionable to pour the wine in first and then dilute it, a
procedure he considers more dangerous than adding wine to water
to bring it up to strength, imagining, I suppose, that the idea of
'watering down the wine' was conducive to a stronger blend than
'flavouring or strengthening the water'.[13] The swirling motion of the
liquids as they were blended together is reflected in the name for
one kind of mixing-bowl, the *dinos* or whirlpool.

There was much dispute about the correct mixture. Athenaeus
records a number of characters in Attic comedies arguing over the
proportions. The majority of fragments refer to a mixture of half and
half, but where the context is clear it seems this is supposed to
designate a particularly excessive and greedy kind of drinking. A
character in Sophilus' play *The Dagger*, for instance, describes wine
so blended as unmixed, *akratos*. Even a mixture of one-third wine
could be considered to go against custom, while a quarter was too
weak. The dilution which seems most acceptable from the comic
fragments lies somewhere in between at two-sevenths, that is five
parts water to two of wine. The resulting liquid could have been as
potent as modern beers and consumed in similar quantities. The wine
and water are considered to be somehow competing with each other,
a poison and its antidote. Even a notoriously heavy drinker, like
Proteas the Macedonian, described in the account of Caranus' lavish

banquet, 'sprinkles a little water' superstitiously before downing six pints of Thasian in one go.[14]

Once the wine had been mixed it was distributed by a slave, first ladling the wine into an *oinochoē* or jug and then pouring it into each cup in turn. The symposiarch would decide not only the measures of water and wine, but also the number of kraters to be mixed. A good decent symposium would be confined to three. Dionysus on stage in a play of Eubulus announces: 'Three kraters only do I propose for sensible men, one for health, the second for love and pleasure and the third for sleep; when this has been drunk up, wise guests make for home.'[15] The number of kraters could be set beforehand or decided as the symposium evolved. Plato's *Symposium* begins with the guests' deliberations about how they are going to drink. Since they are still suffering from the previous night's carousing, moderation is in order. The discussion implies that they will all be drinking the same and need to agree beforehand how much. Apart from the number of kraters and the strength of the mixture, they could vary the number and size of toasts, the size of drinking cups and the frequency of rounds. With such means at his disposal the symposiarch could effectively dictate the pace of drinking, leaving some to complain of forced or 'compulsory' drinking. At public gatherings, officials called *oinoptai*, or 'wine-watchers', were appointed to make sure all drank the same.[16]

The picture of the classic moderate drinking-party which emerges from all these passages must not be seen as a mirror on Greek dinnerparties, held up to themselves by the Greeks for the benefit of posterity, but as a symptom of anxiety about how to drink properly. This anxiety was well founded. Disturbances of the proper rhythm of drinking can be observed at all levels of the ritual. For a start, the drinkers may not finish with the third krater, and the well-ordered symposium, even with its rituals intact, could spiral out of control, its machinery functioning no longer to check excess, but to gather drunken momentum. Dionysus in Eubulus' play goes on to describe what happens if the drinking continues beyond the three kraters he considers advisable: 'The fourth krater is mine no longer, but belongs to hybris; the fifth to shouting; the sixth to revel; the seventh to blackeyes; the eighth to summonses; the ninth to bile; and the tenth to madness and people tossing the furniture about.' Hurtling furniture seems to have been a common manifestation of the symposium's final stage of madness. Disruption could also come from the wrong mixture: 'If you exceed the measure', says the speaker in a comic fragment, 'wine brings hybris. If you drink in the proportion of half and half, it makes for madness. If you drink it unmixed, physical paralysis.'[17]

Despite the risk, *akratos*, neat wine or strong wine, was sometimes consumed. This could be achieved only if the structures of orderly drinking were dispensed with, if the sympotic machinery of dilution and circulation that took the wine from the jars and psykters where it was kept and cooled into the neutralizing krater and then out into the ladle, the *oinochoe* or jug, and finally the cup, was interrupted. One comic character indicates his resolve to get drunk by calling for all the sympotic paraphernalia to be removed, except what he needs to reach his goal. Another refers to men drinking directly from the ladle. More straightforwardly, a determined drinker could simply reach out for the psykter of wine before it had been mixed with water. A character in Menander's *Chalkeia* thought it was a modern habit: 'As is the custom nowadays, they were calling out "*akratos*, the big cup!" And someone would wreak havoc on the poor sods by proposing a psykter for a toast.'[18]

The most famous example of this 'modern' practice comes from Plato's *Symposium*. The drinking-party in Agathon's house has thus far been exemplary. The drinking has been moderate, the symposiarch has not been forcing people to drink toasts, and the speeches have been moving around the room in turns. At this point glorious Alcibiades arrives in a state of high intoxication. He refuses, at first, to join in the rules of the symposium and elects himself symposiarch in order to force them to catch up quickly with his own level of inebriation. Leading from the front he proceeds to drink *akratos* out of the psykter and then gets Socrates to do the same. Before long, however, Eryximachus, the legitimate symposiarch, reasserts his authority and Alcibiades is socialized, brought into the group and into the conversation. Towards the end of the dialogue, however, there is a second disruption of komastic revellers who invade the gathering and force the guests to drink large quantities 'in no kind of order' *en kosmōi oudeni*. With the end of drinking order the symposium itself dissolves.[19]

COMMENSALITY

'There is another correct interpretation of drinking cups:' wrote Artemidorus, the interpreter of dreams, 'they symbolize those who greet us with a kiss. And so, if they break, it means that some of the dreamer's family or friends will die.'

Drinking wine out of the same mixing-bowl forged bonds of consubstantiation among the drinking community akin to the sharing in the sacrificial meat after a religious ceremony. Sometimes the symposiasts enjoyed even greater intimacy by sharing the same cup. The *metaniptron*, for instance, was probably passed around and Critias considered it a peculiarly Spartan custom not to. We also hear of a cup of friendship, a *philotēsia*, which can be pledged in alliance. The strong sense of community forged in the symposium is epitomized in a striking image deployed by Aristophanes. The Chorus in *Acharnians* illustrate their difficulty in handling War by comparing him to a drunken guest who, unlike Alcibiades at Agathon's, refuses to be brought into the group:

> Never will I welcome War into my home, never will he sing Harmodius reclining by my side, because he's nothing but a trouble-maker when he's drunk. This is the fellow who burst upon our prosperity, like a komast, wreaking all manner of destruction, knocking things over, spilling wine and brawling, and still, when we implored him repeatedly, 'Drink, recline, take the cup of friendship', still more did he set fire to our trellises, and violently spilled the wine from our vines.[20]

The symbolism of drinking together is used again in the *Knights* to make a rather more down-to-earth point. At some point in the last quarter of the fifth century a man called Ariphrades had managed to acquire notoriety as a practitioner of cunnilingus. The Chorus expresses its abhorrence quite vividly with a resolution, not, it should be noted, against Ariphrades and his mouth, but against his acquaintances: 'Whoever does not utterly loathe such a man shall never drink from the same cup with me.' The theme of pollution brings us to the festival of Choes and its founding myth. The details are obscure, but it seems that Choes was the name given to the second day of a three-day festival known as the Anthesteria. We hear about it from two classical sources in particular: Dicaeopolis, the hero of Aristophanes' *Acharnians*, is shown enjoying the private peace he has concluded with Sparta by celebrating his own private Choes while the rest of the city prepares for war, and in Euripides' *Iphigenia Among the Taurians*, Orestes describes the origin of the ritual in a banquet held for himself in Athens. Judging from these passages and the ancient commentary on them, Choes seems to have been marked by unusual drinking practices: 'The evening of the twelfth [Anthesterion] was a traditional occasion to invite friends to a party, but the host only provided garlands, perfumes and dessert. The guests each brought their own food and still more significantly their own drink in the form of a wine-jar ... It was apparently the tradition that each drinker consumed his share in silence. This was the complete antithesis of the symposium with its sharing of talk or song.' These unusual practices were supposed to represent the ambivalent hospitality extended by a king of Athens to polluted Orestes, at that time still an outcast from society after the murder of his mother. In *Iphigenia* he describes how he was given his own table, and drank separately from the others of wine poured in equal measure into a vessel touched by his lips alone. There are difficulties in reconstructing the festival, notably in integrating the private and public aspects of the accounts. For our purposes it is enough to note the contrast which was so apparent to a classical author and his audience between the customs of the Choes and the normal practice of Attic drinking, and the way that the perceived contrast is used to demonstrate Orestes' social isolation. The very fact that the drinking at the festival was not from a drinking vessel but from a jug, a *chous* meant for pouring, is enough in Athenian eyes to define that way of drinking as an interruption of the processes of *distribution*, just as Alcibiades' drinking from the psykter indicates an interruption in the process of *mixing* the wine with water.[21]

Another factor which underlines the subversion of drinking rules in the ambiguous hospitality shown to Orestes is the lack of verbal communication. He feasts, says Euripides, 'not speaking and not spoken to'. The abstract concept of sociability was realized in the symposium, as for Brillat-Savarin, in the concrete practices of discourse. Conversation was such a defining feature of the symposium that Theophrastus referred to the notoriously chatty barber-shops as 'symposia without the wine'.[22] In the Greek context, the passage of wine and the passage of words supported and complemented each other, linked metaphorically and structurally. This linkage can be quite formal, as in Plato's *Symposium*, where each guest in turn has to make a little speech. Talking was the paramount purpose of such symposia. Drinking was ancillary, serving only to loosen the tongue and facilitate the flow of words. In practice, however, the primacy of discourse was rarely observed and the advocates of conversation were disappointed. Instead of coming to the aid of dialectic, wine and words competed with one other, an unequal contest that wine usually won and drink for drinking's sake, drinking to get drunk, supervened, destroying rather than cementing the society of drinkers with violence, or binding them closer together in a dangerous collective hysteria.

A proper flow of conversation is accordingly connected with the proper admixture of water and with drinking in small draughts, all practices designed to moderate the effects of the drug. The practice of silent swigging in the manner of the drinking contest at Choes was quite exceptional and, outside the festival, strongly condemned. The contrast was made most explicit in some pages of the manuscript of Athenaeus that were ripped out and survive only in epitome: 'It can even be considered gentlemanly to spend time drinking, provided that one does it with good taste, not drinking deeply (*kōthōnizomenon*) and not swigging it without a breath, in the Thracian fashion, but blending conversation with the drink as a health potion.' Because we don't possess the full text at this point, it is impossible to know if Athenaeus is citing classical sources for this idea or simply expressing his own Middle Imperial thoughts, but older texts than his make the same connection between conversation and moderate drinking. One of Socrates' arguments against huge draughts in Xenophon's

Symposium is that it will mean they won't be able 'to say anything'. 'Let's not forever be taking a pull from cups filled to the brim, but let something conversational strike the company,' says a character in Antiphanes' *Wounded Man*. The same contrast is echoed by characters in several plays of Alexis. 'You see', says Solon in *Aesop*, 'this is the Greek way of drinking, using moderately-sized cups and chattering and gossiping with each other pleasantly.' In contrast, a *polyphagous parasite* in Alexis' play of that name is the image of the silent guzzler: 'He dines as mute as Telephus, nodding his head to those who direct some question to him.' It is characteristic of degenerates, comments Satyrus, foreshadowing the views of Brillat-Savarin and the anthropologists, 'to take pleasure in wine rather than in their drinking-companions'.[23]

Athenaeus' talks of 'gentlemanly' or 'liberal' (*eleutherion*) behaviour, and this emphasis on class (in its broadest sense) also finds echoes in earlier literature. Alexis makes the statement that 'no man who is a wine-lover can be of low character (*kakos*). For twice-mothered Bromius [Dionysus] doesn't enjoy the company of coarse men and a life of no refinement.' A similar sentiment is found expressed at the beginning of *Wasps* where the audience is trying to guess the nature of jury-loving Philocleon's vice. One suggests he is a wine-lover (*philopotēs*) and Xanthias replies, never, since that disease is a 'disease of worthies' (*chrēstōn*). Towards the end of the same play Philocleon's sophisticated son Bdelycleon orders the slave to get dinner prepared so that they can get drunk. His low-class father objects that drinking leads to bashing-in of doors, violence and fines. 'Not if you are in the company of gentlemen' (*kaloi k'agathoi*), replies his son. At this point the audience is probably expecting something along the lines of Athenaeus' remarks about how true gentlemen know how to moderate their drinking with the refinements of conversation, but Bdelycleon's mind is running along a different track. There will be no less violence, but once all the damage has been caused, the gentlemen intercede with the victim for you, or you yourself come up with some witty story, one of Aesop's amusing fables or some tale of old Sybaris which you learned in the symposium; and so you turn it into a laughing matter and he forgets about it and goes off.[24]

TAVERNS

These remarks remind us that although the symposium has been treated as *the* classic context for drinking in Greek society as late as the fourth century, it carries over from the archaic period associations with the lifestyle of one particular group within society, the aristocracy and their emulators. As Oswyn Murray observes: 'However much the fifth-century democracy might try to provide public dining-rooms and public occasions for feasting, the *symposion* remained largely a private and aristocratic preserve.' The lingering connotations of elitism are quite clear in the final scenes of the *Wasps*, in the awkwardness with which an Athenian Everyman, a dikast, like Philocleon, approaches the symposium: 'to the fifth-century Athenian audience, the *symposion* is an alien world of licence and misbehaviour.'[25]

Those beyond the aristocratic pale had to get their liquid refreshment elsewhere, in the tavern or *kapēleion*, a far more demotic and promiscuous space than the private and selective *andrōn*. This well-attested institution does not seem to have been given as much scholarly attention as it deserves. After the reference-filled columns of Hug's brief entry in Pauly-Wissowa's panoramic encyclopedia of the ancient world, it is hard to find any detailed study and few bother even to refer to it. To some extent this neglect is a direct result of the prominence accorded the symposium and the anthropological model of commensality in accounts of Greek drinking. In contrast to the symposium, the *kapēleion* looks out of historical place, foreshadowing the consumerized, individualized drinking which ought to be the prerogative of modern times. In addition there are some philological questions that sometimes cause problems. A *kapēlos* can be both a retailer in general and a taverner in particular, although in comedy and oratory, when it is used without qualification, the latter sense can almost always be assumed.[26]

These taverners seem to have sold wine, vinegar and torches to light the way home at night and offer protection from cloak-snatchers. In some of these establishments, it seems, you could have something to eat as well. The *kapēloi* began as wholesalers and continued to sell wine in bulk to those who could afford to entertain at home. But they also broke the bulk, a practice known as 'half-pinting' (*kotulizein*), and served smaller quantities of wine with water to be drunk on the premises. In *Gorgias* Plato mentions one particular *kapēlos*, called Sarambus, whose skill at 'preparing' (*paraskeuazōn*) wine he compares with the work of Athens' finest baker and Mithaecus, a Syracusan cook, reputed to be the Pheidias of the kitchen. Some translators treat Sarambus as simply a seller of wine, and translate 'prepare' as 'provide', but the fact that he is put alongside creative characters like a baker and a chef suggests that Sarambus is more than a simple retailer. Plato is talking of his skills as a taverner, and in fact it is precisely this passage that the lexicographer Pollux uses to demonstrate that in classical Attica *kapēloi* also mixed the wine. Plato, he says, is praising Sarambus for his *oinourgia*, his 'winesmanship'. What the *oinourgia* of a good taverner consisted of in actual fact is open to speculation; honest measures of good wine, perhaps, from an amphora not long opened, strained of debris, blended with clean, chilled water, maybe a little perfume, served in fine cups with some bar-food, some *tragémata* (desserts) perhaps or *hales* (savouries) as an accompaniment. There is evidence for the suppression of such establishments in Thasos at least and we don't hear much of taverns before Aristophanes, but in his comedies they appear as an already well-worn feature of the urban environment and it would be dangerous to argue from silence that taverns were a late-fifth-century phenomenon, supplanting the older more traditional aristocratic symposia as the fourth century progressed. The two institutions of drinking continued to exist side by side for a long time and they had probably coexisted for some years before they turn up in our sources.

There are enough references in all manner of different texts to indicate that taverns were widespread and popular. In Pompeii they reached a density that compares with the frequency of bars and pubs in modern cities. An assessment of their distribution in Athens must of necessity be rather more impressionistic. But take, to begin with, the laconic remark which Aristotle in the *Rhetoric* ascribes to Diogenes the Cynic: *ta kapēleia ta Attika phiditia* ('taverns are the refectories of Attica'). The impact of the facetious comparison lies in the conjunction of two starkly opposed institutions: the communal dining-halls of Sparta, the epitome of a conservative collective, archetypes of elite commensality, membership of which effectively defined citizenship, and Athenian taverns, a typically democratic efflorescence, quintessentially commercial and apparently plebeian. But behind the sarcasm of Diogenes' comparison there lies an observation about the popularity of taverns in Attica. Just as the common messes feed and water the entire citizenry in Sparta, so the whole population of Attica can be found of an evening thronging the *kapēleia*.[27]

Diogenes' observation is confirmed by the frequent references in comedy and forensic speeches to 'the neighbourhood *kapēleion*, offering a picture of bars spread widely throughout the city. So common a feature of the cityscape were they that the cuckold Euphiletus, justifying his murder of Eratosthenes in cold blood at the beginning of the fourth century, notes that he and his friends were able to buy torches for their expedition late at night from 'the nearest *kapēleion*' so that all could fully witness his wife's adultery before her lover was despatched. Apart from these literary sources, *kapēleia* feature frequently in curse tablets, lead-letters commissioned from magicians and deposited in infernal postboxes, usually graves or crevices, conjuring Hermes and Persephone to spell-bind their enemies. One tablet in particular from an unsuccessful rival, or an impoverished alcoholic, vividly confirms the picture portrayed in comedy and court speeches of Athens with *kapēleia* on every corner: 'I bind Callias, the taverner and his wife Thraitta, and the tavern of the bald man, and Anthemion's tavern near [. . .] and Philo the taverner. Of all these I bind their soul, their trade [*ergasia*], their hands and feet, their taverns . . . and also the taverner Agathon, servant of Sosimenes . . . I bind Mania the bar-girl at the spring, and the tavern of Aristander of Eleusis.' The '*kapēleion* of the bald man' seems to have been a common tag for a well-known tavern which crops up again in an inscription, a tavern of which perhaps Callias and Thraitta were the owners or staff. That a number of these tavern-keepers were slaves is indicated not only by mention of their owners, but also by their names. Thraitta (Thracian woman), for instance, is sometimes used almost as a synonym for slave-girl. The fragment of Alexis' *Aesop* mentioned above refers to the practice of selling wine from carts, and some of these *kapēleia* may have been nothing more than this, conveniently situated by a spring perhaps to enable the wine to be mixed with cold water and drunk there and then. Other more solidly founded bars had wells or cisterns on the premises.[28]

A vase in a private collection, currently on loan to the Ashmolean Museum in Oxford, is almost certainly an illustration of a *kapēleion*. The mouth of the buried cistern or *lakkos* is behind the youth who asks for '*trikotylos*', cheap wine sold at three obols a *chous*. An *oinochoē* or pitcher hangs behind him in case he wants to drink it on the premises. He is either opening the amphora or tasting wine with a sponge, which may symbolize thirst, or greed for wine. In the other hand he carries a bag of money to pay for it. The cup may have been destined for a symposium, juxtaposing hospitality with the market-place by reminding the symposiasts how the wine they are drinking got there and allowing the symposium's plebeian counterpart into the confines of the *andrōn* to show how aristocratic it is, or perhaps it was itself destined for a bar indicating that the *kapēleion* was also perhaps capable of sealing itself off from the world with an imagery of endless self-reflexion.

In the early 1970s excavators in the Agora unearthed a building of the early fourth century BCE which looks very like one of these taverns, adjacent to, or incorporating within it, some kind of eating-place. In 'room six' of the complex they discovered a well which having run dry was used for rubbish and filled with the debris of plates, fish-bones (of course) and a large number of amphora fragments revealing that, apart from the local Attic wine, Mendaean had been poured, along with Chian, Corinthian, Samian and Lesbian. In among these shards of coarse ceramic they found a large number of drinking cups of various types, some of a rather high standard: ' – they suggest that the establishment catered to a clientele of some quality and some indication of the power of that wine and the popularity of the shop is possibly to be inferred from the extraordinary breakage of which our well preserves the record.'[29]

Like fishmongers and other traders, *kapēloi* seem to have been held in low esteem by the general population. In one play Theopompus the playwright compared the Spartans to barmaids (*kapēlides*) because after their victory in the Peloponnesian War they gave the Greeks a taste of freedom, and then disappointed them with vinegar instead. Blepyrus in Aristophanes' *Wealth* mistakes the wretched personification of Poverty for the local barmaid who 'cheats grossly' in her half-pint measures. Again in *Thesmophoriazusae* the herald includes among the public curses imprecations against 'the taverner or the barmaid who cheats without shame on the full legal measure of the *chous* or *kotylē*. It is not long before *kapēlos* and its cognates comes to denote hucksterism or trickery in general; honest barmen were correspondingly prized.[30] The nervous measure-watching atmosphere of the *kapēleion* makes a striking contrast with the generous equality of the symposium.

It seems quite clear that most of our sources (representing something far short of a cross-section of society) see the *kapēleia* as a feature characteristic of democratic and commercial cities, and ascribe the popularity of such establishments to the 'baser' elements of society. This, for instance, is the historian Theopompus' tirade against the people of Byzantium and Chalcedon, taken from book eight of his *Philippica*:

> The fact that they had been practising democracy for what was by now a long time together with the fact that their city was situated at a trading post, not to mention the fact that the entire populace spent their time around the agora and the harbour, meant that the people of Byzantium lacked self-discipline and were accustomed to get together in bars for a drink. And the people of Chalcedon, before they came to share with the Byzantines in their government all used to pursue a better way of life. But when they had tasted Byzantine democracy they fell to decadence and from having been the most self-controlled and moderate in their daily life, they became drink-lovers and squanderers.

Later the historian Phylarchus, echoing Diogenes' observation about Athens, noted that the Byzantines virtually took up residence in taverns. In Thasos, on the other hand, breaking the bulk and selling by the *kotylē* was illegal, a measure intended, it seems, to outlaw taverns altogether.[31]

According to Isocrates the pamphleteer, only a certain type of person would allow himself to be seen at one of these establishments. In a eulogy of the ancient aristocratic council of the Areopagus, for instance, he looks back with nostalgia to the way young men used to behave in the good old days: 'No one, not even a servant, at least not a respectable servant, would have been so brazen as to eat or drink in a *kapēleion*. For they cultivated dignity, not buffoonery.' The same theme is repeated with some elaboration in the *Antidosis*:

> You have brought it about that even the most respectable [*epieikeis*] of the young men are wasting their time in drinking and assignations [*sunousiai*], and idleness and childish games . . . whereas those who are more base in nature spend their days in the kind of degenerate pastimes which not even a decent servant would have dared to pursue in former times. Some of them chill wine at the *Nine Fountains*, others drink in *kapēleia*, there are some who play dice in the gambling-dens and many who loiter around the place where the flute-girls are trained.[32]

Isocrates was not alone in his prejudices. In his speech *Against Patrocles*, the orator Hyperides, a contemporary of Demosthenes, records that 'the Areopagites barred anyone who had breakfasted in a *kapēleion* from going up to the Areopagus'. This was, of course, as much as anything, an attempt to stop drunken deliberations, and it seems likely that when our sources talk of people drinking during the day it is to the *kapēleia* that they are referring.[33] There seems to be an attack on the demagogue Cleon's morning attendance at these watering-holes of the Agora before a debate in the nearby Assembly – if not the actual bar unearthed by the archaeologists then one very similar – contained in the Paphlagonian's boast at Knights: 'I who can consume hot slices of tuna, drink a *chous* of neat wine and then go and screw the generals at Pylos.'

Isocrates allows us to set up an opposition between two kinds of drinking, the *potoi* (sympotic drinking) of the most 'respectable' (*epieikēs*) and the tavern drinking of those 'worse in nature'. Clearly, elements of social prejudice are in operation in his distinction between coarse low-class buffoonery (*bōmolochia*) and decency (*epieikeia*) as the reference to the 'servant' indicates. But we should not give the orator's nostalgic fantasy more credit than it deserves. Even with the limited information at our disposal we can see there were ranks among the taverns, running from high-quality *kapēleia* like the one dug up in the Agora, whose patrons could get hold of the best wines from the best producers, served in good ceramic ware by highly-regarded barmen like Plato's Sarambus through to the small stalls owned by the characters we encounter on the curse-tablets, some of which perhaps consisted of nothing more than a slave-girl and a cart by a spring. The clientele reflects this range. According to the rhetorical sources, the taverns are places where you could meet a member of the Areopagus, or Aeschines the Socratic, or Euphiletus and his friends, picking up torches on their way to kill Eratosthenes. In comedy they are places well known to men like Blepyrus in *Wealth* or slaves in *Lysistrata*, and to women of all levels of society, the citizen women of the *Lysistrata*, *Thesmophoriazusae* and the *Ecclesiazusae* as well as a nurse in Eubulus' *Pamphilus*. In the tavern as in the *andrōn*, wine was drunk mixed, but without all the ritual and regulation of the well-ordered symposium: 'As for me – for there happened to be a large new *kapēleion* across the road from the house – I was keeping my eye on the girl's nurse, for I had ordered the barman to mix me a *chous* [six pints] for an obol and to accompany it with the biggest *kantharos* he had.' Wine in the tavern was mixed for the individual in an individual vessel, with an individual cup to drink it out of. The elaborate rituals of sharing from the *kratēr* which are such a conspicuous feature of the symposium, have no part in the commercial environment of the tavern. Aristophanes uses the symposium as a metaphor for community threatened by unwelcome outsiders, like War or the friends of Ariphrades. The *kapēleion* on the other hand, he uses as an allegory of cheating, the swindling taverners out to exploit to the fullest extent their clients on the other side of the bar. In the *kapēleion* are to be found those who had no part in the symposium: '*des femmes, des esclaves, des barbares*.' It seems, therefore, to fulfil a role as the symposium's Other, on the margins of the Athenian community of citizens, a place where people drink 'in no kind of order' as Plato observes of the drinking which disrupts and dissolves his own *Symposium*. The tavern is a place where wines are identified by their price, where drink is commodified and severed from social ties, a place where drink is for getting drunk, a place where ancient drinking comes to look most like the drinking we apparently do today.[34]

But this is to ignore certain characteristics of this commercial drinking which shine through, even though the evidence is so scattered. First of all, the bars are so often 'local'. They nestle snugly into the neighbourhood. The nurse only has to pop across the road to her *kapēleion*, as do so many others from cuckolded Euphiletus to Blepyrus in the *Wealth*, and there she finds someone to buy her a drink. Blepyrus in that play thinks he recognizes in the goddess Poverty the cheating barmaid from his local and there is certainly an expectation that customers and clients would know each other and their drinking habits. This is a long way from anonymous drinking: 'There is a taverner in our neighbourhood; and whenever I feel like a drink and go there, he knows at once – and he only knows – how I have it mixed. I always know that I'll be drinking it neither too watery, nor too strong.' The bonds between barmen and their regulars are reflected in the practice of drinking on tick. Athens was a city in which borrowing was very common. Ready use of credit is often seen as an indication of a highly developed capitalist economy, but in many societies, and in particular at Athens, it seems to have more in common with pre-money economies based on gift-exchange, a transaction which shifts the burden of trust away from the quality of the coinage and back to personal acquaintance. The practice of '*prodosin pinein*' fatally compromises the impersonality of drinking in a tavern, tying up the free-flowing promiscuous exchange of commodities with bonds of debt and trust. It is a sign of the depths to which insolvency has brought Aeschines the Socratic, that even the local *kapēloi* have stopped advancing him credit.[35]

The distinction between symposium and *kapēleion*, then, was one of class and culture rather than of socialization. The tavern was differently socialized rather than unsocialized and if it was the site of those excesses whose debris so impressed the archaeologists, its reputation at Athens was not worse than that of the symposium. In fact, in the popular imagination it figures, if anything, as less of a threat to public order than the aristocratic drinking-party. For this, of course, was a democratic city with a radical reputation. Non-Athenians like Theopompus and Diogenes or the government of Thasos looked on taverns very differently.

* * *

To a surprising degree the Greeks anticipate modern debates about drinking as a drug or as a social catalyst. They were nervous drinkers and shared the anthropologists' anxiety about the threat wine presented to socialization, agreeing with Brillat-Savarin that the discipline of conversation must restrain it. One important aspect of the Greek problematic of wine finds few modern parallels, however, focusing neither on the community of drinkers nor on the drink, but on something in between.

CUPS

Some of the most surprising texts on the subject of drinking in antiquity are those fragments in poetry and prose in praise of Spartan drinking habits composed by the Spartan-loving revolutionary oligarch, Critias of Athens. In his *Elegies* he contrasted Spartan drinking habits – each man from his own cup, no toasts passed around and, he insists, no drunken excess – with Athenian practice. In a similar work, *The Constitution of the Spartans*, he elaborated his praise of Spartan institutions in prose with an encomiastic examination of the smallest details of their daily life from their footware to their crockery: 'Laconian shoes are the best; their cloaks are the most pleasant to wear as well as being the most useful; the Spartan *kōthōn* is a cup most appropriate for military service and easily transportable in a kit-bag. It is a cup for soldiers, because it is often necessary for them to drink water that is not clean: the liquid inside a *kōthōn* cannot be seen too clearly, and the cup has ridges so that it retains any impurities.'[36]

This fragment of Critias is the first in a strange series of rationalizations penned by the supporters of Sparta's peculiar conventions. Xenophon, for instance, tells us that Lycurgus devised red cloaks for the Spartiates because he believed this costume had least of all in common with a woman's dress. He also permitted men past their first youth to wear their hair long, not for the sake of vanity, but because he thought it would make them look taller, more gentlemanly, more terrifying. Aristotle in his *Constitution of the Spartans* returned to the same theme. Red cloaks were inherently masculine. Their sanguinary dye accustomed the Spartans to depise the flow of blood. Plutarch had a slightly different explanation: the crimson colour was designed to disguise from the enemy the fact that they had been wounded. In the *Rhetoric*, again, Aristotle gives a Veblenian elaboration of Xenophon's views on long hair: 'it is the mark of a gentleman, for it is not easy to perform a plebeian task with long hair.'[37]

It is not difficult to see that this exegesis of the semiotics of Spartan fashion is rather defensive in tone, the self-conscious forging of a myth. The writers protest too much, and the reason for their defensiveness is not hard to find: the habits they describe look rather like luxurious practices to the Athenian eye. This is most obvious with the custom of wearing the hair long, a vogue that, outside the boundaries of Laconia, aroused considerable suspicions, drawing charges of effeminacy and enervation and bringing to mind paragons of long-haired vice like the fictional profligate Pheidippides in Aristophanes' *Clouds* or, on the very streets of Athens, infamous Alcibiades. Similar connotations of luxury hover around other items of Spartan fashion. Laconian shoes are fine pieces of footwear, the shoes of gentlemen in contrast to the felt slippers of the poor. The *phoinikis* too, the scarlet cloak with its expensive vermilion dye, evokes extravagance to an outsider's eye.[38] In democratic Athens the whole get-up would look like something very far from asceticism. The attachment of the Spartan epithet to the paraphernalia of a rich and opulent lifestyle was a continual rebuttal of those citizens of oligarchic tendency who tried to emulate the Spartan way of life, holding it up as an example of moderation and restraint.

Critias' elaborate defence of the Spartan cup falls into the same apologetic category. This too was a suspicious object. Spartan drinking, without the lively conversation, the toasts and the passing of the cup which characterized well-ordered drinking at Athens, looked rude, ill-mannered and dangerous to Critias' audience. The Spartan way of drinking from one's own cup, in silence, bore most resemblance to the transgressive and competitive drinking-to-get-drunk of *Choes*, the feast of the Pitchers. The cup was itself a symbol for the wrong kind of drinking, as Aristophanes made explicit in his lost play *The Banqueters*. The play centres on the activities of a man's two sons, one of them a model of self-control, the other utterly dissipated in every field. An illustration of this dissipation is provided by his drinking habits; no moderate measure for him, no gentle sipping from shallow vessels between anecdotes, but 'Chian wine from Spartan cups'.[39] The *kōthōn*, in an Athenian context, far from being an attribute of the rugged asceticism of soldiers, stands for the worst kind of vinous indulgence practised by urban degenerates. The reason for the cup's infamy seems clear. It was the wrong shape.

The Greeks enjoyed a rich and varied array of cups in all manner of shapes and sizes. There are indications that it was customary to progress from small cups at the start of the symposium to larger ones at the end. The Scythian Anacharsis, who represents for the Greeks something akin to the naive wisdom of the eighteenth-century's 'noble savage', thought this very odd. Why drink from small cups when you're empty and from big cups when you're full? At the drinking-party described by Xenophon in his *Symposium* one of the guests, breathless from an impromptu dancing performance, tries to hurry things along and asks for 'the big cup' to quench his thirst. The host concurs and asks for big cups all round; the others are thirsty too, not from dancing but from laughing at his performance. Predictably, however, Socrates, who is a guest at an alarming number of attested symposia, intercedes and speaks in favour of 'small cups sprinkled frequently, so that we will be seduced into reaching a state of amusement, instead of being forced by the wine into drunkenness'. The moderate drinking practices of the well-ordered symposium call for moderately-sized cups. Drinkers who are getting serious about drinking, on the other hand, typically ask for a big cup, or a bigger cup to show they mean business. The woman in Pherecrates' *Corianno* goes so far as to bring her own well-sized vessel along, rejecting the little *kyliskē* hopefully offered to her.[40]

It is important to observe that in the literature big cups are almost always *deep* cups. The vessels to which they are opposed are flat, shallow, saucerish things. A fragment from a play of Pherecrates makes this relationship between size and shape quite clear. In his play *Tyranny*, which seems to have been a fantasy of women seizing power on the lines of Aristophanes' *Ecclesiazusae*, he describes the women's control of men's drinking as follows:

Then for the men they had cups made which were flat, nothing but a base with no sides, and room for not so much as a cockleful, like little 'tasters'; for their female selves, on the other hand, they had deep cups made, cups like wine-transporting merchantmen, well-rounded, delicate vessels that bulged out in the middle; cups designed with far foresight for maximum consumption and minimal accountability. The result? Whenever we charge them with drinking up the wine they reproach us and swear that they have had no more than a single cup. But this single one is greater than a thousand cups.

A similar contrast is made by Epigenes in his play *Heroine*: 'But the potters don't even make *kantharoi* nowadays, you poor chap, not those fat ones; they all make these low-lying elegant things instead . . . as if it were the cups themselves we were drinking rather than the wine.'[41] The size and shape of the vessels represented a difference in the manner of drinking. Deep cups meant deep drinking, long draughts knocked back from fat vessels, bottoms-up; shallow cups in contrast were drained more elegantly, tilted slightly and sipped frequently between dialectical contributions.

Typical of these vessels of depth was the bat-eared goblet of the Boeotians and Etruscans, the *kantharos*: 'Let's put out into the deep; into the *kantharos*, boy, pour it, by Zeus, into the *kantharos*,' says a comic character to his slave. A huge *kantharos* is what gets the nurse drunk in Eubulus' *Pamphilus* (she drains it dry in one go), and it is a *kantharos* that Hermaiscus is seen knocking back in Alexis' *Cratias*. It is no surprise, then, that it is this cup above all that Dionysus keeps by his side, that, indeed, becomes so closely associated with the god of wine as to constitute an attribute.[42]

The horn-shaped vessels called rhyton and *keras* belong to the same capacious category. A fragment of Epinicus describes three cups of legendary capacity, all of them rhyta. One holding two *choes*, approximately twelve pints, is known as the elephant tusk, to be drunk, apparently, in one go. At least one other source refers to such a vessel; it may be more than a figment of comedy's hyperbolic imagination. Drinking-horns share the *kantharos'* symbolic associations with Dionysus and his retinue, indicating in particular a primitive or barbarian approach to drinking. Often, it seems, they were filled with *akratos*. One striking image from a vase of about 500 BCE shows a foreshortened symposiast dressed up for drinking like a Scythian, a huge drinking-horn silhouetted against him in the foreground. When someone in a comedy asks for a drinking-horn or even for 'cups deeper to drink from than drinking-horns', it is clear that the well-ordered Greek forms of drinking are being ushered out of the door. A striking illustration of this comes from the plastic vases, ceramic cups moulded into figures. The cups come in a variety of forms, but never assume the features of the white males for whose lips they were intended, a striking exception that François Lissarrague in his study of the imagery of the symposium thought significant: 'there are no gods except for Dionysus and Heracles; instead one finds only women, both male and female blacks, Asians and satyrs ... It is as if the anthropology of such moulded vases was meant to define the opposite of the Greek drinker and to hold up to him all the things that he was not.'[43] It is no coincidence that the cups most often used for refashioning into the form of these notoriously immoderate drinkers are the cups of immoderate drinking, the *kantharos* and the horn being particular favourites for makeover.

Drinking-horns presented something of a problem for moralists. For if, as the philosopher Chamaeleon of Heracleia insisted, in his treatise *On Drunkenness*, big cups were an invention of modern decadence and did not exist in earlier times, how was it that the rhyton was an attribute of the heroes of the past? The philosopher had an answer for this objection. The artists represent heroes with large cups, so that it will be seen that their characteristic rage is due not to their temperamental nature, but to their inebriation.[44]

Other rather more obscure shapes share the reputation of the *kantharos* and the rhyton. The *kumbion* was a deep vessel shaped like a boat, a favourite shape of one notorious drinker in the fourth century, known as Euripides. Another deep cup called *lepastē* was associated with the verb *laptō*, which Athenaeus glosses as 'to drink in one go'. A fragment of Pherecrates has a character offering one to the thirsty members of his audience suggesting they swig it like Charybdis. Elsewhere, we find it emptied by old women, and used successfully to charm Lysander when a *kōthōn* had failed. One of these deep cups is actually called a 'breathless cup', because its contents were drunk down without a breath.[45]

Despite the competition, it is Critias' *kōthōn* that comes to stand *par excellence* for deep drinking at Athens. It shares many of the features of those deep cups associated with Dionysus and his followers, emptied in single draughts. A *kōthōn* referred to in a play of Alexis could hold about two pints. In a painting described by Polemon in a fragmentary ecphrasis from his *To Adaeus and Antigonus*, Dionysus is seated on a rock accompanied by a bald-headed satyr holding a *kōthōn*. A woman in Theopompus' *Stratiotides* describes the customary way this cup was drained: 'I, for one, would be prepared to stretch back my throat to drink from the neck-twisting *kōthōn*.' Most commentators suggest that this comic drama played on the consequences of the fantastic scenario of women in the army, and there seems to be more to the *kōthōn*'s military connection than special pleading on the part of Critias. They are found in the hands of soldiers in Archilochus' early archaic *Elegies*, and in Aristophanes' late-fifth-century *Knights*. However, *contra* Critias, the liquid most likely to be discovered inside was not water but wine. There has been some debate over what the Spartan cup actually looked like. Many have been misled by Critias' description to look in vain for a vessel with an elaborate folded-over rim to catch impurities. But the fragment refers more simply to *ambōnas*, meaning 'ridges' or 'ribs'. At least one vase, shaped like a stout mug or tankard, has been discovered with *kōthōn* actually written on the base, and it now seems clear that this shape satisfies most of the literary references. By Critias' time at the end of the fifth century they were being made with vertical ridges all the way round. Normally such ridging was simply decorative, an attempt to make ceramic ware look like silver, but on the *kōthōn*s the ridging is often found on the inside too, apparently a rather pointless exercise that would only weaken the fabric. Some students of vases have suggested this could only be explained as an obsession with imitating metalware taken to counter-productive extreme. But Critias explains it much better. What is the point of having ridges to collect the lees unless you have them on the inside?[46] If such vessels are rarely mentioned in modern accounts of Greek drinking it is because they do not fit the image of the classic elegant sympotic cup, looking more like a medieval tankard. Beazley, the great connoisseur of Greek pots, preferred to leave them nameless, classifying them (despite their lack of a pouring-spout) with jugs.

We are now in a position to subvert Critias' special pleading and to restore to the *kōthōn* its normal connotations. It was a very useful cup for scooping, not from streams of mountain water, but from vats of wine as described with such relish by Archilochus. Its contents would be less visible than in an ordinary flat sympotic cup, not to disguise the dirtiness of the water drawn from mountain streams, but simply because it was a deep cup made for deep drinking. The ridging was suitable not for catching Critias' river-dirt but for saving the swigger from getting a mouthful of lees and all the other bits and pieces left in ancient Greek wine. It may have started as a military cup, but it seems to have found its way into the symposium at an early date.[47] There it will have stood alongside the *keras* and other deep cups as a challenge to the orderly blending and distribution of the wine. The *kōthōn*, with its characteristic single handle does not look like a cup made for sharing.

From the name of this cup the Greeks generated the noun *kōthōnismos* and the verb *kōthōnizein* which first appear in the fourth century. They refer to 'deep drinking': '*je vide la grande coupe*' is how a French commentator begins the conjugation of this interesting verb. The physician Mnesitheus wrote a treatise in the form of a letter around the middle of the century, suggesting that in certain circumstances *kōthōnismos* could be good for you, like an emetic or a purgative. He gives three main points to bear in mind when engaging in such drinking: 'not to drink poor wine or *akratos*, and not to eat *tragēmata* [dried fruits and nuts and other desserts of the second table] in the middle of *kōthōnismoi*. When you have had enough, don't go to sleep until you have vomited more or less. Then, if you vomit sufficiently go to bed after a light bath. If, however, you weren't able fully to purge yourself, use more water and completely immerse yourself in a warm tub.'[48] This kind of drinking had probably always gone on, but it wasn't until the fourth century that the culture of *kōthōnismos* caught the attention of the orators and moralists.

Demosthenes, according to Hyperides, considered it a particular vice of the young. He described them as *akratokōthōnes*, a remark that subsequently became notorious. The parasite known as the Lark demonstrated the wit that excused his gate-crashing by connecting Demosthenes' remark to his notorious readiness to accept bribes, accusing the orator of a kind of metaphorical hypocrisy: 'This man who calls other men *akratokōthōnes* has himself drained the big cup dry.' Such drinking seems to have been social and competitive and may well have taken place in a sympotic context, although it transgressed so many of the symposium's rules. By the early third century *kōthōn* means a cup no longer, but a drinking-bout, or drinking-party. Two kinds are mentioned, *sumbolikos* and *asumbolos*, with and without contributions, the former requiring each participant to bring his own wine, the second providing an open bar. When Lycon the Peripatetic arrived as a student in Athens in the early third century he made great progress in acquiring knowledge of these p.b.a.b. parties as well as the rates charged by each of the city's courtesans.[49]

As Demosthenes' coinage indicates, the *kōthōn* was associated not simply with slugging deep draughts, but with drinking strong wine. This is something it had in common with other deep cups. The notion of 'depth' is the key to the problematic of drinking at Athens, enabling us to draw up a division along two axes. One kind of consumption emphasizes the horizontal plane: the wine is blended expansively with water; it is sipped slowly from smaller shallower cups; there are as a result more rounds, more of those processes of circulation and distribution which make the symposium such a bonding experience; words join water in diluting the wine whose proper role is to facilitate conversation. In this shallow form of drinking the emphasis is not on the wine but on the company of drinkers joined around the *kratēr*, protected from the power of liquor by a whole theatre of mitigation, and the distracting play of discourse and representation. Wine is effectively flattened and rendered negligible. This is the wine of commensality, of Brillat-Savarin and the anthropologists.[50] Opposed to this is the degenerate consumption of the vertical axis, the wine of Baudelaire and the alcoholists: the wine is *akratos*, thick, three-dimensional and strong; the cups are large and deep; drinking is long and breathless. Wine can reassert its primacy and, in the stampede to inebriation, the niceties of social interaction get trampled underfoot. Here wine is no longer a catalyst of conversation. It is a drug once more.

PART II

DESIRE

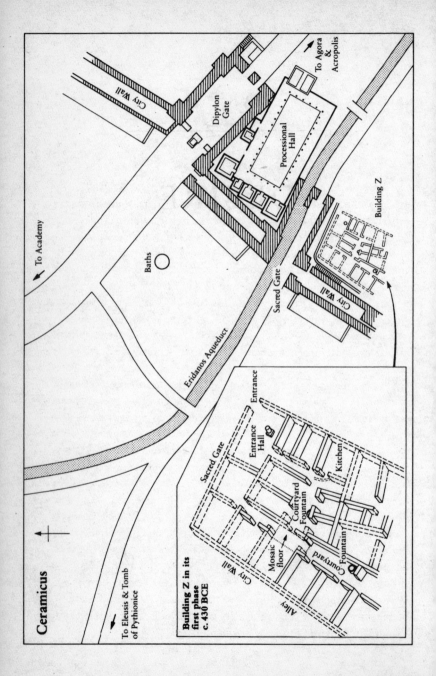

Ceramicus

To Eleusis & Tomb
of Pythionice

To Academy

To Agora &
Acropolis

City Wall

Dipylon
Gate

Processional
Hall

Baths

Building Z

Eridanos Aqueduct

Sacred Gate

City Wall

Building Z in its
first phase
c. 430 BCE

Sacred Gate

Entrance

Entrance

Entrance Hall

Kitchen

Courtyard
Fountain

Mosaic
floor

City Wall

Courtyard

Fountain

Alley

III

WOMEN AND BOYS

THE ORATOR APOLLODORUS is attacking Neaera, a prostitute, in court. He digresses, for a moment, on the uses of women in Athens: 'Hetaeras we keep for pleasure, concubines for attending day-by-day to the body and wives for producing heirs, and for standing trusty guard on our household property.'[1] Ancient literature contains no shortage of attempts by ancient men to put ancient women in their proper sexual place, and a whole lexicon of labels and terms with which to do it: 'two-obol woman', 'ground-beater', 'flute-girl', 'companion', 'wage-earner', 'wanderer', 'wife'. The very act of naming was an important part of policing women and women's sexuality. According to the laws of Syracuse, for instance, the great Greek city on the southern tip of Sicily, a woman was forbidden from wearing 'gold ornaments or gaily-coloured dresses or garments with purple borders unless she admitted she was a common prostitute'.[2] Apollodorus' neat three-kinds-of-women statement has been particularly influential among modern historians and is sometimes cited as a straightforward account of female roles in Athens. It is far from that, however. The speaker himself shows a remarkable level of inconsistency in conferring his titles on Neaera and the whole thrust of the speech is that such distinctions are easily flouted, enabling Neaera's daughter, 'a common whore' (*pornē*), to infiltrate the ranks of decent citizens by marrying the King Archon, even presiding with him over the most ancient rites in the city's religious calendar and risking the wrath of the gods. As the great French classicist Jean-Pierre Vernant comments, the author's 'remarks in this . . . speech indicate better than anything both the desire to establish a clear demarcation . . . and at the same time the impossibility of so doing'.[3]

Other writers are no more helpful than Apollodorus, frequently applying several different terms to the same woman, and thus confounding their own taxonomies. This ambivalence is at the very heart of the vocabulary used to describe women's roles. *Gunē*, wife, can also mean more generally 'woman' (cf. French *femme*), and was sometimes used for a concubine or mistress. The more normal word for a woman in that kind of informal relationship was hetaera, but that could equally well designate a woman of independent means and high fees, or, at the other end of the scale, a slave-girl working for a madam. It is hardly surprising, then, that despite the survival of numerous ancient definitions, attempts to establish clear demarcations between the different categories of women in Athens (to distinguish wives from concubines [*pallakai*] and concubines from 'courtesans' and 'courtesans' from 'common whores' [*pornai*]) are highly problematic, and consensus rarely survives for more than a generation. Most recently, many scholars have become impatient with this inconsistency on the part of ancient writers. Ignoring Vernant's advice they have concluded that one division alone can be made with some confidence, one division that really mattered: the division between Wives and the Rest. The other distinctions represent nothing more substantial than a rich vocabulary with which men could express varying degrees of contempt for the women they used.

This 'two-types' model in works on women in antiquity has had a devastating effect on the career of the courtesan or hetaera who has moved from a position at centre-stage in earlier accounts of prostitution to near invisibility in more recent ones. In the early years of this century, when such subjects as Women and Sex were first considered worthy of attention, the hetaera exercised a strong fascination on male historians. She was represented as a sophisticated lady, a cultured woman of the world, witty, philosophical and flirtatious. In these earlier, idealized treatments a strong distinction was made between high-class courtesans and the *pornai*, the lower-class prostitutes of the brothels and the streets, who alone represented the 'bad' kind of prostitution. Charles Seltman, for instance, writing in the 1950s, maintained:

The framework of social life in Athens was not far different from that of Paris up to 1939. There were brothels, mainly for foreigners of all sorts, licensed under the laws of Solon as far back as the early sixth century BC. The licensing was done to prevent brawling in the streets. Later street-walkers living under the care of a 'Madame' began to appear. All this, of course, is the same as in any Mediterranean city today, a world-wide misfortune. But hetaeras were certainly in a very different class; often highly educated women, foreigners from other Greek states and cities, earning a living sometimes in commerce, business girls, bachelor girls, models.[4]

That the hetaeras who associated with the leading men of the period, who engaged Pericles and Alcibiades in droll conversation, also sold their bodies for sex, was an uncomfortable fact, readily pushed into the background.

The new accounts of women in antiquity, however, influenced by feminist attitudes to prostitution, have reacted strongly against this picture, treating it as an attempt by male fantasists, ancient and modern, to romanticize an inherently obnoxious institution. Women had two roles available to them: the wife or the prostitute; there was no room for any equivocating 'courtesan' in between.[5] Eva Keuls, for instance, in a chapter entitled 'Two Kinds of Women. The Splitting of the Female Psyche', remarks:

If the sexual conduct of the respectable woman is restricted to marital intercourse while the corresponding male is permitted to be promiscuous, it must of necessity follow that the female population is divided sharply into two classes: those who have limited sexual contacts in the course of a lifetime, probably far less than their physical nature could accommodate, and those who have sex in great abundance, far more than they could possibly experience in a meaningful way.[6]

This initially rather radical idea has now settled comfortably into the mainstream of ancient studies: 'Athenian society perfected a quite precise double standard,' claims one textbook, 'which did not involve contradiction, or subterfuge, but rather relied on a clear separation between two categories of women who were not to be confused: legitimate wives (or potential legitimate wives) and all other women.

The first were the chaste mothers and daughters of Athenian citizens; the second were open to free sexual exploitation.'[7] In this version of the position of women at Athens there are only two very starkly contrasted groups, almost mirror-images of one another. They are connected only by the hydraulic operation of male heterosexuality, the prostitutes providing release for the pressures produced by the chaste seclusion of decent women, relief for the sexual frustrations of men not yet married, or forced to marry women whose only attractions were a large dowry or an influential family. She is a sexual substitute for the wife, a body-double or, in the words of a recent German study, an 'Ersatzfrau'.[8]

Under the influence of this transcendental distinction between Wives and the Rest the old distinction made between courtesans and 'common whores', hetaeras and *pornai*, has become obsolete. They both fall more or less happily now into a single modern category. They are all prostitutes.[9] At the same time, important intervening terms like the Athenian hetaera and the concubine have been elided, forgotten or ignored as if all Athenian women were chastely married or about to be, and all hetaeras were foreigners speaking in strange dialects with funny accents. These need not trouble the two-women theory. Either they are 'paradoxical' exceptions whose existence 'paradoxically' confirms the basic truth of the doctrine or they are put into the even more fuzzy class of '*pallakai*' and classed with wives or hetaeras depending on convenience. There are, to be sure, not many references to these native-born courtesans and concubines (they will have found it easier than most to fade into decent obscurity), but they certainly existed, providing an important bridge between Wives and the Rest and muddying masculine distinctions.[10] One cannot help thinking that this dogmatic distinction is a way for scholars to avoid dealing with prostitution altogether and helps to account for the astonishing lack of research in a subject which sits at the intersection of two of the biggest growth areas in modern classics, the study of women and the study of sexuality.

Instead of two stark groups of women and one great undifferentiated mass of sex-workers I want in the next couple of chapters to emphasize the diversity and complexity of the sex market in Athens and to re-establish the importance of the hetaera. There were numerous gradations between the miserable life of the streets and the comfortable existence of the most successful courtesans, quietly encroaching on the territory of the legitimate family and causing consternation to Apollodorus and his fellow-citizens. To talk of 'mistresses' and 'courtesans' may risk glamorizing, romanticizing or exoticizing a life that was in most cases nasty, brutish and short and there are dangers in reconstructing a kind of hierarchy, but, on the other hand, historians are providing no compensation for the wretchedness of ancient women's lives by lumping all 'bad girls' together. Moreover, the sex market in Athens was not just about the exploitation of women. Men were sexual commodities as well as consumers and although male sex-workers were, I think, nowhere near as numerous as their female counterparts, they did take on very similar roles in the city, making prostitution more than a straightforward gender issue.

The terms used to describe women were so slippery that to avoid misunderstandings Athenians had to resort to various, often revealing, circumlocutions. Instead of simply *gunē*, a wife might be described as a *gunē gametē*, 'a married wife', or even a *gunē gametē kata tous nomous*, 'a wife married according to the laws'. A hetaera could be more closely defined as 'one of those women that are hired out' or 'one of those women who run to the symposia for ten drachmas'.[11] It was in law, however, that the categorization of women became a matter of vital necessity. Adultery carried heavy penalties in Athens. One antique law from the Draconian code (*c*. 621 BCE) allowed a man caught in the act of having sex with another man's woman (wife, daughter, mother, sister, concubine) to be slaughtered on the spot.[12] It was thus a matter of some importance to define those women with whom one could copulate in safety and so another ancient law, ascribed to Solon (*c*. 594), specified the women who fell outside the law's protection, referring not to *pornai*, but to 'those who sit in a brothel or those who walk to and fro in the open'.[13]

STREETS

As we have seen, space in antiquity was rarely a neutral concept and its silent dispositions were very often charged with symbolic meaning and ideological distinctions. On the personal level this might involve the opposition between right and left that governs the morality of eating. On a grander scale it provided separate domains for gods and goddesses within the territory of the polis, the cultivated spaces of Demeter, the marginal mountains, meadows and woods that belonged to Artemis and Pan, and the citadels of Athena. One of the most carefully delineated zones within the city was the zone of Hestia centred on hearth and home, opposed to the sphere of Hermes god of the threshold, of the paths that led from it, and of luck.[14] According to this stark symbolic opposition, the women of the streets stood at the farthest remove from the world of the wife who kept to the interiors, 'trusty guardian of what's inside', as Apollodorus puts it. Women who wanted to preserve a reputation for decency rarely strayed out of doors except under pressing necessity and a thick cloak; public activities, such as politics and shopping, were the province of men. Women of the streets therefore lived on the wrong side of the threshold and advertised their availability by submitting to the public gaze. They carried their homelessness in their names, which convey in terse slang something of the monotony of life on foot: 'bridge-woman' (*gephuris*), 'runner' (*dromas*), 'wanderer' (*peripolas*), 'alley-treader' (*spodesilaura*), 'ground-beaters', 'foot-soldiers'.[15] They form an anonymous mass of women, faceless 'ranks', or 'droves'.

Not surprisingly, these women have left little trace apart from their nicknames in the historical record. A roofless existence and a nomadic lifestyle were not productive of long-lasting monuments. But the casual remarks of observers indicate that 'women who walk to and fro in the open' were still very much a feature of the urban landscape long after Solon made them an exception. Xenophon, for instance, records Socrates in the late fifth century observing that the streets of Athens were full of such safety-valves for 'releasing the pressures of lust'.[16] More evidence for this form of prostitution can be gleaned from speeches and comedies casting aspersions on the sexual morality of male politicians. This often obscene innuendo takes us a little beyond mere speculation and sheds some light on the *alfresco* shadowlands of Athenian sexuality.

Most revealing of all is Aeschines' prosecution of Timarchus of Sphettus, whom he accused of having been a common prostitute. It seems quite clear that Aeschines in fact had very little evidence to substantiate his allegations and he relies instead on rumour and insinuation, recalling in particular an event at a meeting of the Council some months previously. Timarchus was lecturing the committee on the need to strengthen the city's defences, but the grave atmosphere had been punctured by giggles whenever he mentioned the 'walls', or 'a tower' in need of repair or someone being 'led off somewhere'. Since Aeschines uses this laughter to prove that the defendant's activities as a common prostitute were common knowledge, it seems clear that the places mentioned were known to be the favoured haunts of 'ground-beaters' and 'alley-treaders'. At a general Assembly of the People held on a winter morning some time later, Autolycus, a distinguished member of the august Areopagus, decided to take issue with Timarchus' proposals: 'You must not be surprised, fellow-citizens,' he began, 'if Timarchus is better acquainted than the members of the Areopagus with this deserted area and the region of the Pnyx . . . we can make some such allowance as this for Timarchus: he thought that where everything is so quiet, there will be but little expense for each of you.' Immediate applause and cheers and loud laughter. Autolycus does not quite get the joke. He frowns and continues, but when he comes to the question of the 'derelict buildings' and 'the wells', the whole Assembly degenerates into a riot. 'Fortunately the modern reader is spared a knowledge of the *double-entente* that made the vulgar listeners laugh – ', claims Charles Darwin Adams in a footnote to his translation of this passage, but if he or she bears in mind that Timarchus was formally charged with prostitution at the same meeting, the modern reader should not find the ancient allusions quite so opaque. *Lakkos*, a well or a cistern, is the most straightforward to decipher. It was used of prostitutes, referring apparently to their enormous sexual capacity, or, more graphically, to their passive reception of effluvia.[17]

City walls, on the other hand, in many times and places have had a reputation as areas for quick and surreptitious sexual transactions, and where they still stand they still do, but here perhaps 'the walls' and the 'tower' might refer more specifically to the red-light district of Athens, the Ceramicus, lying in the north-west around the main entrance to the city, the double Dipylon gate. The Ceramicus took its name originally from the potters who used to dominate the district, but it was distinguished also for the splendid monumental tombs that lined the roads out of Athens, taking the initiated to celebrate the Mysteries at Eleusis, or leading would-be philosophers to the gymnasium of Academy for a session with Plato. When later commentators explained its significance to their readers, however, they fixed on a quite different local feature: 'a place at Athens where prostitutes (*pornai*) stood' was the usual succinct gloss. This green and tranquil park is one of the quieter archaeological sites in Athens, but a passage from Aristophanes' *Knights* helps to bring it noisily to life: the Sausage-seller having knocked the chief demagogue off his perch thinks up a suitable punishment for him: 'he will have my old job, a solitary sausage-selling franchise at the gates, blending dog meat with asses' parts, getting drunk and exchanging unpleasantries with the whores, and then quenching his thirst with dirty-water from the baths.' 'Yes, an excellent idea. That's all he's good for, outbawling the bath attendants and the whores.'[18] Some of the prostitutes lining the streets will have had beds in the brothels nearby, others may have made do with the nearby cemetery itself, enabling Aristophanes to concoct a gross combination of two extra-mural activities, mourning and whoring, in another piece of invective against a public figure: 'Amidst the tombs, I hear, Cleisthenes' boy bends over, plucking the hair from his arse, tearing at his beard . . . and crying out.'[19] In *Peace* Aristophanes outdoes even this gross image and reveals in passing that Athens' port, the Piraeus, was another popular zone for street-women. Flying high above the city on the back of a dung-beetle on a mission to rescue the goddess Peace, Trygaeus catches sight of 'a man defecating amongst the prostitutes in the Piraeus', a disaster if his coprophiliac transport should catch the smell.[20] He calls down to the man quickly to dig a hole, plant around it aromatic thyme and drench it in myrrh.

By the late sixth century if not before, the boisterous street-walkers had competition from the more tuneful *aulētrides*. Often called 'flute-girls', the double-reeded and frequently double-piped *aulos* they played was closer in timbre to an oboe or shawm. The Greeks likened it to the buzzing of wasps at the lower end of its range and the honking of geese on the high notes. Pollux the lexicographer put together a list of Attic words used to describe it: 'wailing, enticing, lamenting'.[21] Along with other music-girls the *aulētrides* played an important role at the symposium, entertaining the guests with music at the beginning and with sex at the end of the party, but just as often they are to be found out of doors, in the docks of the Piraeus where 'just past puberty they take a fee and no time at all to sap the strength of cargo men' or in Athens 'smiling at you on streetcorners'; clearly it was possible to have sex with a flute-girl without taking her to a party first.[22] Unlike the solipsistic lyre which accompanied poetic introversion and repose, the *aulos* was usually found providing music for working and moving, more particularly for *moving off* in the dancing-lines of the procession and the march.[23] It possessed a supernatural power to take over the body; when the *aulos* played, men forgot themselves. The showpiece orator of the Roman period, 'Goldenmouthed' Dio, tells the story of the great flautist Timotheus performing for Alexander. Alexander was so excited by the tones of the music and by the rhythm of the playing that he got to his feet at once and rushed for his weapons like one possessed. Even animals were susceptible to its charms. It was said that the decadent Sybarites made the mistake of acquainting their horses with the sound of flutes and watched helplessly when in mid-battle the cavalry started dancing to the enemies' tune, waltzing off into the opposite camp. In the ancient world all flutes were half way to being magic ones.[24] The flute was an important element in the symposium, providing the rhythm for the mixing and distributing of the wine as well as the singing, but in many ways this narrow space of horizontal drunkenness was rather restricting for the *aulos*. One medical writer knew of a man who was thrown into a panic whenever he heard its tone within the *andrōn*'s narrow confines. It was outside, on the street, that the flute-girls really came into their element, in the *kōmos*, a conga of revellers that took the drinking-party out into the city on expeditions of riot and debauch.[25]

We hear of 'training-schools for flute-girls' where old men like Isocrates thought young men were spending too much time, but Plato implies they could not play very well, and it was not generally for their musical skill that they were so popular.[26] Although a few among them rose to the highest ranks of the courtesans, it seems quite clear that flute-girls were always considered among the cheapest and most despised of hired women. By the fourth century *aulētris* is used almost as a synonym for 'cheap prostitute'.[27] Crucially they shared the same space as the ground-beaters, in the Piraeus, on the streets, or under the walls, providing musical accompaniment when the battlements were torn down in 404 after the victory of Sparta.[28] It was not long before the ramparts rose again, of course, to provide Athens with seclusion, but for about ten years the city, too, knew what it was like to be on the outside.

The streets could be rough. Fighting over prostitutes was a commonplace of low-life escapades and flute-girls were especially vulnerable to being mauled by competing males. Demosthenes refers casually to a member of the board of *archons*, the *thesmothetai*, who had been involved in a punch-up while attempting to carry off a flute-girl. In *Wasps* Aristophanes stages just such a tug-of-war with a father on one side, his son on the other, and a naked *aulētris*, stolen from a party, in between. In *Acharnians* he reduces the origins of the Peloponnesian War from a high-minded feud over sacred land to a squalid dispute over *pornai*, and makes a straightforward equation between naval expeditions, flute-girls and black-eyes.[29] So long as these fights were confined to the symposium, it was a private matter to be sorted out in a private law-suit. On the streets, however, there was a serious problem of public order, and the Astynomoi, a board of ten responsible for keeping the highways of the city open and clear, were empowered by law to sort out disputes peacefully, making sure that the flute-girls and other musicians did not themselves profit from the demand for their services. A maximum fee for the night was set at two drachmas. If more than one man wanted the same woman the matter was settled by drawing lots; she herself was not consulted.[30] This was not an idle statute and we know of prosecution through the heavy-handed mechanism of *eisangelia* (public impeachment) against men who paid more than the law allowed.[31]

The other duties of the Astynomoi involved disposing of the corpses of those who died in the street and making sure the shit-collectors dumped their shit at a requisite distance from the city walls, and this seems a fair summary of the spatial, administrative and symbolic position of street-women in Athens, occupying the places where bathmen poured the effluent of public baths, where those who needed to might take a casual crap, where the city buried its dead. A street-woman was not just on the streets, she was somehow of the streets as well, a 'public thoroughfare' in the words of the poet Anacreon, a public convenience for bodily functions, a 'cistern' for collecting the effluent of surplus sexual desire.[32]

BROTHELS

If the streets were linked in the collective imagination with refuse and sewage, the brothel was more like a mortuary or a tomb: 'I know someone who dreamed that he entered a whore-house and was unable to leave. He died a few days afterwards, as was the logical result of his dream. This place is known as a "common place", like that which receives corpses, and much sperm perishes there. So it is reasonable that this place should resemble death.'[33] The life of the brothel was despised and feared, especially by other prostitutes. The courtesan Adelphasium in Plautus' *Little Carthaginian* does not want to go near these 'women who smell of stable and stall . . . whom hardly any free man has ever touched or taken home, the two-obol sluts of dirty little slaves.'[34] Even for a slave-girl it could be considered a fate worse than death, as Antiphon's speech *Against the Stepmother* illustrates rather graphically: learning that her lover and master was tired of her and wanted to pack her off to a brothel, Philoneos' slave-concubine poisoned his food, killing at the same time a friend he happened to be entertaining. The girl was immediately tortured and executed.[35]

A more cheerful and positive picture of a visit to a brothel is provided by some comic fragments collected by Athenaeus. Here the sex-workers are being celebrated as subsidies for public morality, part of the fabric of the well-organized state, providing an easy and legal outlet for lusts that might otherwise find their way to adultery:

> What the younger men get up to in our city is appalling, quite appalling, wholly insupportable. For there are young ladies here at the brothels who are most amenable, ladies you are not banned from looking at as they sun-bathe with bare breasts, stripped for action in semi-circular ranks; and from among these ladies you can select whichever one you like: thin, fat, round, tall, short, young, old, middle-aged or past it. Much better than going through that adulterous business of a ladder against a wall and tiptoeing about, or climbing in through the vent below the roof, or smuggling yourself in under a pile of straw. With these girls you're the one that gets grabbed. They positively pull you inside, calling the old men 'Little Daddies' and the younger ones 'Little Brothers'. And any one of them is available, without risk, without expense, in the daytime, in the evening, any way you want it; but as for those other women, the ones you may not look at, not properly, at any rate, even if you do manage to get a glimpse, unless, that is, you're prepared to be continually looking over your shoulder, knees knocking, scared half to death, holding your life in your hands . . . How can men ever have sex with such women, Cypris, mistress of the sea, when just as they are getting into it they remember the laws of Draco?[36]

Other fragments provide confirmation of Xenarchus' picture of the fourth-century brothel. The girls seem to have stood half-naked or clad only in diaphanous fabrics arranged in a semi-circle for the clients to make their selection. Eubulus says they sang. A character in a play of Alexis spends three whole days in the Ceramicus in search of instruction in the 'soft life', but usually visits were much quicker.[37] The normal word for a brothel occurring even in Solon's ancient law-code was *ergastērion*, which means nothing more than 'place of business' or 'factory'. The brothel was literally a 'sex shop' or as one poet calls it, a *kinētērion*, a 'fuckery': 'They stand virtually naked, lest you be deceived; take a look at everything. Perhaps you are not feeling up to the mark; maybe you have something [on your mind]. The door's wide open; one obol's the fee. Pop in! No coyness here, no nonsense, no running away, but without delay the one you

want, whichever way you want her. You come out; you tell her
where to go; to you she's nothing.'[38]

The comic poets are, of course, not altogether serious, and we
should not be misled by the impression gained from the comedies
of efficient pleasantness. Eubulus gives the game away when he
describes the girls as 'the ones the Eridanus refreshes with his pure
waters'. By the time the Eridanus had flowed through the city and
reached the Ceramicus it will have been little more than a sewer,
the recipient of the discharge from the city's Great Drain, of the
dirty bath-water (in all probability) mentioned by Aristophanes, and
of much else besides.

We do not, fortunately, have to rely solely on catching the irony
of the comic poets to get a picture of what the brothels were like.
One branch of the Ceramicus' drains led from a mysterious building,
known to excavators as 'building Z', nestling just inside the city
where the wall forms a corner with the Sacred Gate. The building,
originally erected after the middle of the fifth century, went through
a number of different incarnations during the next century and a
half. The first version, however, provided the basic blueprint for the
rest. A door in the shadow of the city bastions opened on to a large
entrance hall. From here a narrow corridor led the visitor past some
small rooms, turning right just before the kitchen into a small courtyard. More doors led off from here on the right and on the left.
Directly opposite, however, was the ante-room of a much larger
room with a mosaic floor. Through here, the visitor gained access
to the west side of the house: a row of larger chambers with red-
stuccoed walls and a second little courtyard at the back. There were
more than fifteen rooms altogether connected by open spaces and
corridors, and the building as a whole must have been labyrinthine.
The archaeologist in charge discovered a large number of feminine
accoutrements, some illustrated with images of Aphrodite and her
cult, and a whole array of sympotic crockery for entertaining guests.
These artefacts together with the size of the site, its location and the
number of its rooms indicates strongly that for most or all of its life
building Z served as a brothel and/or inn.[39]

Its first incarnation did not last long, succumbing after just a few
years, probably to an earthquake. Its later manifestations show the

main courtyard much enlarged. The excavator, Urusla Knigge, found what she thought were gardening tools which might have helped to make it more pleasant. Perhaps this was the site now for those semi-circular displays the comic poets refer to. At the same time the rooms grew smaller and more numerous. The second version built quickly on the rubble of the first in the later fifth century shows the first evidence for a cult of Aphrodite that was characteristic in antiquity of the piety of prostitutes, a fragment of a mixing-bowl, showing the sacrifice of a white goat. This second building did not last much longer than the first, burnt down, this time, in a fierce fire. The charred ruin stood derelict for well over fifty years. Athens' impoverishment after defeat in the Peloponnesian War did not warrant much investment. It must have retained enough of its foundations, however, to supply the ground-plan for a third building on this site around the mid-point of the fourth century. Three great cisterns were added, interconnected through underground pipes and filled by rainwater trickling off the roof, a contemptuous metaphor, as we have seen, for prostitution itself.[40]

A contemporary in a comic play refers to a brothel in the Ceramicus with as many as thirty women and this third version of building Z probably had at least twenty rooms. The women who inhabited these corridors were foreigners, almost certainly slaves, who left traces of their devotion to foreign goddesses in the form of little statuettes. These, together with the jewellery found on the site, suggest they had come from Thrace, Anatolia and Syria, the usual suppliers of slaves to Athens. Among the finds was a silver medallion with a figure that Knigge identified as Aphrodite riding the back of a white goat across the night sky, with Phosphorus, the morning-star, the Light-bearer, in front of her and Hesperus, the evening-star, the Western star, behind, two aspects of the planet Venus, who reigns over this time.[41]

Some other finds presented the archaeologist with evidence of a further function for the building, which can be used to assist with an old problem. The debate about the mysterious 'Spinning Hetaeras' began in the early years of this century with the discovery of an Athenian perfume bottle. A young man with a staff in one arm and a hen in the other approaches a woman standing spinning by a chair.

He is led by a boy, with a bird and an octopus, who is looking backwards at him. The first commentators interpreted this as a scene from family life: a young man and his slave return from a shopping expedition, while the wife spins. In 1919, however, Carl Robert, drawing on his own experiences in Naples, suggested the scene was not quite so innocuous. The woman was a prostitute, the little boy her pimp and the young man a client he had found for her.[42] The scene is far from unique. A large number of vases starting round the beginning of the fifth century show women spinning or winding wool approached by young men with gifts or money-bags. These latter, especially, seem to make the men's intentions quite clear, and in fact nobody really disputes what the men in these scenes are after. What the women are up to, however, is more controversial. The more worldly commentators see the spindles as an exotic fetish. The women are prostitutes turning their clients on with a pretence of wifely virtue. Others, with their delusions still intact, argue that wifely virtue was exactly what men visiting prostitutes were trying to escape from. There must be another explanation. The women were not hetaeras but decent young ladies being lured away from their household tasks by young men with immoral designs and bags of money. After almost a century of debate a small majority of scholars accept that the women are indeed prostitutes and the spindles merely a prop, although Eva Keuls suggested it was not wifely virtue but female toil of all kinds that got Athenian men excited.[43]

The discovery of over one hundred loom-weights in the fifth- and fourth-century levels of building Z seems to indicate that all these interpretations have been barking up the wrong tree. It may well be true that a good wife worked hard at domestic chores, including her weaving, but cloth-manufacturing was also a trade. Practitioners of this trade, slaves and free women fallen on hard times, sat at the loom to survive rather than to impress philosophers.[44] They will have shared the bad reputation of other women who worked, the wine-sellers, wet-nurses and market-traders rather than the good wife who span. After all, the regular word for brothel in Greek is simply 'factory' and for prostitution simply 'trade'. Some epigrams of the Hellenistic period play on the interchangeability of women's work, placing the two major women's professions, Athena's textile and Aphrodite's sex industry, in ironic juxtaposition. Two of them concern dedications by wool-workers of the tools of the wool-workers' trade: combs, spindles, shuttles. Women tired of drudgery turn to a more rewarding profession in the hope of an easier life: 'To Athena she said, "I shall apply myself to Aphrodite's work and vote, like Paris, against you."' One of them makes a bonfire of her bobbins and calls on Aphrodite: 'take one trade and give me another in exchange.' In a third poem the poet plays on two meanings of *ergazomai* ('make' and 'make money'): 'Philaenium slept secretly in Agamedes' bosom and made herself a cloak. Cyprian Aphrodite was herself the wool-worker. Let women's spindles, let women's well-spun thread lie idle in the wool-basket.' Occasionally the pattern is reversed. One describes an old prostitute whose rich conquests are in the past, forced to get by on the loom's pittance.[45] The geographer Strabo tells an anecdote that shows wool-working and prostitution were far from being mutually exclusive careers. A Corinthian hetaera is accused of not working hard enough at her loom. 'But I have had it up three times already in this short time,' she complains.[46]

With the help of Strabo's dirty joke, the finds from building Z and the Hellenistic epigrams, the 'Spinning Hetaeras' look less mysterious. More than one vase shows wool-working in what most commentators agree is a brothel, and one particular water-jar currently in Copenhagen has a seated woman apparently instructing a naked prostitute to spin wool.[47] Clearest of all is a late-sixth-century cup by the Ambrosios painter in a private collection. I have not had an opportunity to view it myself, but the description seems unequivocal: 'On the far right of one side a girl is spinning as a man tries to opportune [sic] a companion who is playing the pipes. On the left a more patient customer watches two hetairai packing away full spindles of wool into a basket. That these women are hetairai is made very clear by the names the painter has given them – Aphrodisia and Obole.'[48] The same pattern can be seen in some other vases. When men are around, the wool is pushed to one side or carried off.[49] A greedy slave-owner did not need to let his slaves sit idle while they waited for night to fall. The brothel, especially a cheap brothel, would have to double as a textile factory.[50]

There were certainly wool-workers who did nothing but work

wool, and prostitutes who never touched a spindle, but it seems an unavoidable conclusion that a large group of women in ancient Athens fell between these two stools and were forced (or chose) to moonlight in the other profession, tainting the reputation of the textile industry. The symbols of virtuous dedication were transformed into something altogether more suggestive, sticky threads of seduction and enchantment, woollen webs and spider-snares.[51] This cuts the Gordian Knot of the 'Spinning Hetaeras' and reduces the need for excessive reliance on those favourite tropes of the modern iconologists: paradox and ambivalence. The masculine invasion of a feminine environment that the vases continually enact is not simply an artistic device, a clash of opposed worlds for the sake of it, but reflects the actual daily invasions of this normally man-free zone by the brothel's male clients. It had always seemed rather curious that the *andrōn's* sympotic vases should include among their scenes of drinking and pleasure images of virtuous wives engaged in household chores, but both loom-weights and wine-cups were at home in building Z. Here the spindle and the wool-basket are symbolic not of virtue but of the time of day. The vases show the precise moment when one kind of work is put aside and an altogether different labour is taken up, a dramatization of the onset of the night-shift, a mirror-image of the scene on the silver medallion from building Z, where Aphrodite rides in the space between the morning- and the evening-star. The young men are depicted as over-eager, perhaps, to be first inside, or perhaps they belong to that group of degenerates who visited brothels during the day to engage in what Demosthenes called 'middle-of-the-day marriages'.[52] A cup in Berlin has a different satirical target. One woman continues to spin and wait while her colleagues receive clients. She is painted staring directly at the drinker in the unusual full-frontal pose the Greeks used to arrest the viewer's attention. She is supposed, perhaps, to be old or ugly, thus fore-shadowing the Hellenistic epigram for the prostitute who has to turn to weaving in old age, or perhaps she is a Madam, one of those who 'entwine you in their threads'.[53] Another frontal face stares out from the bottom of a cup in Paris. It's not the drinker draining his cup she is staring at, however, but herself in a hand-held mirror. Her naked body is visible through the folds of her chiton and an inscription tells us she is 'beautiful'. She too has a wool-basket, just visible on her left in the corner of the round frame but it stands neglected. She has other things on her mind.[54] By spying on the brothel's off-peak hours the vase-painters were anticipating the fascination of French artists of the nineteenth century. Like them it was not women's work which the Athenians found sexually intriguing, let alone 'wifely virtue', but feminine *ennui*, the erotically charged tedium of the women waiting in the women's quarters.

Z3 succumbed to the same fate as Z1, victim probably of an earthquake some time around the end of the fourth century. The finds discovered over two thousand years later may indicate that it struck during the day when the women were still at their looms.

Men do not seem to have worked in large brothels (*porneia*), but both men and women are sometimes described as 'sitting in an *oikēma*' (cubicle), which probably refers to a slightly different kind of institution. Aeschines, as usual, is the most forthcoming on the subject, keen to be as explicit as possible in the hope that some of the mud he spatters throughout his speech will stick to Timarchus too:

Picture those men who sit in the stalls [*oikēmata*]. They make no bones about the kind of profession they serve, but they do, nevertheless, make an effort at modesty and keep the doors shut when they are engaged, trying 'to make ends meet'. But doors or no doors, if you were walking along the street and someone were to ask you what the man was doing at this moment in time, you could put a name to it. You wouldn't need to actually see it. You wouldn't need to know who had gone in there with him. You could work it out from your knowledge of the man's professional vocation.[55]

We know of at least one exception to Aeschines' rule. Plato's *Phaedo* is perhaps his most moving work, an account of Socrates' death told by a close friend, who gives his name to the dialogue. While the executioner is mixing the hemlock that will slowly kill him, Socrates plays with Phaedo's long hair (soon to be cut short in mourning) and discourses on the immortality of the soul. What Plato does not tell us is that Phaedo, too, had once been stationed 'in an *oikēma*'. When he 'put the door to', however, it was in order to participate in philosophical not sexual intercourse, with Socrates, who eventually induced some wealthy friends of his to buy back his freedom.[56] From these two accounts the *oikēma* sounds rather different from the *porneion*, or brothel. There is no mention of the semi-circular exhibition of prostitutes that we hear about in the comic fragments. Something much more like an individual cubicle is envisioned, with doors opening directly on to the street, its occupant on show inside.

Phaedo, a member of an aristocratic family from Elis apparently, had been enslaved when his city was captured, and most of the men who sat in the cubicles will have been forced like him to do so. But some male prostitutes enjoyed free status with a free man's privileges and no need of a pimp to act for them or to defend them, and more opportunity than women to set up on their own. In Plato's *Charmides*, 'sitting in an *oikēma*' is listed alongside 'selling salt-fish' and 'making shoes' as a most disreputable but not inconceivable profession. Aeschines cites one case which had become notorious. Diophantus, 'known as "the orphan"', had arrested a foreigner and dared to bring him before the eponymous archon (an important magistrate who gave his name to the year) responsible for orphans' interests, alleging the man had cheated him out of four drachmas. It was an occupational hazard for any prostitute. In the nastier parts of the underworld, claims Aristophanes, alongside those who break the laws of hospitality are those who 'steal the pay, while having their way with girls and boys'.[57]

SYMPOSIUM

'When promoting the pleasure of a forthcoming social event, it is standard practice in certain LA circles to mention the likelihood of "beautiful girls" or "babes" being present . . . A lot of the time [the information] is offered in much the same spirit and tone that one might augur champagne and canapés – as an assurance that all the appropriate catering arrangements have been taken care of.'

(ZOE HELLER, *Sunday Times*, 7 July 1996)

Between them, the brothels, the streets and the *oikēmata* must have accounted for the majority of available bodies. From this low-point anything was an improvement. The first women who could properly be called hetaeras are the so-called 'wage-earners', the *misthamousai*, women hired for an evening or longer as escorts, rather than being paid like the *pornai* simply for sex. Just as *ergastērion* (factory) can indicate brothel and *ergasia* (trade) prostitution, so, when used of women, *misthameín* (work for hire) implies the professional hetaera.[58] This is where Neaera herself started out. Apollodorus says she entered the trade as a young girl, bought as a slave by a woman based in Corinth called Nicarete who pretended to be her mother. She and her 'sisters' were hired as escorts by wealthy and distinguished men, poets, foreign aristocrats and masters of the art of Greek prose composition such as Lysias. They were taken to festivals and were seen at dinners and drinking-parties all over Greece: 'Simos of Thessaly had Neaera with him when he came here to celebrate the Great Panathenaea. Nicarete came too as her chaperon. They stayed with Ctesippus, son of Glauconides from Cydantidae, and this woman here, this Neaera, went to the dinners and the drinking-parties in the company of many men as if she were a hetaera.' They were often controlled by a man, a *pornoboskos*, whose name means literally 'whore-pasturer', driving his herds of women around Greece following the seasons and the festivals.

Working as an escort did not always imply foreign travel, and Neaera spent most of her time in Corinth, a centre of the sex-trade, where she established something of a reputation. During this period, claims Apollodorus, she plied her trade openly and had many lovers. He names two Athenians in particular and gets one of them to testify that he had indeed hired her in Corinth 'as a hetaera who is hired out' and that she drank with him and his friend. These references to 'drinking with men' that Apollodorus is so keen to multiply in his attack on Neaera refer, of course, to the world of the symposium that is the most familiar face of Greek prostitution. Getting hold of women was as much a part of preparations for a dinner-party as going shopping for fish, wine and perfume. Some of the girls, the *mousourgoi*, could entertain with instruments, usually the 'flute' or harp, others could dance or sing. In Xenophon's *Symposium* these entertainments are highly elaborate, culminating with a kind of mythological tableau. The musicians played variations of well-known cult tunes: 'The other flute-girls are to be seen playing "Apollo's theme" . . . and "Zeus' theme"; but the only theme these women play is "The Grasping Hawk".' Some were more creative and made up their own music, maybe their own pageants too. Aristophanes refers to one Charixene, whom the later lexicographers describe as an 'ancient flute-girl and composer of musical pieces . . . a writer of songs' and 'a composer of *erōtika*' and it is possible the scene with the three old women at the end of the *Ecclesiazusae* is a parody of such a show; in the Hellenistic period, the 'tunes of Glauce', another female musician, were famous.[59] There were many, however, like Neaera herself, apparently, who had no instrument at all and were known curiously as 'the heifer infantry' according to one source, relying solely on their looks and their conversation.[60] For the symposium was the place where beautiful and witty girls exchanged jokes and *double-entendres* with artists and politicians, illustrated and celebrated on drinking cups and mixing-bowls. Collections of these obscene witticisms of hetaeras and of their male counterparts, the gate-crashers or 'parasites', became almost a sub-genre of literature. One, Machon's *Chreiai*, partly survives in long fragments, an ironic versified counterpart to the collections of philosophical anecdotes such as Xenophon's *Memoirs*. Some of the jokes are highly sophisticated, punning on lines from tragedy, but if we acknowledge that Machon, like Xenophon, put something of himself into the collection, that does not mean that the witty hetaera is any more a fabrication than the wise Socrates.

The presence of the rich and famous in a relaxed mood, and with their trousers down, made the symposium a suitable place for staging a coup, allowing the world of the sympotic hetaera to make a rare appearance in History. Xenophon, for example, tells the following story of how in winter 379 the city of Thebes was liberated from the control of a Spartan-backed faction and launched (briefly) as the dominant power in Greece:

The junta always celebrated a festival in honour of Aphrodite on leaving office, and Phillidas had long promised, among other things, to bring them the classiest, most beautiful women in Thebes. This promise he would now fulfil, and they expected to be spending the night very pleasantly (for that was the kind of men they were). When they had finished eating and, with his enthusiastic assistance, were quickly drunk, he finally acceded to their requests to bring in the hetaeras. He left the room and brought in Melon and his party, three of them dressed as ladies, the rest as their attendants.

The 'hetaeras' out of modesty asked for the servants to be dismissed and entered the room, their faces covered. Phillidas sat one at the side of each officer. As soon as they were seated the revolutionaries lifted their veils and drew their daggers.[61]

The international demi-monde of the drinking-party looks glamorous and was certainly an improvement on the brothels, some of which, it seems, tried to emulate a sympotic atmosphere if the finds at building Z are anything to go by, but it could, if necessary, be painted in rather a different light: Demeas in Menander's *Samia* thinks mistakenly that his mistress, Chrysis, the eponymous 'Woman of Samos', has been sleeping with his adopted son Moschion and has had a child by him. He threatens to throw her out of the house: 'You think you're so fine. Go to the city and you will see what kind of a woman you really are. They live in a different world those other women, paid a paltry ten drachmas for running to dinner-parties and drinking neat wine 'til they die, and if they hesitate or demur, they starve. You will learn the hard way like everyone else, and recognize what kind of a mistake you made.'[62] Demeas omits from his account the most frightening aspect of this way of life, the pimp or *pornoboskos*, who appears in comedy as an evil, manipulative, money-grubbing character, always threatening to dispatch his women to a brothel. If comedy exaggerates their worst characteristics, real-life examples of the profession were certainly not well-liked. For lovers, pimps stood in the way of romance, for philosophers they represented avarice without shame and for the general public they charged too much (like the fishmongers and the taverners) for desirable commodities. The thought that their beloved Neaera might end up in the power of a *pornoboskos* motivated her lovers to raise large amounts of money to buy her freedom.[63]

Another conspicuous omission from Demeas' account of this way of life is sex and in fact the significance of sex in the hired girl's job-description can be rather difficult to gauge. Clearly there was a certain expectation on both sides that copulation was on the cards. The members of the Theban junta seem to have been working on that assumption (though Xenophon, interestingly, thinks their assumption is characteristic of a particular type of man) and Habrotonon the harpist in Menander's *Arbitration* thinks it very odd that Charisius pays twelve drachmas a night to her *pornoboskos* but shows no sexual interest in her at all. Demeas, on the other hand, is keen to exaggerate the nastier side of the experience of a hetaera *mistharnousa* and the fact that he does not mention sex must be taken seriously. Hetaeras who were paid for the evening must be strongly distinguished from *pornai* who were paid for the deed. The social intercourse of the symposium, the 'drinking with men' that Apollodorus is so concerned to demonstrate in Neaera's past, should not be seen as a euphemism for sexual intercourse, or as an unimportant prelude to the real business of the bed. 'Love-making' had a more varied frame of reference than the sexual act it denotes today. The careful seclusion of respectable women in Athens ceded a huge territory of feminine intimacy to the hetaera. There was unaccustomed female intercourse as soon as women entered the *andrōn* and removed their veils, and flirtation could be elaborated a long way in looks and stares, jokes and innuendo, kisses and caresses before the question of bed arose. One jealous suitor in Plautus' *Ass-dealer* tries to ban his girlfriend from any kind of flirtation and in so doing elaborates for us the varieties of coquetry available in the symposium including sharing cups with a man, passing him the dice or calling on his name while she throws them, treading on a man's foot, taking his hand when she gets off the couch, or making a pass when the light gutters out, coughing and showing her tongue etc. Her company in the broadest sense was what a hetaera, a 'companion', had to offer, and despite the daydreams of wool-workers, she worked hard for the money.[64]

One thing that makes it difficult to discover the proper place for sex in the symposium is that the two most detailed accounts of the institution, by Plato and Xenophon, take great pains to avoid intimations of fornication. There are no hetaeras among the guests at either party and Plato even has the flute-girls sent away, forcing the erotic atmosphere to be discharged in amorous philosophy. Xenophon's version looks at first sight much more typical. The occasion, again, is one of the festivals that were so frequent in ancient Greece and which helped a world without weekends to structure the months and years. Callias throws a dinner party for his 'boyfriend' and his father to celebrate the boy's victory in wrestling at the Great Panathenaea. After dinner the tables are cleared away and a man arrives. He is from Syracuse and makes a living by choreographing sympotic spectaculars. Xenophon is often coy about such things, but it seems clear the man is a *pornoboskos* or something close to it. He has with him a 'good flute-girl, a dancing-girl who could do amazing tricks and the most beautiful boy who played the cithara and danced, beautifully'. They perform a whole range of daredevil flings and complicated acrobatics culminating in a pageant of *Ariadne auf Naxos*, with the *abandonata* dressed as a bride awaiting Dionysus. The spectators find the performance very real. The dancers kiss and exchange sweet nothings. Finally they embrace and head for the bridal couch. This vision of marital bliss has a powerful effect on the guests. The bachelors swear to get married and the husbands ride off to their wives. With less subtlety than Plato, Xenophon tries to tame the naughty symposium, bringing it safely within the libidinal confines of the family.[65]

During the discussions that precede this ballet, the Syracusan reveals he is worried about the beautiful multi-talented boy who, it transpires, also shares his bed. It has come to his attention that some men are plotting to seduce him and thereby 'ruin' him. From this it appears that professional *musiciens* in the symposium were just as vulnerable to sexual advances as their female counterparts. 'Citharaplayers' seem to have been especially popular. One of Timarchus' alleged ex-lovers, Misgolas, was famously addicted to them.[66]

If a client wanted more than just one night with his 'day-labourer' he could negotiate a contract for a longer period. Outside comedy most of our information on these contracts concerns men, and again Aeschines is our main source. He anticipates that Demosthenes in defending Timarchus will counter the rumours and innuendo by asking for facts and documents, arguing that 'no man has been "an escort" unless he has been hired under contract'. Aeschines forestalls this attack, revealing in the process that such contracts between men were in practice probably unworkable. He is able to cite only one example of such a document and names neither party to it. Even this obscure allusion looks like more innuendo, another opportunity to cast aspersions on Timarchus and his friends rather than a real case.[67] In fact the only actual contract we know of is one alleged to have been made between a certain Simon and Theodotus of Plataea, a refugee like Phaedo from a sacked city, though not necessarily like him enslaved. Simon claimed to have paid as much as 300 drachmas to the boy, although for what, or for what length of time we do not know. The contract does not seem to have been produced in court. Perhaps Simon was lying or perhaps Aeschines was right that the clauses of such agreements between men were so shameful that they were unenforceable. At any rate Simon chose to prosecute the boy's rich new lover for assault during an argument rather than sue the boy for breach of contract.[68]

Contracts with women are referred to on several occasions in Roman comedies, which were translations of, or versions of, Greek originals. There are some in the plays of Plautus, with one very extended example (called by its Greek name *syngraphus*) given verbatim. It concerns arrangements between Diabolus and Cleareta for the services of Cleareta's daughter Philaenium. There are some basic terms – that Philaenium should spend all her days and nights with Diabolus for one year at a price of twenty minae (2000 drachmas) – which take up four lines in the text. They are followed by forty-six lines of paranoid sub-clauses. We have already mentioned those which attempt to stop the girl flirting with other men in the symposium. There are others besides: she must let absolutely no one else inside her door and not even look at another man, she must have no access to writing tablets; she must swear only by female deities and use only words which have no double-meaning; she must speak only in Attic Greek.[69] Clearly this is a satire on the insane jealousy that afflicts men in love with hetaeras, but the contract does seem to share some formulaic clauses with others known from comedy guaranteeing exclusive access to the girl.

AT HOME

If the woman you loved was a slave, however, there was a much better way to establish rights over her than by signing contracts. You could buy her. This is what happened to Neaera after she had lived and worked in Corinth for a few years as a 'hired girl', her reputation growing. Two of her lovers, Eucrates of Leucas and Timanoridas of Corinth, found that they were paying so much to Nicarete that it was cheaper to purchase Neaera lock, stock and barrel. They clubbed together and paid out 3000 drachmas for which 'they kept her and used her for as long as they liked'.[70] Slave-concubines are comparatively rare in the sources but this does not mean that they were rare in reality and their existence is attested for all periods of Athenian history. They were, apparently, already around in the seventh century at the time of the Draconian law which grants immunity to the man who kills a man caught with a 'concubine kept for the production of *free* children', and implies thereby the existence of concubines kept for the production of children who were not. Philoneos, as we have seen, was poisoned by his slave-mistress in the fifth century and a hundred years later Menander's *Hated Man* opened with the soldier who gives the play its title, distraught that his mistress Cratia, a captive taken in war, does not return his affection. Normally in Menander the relationships already established at the beginning of the play are with free or freed women, although the ramifications of raising enough money to purchase girlfriends from the *pornoboskos*, without letting father find out, fuel the plots of many Roman comedies. It is not surprising that we do not hear more of slave-mistresses in oratory. Relations between a master and a slave with almost no rights did not often make it into court. No one was interested in Philoneos' murderous concubine. If we know of her existence at all it is thanks to later accusations against the friend's free wife.

Of course, any domestic slave-girl was sexually vulnerable to her master's sexual advances. 'Kissing Thratta the slave-girl, while the wife's washing' is treated as a commonplace of normal peacetime life in Aristophanes, and in Menander's *Necklace (Plokion)* the ugly heiress makes her husband get rid of a servant who works well but is too pretty for comfort. One scene from Lysias' speech *On the Murder of Eratosthenes* makes these allusions to domestic tension much more real. Euphiletus comes home early one day. He and his wife have dinner together. Upstairs the baby starts crying. He tells her to go and see to it. She feigns reluctance. He only wants her out of the way 'just so you can have a go at the maid down here; it wouldn't be the first time you've got drunk and forced yourself on her'. She leaves the room in a sham stomp, locking the door behind her. He laughs and falls into a post-prandial doze, oblivious to the fact that his wife's lover, Eratosthenes, is waiting for her upstairs and that the whole scene has been carefully stage-managed.[71] We should not see the wife's maids as necessarily the husband's harem, however. The below-stairs affairs that are a commonplace of eighteenth-century novels are rare in Greek literature and a strong distinction seems to have been made between mistresses and maidservants. It was in fact considered disgraceful to keep a lover in the same house as one's wife or other female relatives. The speech-writer Lysias knew how to behave; when he had Metaneira, one of Neaera's 'sisters', to stay with him in Athens he lodged her at the house of an unmarried friend. Alcibiades was not so considerate; his wife tried to divorce him, it was alleged, because he introduced hetaeras, free and slave, into his home.[72]

Once the money had been raised, the lover had two choices: to buy the slave's freedom or simply to buy the slave. The first alternative carried obvious risks for insecure lovers, and meant denying yourself the possibility of realizing the resale value when you got bored. A case from a speech of Hyperides throws light on this strange and obsolete romantic dilemma. Epicrates has fallen in love with a boy who works in a perfume shop and offers to buy his freedom from the owner, an Egyptian called Athenogenes. The boy persuades Epicrates to include his father and brother in the deal. When they come to clinch, however, Athenogenes makes an unexpected offer; instead of freeing them why doesn't Epicrates buy them off him: 'I will sell them to you properly, so that no one will pester the boy or ruin him, and they out of fear won't attempt to make any trouble. Best of all, whereas now it might look as if I am responsible for freeing them, if you buy them properly then you can free them yourself later whenever you like and they will be twice as grateful.' Epicrates is convinced and seals the contract. Only later does it transpire that Athenogenes has included in the deal enormous debts the slaves have incurred through the perfumery, for which their new owner is now responsible. 'Freeing a little whore' is a commonplace in comedy for the heedless extravagance typical of young men in love. In Aristophanes' *Wasps*, Philocleon, the vulgar old juryman, delivers a series of stock promises to the flute-girl he has stolen from the symposium, comically inverting the roles of father and son:

> You see how neatly I sneaked you away, just before you started sucking off the guests; you can repay the favour to this dick here. But no! I know you'll get out of it, you won't do it, I'll end up the poor sucker instead and you'll have a good laugh at my expense; I wouldn't be the first. But look, I'll tell you what, if you are a good girl, my little pork cuntlet, when my son dies I'll buy your freedom and keep you as a concubine. The thing is I'm not now in control of my finances. I'm young you see. They keep an eye on me. That little son of mine won't let me out of his sight he's such a bad-tempered tight-fisted penny-pinching skinflint. He's afraid I'll be ruined. I'm the only father he's got.[73]

As Athenogenes points out to poor Epicrates, there was a big difference between paying a *pornoboskos* for a slave's freedom and freeing him or her yourself after purchase, for freedmen maintained very close relationships with their former masters, relationships that were reinforced by ill-defined but legally binding obligations. Neaera's history, again, is a good example. After keeping her for a while as their slave and mistress, Timanoridas and Eucrates decide to find proper wives and settle down. Unwilling to see her in the power of a *pornoboskos*, they offer her a discount of a third off the price of her freedom, providing she can find the rest of the money herself. She raises a substantial sum from her own savings together with some contributions from her old lovers. This she gives to an Athenian called Phrynion who puts up the remainder and so purchases her freedom. But this freedom is heavily compromised. Her old masters are able to insist that she never offends their sensibilities by working in Corinth again. Phrynion too has power over her:

He took her everywhere with him, to dinners, to drinking-parties, on expeditions of debauchery. He enjoyed her intercourse quite openly everywhere, whenever he wished, showing off his entitlement to any who cared to see. One of the many beneficiaries of the pair's riotous visitations was Chabrias of Aixone who was holding a banquet at Colias to celebrate his victory in the chariot-race at Delphi . . . And there while Phrynion was asleep and Neaera lay in a drunken stupor she was visited by a whole host of men, including the attendants who had served the meal.

Apollodorus appends the statements of some other guests who happened to be present and who 'noticed people getting up in the night and going to Neaera and in particular some of the servants, who were Chabrias' household-slaves'. Offended at such outrageous treatment Neaera packs her jewels and leaves for the city of Megara next door. It is hard to make a living, however, among the niggardly Megarians and when another Athenian, one Stephanus, comes knocking at her door and asks her to go back with him, she jumps at the chance. She is not long in Athens, however, before Phrynion finds out and presses his claims over her. The dispute eventually goes to arbitration; Neaera's independent status is confirmed, but she is required nevertheless to divide her time equally between Stephanus and Phrynion, her present and former lovers. Freedom for a freedwoman was a relative not an absolute thing, and as precarious as it was ambivalent.[74]

It is sometimes argued that a woman in a permanent relationship has ceased to be a hetaera and enjoys the status instead of a *pallakē*, or concubine. There is, however, little point in following Apollodorus in his attempt to drive a wedge between the two categories.[75] At any rate we often hear of Athenian men who live in a permanent relationship with 'hetaeras' (and occasionally even with their male equivalents), forming a kind of alternative household with them. When Trygaeus, having successfully distracted his dung-beetle from the smell of the Piraeus and having made it all the way to Olympus, allows himself to dream about a world without War when the goddess Peace has returned to Earth, he talks of spending his life with a hetaera, not a wife, by the fire-side. When, after Athens' defeat at Chaeronea, Leocrates takes his hetaera with him to Rhodes, his 'business-trip' can be represented as a full-scale evacuation of his household, an act of treachery when the city was on its knees. These permanent hetaeras become closely associated with their lovers and are identified with reference to them: 'Olympiodorus' hetaera', 'Athenogenes' hetaera', etc.[76]

For most men these kinds of relationships were either pre-marriage or post-marriage. Trygaeus seems to be a widower and Stephanus will respond to Apollodorus that the children he has introduced to the citizen-body are not born from Neaera's foreign womb, but the product of a marriage with a citizen-woman that pre-dates her. Likewise, according to Plutarch, Pericles took up with Aspasia only after his first marriage had been terminated.[77] Timanoridas and Eucrates, on the other hand, used Neaera to keep their beds warm in their bachelor days before they had to settle down. Others managed both to have their cake and eat it, with a marriage and a mistress on the side. One of the speeches of Isaeus, a teacher of Demosthenes, describes how Euctemon, a very wealthy old man, had become familiar with one of his slaves, a former prostitute who now managed a tenement-block for him. Short visits to collect the rent became longer as he stayed for dinner, until he ended up abandoning his wife and family and living with her permanently, even passing off her children (allegedly) as his own. Apollodorus, despite his attacks on the domestic arrangements of Stephanus and Neaera, was not beyond a little fornication himself, and was attacked for having freed one hetaera and given away another although he was married. Both Euctemon and Apollodorus were fabulously rich men, and it was considered a mark of prosperity or of extravagance to keep more than one woman.[78] The orator Hyperides made so much money from the proceeds of politics and from writing speeches for people like Epicrates that he could afford to keep three mistresses in various homes throughout Attica. He installed Myrrhine in the family home in Athens, throwing out his own son (since there is no mention of an offence to his wife, she was presumably dead), Aristagora in Piraeus, and Phila in Eleusis. The latter he purchased for a very large sum and kept as a freedwoman, later setting her up as mistress of his household 'oikouros'.[79]

Occasionally we hear of men cohabiting with hetaeras not merely as a supplement to marriage, but apparently as a substitute for it.

Pyrrhus looked all set to die without issue when he took a citizen hetaera into his house. On his death the estate passed as planned to his adopted son and Pyrrhus' dalliance must have seemed like a harmless bit of fun. Twenty years later, however, a woman turned up claiming the hetaera had been a wife, that she was her legitimate daughter and that Pyrrhus' vast estate belonged by rights to her. Other confirmed bachelors had the audacity to shack up with foreigners, even slaves, waiving their responsibility to maintain the autochthonous Athenian stock (not immigrant, they boasted, but born from a piece of Attic soil where Athena dropped the wool she used to wipe away a shot of sperm from an overexcited Hephaestus). Such an affront to family values did not pass without comment:

> This man here, this Olympiodorus, has never married a citizen woman in accordance with your laws. He has no children and has lost none. He does have a hetaera, however. He bought her freedom and keeps her at home, and it is she who has brought ruin to all of us, turning his mind to ever greater acts of lunacy . . . It is not just for myself I am engaged in this struggle, but for his sister, born of the same father and the same mother, who lives with me as my wife, and for his niece, my daughter. For they too are wronged, more even than I. Who will deny it? Who will deny that they suffer appallingly whenever they see this man's hetaera on one of her outings, showing off with a great mass of jewellery and fine clothes beyond the bounds of good taste, recklessly vaunting herself at our expense, while they are too poor to afford any of it?[80]

In comedy, too, we find a number of men living with women to whom they are not married in apparently permanent monogamous relationships. Demeas in Menander's *Samia* had been an old bachelor. Late in life he falls in love with a Samian woman and is persuaded by his adopted son to take her into the house, preserving her thereby from the hands of younger suitors. The attractions of such a partner were obvious. Hetaeras were well-versed in the arts of making men feel good. They could dine with them and drink with them and flirt with them and flatter them. Their vulnerability made them complaisant, as one comic character was well aware: 'Apart from that it's easier, isn't it, to get along with a "married" hetaera than with a wedded wife. Of course it is. A wife stays indoors, her haughtiness licensed by law, a hetaera, on the other hand, knows that if she wants to keep her man she must pay for him with good behaviour, or go and find another one.' In some other plays of Menander, *The Haircut* (*Perikeiromene*), *The Man from Sikyon*, *The Hated Man*, the men involved in these unmarried relationships are all professional soldiers, in accordance with a long-running stereotype about the domestic arrangements of mercenaries to which Plato too subscribes. There may have been some truth in it. According to Xenophon, hetaeras accompanied the mercenary army known as the Ten Thousand on their great expedition into the heart of the Persian Empire.[81]

One last group of women needs to be considered, the great *megalomisthoi*, or 'big-fee' hetaeras, who were able to maintain independent homes to which they invited whichever lover they happened to be seeing at the time. Some of these establishments could be quite lavish, especially in the Hellenistic period. The historian Polybius was disgusted to discover on a visit to Alexandria that the finest houses in this fine city were known as 'Mnesis's' and 'Potheine's', 'and yet Mnesis was a flute-girl, and Potheine too'. Machon talks of a symposium at Mania's, and of a visit to Gnathaena's where Diphilus, a comic poet, makes an obscene joke, which is old now even for us, about the frigidity of her 'cistern' (she keeps it cold, she retorts, with the prologues of his humourless plays). The same woman provided a more direct record of her establishment by adding a footnote to the tiny corpus of classical literature written by women, a 'Rules of the House' (*nomos sussitikos*) in three hundred and twenty-three lines, telling guests how to behave when visiting her and her daughter, a parody of the similar *nomoi* written by the philosophers, just as Machon's *Chreiai* was a parody of their wise sayings. Gnathaena's *Rules* found its way to the great Library of Alexandria and was catalogued by the librarian-poet Callimachus who recorded for posterity its mocking first line: 'The Rule here written down is equal and fair for all . . .'

References to the houses of hetaeras go back well before the Hellenistic period. Aristophanes mentions 'darting into the dancing-girl's place' as a pastime typical of the late fifth century's decadent youth, and Amphis describes the god Wealth 'paralysed at home with Sinope, Lyca, Nannio and other traps of livelihood and never coming out'. Neaera had a house in Megara where Stephanus stayed and had sex with her, and once back in Athens she set up shop in his house, according to Apollodorus, and began to extort money from foreigners simply to meet her huge living costs, for she was accustomed to a far from lowly way of life. Having freed one hetaera himself and 'given another away in marriage', Apollodorus must have known what he was talking about. Xenophon's *Memoirs of Socrates* contains a coy but unambiguous account of one of these independent women in the comfort of her own home. He narrates the visit of Socrates and some friends to the house of Theodote, 'a beautiful woman'. The philosopher is astonished at the splendour of her establishment, 'noticing that she was richly dressed, and that her mother at her side was also wearing fine clothes and jewellery, and that she had many lovely-looking maidservants also well-looked after and that her house was furnished lavishly'. He wonders if she is a landowner, but her source of income turns out to be rather difficult to pin down.[82]

The independence of the 'high-fee hetaeras' was once again a highly compromised form of independence, maintained only perhaps by playing different lovers off against one another, and it must remain in doubt that, in Athens at any rate, it was ever possible for women to own real property. It is noticeable that Neaera, though described as 'herself mistress of herself' (*autēn autēs kurian*) prefers to live under Stephanus' roof, and it is Stephanus who acts as her lord and master (*kurios*) when extorting money from unsuspecting foreigners for adultery, although perhaps he is pretending to be her husband. Theodote herself is described elsewhere as Alcibiades' loyal mistress, which perhaps makes her sense of her own independence in Xenophon's account mere self-delusion.[83] We could, however, look at the same relationships the other way around. Apollodorus claims that Stephanus is supported by Neaera's income and some other hetaeras are reported to have had male dependants who could be used as representatives or protectors when necessary. Machon and Lynceus of Samos make a play on the role-reversal involved in these relationships: the stomachs of kept men swell like the stomachs of kept women, not with babies but with food. In particular, we hear of one Gryllion ('little grunter'), a member of the Areopagus, who was

Phryne's parasite, and Satyrus of Olynthus who played the same role for Pamphila.[84]

These *megalomisthoi* hetaeras are the rich and famous ones, the ones catalogued in scholarly treatises, who had plays written about them and speeches composed on their behalf, the ones whose *bons mots* were recorded in anecdotal collections like those of Machon and Lynceus of Samos. Thanks to Apollodorus' speech and a comedy of Timocles named after her, Neaera herself could claim a place on this exalted list along with Laïs the younger, Laïs the elder, Sinope, Mania, Gnathaena, Naïs, Thaïs and many others. Of all of these Phryne was perhaps the most renowned. Like Theodote, she allowed artists to paint her. It was she who modelled for Praxiteles, it was said, his revolutionary female nude, first of its kind, known as the Venus of Cnidus, and, for Apelles, the *Birth of Venus* that was reimagined so famously by Botticelli. Another statue *sua ipsa persona*, again modelled by Praxiteles in gilt or gold, was dedicated at Delphi and placed between Philip of Macedon and Archidamus, King of Sparta. It was a dedication, said the Cynic Crates, to Greek self-indulgence. These works of art not only immortalized the form of Phryne for posterity but spread her image throughout Greece. According to Callistratus in his work *On Hetaeras*, she became so rich that after the Macedonians had razed the city of Thebes to the ground she said she would pay for the city wall to be rebuilt, providing the citizens put up an inscription: 'Alexander may have knocked it down, but Phryne the hetaera got it back up again', one of the very few occasions when these women gave themselves the label.

The late fourth century seems to have given even greater scope to famous ladies, as the squabbling cities of old Greece found themselves mere suppliants of rich and powerful individuals, mercenary commanders and Alexander's agents and successors who all had their girlfriends and boyfriends. As early as the 350s the Phocian generals funded their armies from treasures plundered from Delphi, setting aside from the spoils choice items to give as presents for their lovers. But their activities were soon eclipsed by the activities of Harpalus, Alexander's renegade treasurer, who was so upset at the death of his mistress Pythionice that he organized a great funeral for her and set up two great shrines in her memory, one in Babylon and one among the tombs outside Athens' Dipylon Gate on the road to Eleusis: 'a monument which has no equal in size. At first you would say, not without reason, that it must be a memorial of Miltiades, or Pericles, or Cimon, or another from among the ranks of the great and good, a public monument, at least, built by the city or by the city's decree, but when you examine it again and discover it is a monument to Pythionice the hetaera, what must one be led to expect?' The tomb at Athens was said to have cost the enormous sum of thirty talents, but Plutarch who saw it about four hundred years later thought it very ordinary. Theopompus in an open *Letter to Alexander* estimated the cost of both tombs even higher at 200 talents and even claimed that Harpalus had established a sanctuary he dared to call the temple of 'Aphrodite Pythionice'. Harpalus' actions and the publicity surrounding them led to severe inflation in hetaeras' expectations: 'You will be queen of Babylon, if things turn out; you know, don't you, about the famous Pythionice and her Harpalus?'[85]

Pythionice's grandiose memorial was only a few miles down the road from the women who stood noisily in the Ceramicus at the Dipylon Gate, a graphic indication of the range of lives covered by the single modern term 'prostitute'. Not many women managed the journey between the two points, but some did. Along the route all kinds of other women were to be found, the street-walker who rarely had the resources to look beyond the next twenty-four hours, the slave-girl installed in a brothel to make profits for the brothel-keeper, and the professional party-girl who lived off her musical talents and complaisance. It included a large number of women who became the free mistresses of the better-off and even one or two women whose success had brought them control over their own lives, and a degree of choice among their lovers. The world of these 'prostitutes' encroached at many different points on the world of the men they consorted with and it is as absurd to generalize about them as it is to generalize about their clients. There was movement also between these female stations. Lysias provides a list of women who had been prostitutes in their youth but had since moved on and there is plenty of evidence that the invisibility of women in Athens, which has been seen as part of an effort to keep them under masculine control, often gave them greater freedom to move between these different existences, rising up the ladder or falling back into ignominy all unseen, even on occasion daring to insinuate themselves among the ranks of the wives or to place their children on the list of citizens.[86]

IV

A PURCHASE ON THE HETAERA

ALTHOUGH APHRODITE'S WORLD seems rather shadowy and mysterious, we can make out certain recurrent themes within the murk. One of the most important of these is the attempt to draw a sharp distinction between two kinds of amorous intercourse: the romantic strategy of courting, wooing and seduction and the more direct approach of buying and selling sex. The distinction is implicit in many discussions of the proper way to behave with lovers and occasionally it is brought out into the open and subjected to a rigorous examination by cynics like the slave Cario in Aristophanes' *Wealth*. His master is discussing the power of money:

'They do say those Corinthian hetaeras pay no attention whatsoever when a man without means tries to seduce them but if a rich man comes along they bend over and present themselves in no time at all.'

'Yes and they do say that boys do the same, not for the sake of their lovers, but for money.'

'Only the whores among them, not the decent ones; decent boys never ask for money.'

'And what do they ask for, then?'

'Well, one might ask for a thoroughbred, another might ask for a pack of hunting dogs.'

'That's just euphemism. They are ashamed to ask for money and gloss over their vice with words.'

Aristophanes is here touching on something of central importance in modern anthropology: the distinction between commodity exchange and the exchange of gifts, between payments and presents.

This is not always an easy distinction to grasp, but that, as I hope to show, is precisely why it is so important. Commodity exchange establishes a relationship between *objects*, a relationship expressed in terms of price. Commodities are interchangeable, easily measured and compared, their quantity and quality can be broken down into units, often into units of currency. They are somewhat featureless, rather anonymous articles and the exchange of commodities reflects this anonymity. The transaction is clean and final, the goods are forever lost to the seller and transferred into the possession of the buyer.

Gift exchange, on the other hand, establishes relationships not between objects but between people, who are thenceforth linked by ties of patronage and friendship. Consequently, gifts are personal. They should be unique, individual, resistant to objective evaluation. Unlike commodities, gifts are sticky objects. A gift is never completely lost to the giver. A nice illustration of this principle in Greek culture is the way that when a city makes a gift to a god at a panhellenic shrine like Delphi or Delos the gifts remain in the city's own specially built treasury. A gift also maintains a connection by burdening the receiver with debt and obligation. An exchange of gifts, similarly, is far from final, merely the latest episode in a long history of giving and repaying favour.

The distinction between these two kinds of relationship is not simply the difference between an exchange of objects and a payment of money, although thanks to its interchangeability, money naturally tends to establish more impersonal relationships. If someone goes every morning to a specific place to barter a specific amount of milk for a specific amount of honey with a complete stranger it looks very much like a commodity exchange even though no coins change hands. Nor should we imagine gift exchange as a more primitive stage of development that cultures grow out of as they become more sophisticated. Gifts and commodities are to be found within the same societies. The separation, then, is relative rather than absolute. Something can be more of a gift or less of one and anthropologists can talk of objects (and people) being commoditized and decommoditized and recommoditized, when an heirloom is auctioned off, for instance, or when a slave becomes a mistress, when a silver votive-offering is evaluated by weight and used to pay off mercenary soldiers, when the paymaster is a lottery-machine, when a sex-session is timed.

We are talking above all of a symbolic distinction which has to be maintained and enforced by societies. There might be sharply contrasted spaces: the market-place versus the home; or times of the year: a market-day versus Christmas. Above all there is language: 'friendship', 'favours', 'giving' on the one hand, and 'paying', 'buying' and 'selling' on the other. We should not think of these distinctions as obsolete in modern culture. A very small part of the modern economy functions as gift exchange, but it can be very important. We still worry about leaving the price on presents. We carefully assess the value of the gifts we exchange but object if someone too blatantly compares what has been given with what has been received, or, worse, has a keepsake valued. We especially appreciate presents which have been made for us or which have sentimental value for the giver. We wonder whether politicians should accept invitations to stay at the villas of wealthy interested friends. We protest, on the other hand, if a payment for services rendered is represented as an act of generosity for which we are supposed to be grateful.

As these examples show and as the slave Cario (himself a commodity) points out to his master, there is a large degree of dissimulation or even hypocrisy at the very heart of gift-giving. The giftness of the gift depends on a general practice of what the anthropologist Pierre Bourdieu calls *méconnaissance*, of misrecognition, of pretending that the gift has no value placed upon it and requires nothing in return. The favour which is expected in response must be presented as something completely at the discretion of the receiver, who emphasizes his freedom of action by choosing the time and the manner of his response. It helps if the gifts are slightly mismatched. It helps if there is an interval, but not too long, before it is reciprocated. If a present follows too hard on the heels of a favour it is a gift no longer, but a payment for 'services rendered'.

The difference between these two kinds of relationship becomes even more fraught when one of the items exchanged is sex. In classical Athens it is never simply a question of whether you 'do it for money' or 'do it for gifts'. To turn sexual intercourse into an exchange of alienable commodities involves a great effort of reification. What is it the prostitute is selling? A length of time? A sexual act? A body? A part of the body? Hetaeras, on the other hand, who are seduced by gifts, must make full use of the possibilities of discretion to avoid being seen as common prostitutes, while their enemies use all the language of the market-place to bring them back into line. Specifying is itself an issue in the sexual economy. If ancient men and modern scholars find it difficult to get a purchase on the hetaera this is not simply because the world of women is complicated. The hetaera goes to great lengths to avoid having herself and her relationships with men made explicit. Otherwise she would not be a hetaera.[1]

LOVE AND MONEY

Because the gift and the commodity define themselves in mutually exclusive opposition, we cannot know the one without knowing the other. We need to take a close look at how people and sex were transformed into goods for sale, before we can see how the hetaera avoided it. One of the most important diagnostics was space. In the Solonic law on adultery, as we have seen, space was the primary indication of whether it was legal to have sex with a woman. If she was one of those who 'walk to and fro in the open' or 'who sit in an *ergastērion*' (factory or shop) she was a whore and not available for adultery. These public spaces, the streets, the agora, brothels, sex-stalls (*oikēmata*) and 'shops' were contrasted with the private space of the *oikos*, which means both 'home' and the people who live there, the family, or the household. They might be considered 'zones of commodification', magic spaces that turn people into products, enabling uncomplicated transactions a world away from 'love-affairs' and 'seduction': 'The door's wide open; one obol's the fee. Pop in! No coyness here, no nonsense, no running away, but without delay the one you want, whichever way you want her. You come out; you tell her where to go; to you she's nothing.'[2]

The women of the truly public spaces presented few problems of definition. Outside is outside. The streets are the streets. But the second group of women, the women of the brothel, presented more difficulties. It might be rather awkward to tell a house from a house of ill-repute. What kind of building is Pyrrhus' home when Phile's mum, 'a woman shared by all who wanted her', comes to stay, a house surrounded by scenes of disorder, visited by bands of revellers? And when someone caught in Stephanus' house having sex with 'his daughter' Phano is let off on a charge of adultery it is hard to know which of the implications is more alarming: that the girl is therefore a common prostitute, or that Stephanus' home is therefore a brothel.[3] The *ergastērion* turns sex into an object for sale but the roles can be reversed. A whore can turn a home into a bordello.

We should not expect Aeschines to forgo this useful piece of sophistry in a speech that represents one of the most energetic attempts to turn 'friendships' and 'love-affairs' into business transactions, the speech *Against Timarchus*. It seems clear that part of the debate in this trial of a politician for prostitution concerned the kind of places in which intercourse was alleged to have taken place. If Timarchus was really a prostitute the prosecution should be able to point out the places he worked. Aeschines at first pretends to be disgusted by this line of argument:

> The defence which Demosthenes persuades you to make is not the defence of a free man, but the defence of a prostitute quibbling about places. But since you do take refuge in the names of premises and since you seem to think we should specify every single cubicle [*oikēma*] you've ever sat in, to prove our case. We will. But you'll regret it when you hear what I have got to say. Never again will you resort to such an argument if you've any sense at all. For premises don't label people. It's people who label premises: when a whole group of men rent a place and take possession of it, sharing it between them, it's called 'apartments'; when there's only one man it's called a house. And if a doctor moves into one of these shops [*ergastēria*] on the streets, it is called a clinic; if he moves out, and a smith moves in, then it is a smithy; if a fuller moves in, it is a fuller's; if a carpenter moves in, a carpenter's, and if a pimp moves in with his whores, it's called a knocking-shop [*porneion*], from the business that goes on inside. So that you have made many a house a brothel by the facility with which you have plied your trade.[4]

It is no coincidence that the occupants of the building described by Aeschines number five, beginning with a doctor and ending with whores and that Timarchus, according to Aeschines, moved in with five different men, the first of whom was a doctor and the last also 'a prostitute'. When Timarchus lived with the doctor the clinic became a brothel, a transformation he performed wherever he resided. The building Aeschines describes is an anonymous space, a far cry from home. It is a promiscuous space, sometimes occupied by a number of men and shared out between them or quickly passing through the hands of a series of different owners. One does not have to be oversubtle, I think, to notice that Aeschines is taking the relationship between people and places one stage further. The 'shop on the street' is, of course, Timarchus himself, his body, 'hired out' to each man in turn. The body = building metaphor is not unique to Aeschines, and a self-confident immoralist could use the same comparison to make a quite different case. When Diogenes claims his girlfriend Lais is a communal whore (*koinē pornē*), Aristippus asks whether he would object in that case to living in a house other men have lived in, or sailing in a ship other men have sailed in.[5]

The brothel, the agora and the streets do not exhaust the range of marketing spaces. From Persaeus of Citium, a Stoic philosopher, we learn that even the symposium could be turned into a market-place with the staging of auctions at which the guests bid for slave-girls. From Antigonus of Carystus we learn that Persaeus himself once 'bought a flute-girl' at a symposium, though hesitating to take her home, because he lived with his lover Zeno. We must be on our guard here, for we are ourselves perfectly familiar with the idea that prostitutes 'sell themselves' and it causes no surprise that the ancient Athenians used this language of buying and selling too. So Aeschines can talk of Timarchus 'selling himself by choice', although he was not, of course, sold or bought by anyone. Aeschines is simply deploying the language of sale to turn Timarchus into an object and to separate his relationships with his 'clients' from the honourable relationship of a lover (*erastēs*) and his beloved (*erōmenos*). But Athens was a slave-owning society in which men quite literally bought other men and women and enjoyed full property rights over them. In this context the notion of 'buying women' is rather more problematic, since so many *pornai* were slaves and the property of the pimp who 'sells', or 'hires them out' in turn. When Demosthenes, for instance, denounces Philocrates for betraying the city for money, he describes him spending it 'buying fish and prostitutes'. The word he uses, *agorazō*, 'going shopping', 'haggling over', conjures up most vividly the commercial transaction, but there is no reason to think that the women in question were ever taken into Philocrates' possession permanently. In fact Demosthenes is emphasizing the trivial use the money was put to. Nor should we necessarily imagine that Persaeus actually took possession of the girl he had bid for at the party auction. Even undisputed commodities had a use for the discourse of commodification. They could use it to isolate and detach some discrete commodity separate from their own commodified selves, although it is not always clear what it is.[6]

Time, of course, is one possibility. This is clearly what Neaera was selling during her early years as a *misthamousa* or wage-labourer, in Corinth. A sympotic hetaera was paid for her company for an evening, and if, like Habrotonon in Menander's *Arbitration*, her client asked for nothing more, she may have been surprised but she would still have earned her fee. Apollodorus when attacking Neaera represents her activities as 'trade' (*ergasia, ergazesthai*) and at one point asks rhetorically; 'Where has Neaera not gone in search of her daily wage?' A more extreme example of this kind of purchase is reflected in the stories about the woman known as Clepsydra, the Water-clock. She seems to have become famous around the middle years of the fourth century and was the subject of a comedy by Eubulus. According to one source she got her nickname because she timed her sessions and stopped having sex when the water-clock ran dry, thus transforming her time very effectively into a series of discrete products. The water-clock which allowed one vessel to drain at a regular rate into another conjured up, like the 'cistern', an appropriate metaphor for sex itself.[7]

Another possible candidate for commodity status was the body: 'select whichever one you like: thin, fat, round, tall, short, young, old, middle-aged or past it' says the brothel's encomiast in Xenarchus' *Pentathlete*. The body for sale is a favourite theme of both Apollodorus and Aeschines. For the former, Neaera is a woman who 'trades in her body' – she is in 'the body business' – and Aeschines paints Timarchus as if he is somehow quite separate from his corporeal self.

He is someone who 'let out his body for hire'; 'He has used his own body with scorn and contempt'; 'he sinned against his own body'. His lovers didn't commit wrongs and acts of hubris against Timarchus but 'against the body of Timarchus'; the men who visited him when he was residing in the house of the physician didn't pay to have sex with Timarchus but they 'used the body of Timarchus'. By talking always of Timarchus' carcass Aeschines is turning this well-known politician into a depersonalized anonymous object.[8]

At a further level of detachment it is not the body so much as a specific part of the body which is on the market. This stuff is too strong perhaps for Apollodorus' audience, or Aeschines' but we can trust Aristophanes to go the whole hog. 'Piggy', *choiros*, as it happens, is Greek slang for the genitals of girls or the smoothly-shaven pudenda typical of hetaeras. When the old man gets hold of the flute-girl at the end of *Wasps* he shows clearly how he sees her by addressing her as 'cuntlet', *choirion*. The comic writers did not let such an opportunity for jokes pass. Coming across the phrase 'piggy-selling' in Corinth, the later lexicographers explained to the bemused readers of Byzantium that this was a reference to the city's famous prostitutes. Since Corinth was a great centre for prostitution, temple and otherwise, it must have meant something like 'selling coals to Newcastle'. In *Acharnians* the marketing metaphor is developed much further. The hero of the play, Dicaeopolis, has had enough of fighting the Peloponnesians and decides to make his own private peace in the midst of a city preparing for war. He is determined to enjoy the benefits of commerce with hostile nations although their goods are under embargo and sets up his own free trade area in the market-place. He is approached by a man from neighbouring Megara, whose population is suffering the effects of an Athenian blockade and regular scorching raids. He has disguised his daughters as piggies in order to sell them and make some money. Dicaeopolis quickly sees through the disguise and starts bargaining. It is impossible for the audience at any one time to see if what is being talked about and traded are pigs, girls or vaginas. Two sets of mistaken identities are in operation. The Megarian's daughters cover up their female attractions and become little pigs, but at the same time, by means of the pun, the little pigs become nothing more than vaginas. The superficial gaze, which sees 'piggies for sale', and the penetrating gaze, which sees through their costume 'girls for sale', produces a third image, 'cunts for sale', the essential truth behind the façade, the answer to the puzzle. By means of this complex network of puns and disguise the girls are reduced to the level of sex-organs.[9]

From this brutal illustration of how bodies are turned into goods we come to what is a more acceptable metaphor, 'selling sex'. There is a certain amount of evidence that the Greeks considered sex between lovers different from bought sex. The former simply continued the reciprocal exchange of gifts and favours on a more physical level, the latter was hubris. The precise meaning of hubris has caused problems for many generations of students of Greek. It is one of those things the Greeks have a word for that we do not, covering violence, insolence and presumption. Aeschines puts it in a sexual context: 'He who hires', he says, 'commits hubris.' It seems to have more or less the same connotations as our phrase 'use for sex'. Aristotle, for instance, tells the story of Hellanocrates of Larissa whose lover refused to fulfil a promise to restore him to his country, 'thus making it clear that the connexion between them had originated not in erotic desire, but in hubris'. Hellanocrates felt used and killed him. Perhaps, then, sex becomes hubris when it is reduced to an impersonal activity, a mere commodity, sex that means nothing, rather than sex that reflects mutual attachment. It is not too difficult to see how the whambamthankyouma'am kind of sex celebrated in comic visits to the brothel could be associated with a word that elsewhere denotes insolent behaviour.[10]

The word *pornē* itself derives from a verb (*pernēmi*) which refers to selling or more probably being sold. More importantly this relationship between the two words seems to have been quite transparent: '*pernatai* = sells; whence also *pornē*, she who sells sex (*mixin*).' It is a small step from here to comic descriptions of the brothel as a *kinētērion*, a 'fuck-factory' as if it were a workshop producing sexual commodities. Its product range might have been quite extensive. The fourth century saw an explosion in manuals and handbooks which soon covered everything from 'how to cook' to 'how to survive a siege'. Among them were sex manuals, which included advice on flattery and seduction, as well as a range of sexual positions.

Aristophanes mentions a hetaera called Cyrene who had apparently mastered twelve. To most of these we can't even put a name, and those we can, like the so-called 'lion on the cheese-grater', leave us none the wiser, but three of them are mentioned quite frequently. Two of these involve penetration from behind: *kubda*, 'bent-over' is standing up with the woman bending forwards and *lordō*, 'bent-back' has the penetratee leaning back against the penetrator's chest. The third is *kelēs*, or 'racehorse' in which the penetratee sits astride the man and rides him like a pony. Different positions were charged at different fees. In a spoof sacrifice to porno-gods in a fragment of comic Plato, Bent-back gets a drachma, Bent-over three obols (half a drachma) and Racehorse the *derma* or skin, almost certainly a satire on a prostitute's price range. Apart from the obvious possibility of obscene allusion, the skin of a sacrificed animal was the most valued prerogative and 'racehorse' certainly seems to have been the most expensive position. Bent-over, on the other hand is the cheapest kind of sex, often priced at three obols. It is found as a commodity in one of Machon's anecdotes about the *grande horizontale* Gnathaena: long past her best, the distinguished lady goes to market and notices a handsome young butcher weighing some meat. She approaches him and asks 'How much?' He smiles and turns her question on its head. 'Three obols', he says, 'bent-over.' We are now in a position to understand the full implications of the behaviour of the Corinthian hetaeras mentioned at the beginning of the chapter. With all their airs and graces, they show themselves no better than 'two-bit' tarts when they bend over for a rich man.[11]

The fact that there seems to be a standard price for *kubda* helps to transform it into a recognizable sex-product and a distinctive feature of the language of commodity is a concern with fixed prices. When Theopompus wants to transform the great Pythionice into a common whore he observes that apart from being three times a *pornē* and three times a slave, she is one 'whom everyone knew had been shared by all who wanted her *at the same price for all*'. Elsewhere we find a fixed price inscribed even in women's names. One of the women, we recall, in one of the brothel/cloth factory scenes is called Obole, the price referred to in Philemon's account of the brothel: 'The door's wide open; one obol's the fee. Pop in!' Another woman was known as Didrachmon, 'Two-drachmas', because 'she visited anyone who wanted her for two drachmas'.[12]

Cash itself does not necessarily define commodity-exchange, but it certainly helps the concept along and there does seem to be a strong symbolic association between coins and promiscuity that runs both ways:

> Only a monetary transaction corresponds to the character of a completely fleeting inconsequential relationship as is the case with prostitution. The relationship is more completely dissolved and more radically terminated by payment of money than by the gift of a specific object, which always, through its content, its choice and its use, retains an element of the person who has given it. Only money, which does not imply any commitment, and which in principle is always at hand and welcomed, is the appropriate equivalent to the fleetingly intensified and just as fleetingly extinguished sexual appetite that is served by prostitution . . . In as far as one pays with money, one is completely finished with any object just as fundamentally as when one has paid for satisfaction from a prostitute . . . we experience in the nature of money itself something of the essence of prostitution. The indifference to its use, the lack of attachment to any individual because it is unrelated to any of them, the objectivity inherent in money as a mere means which excludes any emotional *relationship* – all this produces an ominous analogy between money and prostitution.

Simmel's *fin-de-siècle* perspective seems to find support in classical Athens where coins reflect and define the anonymous exchanges of promiscuity. Thus the brothel-women in Eubulus fragment 82 are 'coin-traps' and in fragment 67 we learn that you can purchase your pleasure from them for 'a small coin'. It is with coinage that Epicrates illustrates the decline of the hetaera, Laïs, when he contrasts the period of her prime, when staters (two drachmas) made her wild with rage, and her current decrepitude, when she accepts even a triobol (half-drachma) with meekness and mildness. There are hints in the classical period of a simple identification of money and sperm, two aspects of a man's substance. These hints later become much more explicit. This is the logic that leads Artemidorus in the second century of our era to conclude that when men dream of sex with their sons it indicates they will drain away money into them: school-fees, or a transfer of property. According to the same principle, the golden rain that falls impregnant into Danaë's lap on classical vases later turns Titian-like into a shower of gold coins pouring into the lap of a harlot. It is not so far from Eubulus' view of prostitutes as 'coin-traps' to Simmel's and Baudrillard's view of capitalism as promiscuity.[13]

Clearly there are strong currents of hatred and contempt running through the presentation of prostitutes as objects for sale, but it is unhelpful to regard the discourse of commodity-exchange as inherently, intrinsically, positive or negative. So long as there is prostitution, this kind of language and symbolism can be used to protect prostitutes as well as to denigrate them. With such strategies women and men without means can endow themselves with products in demand, and place themselves in the position of sellers. It is not surprising then that sociologists find that many prostitutes claim to experience their first sense of power when negotiating their first transaction. Many prefer to call themselves sex-workers. It is the clients who fantasize about a special relationship, coming up with stories of the girl who fell in love with a client and refused a fee.[14] It is Clepsydra, remember, who resorts to the clock.

JUST GOOD FRIENDS

The world of the grand hetaera is a million miles away from Clepsydra's temporal fractions. Nothing could be further from a knocking-shop than Theodote's well-appointed residence, where in rather luxurious surroundings she receives Socrates' visit. The philosopher is notably impressed and cannot help being curious about her means of support. Does she have a farm? A house? Some craftsmen working for her? To each question Theodote answers in the negative. Her sole source of income is her 'friends'. This appears a somewhat fragile living to the philosopher, who turns anthropologist and reflects on methods by which such a haphazard arrangement could be fixed more securely. Friendship can be strengthened and reinforced by visits at appropriate times for instance. Theodote is appalled at the thought of such self-consciousness. Socrates changes tack, comparing friendship to hunger and favours to food (a favourite analogy for desire), using the metaphor to outline a libidinal economy of appetites whetted and satisfactions deferred. So impressed is Theodote by Socrates' true understanding of friendship that she offers to engage his services.. Socrates says he is too busy. He would rather she came to him.

This famous episode so full of ironic allusion must be the starting point for any investigation into the relationship between the hetaera and the gift for, of course, although neither Socrates nor Xenophon ever says so explicitly, Theodote is a courtesan. References to clients and prices and payments and sex are carefully avoided. The talk is all of friendship and favours. The philosopher sets the tone as soon as the visitors arrive, worrying his companions with the question whether they now have a favour to repay to Theodote for agreeing to see them or she to them for their attentions. When the beautiful woman herself appears, her conversation never ventures outside the language of friendship, gifts, benefaction and gratitude. 'If someone who has become my friend wants to benefit me . . .' is how she describes her livelihood. The language game is continued by Socrates, who outlines a plan by which her acquaintances 'might become the greatest friends, and continue in friendship for the longest time, and confer the most benefits.'[15]

There are numerous occasions in comedy and elsewhere where hetaeras are associated with gifts. The herald in Aristophanes' *Thesmophoriazusae*, for instance, curses 'the hetaera who receives gifts and then cheats her friend', but the most famous example of a gift between a hetaera and her lover, and in many ways the classic case, is Praxiteles' gift to Phryne of a sculpture of the god Love. Many stories were told about this famous gift. Athenaeus quotes an epigram reported to have been attached to this or another version by the sculptor himself: 'Praxiteles portrayed with precision the Love which he suffered, hammering out the archetype from his own heart. To Phryne he gave me, in return for me.' In some accounts the statue is not made for Phryne but is chosen by her from the sculptor's oeuvre after carefully working out its value, but the epigram presents the statue in terms of a perfect personal gift. The statue is a rendition of his love, the love he felt for Phryne, the love Phryne gave him. It is a precise match, a precise replica of it – 'me in return for me'. It is perfect too in that it conforms so neatly to the modern definition of a gift, as a personal relationship between people. What represents a relationship between two lovers better than Love? The statue maintained its career as a gift for quite some time. Phryne gave it to the god himself, *Love* to Love for love, placing it in the sanctuary of Eros in Thespiae. There it remained, the city's sole tourist attraction, until it was removed to Rome under the emperors only to be destroyed in a fire.[16]

The journey from love-gift to temple dedication could be reversed. In his work *On the Funds Plundered from Delphi* Theopompus catalogued the gifts of priceless ancient treasures made to their male and female lovers by the tyrants of Phocis while the sanctuary was under their control: 'To the flute-girl Bromias . . . Phallus gave a silver *karchesion*, a votive offering of Phocaea, and an ivy wreath of gold, the offering of Peparethus . . . To Pharsalia, the dancing-girl from Thessaly, Philomelus gave a laurel crown of gold, a votive-offering of Lampsacus.'[17]

Judging from the Roman versions by Plautus and Terence, new comedy was perfectly sensitive to the importance of gift-exchange in the world of the hetaera (in Latin *meretrix*). The author of one study comments: 'In the vast majority of texts relating to the maintenance of the *hetaira/meretrix* in the Classical world, it is quite clear that gifts, whether in kind or in pecuniary form, were not merely a customary manner of payment, but where a more or less durable relationship . . . was concerned, almost the only one.' Sometimes these gifts are a major part of the plot. Terence's *Eunuch*, for instance, which takes its title and much of its plot from a lost play of Menander, centres on gifts of a slave-girl and a eunuch made to the hetaera Thais by competing suitors. Apart from Roman copies, there are two passages preserved on papyri which together capture the complicated relationship between language and reality in the area of giving gifts. In the first, a new fragment of the *Hated Man* first published in 1977, the soldier Thrasonides complains about his treatment by the captive

Cratia, who seems to hate him despite all his gifts to her: 'I bought her, [gave her] her freedom, proclaimed her [the mistress] of the house, gave her maidservants, gold ornaments, cloaks, treated her as a wife.' The second is from the play *Theophoroumene* (*The Girl Possessed*). An eavesdropper, it seems, has seen a strange girl talking distractedly about 'my gifts' and how they have been stolen from her. Such language labels the girl immediately as a *Hippoporne*, a Mega-whore. Together the two passages nicely illustrate the shifting sands of hypocrisy and cynicism involved in ancient gift-giving. In the first the soldier's gifts to Cratia are placed at a great distance from payment to a prostitute, evidence to support his claim to have treated her as a free woman, even as the mistress of the house, his wife. It is almost certain, however, that she is (or was) in fact a slave-concubine. In the other fragment, references to gifts are immediately 'seen through' as a hetaera's conceit, and the woman identified as a whore, although, since the character is almost certainly a virgin, the designation will turn out to be quite wrong. What these fragments show, along with Xenophon's account of Socrates' visit to Theodote, is that the Greeks were wise to the gift. They could see as well as any anthropologist how it worked, that it might be no more than a game, a self-conscious game whose rules must never be mentioned, a game at which the hetaeras were Grandmasters.[18]

Of course, these gifts were not free gifts. The women were obliged to give something in return – at their own discretion, of course. Praxiteles' epigram makes it clear that his gift of *Love* is in return for Phryne's love. What Theodote has to give in return for her friends' favours, on the other hand, is not made absolutely clear. Socrates helps her along. Perhaps she repays the favour with visits when the friend in question is sick, with congratulations when he has enjoyed some success, with words, with a glance. If he is especially keen, she can gratify 'with all her soul' (whatever that means). Socrates is beating energetically about the bush: 'I know too that you lead your friends into thinking they are amenable to you, not only by what you say, but also *by what you do*.' Later he talks of her making a gift of *ta para seautēs*, 'things from you', of benefactions, of *pleasure*. Now he's getting warmer. Machon is not so coy. What his hetaeras have to give is similar to what the *pornai* sell. He tells an anecdote about the hetaera Nico and Sophocles' boyfriend Demophon: 'it is said that she had a very attractive bottom, which Demophon once asked if he could possess. And she laughed and said "be my guest, my friend, take it and give it to Sophocles as a present from me."'

A similar anecdote is told about Mania and Demetrius the Besieger, a Hellenistic dynast: 'They say that on one occasion when Demetrius the king was after her behind, Mania asked for something in return. He granted it to her, and shortly afterwards she turned around and said "Son of Agamemnon, *now* you may".' That 'shortly afterwards' is crucial. The women of the brothel according to the comic encomia must do it instead 'without delay'. As Bourdieu remarks: 'the operation of gift exchange presupposes misrecognition [*méconnaissance*] of the reality of the objective "mechanism" of the exchange, a reality which an immediate response brutally exposes.' This confrontation with which anthropologists are only too familiar between the external vantage-point of outsiders and the experience of those who actually participate can be seen in the case of Socrates' visit to Theodote. At one point the hetaera objects to Socrates' careful discovery of the rules of the game: 'By Zeus,' she swears, 'I myself contrive none of these things.' Socrates, only slightly abashed, agrees: 'Quite so; it is very important that your behaviour to people be natural and genuine.'[19] Mania's small delay before giving Demetrius his wish, Theodote's outrage at Socrates' cynicism are both necessary to maintain a defence against the world of buying and selling. Misrecognition, beating about the bush, the avoidance of specifics, the uncertainty of favours in return, are all strategies designed to keep 'friendship' out of the market-place.

This is more than a question of sensibilities. There is an atmosphere of secrecy and subterfuge in the world of the hetaera. With definition came dangers, taxes, limits, laws. Women who worked in brothels were registered and had to pay the *pornikon telos*, the whore-tax. Flute-girls could charge no more than two drachmas a night and were forced to go with whomever the Astynomos allotted them. Women of the brothels and streets had been excluded from the protection afforded to other women since Solon or Draco. Athenian women who practised this way of life could be exposing themselves and their lovers to the laws of adultery, even death. Hetaeras had a powerful interest in this game. Upon the fragile status of the gift depended their fragile status as 'companions' rather than common prostitutes. The avoidance of calculation in giving, the naturalness of friendship, on which Theodote insists, and with which Socrates ironically concurs, can be used by women themselves to elude definition, quantification and commodification.

The choice a hetaera exercises over whom she sleeps with is a prerogative of central importance. Theodote does not go with whoever wants her, but with whoever 'persuades' her. In this respect hetaeras are closer to (adulterous or potentially adulterous) wives than prostitutes. The appropriate verb is not buy, but *peithein*, 'persuade, seduce', or *peiran*, 'to make trial of someone or something for the purpose of ruination or sex' as Photius puts it. It can be used of assaults by armies on cities or countries, but also of attempts on sexual 'honour'. It is used in the New Testament and translated as 'temptation', but it is also found in the tiny surviving fragments of the ancient world's most famous sex-manual ascribed to Philaenis of Samos. The top of column two of the first papyrus fragment is headed *Concerning Techniques of Seduction* (*Peri Peirasmōn*). What follows seems to be advice on different modes of flattery and seduction addressed to *ton peirōnta*, the tempter (masculine). *Pornai* in contrast, have to have sex with *ho boulomenos*, 'whoever wishes'. Apollodorus is keen to stress that in her early career as a slave-girl under Nicarete, Neaera 'hired herself out *to whoever wanted* to have sex with her', and according to Isaeus, Pyrrhus' 'wife' and Phile's mother was not just a hetaera but 'a woman available to anyone who wanted', just as Pythionice according to Theopompus 'was readily available *to all who wished* at the same price for all'. The same rules applied, of course, to men. Elsewhere in Xenophon's *Memoirs* Socrates claims that someone is called *pornos* if they sell their youthful bloom to *whoever wants it* and Aeschines argues that what distinguishes a common prostitute from an 'escort' is that he 'does it with many men *without discrimination*' (*eikēi*).[20]

Another basic rule is capriciousness. A hetaera must always have freedom to exercise her whim and keep alive the possibility, however small, of doing something for nothing or of not returning the favour at all. There is of course a rational explanation for this irrational behaviour: 'The simple possibility that things might proceed other-wise than as laid down by the "mechanical laws" of the "cycle of reciprocity" is sufficient to change the whole experience of practice and, by the same token, its logic. The shift from the highest prob-ability to absolute certainty is a qualitative leap out of proportion to the numerical difference.' Machon's collection of witty sayings is full of arbitrary behaviour: 'Moerichus was attempting to get Phryne into bed (*peiran*). When she asked him for a hundred drachmas he said, "You ask for a lot. Did you not yesterday stay with a stranger, though you only received two gold pieces?" "Well then," she said, "the same applies to you. Wait until I want to have sex, and I will take that amount."' This is a long way from the 'fixed price' of two-drachma Didrachmon. Laïs is said to have had a large crowd of lovers and not to have distinguished between rich and poor. The philosopher Aristippus was reproached because he gave Laïs so much money, although she rolled about with Diogenes the Cynic for free. No matter how many times he asked, Gnathaenium (daughter or grand-daughter of the great Gnathaena) refused to 'ride the racehorse' with her lover Andronicus, an actor, although they were virtually married. She did, however, grant this favour to a good-looking coppersmith while Andronicus was away: 'she couldn't bear to accept a fee, but he persevered in his entreaties and spent on her a great deal of gold and so had her.' Unfortunately the coppersmith had no breeding and boasted of his conquest in the shoe-maker's shop. Her lover found out and confronted her with the information. She had a ready reply. She had no desire, she said, to embrace the copper-smith's dirty body and contrived to touch only the part that was smallest in size and projected furthest from him.[21]

The difficulty involved in defining a hetaera, then, is all part of the hetaera's plan. A hetaera remains a hetaera only so long as she can foil attempts to pin her down. This uncertainty keeps her on the right side of laws and taxes and builds a glass wall between what she does and what goes on in brothels. Much more than that, how-ever, it makes her sexy: 'What a difference there is between spending a night with a street-walker and spending a night with a girl [*koriskē*]. Ah yes, the firmness of her body, the colour of her skin, her breath, ye gods! That everything is not too ready for business, that you have to struggle a bit, get slapped and punched by gentle hands; a great pleasure, by Zeus, the greatest!'[22]

THE ECONOMY OF LOOKING

The hetaera's avoidance of economic definition finds a parallel in her careful avoidance of the masculine gaze. Decent women in Athens were supposed to be secluded, avoiding the company of men outside the family and not even having their names mentioned in public. So invisible were they that in extreme cases their very existence might be called into question. The crucial issue in the speech *Against Neaera* is whether there had ever been a citizen-wife in Stephanus' house to make his children legitimate citizens. Whether seclusion was an ideal or a common practice, and whether keeping women out of sight indicated honour and respect or fear and contempt are questions that have generated plentiful discussion.[23] Argument tends to swing backwards and forwards from one point of view to another, without generating much light. Seclusion is seen as a static condition, the absolutely private contrasted with the absolutely public to divide the world of women in two, a straightforward split which is inevitably related to the division of women into two categories: Wives and the Rest. At best visibility is treated as a reflection of something else, an indication of attitudes to women, a mark of status. The most obvious aspect of seclusion, that it is about sexuality, about female desire and about the power of female attractions, has been strangely neglected. If it is connected to sexuality at all it is seen in terms of substitutions and compensation. Sexuality is viewed in terms of a hydraulic model: Athenian women were kept out of sight, therefore men had to turn to slaves and prostitutes. Slaves and prostitutes were not intellectually or spiritually fulfilling enough, therefore men turned to homosexual relations with each other, etc. In these treatments, seclusion challenges, diverts and distorts a fully formed force of desire, as if men maintain a constant level of lust that can only be managed, released or diverted. That seclusion might actually produce desire, that it might construct attractions in particular ways, that it might be active in the field of sexuality and not just passively reflect existing drives is rarely considered.

It seems to me more fruitful to treat public and private spaces not as two distinct worlds, but as two extreme points in a single system or economy. An economy which actually helps to stimulate desire rather than just managing it, an economy that constructs lust in particular ways. The whole business of hiding women only to discover them later places them in a spectacular system, what Luce Irigaray calls a 'dominant scopic economy . . . she is to be the beautiful object of contemplation . . . her body finds itself thus eroticized, and called to a double movement of exhibition and of chaste retreat in order to stimulate the drives of the "subject".' The public space of the streets and the secluded zones of the women's quarters are not static zones, but extreme points on a shifting scale of titillation: 'Come and accept our offering, greatly honoured one', says the servant to the figure of Peace personified in Aristophanes' play, 'and for god's sake don't do as the adulterous women do. For they let the door stand a little ajar and lean out, and if someone happens to notice them they go back in; and then if they go away, they lean out again. Don't do that to us.' Or, from the woman's point of view: 'And if we lean out of the door, you try to get an eyeful; and if out of a sense of shame she withdraws, then every man desires much more to look at that "bane of our lives" bent over.'24 The sight of a woman therefore has a charge, a specific symbolic value. All but the most invisible women are revealing something. All but the most completely naked and exposed have something more to reveal. For the men of Athens the women of Athens are in various stages of undress. The extreme exposure of the brothel prostitute and the complete invisibility of the decent lady force all other women to dance a striptease on points in between.

An economy of the gaze may seem like an uncomfortable mixture of metaphors but it does have an ancient precedent. If we look again at Socrates' visit to Theodote, we notice that his very first question manages to frame the whole visit in terms of an exchange not of gifts, but of seeing for showing: 'My friends, ought we to be more grateful to Theodote because she has shown us her beauty, or she to us because we have come to see her? For isn't it true that if her exhibition [*epideixis*] of herself is of more benefit to her then she should be grateful to us, but if the sight [*thea*] of her is of more benefit to us then we are indebted to her.' Socrates, the anthropologist, having made these ineffable exchanges explicit has the cheek to attempt a calculation, to find out which of the two is more valuable. In so doing he connects looking to lusting, the scopic to the libidinal economy: 'We already desire to touch what we have seen and will leave with our appetites whetted, and once we have gone we will be afflicted with longing. It is reasonable, I conclude, to say that it is we who are performing a service and she is the one who is being served.' 'Then of course', said Theodote, 'if that is so, I ought to be grateful to you.'

Theodote is by no means a secluded wife, but neither is she a public prostitute. Nevertheless, from the beginning of the episode she is placed in the context of the masculine gaze, her visibility, her dress, her undress are all assessed and given values within the scopic economy. She is introduced to Socrates as someone whom artists visit to observe and paint. She shows these artists a carefully calculated portion of herself, 'as much as is proper'. Indeed, when the philosopher and his cronies arrive at her house to view her, she is already under the gaze, sitting for a painter. The visitors observe her being observed. This gaze eroticizes her body. Looking is linked automatically to possessing. The men desire to touch what they have seen. Theodote's exhibition of part of herself only serves to produce a longing for more of her. Her revelation only serves to concentrate attention on what still remains covered, what remains to be revealed.[25]

Athenian women, then, are rather like Russian dolls. The first obstacle the searching eye comes across are the walls of the house in which the women are enclosed. Once inside the house the women may still be unseen, secreted in the next layer, the *muchos* or women's quarters. Behind these doors they still remain hidden in the folds of their drapery. Behind that level is the female body, and secreted in the remotest part of that structure is the vagina, the receding point. Women can place themselves at various points along this continuum of exposure, turning from visibility to invisibility. The body is itself like a building, with its own recesses and secret places. We have already seen this happening with Timarchus' body, when Aeschines compares it to the promiscuous and public space of a 'shop on the street'. Aristophanes uses a similar body/building comparison to quite opposite effect in his fantasy of feminine revolution, the *Ecclesiazusae* or *Women in Power*, creating an evocative image of the privacy, secrecy and hidden sexuality of the world of women. The play opens with an encomium to a lamp, or rather, the lamp's 'shining eye', which performs indoors the 'bright offices of the sun'. Because of its previous record of keeping secrets, Praxagora the leading conspirator will confide the women's plot to take over the government. There is little sense here of seclusion as a desexualized space, a safe haven from desire. Rather, secrecy and sexuality are intertwined to produce a powerfully erotic effect: 'You alone we allow to see, when within our walls you dance attendance on our erotic feats, and no one shuts the door on your eye, the overseer of our racked flesh. You alone bring light to our thighs' confidential crevices, singeing away the hair as it pokes through.' There is word-play here between *muchos*, as the innermost part of a house, the women's quarters, and *muchoi*, the recesses of the body, i.e. the vagina. But Aristophanes is simply elaborating a very common metaphorical vocabulary, which sees the body as a building or a space, and the vagina, either as a door opening into it or a recess within it. This notion of the body as a covering produces some rather odd images. Socrates talks of Theodote's body as if it were a 'net' and Athenaeus tells a smutty anecdote about the poet Menander going to visit the hetaera Glycera, getting on in years. 'She brought him some boiled milk and encouraged him to drink it down; but he said, "I don't want it", for "hag's-skin" scum had formed on it. And she said, "Blow off the hag's skin and use what's underneath." '[26]

All the other differences between women in Athens have echoes at the level of looking. The general accessibility of the brothel prostitute, the ease with which you can have her, her cheap price, the simplicity of the sexual transaction, her obviousness, find a parallel in her transparency, her openness to the masculine gaze. On the other hand, the difficulties in classifying the grand hetaeras, the difficulties in getting them into bed are bound up with the difficulties in seeing them. This is the contrast pointed up most plainly in comic praise of the brothel. *Pornai* stand in the sun, 'half-naked'; they are women 'it is permitted to look at', 'lest you be deceived'. 'Take a look at everything', says the speaker in one fragment, '. . . the door is open.' They are being contrasted, according to Athenaeus, with free women, in particular the great hetaeras. These are the women described in Xenarchus' praise of the brothel as 'those you are not supposed to see'. 'How', the speaker continues 'can men ever have sex with such women . . . when just as they are getting into it they remember the laws of Draco?'[27]

It is controversial, to say the least, to put hetaeras among the ranks of the women of the interior, protected by Draco's laws absolving enraged husbands and fathers from on-the-spot murder, but Athenaeus is quite explicit and there is no reason to think that he has got it wrong, precisely because it is a rather odd, counter-intuitive thing to say. The laws themselves are quite unequivocal. Draco clearly included within his remit 'concubines who are kept for free children' and Solon did not exclude them, referring, as we have seen, only to the women of brothel and street. Modern scholars with their simplistic approach to women in Athens tend to forget or elide difficult categories like the mistress and the concubine. The traditional view of *moicheia* in modern scholarship is 'illegitimate intercourse with any female *member of the family*', omitting mistresses altogether. But Athenian law is a law of authoritative original documents, publicly displayed and open for anyone to bring into the court-room. So long as those laws of Solon and Draco were inscribed in stone and remained as part of the law-code they were open to literal readings. As such they make a very clear distinction between slaves, and women of the streets and the brothels, but no distinction between wives and free concubines. The possibility must, therefore, be borne in mind that both of these laws could be used by offended parties to protect the honour of their mistresses, and there is some evidence that this, in theory, if not in practice, was the case.[28]

We have already seen some examples of hetaeras being treated as wives. And on more than one occasion we find that the language of 'adultery' (*moicheia*) is used when other men, apart from the men they live with, have sex with them, or get too close. Moschion in Menander's *The Haircut* is called 'adulterer' (*moichos*) three times by the slave Sosias for the attentions he pays to his master's mistress. This is usually assumed to be a case of hollow threats on the part of the slave and self-delusion on the part of his master. But the charge seems not at all inconsistent with the laws of Draco and Solon and the fragment of Xenarchus. A similar use of the term is found in another anecdote from Machon. He tells of how Leontiscus the pancratiast wrestler kept the hetaera Mania for himself alone, 'in the manner of a wedded wife'. Later he notices that she is being 'seduced into an adulterous affair' (*moicheuomenēn*) by a rival in the sport, Antenor. Also significant is the fact that there seem to be no intervening terms between Draco's protected mistress and Solon's excluded whores. When a charge of 'adultery' is dismissed against Neaera's daughter's seducer, the effect is to evoke Solon's categories, with Stephanus' house cast as a brothel. The only conclusion, it seems to me, is that in all these cases, the old categories defined in the laws of Solon and Draco are the valid and current ones, when *moicheia* is at issue.[29] In practical terms it may have been difficult to bring such a charge unless your mistress was an Athenian, since at some point a law was introduced forbidding 'cohabitation' or 'marriage' (*sunoikeîn*) with foreigners, although since so many Athenians quite clearly did cohabit with foreigners the prohibition cannot have been so straightforward. What seems clear is that on a day-to-day basis, for some men and perhaps for many women too, the difference between wives and mistresses could be rather blurred.

Perhaps we should look at it the other way round. Heterosexual eroticism in Athens was centred neither on sex within marriage, nor on quick visits to the brothel. It was constructed on a shadowy middle ground of uncertainty, on the seduction and temptation of women whose availability was not clear. I have argued elsewhere that the love-songs and pageants performed by the musicians of the symposium were particularly concerned with 'adultery' as we can see in comic references to the 'nocturnal' '*moichikos*' songs of the mid-fifth-century poet Gnesippus and his chorus of filthy female 'pluckers'. This is the world inhabited by Philaenis, who advises her 'tempter' not to seem to 'the woman' to be 'on the job'. What kind of woman is this?[30]

In terms of their visibility, then, the great hetaeras are closer to wives than to the *pornai* who ply the streets and sit in brothels. Like them they are women it is not permitted to look at or only if you dare: 'The houses of the hetaeras are places of tabu fallen from heaven' (*diopeteis*), says one comic character, 'they have become places it is forbidden to approach.' 'When Laïs was a fresh young chick . . .', says another, 'you would have got a sighting of the satrap Pharnabazus sooner than her', but in her decrepitude, 'it is easier to see her than to spit.'· Hetaeras, like married women, can be caught sight of at festivals, like the Eleusinia or the Posidonia, or on trips to the well. When they step out of doors, they keep themselves covered up, but it is on such occasions that the imagination can be excited by what is hidden underneath the garments. Machon tells a story about Gnathaena and her daughter Gnathaenium, attending a festival of Cronus, and being approached by an ancient general, whose desires are aroused by 'studying the girl's shape underneath her clothing and her rhythms' as she moves. No questions are asked when the men disguised as hetaeras in the Theban coup arrive at the symposium covered up and ask the servants to leave before they will come in the room. It is only when they sit down that they reveal their masculine faces along with their knives. Of course the hetaera unlike the decent wife covers herself up not out of chastity but to mislead and delude and to maintain her market value. They are contrasted with Philemon's praiseworthy *pornai* who stand naked 'so that you're not deceived'. According to Antiphanes' *On Hetaeras*, 'Nannio was nicknamed Proscenium (Stage-set) because although she possessed refined features and wore golden jewellery and dressed herself in expensive fabrics, without her clothes she was very ugly.' Alexis takes this line of argument even further: 'One happens to be small; a cork platform is sewn into her slippers . . . One has no hips; she stitches something up and puts it on as an undergarment, so that those who look at her are impressed at her fine backside and call out.' A fat stomach? That's sorted out with a girdle. 'One has a part of her body which is beautiful; this she can afford to leave uncovered making an exhibition of it.'[31]

No such suspicions attached to Phryne, the greatest of the hetaeras and the cleverest manipulator apparently of this scopic economy, carefully rationing out sightings, carefully calculating withdrawal and disclosure. Although what she revealed was beautiful enough, according to Hermipppus of Smyrna:

> In fact she was more beautiful in those parts not exposed to view. Because of that it was not easy to see her naked. She always wore a little chiton clinging to her flesh and did not use the public baths. But at the great festival of the Eleusinia and that of the Posidonia in full sight of a crowd that had gathered from all over Greece, she removed her cloak and let loose her hair before stepping into the sea; and it was from her that Apelles painted his likeness of Aphrodite coming out of the sea.

Since she seems to have kept her tunic on, the sight might have been more like a wet T-shirt contest than Botticelli's nude. Phryne does not keep herself entirely from view, nor does she expose herself completely. Complete invisibility and complete exposure arrest movement along the continuum, and thereby neutralize desire. By revealing a lot, but keeping her clothes on, Phryne keeps herself within that economy and arouses longing for what is hidden. On one occasion, apparently, Phryne did expose her flesh in public. She had been charged with impiety, for introducing new gods. She was defended by Hyperides, one of her lovers, who produced for the occasion what antiquity regarded as his finest speech. It failed, however, to impress the jurors. Seeing that he was making little headway 'he led Phryne herself into view, tore off her tunic-layers, exposed her breasts and finished his speech with a pitiful finale. He filled the jurors with religious awe and stopped them from condemning to death Aphrodite's representative and attendant, as they indulged their feelings of compassion.'[32] If she had made herself more available Phryne could not have expected to produce such an impact, but thanks to years of glimpses and rumours and guessing, her sudden exposure must have had an effect rather like the *dénouement* at the end of a complicated plot.

Hetaeras produced a vast array of material. Speeches were written about them, plays put them in performance, images were made of them, dialogues discussed them. Yet modern scholars and ancient men have great difficulty in working out precisely where they fit into Greek society. This is less of a paradox than it appears. We can perhaps now see that difficulties in defining hetaeras are intimately bound up in what they were. They live in the uncertain economy of the gift and have made the gift's essential misrecognition the centrepiece of their amorous strategy. The very name hetaera – 'companion' 'friend' – is ambiguous, a euphemism. Their language likewise is characterized by double-meanings, notoriously enigmatic, parodic and punning. This is the point about the hetaera's facility with literary quotations, not to demonstrate her erudition but her ability to disguise with a high-sounding quote an obscene proposition hidden within its innocent references. Anaxilas compares hetaeras to the deadly enigmatic Sphinx: 'nothing they babble is straightforward, on the contrary it's all in riddles: how they love "to be in love", and "to be friends" and "to go with someone".' Philaenium's suitor in Plautus' *Ass-dealer* tries to clamp down on her two-timing tongue, by forbidding her from using any 'bendable words' at all. The language of hetaeras moves back and forth between meanings like a saucy woman on a threshold; at any one time they might be simply quoting a line of tragic poetry or mouthing obscenities. This resistance to closed meaning, to definition, to purchase, to possession keeps them away from laws of adultery and the buying and selling of the brothel. But it is not surprising if at the same time this enigma, the problematic of possession, provokes efforts to control them, to capture them in images, to capture them in print. Is it a coincidence that Phryne who was so notoriously difficult to see naked was the model for the first proper female nude, the Cnidian Aphrodite? Of course painters wanted to paint them. Of course sculptors wanted to carve them. Of course poets wanted to write about them. Hetaeras had worked hard to make themselves fascinating. Here at least on the fantasy plane the fantasy did as she was told. The hetaera might elude purchase and escape male meanings and the masculine gaze, but she could always be manipulated on the male stage or on the male page or in the masculine imagination:

All night long my dream laid Sthenelais naked by my side, she who has set the city on fire, she who commands hefty fees, she who roars 'GOLD!' to those who line up for her services. Right up until dawn she lay next to me, granting her favours for nothing. No longer will I get down on my knees before a barbarian woman, no longer will I shed tears for myself, now that I have sleep to give me what I want.[33]

PART III

THE CITIZEN

BODIES

'It is notorious that in Bristol he went so far as to hire men – porters, hackney-coachmen, and others – to oppose by force his entrance into any druggist's shop. But, as the authority for stopping him was derived simply from himself, naturally these poor men found themselves in a metaphysical fix.' (Thomas De Quincey, *Confessions of an English Opium Eater*, on Samuel Taylor Coleridge)

ANCIENT ADDICTIONS

Aristophanes' *Wasps*, first performed in late January 422 BCE, opens with a scene of mystery and suspense. It is just before dawn. Two slaves have been standing vigil outside a house. Another man sleeps on the roof. What they are guarding is described only as 'a bizarre creature'. It inspires fear and trepidation. Eventually they reveal more. The man on the roof is their master. The monster he keeps locked up inside is his own father, who is suffering from 'an extraordinary disease' (*nosos*). They challenge the audience to guess what is wrong with him, one of them pretending to hear suggestions of their own characteristic vices from various notorious citizens, the other telling them if they are wrong or right: 'Amynias, here, says he is a gambler, a dice-ophile . . .' 'No, Amynias, but it is an -ophile kind of problem.' 'Sosias, here, is telling Dercylus he's a drink-ophile.' 'Never, that's a disease reserved for the great and good.' 'Nicostratus has another suggestion, he's a sacrificial-feast-ophile . . .' This guess too falls wide of the mark. The slaves decide to tell the audience the answer. The monstrous creature inside the house is a 'court-ophile'. The disease that afflicts him is an incessant desire for jury-service. They have tried everything to stop him, even taking him across to the Temple of Asclepius on Aegina to be cured, but still he manages to slip through their grasp and joins the front of the queue every morning for court duty. The audience is soon given a vivid demonstration of Philocleon's affliction. The old man wakes early and tries every possible exit to make his escape, through the chimney, out through the plug-hole, and in an obscene mockery of Odysseus' flight from the Cyclops, clinging to the underside of a donkey.

Like most of Aristophanes' plays, the *Wasps* contains much parochial detail. Modern stagings would need either to adapt the play substantially to make it intelligible to modern audiences, or to include in the programme several pages of notes explaining the technicalities of Athens' super-democratic legal system (large panels of older citizens selected to act as judge and jury for various usually squalid and often petty disputes on the basis of flimsy pieces of evidence) and a survey of the politics of the 420s around which the play revolves. Even the most learned commentators have had to pass over a good many punchlines without understanding the joke. But behind the specificities of local satire the dramatic premise seems utterly contemporary: the old man is that most familiar twentieth-century specimen, an addict.

Cultural historians, however, have argued that this distinctive character burst into public consciousness no earlier than the late eighteenth century of our era. The opium-addict was one of the first, closely followed by the alcoholic who remains the most familiar manifestation of the type.[1] To these were added briefly at the close of the last century the nymphomaniacs and satyriasics. Very recently the model of addiction has reached a point of apparently universal applicability to match the language of the *Wasps*, so that we can talk freely of 'chocoholics' and 'shopoholics' and 'soap-addicts'. These examples may be deployed flippantly, but the addiction model itself has achieved remarkable currency and respect, turning decadents and sinners into victims and patients and transforming censure into sympathetic understanding. If 'twelve-step programs' to cure addiction to body-piercing ('metal-fever') and jogging still seem rather exotic, it is quite uncontroversial to talk of 'alcoholism' as a disease, even a hereditary disease, that can never be cured and can only be managed through complete abstinence, even of people born with a hereditary disposition to be alcoholics.[2]

The opening scene of the *Wasps* does not quite justify in itself a rewriting of the history of the idea of addiction as an illness. Its language is quite unique. No other ancient source seems to provide so clear a typology of addictive characters under the rubric of disease, not even in jest. As a result it is most likely that Aristophanes' audience would read the scene as another example of the poet's famous talent for conjuring up *eikones* (vivid satirical images), rather than as a banal and familiar view of predilection. To call love of dicing or love of drinking an illness was simply a startling and prescient joke which would not be taken in earnest for two thousand years. The prevailing view of such passions in Aristophanes' time was almost the exact reverse.

At the risk of preposterous overgeneralization, we might say that in modern times we approach the consumable world with relative tranquillity, having achieved a kind of equilibrium with our appetites. While we might seek to moderate and control them, they are not normally massive forces in our lives. Those who *are* engaged in a fierce struggle against appetites are the exceptions. They have taken some substance they should not have or have overindulged in some less dangerous substance to an extreme degree, so that they now find it difficult to live without it. Because of long-term habituation or the inheritance of an addictive tendency or brief exposure to some powerfully addictive drug, they are taken over by severe compulsions. There is something wrong with them that marks them out from the rest of the population, something which can be classed as an illness to distinguish them from the healthy, normal, serene population. In accordance with this medical or pseudo-medical notion of addiction, the typical quarry of this errant appetite is classed as a drug which has transformed the consumer, creating in him or her a dependency. This dependency produces compulsive desires and burning necessities, which dominate his or her life to the exclusion of all other considerations. This compulsion, strangely, is considered quite different from a desire for pleasure. It is a long time since alcoholics and smokers and heroin-addicts have been considered mere voluptu-aries. In fact, pleasure has been so ignored in modern accounts of addiction that enjoyment often comes as a complete surprise to those who dare to indulge for the first time, thinking that the dangers of a dangerous drug, its power to seize its subjects, to hook them, lay in some more occult process. This has the effect of erecting a great barrier between desire for things classed as 'drugs' and all other consumables. Controlling a desire for bacon sandwiches or beach holidays or the rhetoric of evangelical preachers or a bestselling novel is (for the moment) treated as a quite different exercise from control-ling desire for alcohol or cigarettes or cocaine. When similar 'compul-sive' or 'excessive' behaviour is observed with regard to non-drugs, the response is not to question the distinction, but to reclassify the object as a drug or drug-like, turning the definition on its head. It is possible to envisage a time in the near future when this distinction between drugs and non-drugs will evaporate, when our own body's chemicals, our endorphins and adrenalin, will have been reconceived as substances we can 'abuse', and a vast range of human activities is considered susceptible to addiction, with pleasure itself reclassified as just another drug. For the time being, however, the official and unofficial list of dangerous drugs is limited; true addicts are still abnormal and rare; and only a few common activities, smoking, for instance, and drinking, are universally thought to require constant careful invigilation.

The Greeks, in contrast, distinguished no special category of con-sumables as particularly open to abuse, but considered a fierce struggle against desire a normal state of affairs. They saw themselves as exposed to all kinds of powerful forces. The world's delights were lying in wait to ambush them around the next corner. The pleasures of the table, eels and fried tuna-steaks, fragrant wine, and above all human beauty naturally exerted a strong influence on all those who came within their gravitational field. There was no special mechanism at work to produce a particular addiction. People naturally wanted to indulge as much as possible in things that were enjoyable – the rhetoric of orators, the delights of theatrical spectacle, the pleasures of the flesh. This led to a prevailing model of addiction that looks like an exact inversion of our own. People who overindulged in something had not developed an abnormal dependency on it, driven by unique compulsions. It was simply that their capacity to resist the regular, natural, insistent pleasures of the world was lower. Compulsion was seen as a function of enjoyment. The objects of appetite and desire, whether alive or dead, were seen as lively, provocative and flirtatious, marshalled and enhanced by chefs and symposiarchs and the feminine arts of seduction. Normally this struggle was seen as a straightforward battle between the Self and the World, but for those of a more philosophical bent, the Self itself was divided in two parts, the Soul and the Body. The latter acts as a traitor within the gates, pleasure's fifth column. The war is really a civil war, an internal struggle. This influential theory is spelled out most categorically in Plato's *Phaedo*; as Socrates approaches his execution the separation of soul and body is of crucial interest. The dialogue ends with a sensational image of that separation as the philosopher gradually feels the hemlock taking effect and loses contact with his body from the feet upwards. The body's endless demands are progressively muted before being silenced for ever, while his immortal soul prepares for take-off into a world of undistracted contemplation.

Whether the struggle was between you and the world's pleasures, or between you and your body, this state of conflict was normal and natural. What was abnormal was to put up no resistance, to be continually and instantly overwhelmed. Such feeble characters threw in the towel without a fight. They were defeated and enslaved by their desires. They were known as the *akolastoi*, the uncorrected, the unchecked, the unbridled, or the *akrateis*, the powerless, the impotent, the incontinent. They came in several forms. Most of them were terribly mainstream, engaging to excess in activities to which all, to some extent, were prone. Some were more exotic and strange. Most prominent were those who had surrendered to the pleasures of the flesh, the greedy fish-eating *opsophagos*, the drink-lover (*philopotēs*) and various characters whose sexual desires had overwhelmed them, including one particular ancient 'monster' who provides a rather close parallel to the modern notion of the addictive personality, though in a rather unexpected guise. They are distinguished not only by the size of their appetites – a great fish-consumer perhaps would testify only to the great desirability of fish – but also in the manner of their gratification. All men felt the draw of pleasure very powerfully and most at one time or another succumbed. What distinguished these fragile souls was their readiness to surrender on each and every opportunity even when resistance was required by law, society and good manners, even when it was enforced on pain of death.

THE *OPSOPHAGOS*

As we have seen, philosophers and intellectuals argued about what exactly it was about the *opsophagos* that constituted *opsophagia*, but in practical terms it was usually a very straightforward matter to identify the creature himself. There he was, on the other side of the room, grabbing his *opson* without bothering with any bread to dull his sensual experience, not any old *opson* of course, but almost always *the opson*, hot slices of fish. Those who were not invited to such dinner-parties could watch for *opsophagoi* in the market-place instead or at the harbour:

> Euthynus, with a ring on his finger and sandals on his toes and anointed with perfumed oils was settling some little *opson* matter, I don't know what; but then Phoenicides came along and dear, dear Taureas, each of them a veteran *opsophagos*, the kind of men who gulp down fish-slices in the agora. When they saw what he was doing they almost died, outraged at the fishlessness [*anopsia*], terribly outraged. They gathered crowds around them and made a speech to the effect that they could not live with such a situation, that it was unendurable that some of you should be spending great sums of money to fight for marine ascendancy, while not even a bit of fish was making it into port. What was the point of having island-governors? It should be possible to pass laws to force compliance, a naval escort should be provided for the fish. As it was, Maton had monopolized the fishermen and Diogeiton, in heaven's name, had persuaded them to bring the catch to him.[3]

The categorization of various citizens as fish-eaters seems to have been quite consistent, and we find different poets over a period of time satirizing the same people for the same characteristic vice. Phoenicides, for instance, the outraged speech-maker of the previous passage, turns up again in a play of Euphanes scarcely able to restrain his 'passionately agitated' hands at the sight of a casserole full of fish.[4] Two characters in particular were quite notorious, separated from each other by about a hundred years. Melanthius, a great-nephew of Aeschylus, was satirized for his degeneracy and *opsophagia* in numerous comedies at the end of the fifth century, and in spring 421 all three plays in competition at the City Dionysia chose to hold him and his eating habits up to ridicule. One of these plays survives complete. In *Peace* Aristophanes describes him and his brother as 'a pair of Gorgon *opsophagoi*, skate-hunting harpies . . . fish doom'. On another occasion, the comic poet Archippus conjured up on stage a chorus of fishes, who were willing to call a truce in the long war they had been waging against mankind, on condition that Melanthius be handed over to them in chains to suffer the same fate he had inflicted on countless numbers of their relatives. According to the philosopher Clearchus he had outdone Tithonus who asked for immortality and was forced to spend eternity without pleasure as a shrivelled husk. Melanthius prayed instead for the throat of a long-necked bird to prolong the pleasure of the moment.[5]

His fourth-century counterpart was Callimedon, known popularly as the Crayfish, either because this was his favourite delicacy or because his eyes stared in different directions. He was a contemporary of Demosthenes and aspired like him to be a public speaker, though he had not by all accounts a natural talent in this direction. At any rate his political pretensions brought him to popular notice, providing an excuse for playwrights to place his dainty eating habits and his vaunted statesmanship in ironic juxtaposition. His tenacity with regard to food was proverbial and was invoked in comic oaths: 'I'd as soon give up my purpose as Callimedon would give up the head of a grey-fish.'[6] One character mocked his political ambitions, implying that the only people who would honour him with a statue would be the fishmongers. Another poet played up his gourmandise to heroic proportions: 'Other men who have grappled with the gods . . . are joining forces with Crayfish, who alone of mortal men is able to gulp down whole fish-slices from bubbling casseroles, so that nothing whatsoever is left.'[7]

The most fabled *opsophagos* of all, however, was not an Athenian but Philoxenus, a dithyrambic poet from the Spartan territory of Cythera. There were many stories told about his exploits, although he was often confused with at least one other Philoxenus and possibly several more. Since all these Philoxenuses seem to have been equally devoted to gourmandise anecdotes about them were more prone than usual to go wandering. Machon included Philoxenus, alongside the hetaeras and gate-crashing *parasitoi*, in his collection of anecdotes: 'They say that Philoxenus of Cythera was an *opsophagos* to an extraordinary degree. So then, one day he bought in Syracuse an octopus three foot long, prepared it and swallowed it whole, almost, leaving only the head. He became very ill, seized by dyspepsia.' A doctor is called and, seeing the gravity of the situation, he asks if all Philoxenus' affairs are in order. The poet commends his poetry to Aphrodite and Dionysus, and makes one last request: ' "Charon . . . won't allow me to hang about and shouts me all aboard. Darkling Fate calls me, whose call I can but heed. And so that I may take my all on my downwards dash, give me back the rest of my octopus." ' Machon records of him that, like Melanthius, he prayed for a throat three cubits long, 'So that I can swallow for the longest time and may have the pleasure of all the foods at the same time.'[8]

It should be clear by now that the best way to recognize an *opsophagos* is not in the quantity of his consumption nor in its exotic refinement (there are no larks' tongues in the annals of Greek gluttony) but above all in the intensity and immediacy of his desire. Typically he does not stand on ceremony but grabs the fish straight from the pan while still hot. So the Paphlagonian demagogue Cleon is being satirized as an *opsophagos* when he boasts in *Knights* of 'consuming hot slices of tuna' or is cursed with a death from choking on squid still sizzling from the pan.[9] This does not mean that the Greeks prized food that was served at very high temperatures, but that a fish-lover was so desperate for his fish that he could not wait five minutes for it to cool down. This was a long way from aesthetic appreciation as one comic fisherman observed: 'While the results of a painter's exquisite labours end up the object of admiration, hung on a wall, the fruit of our efforts is snatched from the dish without so much as a "by your leave" and disappears directly from the pan.'[10] Sacrificial meat was made for sharing, but fish in contrast was made for keeping to yourself, for grabbing selfishly and swallowing whole. Fish inspired a kind of competitive eating that was quite inappropriate at a public sacrificial banquet. As a consequence it was in the speed of consumption that ancient eating was elaborated to excess, and 'Philoxenus' was naturally accredited with some of the most ludicrous of these developments. According to the Stoic Chrysippus, he made his hand heat-tolerant by thrusting it into hot water at the baths, and gave himself an asbestos throat with a similarly scalding gargle, persuading the cooks to serve the dishes very hot so that he could finish them off alone before anyone else could touch them. Another *opsophagos*, one Pithyllus, was said to have exceeded even these glut-tonous measures and had a special membrane fitted over his tongue, and finger-shields too, so that he could leave his fellow-diners standing.[11]

THE DRINKER

While we may find the Athenians' characterization of gourmands and their love of hot fish rather curious, we would scarcely bat an eyelid at their categorizing of individuals as drinkers. Of all the twentieth-century's labels for addictive and malfunctional types, 'alcoholic' looks the most resilient. After years of critical examination it still seems a meaningful diagnosis, an objective classification which is applied across cultural and historical boundaries. Yet it has been argued with some cogency that the idea of alcoholism as 'a progressive disease – the chief symptom of which is loss of control over drinking behavior, and whose only remedy is abstinence from all alcoholic beverages –' is a modern idea, no more than about two hundred years old. Taking a lead from this, some anthropologists have gone even further arguing that not just the terminology, but the thing, alcoholism, itself, is a thoroughly modern phenomenon: 'Alcoholism – even in the general sense of problems associated with drinking –

is rare in the vast majority of the societies of the world. One might even go so far as to note that it is almost unknown outside the mainstream of Western culture, although it is becoming a widespread concomitant of acculturation which often accompanies the impact of modern industrial society.'[12] Although there have been a number of studies on ancient drinking from an alcoholist perspective published since the nineteenth century, some of them quite recent (John Maxwell O'Brien's 1981 study of Alexander's drinking problem in the *British Journal on Alcohol and Alcoholism*, for instance, or J.-C. Sournia's chapter on the ancient world in his 1990 *History of Alcoholism*), most modern work on ancient drinking, which has been greatly influenced by the anthropological approach, tends to share the anthropologists' scepticism about applying the category cross-culturally.[13] Moreover, alcoholism, as opposed to the physical deterioration caused by excessive drinking (which is not the same thing), is a rather nebulous condition to pin down even in our own society. It is diagnosed not by any medical test, but by self-fulfilling questionnaires which place great emphasis on paranoid anxieties: 'Have you ever considered you might be an alcoholic?' Since we cannot inflict such questionnaires on ancient Athenians, it would seem a rather futile task to go looking for an ancient alcoholic who would stand up to modern diagnosis. On the other hand, the Greeks did record men who drank prodigious quantities of wine, and they did characterize certain individuals as prone to drinking, characterizations that reveal illuminating differences and similiarities with the modern alcoholic which are worth exploring.

One of the audience's suggestions as to the nature of the old man's affliction made at the beginning of the *Wasps* was that he was *philopotēs*, literally 'a lover of drink' or 'lover of drinking-sessions'. Unlike some of the other guesses (sacrificial-feast-ophile, etc.) this term does not seem to have been Aristophanes' own invention. Various characters in contemporary histories, in medical and philosophical treatises and on the comic stage are described in those terms. Cimon, for instance, a great figure of the early classical period, who dominated Athens for almost a generation after the Persian Wars, seems to have been remembered as a drinker many years after his death. Someone in Eupolis' *Cities* describes him as 'by no means a bad man, but simply a drink-lover, without a care' (*amelēs*). The historian Theopompus of Chios, as we have seen, was supposed to have actually provided a list of 'drink-lovers and drunks' in history. The many surviving fragments of his work certainly contain numerous drunken tyrants and whole drunken populations, giving the impression that Theopompus was somewhat obsessed with people's drinking-habits. In the thirty-ninth book of the *Philippica*, for instance, he wrote of Apollocrates, the son of the tyrant Dionysius of Syracuse, that he lacked self-restraint and was a drink-lover. In the twenty-third book he wrote of Charidemus of Oreus: 'It was plainly seen that he carried on a daily routine that was licentious [*aselgē*] and so contrived to be always drinking and getting drunk.'[14] Of course the fact that so many of the fragments have been preserved by Athenaeus who had a particular interest in the pleasures of the flesh gives a distorted impression. On the other hand, it can be shown that references to drinkers and drinking were broadly distributed throughout his works. Despite the frequency of his accusations, however, Theopompus did not make such charges lightly, and considered himself something of an expert on the subject, ready to jump to the defence of those who, in his opinion, had been wrongly labelled. The Spartan general Lysander, conqueror of Athens, was one such, wrongly characterized as a drunk by earlier historians and (Athenian) comic poets. In the tenth book of his *Greek History*, Theopompus came to his defence: 'he was restrained and self-controlled with respect to all pleasures; at any rate, when he had become lord of almost the whole of Greece, in none of the cities can he be shown to have been prone to sexual indulgences or to have engaged in drunkenness or drinking at the wrong time.'[15]

A rather different perspective on drinking is offered by comedy. It was only natural, after all, that drinking should figure prominently and positively in dramatic competitions in honour of Dionysus the god of wine. Even the tragedians had to append to their highfalutin' tragic trilogies a ribald satyr-play. Judging from the surviving examples by Euripides and Sophocles, these little dramas did not make much of an effort to break the typecasting of their bestial cast as passionate devotees of wine. The comic poets were determined not to be outdone in the league-tables of alcoholic burlesque and later students of Old Comedy were left with the impression that the fifth-century stage had been filled with stage-drunks. They identified one early poet in particular, Crates, as the originator of this popular innovation. From that point on there was no looking back. Drunken women and tipsy slaves were a staple of the acting repertoire, drinking-parties and sympotic preparations were staple scenes, drunken lawlessness a useful resort of plots: 'It was the wine . . . Whatever it forced me to do I did. This is the villain, here, this wine.'[16] Aristophanes in the *Frogs* mocks his rivals for such comic clichés but even his corpus contains many scenes of drunken slapstick. The *Wasps* itself begins with the two nightwatchman slaves scarcely able to keep their eyes open thanks to the bottle each of them carries. It ends with the old man fresh from a symposium engaging his son in a drunken tug-of-war over a flute-girl. In this generally drunken atmosphere it is rather difficult to isolate particular accusations of excessive indulgence made against individuals. Characters who could hardly stand were in no position to criticize members of the audience for their drinking-habits. Nevertheless, as we have seen, in the cases of Cimon and Lysander, some public figures do seem to have been labelled drink-lovers.

The demagogue Cleon who stands behind the mask of the Paphlagonian in Aristophanes' *Knights* is not just an *opsophagos* but a drunkard as well and boasts of washing down his hot slices of tuna with a jugful of neat wine. Already at the beginning of the play he is described as suffering from the effects of such habits, lying unconscious in a drunken slumber quite oblivious to the light-fingered pickpockets who make off with the oracles that predict his demise. Another character who seems to be mocked by Aristophanes for his drinking is Cratinus, a rival poet. A year after the rebuke Cratinus responded with an extraordinary play, *Putinē* or the *Wine-flask*. This unique drama, of which, unfortunately, only a few fragments survive, put the author himself on stage as a character. He had been married to Comedy, but she has now left him pleading maltreatment. Friends visit and ask her the cause of the quarrel. She complains that he no longer writes comedies but spends his time in drunkenness. Not much more is known about the plot, but it seems to have included a vigorous defence of wine's creative

A fourth-century fish plate from Athens. A large number of these dishes have been found, especially in South Italy, a testament to Greek fish mania. The painted fish tantalized diners with slow reflexes with images of what their quicker neighbours were now enjoying.

The interior of a cup by Exekias, late sixth century. Dionysus cannot be contained. He fills the ship of his abductors and his vine covers the mast. A red sea of wine laps the sides of the cup, obliterating the frame of the tondo. The pirates [or kidnappers] are transformed into dolphins.

The tondo of a fifth-century cup. A youth buys wine in a tavern. On the wall hangs a jug and behind him the mouth of a giant cistern (*lakkos*) can be seen. The *lakkos* would be filled with rainwater, necessary to dilute the wine, but also an intimidating image of insatiable appetite, sexual and otherwise.

A fourth-century silver medallion, found in 'Building Z', just inside the city walls in the Ceramicus district. Aphrodite rides a billy-goat across the night sky, as Lucifer, the Morning Star, lights the way.

A fifth-century perfume bottle. A seductively dressed woman, spinning wool, is approached by a boy and a youth carrying gifts of sea-food and game. This vase started the debate over whether women who span represented the seducers or the seduced.

A ribbed *kōthōn*, the 'Spartan cup' or canteen. The pro-Spartan, Critias, claimed the ribs were for filtering mud from river water when soldiers were on campaign. Athenians used it to get drunk as quickly as possible.

Another fifth-century perfume bottle. This 'spinning hetaera' hides modestly behind a veil, her wool basket just visible behind her chair. A beardless youth tries a direct approach and offers her money.

The tondo of an early-classical cup. This 'hetaera' carries a perfume bottle and stares out, not at the drinker, but into the mirror she holds. The inscription tells us that 'she is beautiful'. Her wool basket has been pushed aside to the right of the frame as she prepares for work of another kind.

The outside of a cup, circa 470 BCE. There seems little doubt that this is a brothel *and* a cloth factory. One girl puts her work away, while another receives visitors. The woman in the middle continues to spin, perhaps she is one of the 'madams who ensnare you in their threads'.

The inside of an Italian cup. A comic actor, dressed as an old man, holds a wine jug, and the inscription reads 'drink-lover' (*philopotēs*). It has been suggested it is Cratinus, Aristophanes' rival, who portrayed himself in one of his plays as a drinker torn between his duty to Comedy and his love of wine.

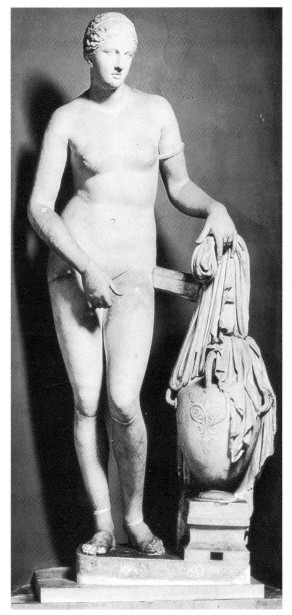

A copy of Praxiteles' Aphrodite of Cnidus. The first true female nude, this statue is said to have been modelled on the great hetaera, Phryne. There are stories of men crying over it, having sex with it and staining it with semen. Pornographic pictures were sold to tourists nearby.

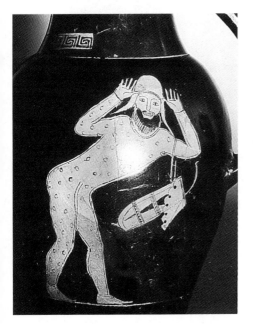

The early-classical 'Eurymedon Vase'. A man holding his penis runs towards a bent-over barbarian on the other side of the wine jug. The inscription between the two figures reads 'I am Eurymedon I stand bent over'. The scene is commonly (but wrongly) interpreted as one of triumph – 'We've buggered the Persians!' – but perhaps the key to its meaning lies in the empty space between the men.

Demosthenes, the great orator of the later fourth century. He looks pensive and humble, but appearances could be deceptive: 'If someone were to unravel you from those lovely draperies of yours and the soft little chitons underneath . . . and let the jurors hold them in their hands, I think they would be quite unable to tell whether they had taken the clothing of a man or of a woman . . .' claims Aeschines.

potential by the poet: 'A water-drinker would never give birth to anything ingenious.' The play went down well and won first prize at the Dionysia of 423. The tondo of a cup from South Italy depicts a comic actor dressed as an old man with a bottle in hand and the legend *philopotēs*. It is possible he is supposed to represent Cratinus himself.[17] The play is a wonderful early example of the confessional, autobiographical mode which will come to play so prominent a role in the Western history of addiction. Cratinus escapes from his drink-induced period of silence with a successful play about his drink-induced silence.

All of this is enough to indicate that the *philopotēs* was a well-recognized type, a label that could stick. At the same time comedy seems to make it clear that it was not considered a very serious charge and there is some evidence that it brought more shame on the accuser than the accused. When Demosthenes wanted to attack various youths for their drinking-habits he had to coin a new term, *akratokō-thōnes*, to distinguish their dangerous kind of drinking from the harmless activities of the *philopotēs*, but even so it was the remark and not its target that became notorious, laying the orator open to the more serious charge of being a water-drinker.[18] It is difficult not to conclude that while the Athenians may have disapproved of deep drinking and lived in trepidation of the violence and vandalism that emerged from the uncontrolled symposium, they were very tolerant of drunks, an attitude that has been a source of great disappointment to historians of alcoholism who trace back to the ancient world a whole range of positive associations that persist to this day, contributing to a mythologizing of alcohol in Western culture, 'an irrational force driving men to drink'.[19] But there is evidence for a much more negative view and not only in the works of Theopompus. The sophist Antiphon in his treatise on statesmanship advised his readers 'to avoid being tagged a "drink-lover" and being thought to neglect your affairs overcome by wine'.[20] So how do we resolve the apparent discrepancy in our sources between the harmless vice we find in comedy and the grave symptom of moral incapacity condemned by some of the philosophers and historians? Was the charge of being a drink-lover something to be taken seriously, something that could damage one's reputation or was it a rather endearing peccadillo? To answer this question we need to look at what kind of behaviour was thought to characterize ancient drink-lovers.

First of all it should be noted that the compulsion that identifies the modern alcoholic is not an obvious feature of the Greek characterizations of the *philopotēs*. Of course there was greedy drinking, in particular, there was *kōthōnismos*, but this was connected with a particular type of drinking rather than a particular type of person.[21] The *philopotēs* does not share the acute craving of the fish-lover for his fish. He is not desperate for immediate gratification. Such earnestness in fact is beyond him. We do find references to people being 'overcome by wine', as Antiphon says and even as 'slaves of drinking', but close examination reveals that it is the effect of wine, rather than desire for wine that is being described.[22] Wine enslaves people by making them do things they would not otherwise attempt, or conversely by making them too apathetic to do anything, not by forcing them to drink. In fact the drink-lover's love of drink is elaborated in the opposite direction to the pressing need of the *opsophagos*. Whereas the latter is identifiable from the speed of his consumption, devising techniques for grabbing his food as quickly as possible straight from the pan, the drink-lover is characterized by the length of his periods of drinking, and the chronic nature of his condition. Aristotle knew a story of one drink-lover from Syracuse who put an egg under his mat and sat on it, resolving to remain there drinking until the egg hatched, and the writer of the Aristotelian *Problemata* claimed to know of many drunkards 'whose entire diet consists of strong wine' and who suffered from severe trembling as a result.[23] Drink-lovers drank the whole time. They even drank in the morning, an invention Eupolis ascribed to Alcibiades. Anecdotes about a notorious drinker like Philip of Macedon stress this incessant intoxication. He was said to take his sympotic paraphernalia everywhere with him, even sleeping with a gold cup under his pillow. Theopompus asserted that when the ambassadors came from defeated Athens, Aeschines among them, to see how he would settle the affairs of Greece after his crushing victory at Chaeronea, he was already drunk having spent the night in non-stop carousal. Sometimes he even went drunk into battle. A story was told of a woman who dared to appeal against one of his judgments. 'To whom are you going to appeal?' he asked her. 'To sober Philip,' she replied, instantly sobering him up.[24]

It seems clear that his son Alexander was no better and was remembered on the Attic stage several years after his death as a prodigious drinker. In Menander's *Flatterer*, composed probably only eight or nine years after Alexander's death, the boastful soldier boasts of draining a ten-*kotylē* cup three times over (altogether about fourteen pints), that's more even than Alexander, says the flatterer. 'It's certainly not less than him,' says the soldier. 'And that's a great deal,' says the other.[25] In fact, Alexander's drinking-problem was the subject of a scholarly debate that was still going many centuries after his death. This debate was fuelled by a rather strange document available to Plutarch and other ancient historians and known as the Royal Diaries, which purports to give an account of how the king spent his days, especially towards the end of his life. The journals seem to describe an apparently never-ending series of drunken parties followed by days of unconsciousness. Aelian includes a precis of one month's entry in his list of some 'bad things' about Alexander:

> They say on the fifth day of the month Dius [October/November] he was drinking at Eumaeus' house, then on the sixth he slept it off, and for as much of that day as he was conscious [*ezēsen*] he rose from his bed and did business with the generals concerning the following day's journey, saying it would start early. On the seventh he feasted with Perdiccas and drank again and on the eighth slept. On the fifteenth day of the same month he was at it again, drinking and on the following day he did the usual things that follow drinking [i.e. he slept?]. He dined at Bagoas' on the twenty-fourth and two days later was still sleeping – accordingly one of two conclusions must be true, either Alexander damaged himself through drinking so many days in a month, or those who wrote this are lying. For you can have an idea of what happened the rest of the time from these extracts, since they say the same things.[26]

Few modern scholars consider the Royal Diaries genuine. One extract preserved in another author contains an obvious anachronism, and different historians seem to have come across rather different versions. A forgery, on the other hand, is a real possibility – diaries were a recognized literary form in antiquity and one soap-operaish example survives purporting to be a diary of the last days of Troy – although the forger's motives for producing this particular document remain obscure. Some have argued he was concerned with proving that Alexander died from drinking too much rather than, as was suspected, from poisoning. Alternatively it might have been a piece of subtle invective to show that Alexander the Great was a drunk. Certainly Aelian sees the journal as a damning indictment of the great man, and Alexander's defenders, from Aristobulus, his contemporary, to Plutarch, four hundred years later, were anxious to repudiate the Diary's portrayal of the Great one as a drink-lover.[27] Even as a forgery, however, the document has historical value, since it shows how someone in the ancient world might reconstruct the diary of a drinker, a plausible portrait of the *philopotēs* in action. It is rather different from the way someone today might forge the daily life of an alcoholic, I think, which would focus on secret and solitary potations, on oblivion and a large degree of self-deception.[28] Alexander too has his lost weekends but his drinking is done in company. It is always social. It is excessive only because it is habitual.

By describing the day-to-day existence of a typical drink-lover the Diaries help to resolve the apparent contradictions in ancient attitudes to drinking. The failing of the ancient drink-lover is not ordinarily his ill-health, his violent rages, or his waking up in strange places but indolence caused by incessant drunkenness, a well-established feature of modern characterizations, it has to be said, as well. Alexander's drinking leaves him incapacitated for days after a drinking-session, a grave dereliction of responsibility. This is quite typical of the drink-lover who is often described as *amelēs*, negligent, careless (or, with a more positive spin, carefree). This negligent quality was ascribed by Eupolis to the drink-loving general Cimon in the *Cities*, and it is because of this that Antiphon advises the potential statesman to avoid a drink-loving reputation. We can see this connection between idleness and drunkenness in numerous passages. Herodotus, for instance, recorded that Amasis who staged a coup and took control of Egypt in the sixth century had been rather happy-go-lucky as a private citizen: 'It is said that he was a drink-lover and fond of jokes, a man completely lacking in seriousness, and if ever he found himself short of the means to sustain his life of drinking and pleasure, he would go out and steal things.' According to Theopompus, the people of the Chalcidice were 'disdainful of the noblest activities, but were quite devoted to drinking and idleness and extreme self-indulgence'. In book fifty of the *Philippica* he turned to the people of Methymna, a city of Lesbos, who always had a drink to accompany their daily necessities and 'never achieved anything worthy of their expenditures'.[29] Cratinus' abandonment of his writing in the *Wine-flask* is another clear example.

A lack of earnestness is a prerequisite for comic characters and fun-loving satyrs and no more than what was to be expected of women, slaves and barbarians, but for the politicians, generals and monarchs who are attacked by Theopompus it was a serious disqualification. The woman who rejected Philip's drunken ruling was already speaking in accordance with a long tradition of political philosophy. Drinking clouded the judgment. In fact it was considered quite impossible for a drinker to achieve anything worthy of note. Theopompus contradicts the claim that the Spartan general Lysander was *philopotēs* by noting that he was *philoponos*, a workaholic. He could not have been both. Likewise Plutarch discusses the picture, painted by the Diaries, of Alexander as an incessant drinker and asserts that he must have been talking rather than drinking at all those parties: 'His life itself provides the proof, for although it was short, it was full to the brim with extraordinary deeds.'[30] The contrasting attitudes to drinking found in people like Theopompus and Antiphon on the one hand and in comedy on the other are based on a strong distinction between public and private citizens. There is a quite clear double-standard in operation. This makes it more likely that the Diaries' tedious emphasis on Alexander's days of drunken stupor was part of an attempt to damage his reputation, perhaps to accredit some of the unpopular measures he took in the last years of his life to the drinker's characteristic negligence or to blame a drinker's indolence for the absence of spectacular new conquests after his retreat from India. It could have been dictated by Theopompus.

The same logic helps to account for what looks at first sight like an exception to this rule, the Athenians' negative attitude towards politicians who drank water. In opposition to wine, water-drinking was a sign of extreme care and industriousness. Demosthenes was the most famous of these teetotallers and was often attacked for it, as he tells us himself: 'They say because I drink water I am ill-tempered and surly', he claims in the *Second Philippic* and recalls a joke made by his enemies during the rancorous debates which followed the 'appeasing' Peace of Philocrates: '"It's not surprising," said Philocrates, "that Demosthenes and I disagree, men of Athens. He drinks water I drink wine." And you laughed.' Lucian records a joke made by another of Demosthenes' enemies, Demades, that whereas the other orators spoke 'to water' (i.e. against the water-clock), Demosthenes actually wrote 'to water'.[31] There is probably some validity in Demosthenes' own interpretation of the jibe. People who did not drink might be considered anti-social and unsympathetic characters, but it seems clear that he is avoiding the main point of the accusation. It was not just anybody who was accused of water-drinking, but specifically orators. As Demades' joke makes clear, writing speeches while drinking water is a sign of an earnest professionalism and laboriousness inappropriate to plain speaking straight from the heart. We remember Cratinus' words in the *Wine-flask*: 'A water-drinker would never give birth to anything ingenious.' The demagogic Paphlagonian illuminates the logic behind the prejudice more directly in the *Knights*, when he attacks his sausage-selling political rival: 'O, so he's an orator, is he? . . . I think I know the type. There was some trivial little case against a foreign resident or something and all night long he mumbled over what he was going to say. He muttered it to himself in the street, he drank water, and then having exasperated his friends he MADE HIS SPEECH and it WENT WELL, and now he's got the idea he's an orator.' The Paphlagonian himself, on the other hand, needs no such laborious preparation and boasts that he can come straight from his hot slices of tuna and jugfuls of neat wine and still rouse the Assembly with speeches of great moment.[32] By claiming that Demosthenes wrote his speeches while drinking water, his enemies undermined his claim to speak sincerely and passionately and angrily. All that famous 'bitterness', all that feeling, all that spontaneity had been carefully manufactured, meticulously prepared with a clear head the night before.

This opposition between the industrious teetotaller and the idle drunk is found also in the medical writers. The early treatise known as *Airs, Waters, Places*, for instance, makes some preliminary remarks about the background knowledge a doctor needs to make a diagnosis. Climate is very important, but it is necessary also to note what kind of people you are dealing with, whether they are 'drink-loving, snack-eating [*aristētai*, lit. 'breakfasters'], workshy types, or teetotallers fond of exercise and hard work and proper eating' (*edōdoi*).[33] It was perhaps inevitable that wine would feature prominently in ancient medical theory. Wine has more immediate and obvious effects on the body than food and performs more durable transformations than sex. Moreover it seemed to have a major role to play in that careful balance of elements, the hot and the cold, the wet and the dry, that constituted the foundations of ancient medical thinking. As we have seen, wine was often considered a remedy rather than a poison, a very useful tool for restoring the proper balance of elements, or for purging the body of accumulated acids.[34]

One of the most interesting of these medical investigations into the effects of wine is contained in book three of the Pseudo-Aristotelian *Queries*. Some of the questions, but few of the answers, will look familiar to modern readers: Q.24: 'Why are the drunken more easily moved to tears? Is it because they are hot and moist and therefore lacking in self-control and, at the same time, moved by small impulses?' Q.11: 'Why are the drunken unable to have sex?' Because for sex one part of the body has to be hotter than the rest and inebriates are hot all over, thus destroying the differential. Q.10: 'Why to those who are drunk does one thing seem to be many?' Q.17: 'Why does cabbage put an end to hangovers?'

Question 23 concerns death through drinking: 'Why do men die from drinking strong wine, if they drink a large amount, being already rather desiccated?' The answer – the body's heat is extinguished by an excess of heat – is not so interesting as the question's assumptions about the conditions necessary for a drinking fatality. In the modern world it is alcohol's chronic effects on the body in general and the heart and liver in particular which are the source of anxiety. It takes a long time to drink oneself into an early grave. There are very occasional hints that the ancient world was not completely oblivious to the dangers of a lifetime's indulgence – Aelian, as we saw, thought Alexander had damaged himself by drinking so many days a month

– but normally those who died from drink perished suddenly and unexpectedly.[35] Fever followed a single unrelenting binge of large quantities of 'unmixed' wine drunk without pause, or even from one single draught of the stuff. The Greek attitude to neat wine was in this respect rather like the popular modern attitude to Ecstasy. You might take it regularly and suffer no ill-effects and then suddenly and mysteriously it would kill you. The dangers of unmixed wine were remembered in sympotic rituals and the stories told to account for them, the homoeopathic sip of neat wine taken as a prophylactic in honour of the Good Spirit, the first bowl mixed for the goddess Health or Zeus Saviour. It was remembered also in stories about the fate of people who broke the rules and dared to drink wine undiluted, men like Cleomenes, ruler of Sparta, who learned to drink neat wine from the Scythians and died a raving death as a result. When one of Alexander's toasts was offered to Callisthenes, the expedition's historian, he turned it down: 'I don't wish to be in need of one of Asclepius' curative cups after drinking from one of Alexander's', he is said to have said. Hephaestion, Alexander's soulmate, was not so faint-hearted. In the winter of 324–3 he contracted a fever and was put on a strict diet. He waited until his doctor had gone to the theatre and then got up and ate a boiled chicken for breakfast washed down with a large psykter of wine. He died soon afterwards, a textbook death from drinking.[36] The psykter we remember was a vessel used to cool neat wine before it was mixed with water; the fever will have made him already desiccated.

Alexander himself died the next summer and his drinking was implicated in almost every account. One of the earliest descriptions is from a contemporary, a hostile source, Ephippus of Olynthus in the Chalcidice, who describes a drinking competition with a formidable adversary called Proteas. Alexander called for a two-chous cup (around twelve pints) and drank his health. Proteas then took the cup and drank it while everybody applauded. A little later Proteas took the cup again and pledged the king. Alexander tried to meet the challenge but could not manage it. 'Instead he fell back on to his cushion letting the cup fall from his hands. And as a result he became ill and died.' Diodorus' account was even more dramatic. Medius, a Thessalian, threw a party. 'There he drank a great deal of neat wine in commemoration of the death of Hercules. He filled a huge cup and drained it. Suddenly he gave out a loud moan as if he had been struck with great force.' Medius' fateful party is mentioned also in the Diaries, although it makes no mention of neat wine and titanic draughts, simply recording a long and late drinking-session as usual. It has been suggested that by omitting mention of the draught from the cup of Hercules and the sudden seizure that followed, the author of the Diaries was trying to disprove the possibility that the king had been poisoned, but it seems quite clear that the more dramatic accounts conform more closely to the Greek idea of a natural 'death by drinking' with their references to unmixed wine and deep draughts.[37] By omitting these important details of *how* Alexander was drinking, the Diaries do little to prove a death by natural causes. The Greeks were perfectly well aware, on the other hand, of poisons in small doses that could take a long time to take effect, like the one poured into his wine by Philoneos' slave-concubine which killed her master instantly, but his friend only twenty days later. So the Diaries might just as well be thought to prove the opposite conclusion: Alexander must have been poisoned, since his drinking that night was no different from countless other occasions which he had survived unscathed. More probably the Diaries have no bearing on Alexander's death at all.

WOMANIZERS AND LOVERS OF BOYS

If the classic modern addiction is alcoholism, producing recognizable variants in chocoholics, workaholics and shopoholics, ancient predilection was more often expressed as a *-philia*, a love of something, which is why the list of addicts at the beginning of the *Wasps* includes not only our friend the drink-lover, but the 'dice-lover' and the 'sacrifice-lover' as well. In line with this language, it was commonly agreed that love in all its degrees and variations, from attraction to beautiful people to sheer animal lust, exercised the greatest force in human affairs. Faced with a choice between worldly power, military glory and feminine beauty it was only natural that Paris would plump for Helen and give the golden apple to Aphrodite. It was only natural that the consequence would be catastrophic disaster. Love was profoundly connected with folly. On the battle-field of the Trojan plain, Homer shows Aphrodite as a rather ineffectual deity, but she alone of the Olympians had the power to prevail over Zeus. Only by borrowing the powers invested in Aphrodite's girdle could Hera hope to overcome her otherwise omnipotent husband and keep him distracted for long enough for her to turn the tide: 'when he saw her, desire smothered his strong mind.' In a lost play Euripides ascribed similar power to Aphrodite's son: 'Whoever judges Eros a god less than great is either a fool or one who has no experience of the beautiful and remains in ignorance of the god whose power in human affairs is the greatest.'[38] The philosophers agreed with the poets on this issue. In Plato's *Republic*, 'Aphrodite's pleasure' is described as the greatest and sharpest pleasure of all and also the most maddening. In *Laws*, the Athenian notes that men are driven by three needs or desires. Two of these, desire for food and drink, are present at birth, the third appears only later, but it is 'the fiercest desire and the most despotic, urging men most powerfully to all kinds of lunacy'. The sophist Prodicus put it more succinctly: 'Desire doubled is Eros', he said and, 'Eros doubled is madness.'[39]

Sometimes we find this theoretical and metaphysical power actualized in extreme examples: Hyperides' exposure of Phryne's naked beauty at her trial, instantly overwhelming the jury's resistance and securing her acquittal; Plato's description of the utter consternation at the exercise-ground when the youth Charmides appears in full adolescent bloom; Socrates' advice to Critobulus on kissing Alcibiades' handsome son:

> Don't you realize that this beast they call 'young and handsome' is more terrible than a scorpion, inasmuch as it does not even need to touch you as the scorpion must, but pierces anyone who looks at it even from a distance and makes them mad ... I advise you, Xenophon, to take to your heels and run whenever you see a beautiful man, and you Critobulus should spend a year abroad. It will take you at least that long to recover.[40]

On a more basic level, the overwhelming power of sexual desire is the premise of Aristophanes' *Lysistrata*, in which a sex-strike brings the men of Athens and Sparta quickly to their knees.

We can add to the list of witnesses all those individuals we have already come across in the law-courts, who were, by their enemies' contention or by their own admission, firmly in the clutches of a strong passion: Olympiodorus, whose hetaera had made him quite mad; Euctemon, who in old age fell victim to the occult arts of love and left his family to live with Alce; Simon, who was so besotted with Theodotus that his new lover was forced to take the boy out of the country; Epicrates, whose head was so befuddled with love for the perfume-seller's son that he allowed himself to be conned out of a fortune. Of course, in all these cases there are good reasons for the speaker to play up love's power to account for foolish or regrettable behaviour, but they were doing so to an audience that found such arguments eminently plausible and had already heard countless sorry love-stories that started with a kiss and ended in violence and madness.

Just as the drink-lover tends to disappear in the drunken atmosphere of comedy, so it is difficult to discern specific devotees of sex, when all agree that the power of Eros can subdue anyone at all. But from time to time certain individuals were identified whose behaviour indicated a definite propensity towards amorous or sexual encounters beyond the norms of human susceptibility, certain men who could be distinguished in terms of their sexuality, among them the *gunaikomanēs*, the woman-mad, the *philogunēs*, the woman-lover, the *moichos* or adulterer, and the *philopais* or *philomeirakios*, like Sophocles, who was passionately devoted to youths. Last but not least there were bizarre sexual monsters called *katapugōn* and *kinaidos* whose characteristic vices are rather more difficult to pin down.

Unlike *paiderastēs* and *philopais*, terms like woman-mad and womanophile are, in fact, very rare in classical authors, not because the whole society was oriented homosexually – our study of prostitution and the hetaeras should have dispelled that misapprehension – but because, on the contrary, in a predominantly heterosexual environment a man's devotion to the female sex had to be extreme to be worthy of comment. One kind of gynophile is illustrated in a comedy of Antiphanes: 'So then, am I or am I not a woman-lover good and proper [*ou dikaiōs*], with all these hetaeras to enjoy? Just for starters, what you're doing to me now, rubbing my feet with your lovely soft hands, it's quite magnificent.' The most conspicuous example of the breed walking the streets of Athens was Callias the younger, born one of the richest men of his time, and a ubiquitous figure in classical literature, often hovering in the background of aristocratic gatherings, the host of Xenophon's *Symposium*, and of the grand philosophical and rather comic seminar that Plato describes in the *Protagoras*. Outside philosophy, however, he appears as a less elevated personality. In the *Frogs*, Aristophanes describes him Hercules-like wearing the pelts of his conquests, not in this case lionskin, but 'pussy-fur'. In case we haven't got the joke, a later commentator explains that Callias was satirized by the comic poets as one 'mad for women'. In the *Birds* he is described as 'plucked by females and litigious pests' (*sykophantai*) and in 421 Eupolis wrote a whole play, *The Flatterers*, about him and his hangers-on (among them Protagoras) which took the prize for best comedy ahead of Aristophanes' *Peace* (maybe the scatological farce with the dung-beetle in the opening scene was too much for some judges). His womanizing seems to have taken many forms. Some later commentators claimed he had been satirized as *pornomanēs*, 'whore-mad'. Cratinus, on the other hand, points to adultery, claiming he was forced to pay a huge sum to an aggrieved husband whose wife he had seduced. But the most extreme example of his madness is described by the orator Andocides in his speech *On the Mysteries*: 'Callias married a daughter of Ischomachus; but the marriage was scarcely a year old before he took in the mother as well, and cohabited, the villain, with mother and daughter together.' The daughter, according to Andocides, tried to kill herself and eventually ran away leaving her mother, Chrysilla, to marry Callias. The mother too fell out of favour, and was thrown out. She claimed she was pregnant and got her relatives to challenge Callias to recognize the child while he was officiating at a festival marking the admission of new members into the distinguished family of the Kerykes: 'They came to the altar with the child and a sacrificial victim and told him to begin the ritual. He asked whose child it was. They said it was the child of Callias son of Hipponicus. He said, "But I am Callias." They said, "Yes and the child is yours."' After several years he was reconciled with Chrysilla and he formally acknowledged the boy, a baby no longer. Perhaps, suggested Andocides with understandable outrage but less than impeccable logic, they should have called him Oedipus. It is notable, I think, that hetaeras have a very low profile in the characterization of Callias as 'mad for women' although there were hetaeras around him to provide fuel for gossip; they appeared in Eupolis' play about him, but only as prizes for which the flatterers competed, which is why the more careful of the marginal commentators observe that he was satirized not as *pornomanēs*, whore-mad, but as *pornoboskos*, a pimp.[41] If men succumbed to the allures of hetaeras it was a reflection of the powers and skill of women, but if men went around seducing other men's wives, their own wives' mothers, or even their own daughters, it was more obviously their own sexual incontinence that was at issue.

Hetaeras figure more prominently in attacks on Alcibiades, another public figure with a reputation as a womanizer, but in his case too it was his seduction of other men's wives that crystallized most clearly the image of his sexual intemperance. In exile in Sparta he was widely rumoured to have made the wife of the king pregnant, since the king himself had not slept with her in ten months, an earthquake having frightened him out of her bed. In Abydus he surpassed even Callias in his perversity, at least according to the version told by Lysias: Alcibiades and his friend Axiochus had gone to Abydus on the Hellespont, claimed the orator, and had married the same woman. 'When a daughter was born to her they claimed they couldn't tell whose child it was, but cohabited with her also as soon as she reached a marriageable age; whenever Alcibiades enjoyed possession of her he would say she was the daughter of Axiochus; but when Axiochus did so, he would say she was the daughter of Alcibiades.' The accusations of the philosopher Antisthenes went even further. Alcibiades, he said, 'enjoyed intercourse with his mother, his sister and his daughter, just as the Persians do'. If the *opsophagos* becomes conspicuous in the speed of his consumption and the drink-lover in the duration, the man excessively devoted to women reveals himself in his disregard for the norms of law, society and nature, in his perversity, a principle neatly compressed by Aristotle in a list of things people are ashamed of: 'and having intercourse with those you mustn't, where you mustn't, when you mustn't, because such activities derive from incontinence' (*akolasia*).[42] There is a good reason for this attitude. As we have seen, a man who found someone sleeping with his wife could kill him with impunity. More often, an adulterer was granted his life in return for paying a large amount of money to the cuckolded husband, who had, it appears, a right to keep him prisoner and inflict on him whatever tortures he could think of so long as he did not use a knife. This is probably where the famous punishment of a radish up the arse came into play, the penalty of *aporhaphanidosis*, although as Kenneth Dover points out, in all probability this 'radish' 'was not simply the very small root we call "radish", but a generic name covering some much larger species'.[43] It was because the penalties were so terrible that the *moichos* got a reputation for sexual excess. To risk massive fines, torture and sudden death, an adulterer in Athens had to be quite devoted to his profession and to his female prey. If we look again at Antiphanes' happy and relaxed gynophile, a rather different emphasis now becomes apparent. If he is a 'woman-lover *good and proper*' it is because his desires are uncharacteristically being kept within the law. The women he surrounds himself with are merely hetaeras and, so far, they are only massaging his feet. But of course by behaving so properly, he is not a proper womanizer at all.

While an *opsophagos* or a drinker could be identified from their behaviour in public or semi-public contexts, in the agora, a dinner-party or a *kapēleion*, a *moichos* had to be identified by more circumstantial evidence. The mystery that surrounded their activities seems paradoxically to have led to a more rigid and canonical stereotype. The fact that the adulterer kept his vice secret, out of dire necessity, put greater pressure on anxious citizens to identify the visible signs of this dangerous character and to extrapolate from there the characteristic deed without having to see him in action. Rhetorical handbooks are full of references to identifying the adulterer. In the Aristotelian text *On Sophistic Refutations*, we learn that you can show your opponent is a *moichos* simply from 'the fact that he is a dandy [*kallōpistēs*], or is seen wandering about at night'. So strong was the stereotype of the beautified seducer that unattractive men who committed adultery were likely to get away with it, suggested Aristotle, like weak men accused of assault. In the *Rhetoric* he advised those who were not so blessed with ugliness how to escape from the charge: they should show that the same grounds for prejudice existed in someone who was by common consent quite beyond suspicion, 'for example, if he is supposed to be a *moichos*, because he is smartly turned out [*katharios*] then so-and-so [some dapper paragon of virtue] must be as well'. The law of Syracuse, according to Phylarchus, allowed no scope for such sophistic refutations and gave well-dressed citizens no benefit of the doubt, stating: 'a man might not make himself look beautiful or dress elaborately and conspicuously unless he confessed to being an adulterer or a *kinaidos* (a male seducer of men).'[44]

As in Renaissance England, the woman-lover and especially the adulterer was considered to have been himself somehow womanized by his womanizing and was pictured as an effeminate. Aegisthus, who kept Clytaemnestra's bed warm while Agamemnon was away at Troy, is addressed as a woman by the Chorus in Aeschylus' *Oresteia*, and on a Corinthian vase which depicts Tydeus stabbing his adulterous wife Ismene to death, the artist has painted her lover Periclymenus white, the colour of women's flesh according to the convention.[45] The comic poets seem to have relished this paradox especially when the subject of Alcibiades came up. One described him as 'a woman's man, apparently, as far as all the women are concerned, without actually being a man', and a character in Eupolis' *The Flatterers* ordered him 'out of the ranks of women'. A similar insinuation perhaps lies in Timocles' epigram about the fourth-century profligate Ctesippus: 'he cuts a brilliant figure amongst the women, but not amongst the men.' The most extraordinary and vivid example of this ancient logic which seems so alien to us now is an often-repeated tale from the Orient. The notorious Sardanapalus whose tomb made light of human ambitions and directed passersby to devote themselves instead to 'Eating, drinking and rutting' (or in some versions 'playing') was reputed to have kept himself locked away in his harem:

Arbaces, a Mede by birth and one of the generals of his realm, entered into an intrigue with a eunuch named Sparameizes to obtain a view of Sardanapalus, and the king reluctantly giving his consent, an audience was permitted him; when the Mede entered he saw the king with his face covered with white lead and bejewelled like a woman, combing purple wool in the company of his concubines and sitting among them with knees uplifted, his eyebrows blackened, wearing a woman's dress and having his beard shaved close and his face rubbed with pumice, and when he looked upon Arbaces he rolled the whites of his eyes.

If it was not for the exhortation to 'rutting' inscribed on his tomb-stone and the description of his women as concubines, we might be forgiven for thinking that Sardanapalus' only interest in the harem was to exchange knitting patterns, but this paradoxical image is for the Greeks typical of the womanizer who is corrupted by the women's quarters.[46]

Those men whose passions were directed towards the male sex did not have to resort to extremes of lawlessness and perversity to distinguish themselves. We have already come across Misgolas who was famous in oratory and in comedy for his special delight in cithara-players. Others who enjoyed a reputation among later generations as lovers of boys were Alexander and Sophocles. The latter earned his reputation from stories which were already circulating during his life. He featured in a curious work of the fifth century written by Ion of Chios, who wrote in prose a book called *Visits* (*Epidēmiai*) which told stories of famous contemporaries who had stayed in Chios and of their amusing conversations at dinner-parties. Among these distinguished foreign visitors was Sophocles whose techniques of seduction are described in a long fragment: 'the wine-pourer appeared, standing by the fire, handsome and red-faced. Sophocles was obviously stirred and said, "Do you want me to drink with pleasure?" The boy said he did. "In that case take your time when you approach to fill my glass and do not be in a hurry to withdraw."' The boy blushes, dying his complexion an even deeper shade of crimson, provoking the learned company into a digression on the terminology of colouring. At length the poet returns to his quarry. He asks the boy to blow away a piece of vine-debris that has been left in his cup, stealthily bringing it closer to his own lips as the boy leans over. When his mouth is in range he pounces for a kiss. Another story of Sophocles' sexual exploits was told by a later writer. He had sex with a boy outside the city wall, but when they had finished the boy ran off with the fine cloak they had used as a blanket. It was said that Euripides taunted him about the incident, claiming Sophocles had been treated with contempt for his 'intemperance' (*akolasia*).[47]

A kiss was also used to illustrate Alexander's enslavement to homosexual desire. Dicaearchus, a student of Aristotle, claimed that in full view of a theatre full of people Alexander had bent over to caress his boyfriend, the eunuch Bagoas, and when the audience responded with applause he bent over again and kissed him.[48] These stories seem rather mild examples of intemperance especially in comparison with the activities of the *moichoi*. It is difficult to see how they illustrate a particular mania on the part of Sophocles or Alexander and perhaps it was only later generations that interpreted them in those terms. On the other hand, they could fit in quite well with Aristotle's formula for sexual incontinence, involving the wrong people, the wrong time and the wrong places.

THE *KATAPUGŌN* AND THE *KINAIDOS*

Of all those who had surrendered to desires, none provoked more extreme outrage than the class of sexual degenerates known variously as *katapugones* or *kinaidoi*, the latter term apparently succeeding to the semantic field of the former some time around the beginning of the fourth century. Like adulterers, they were easily spotted because of their love of fine, seductive or womanish clothing. The man who was unlucky enough to be caught in Syracuse in a state of beautification, dressed in 'elaborate' or 'conspicuous' attire, had a choice, we remember, of being labelled either *moichos* or *kinaidos*. Likewise when Aeschines, pausing for a moment from his long savaging of Timarchus, turns on his backer Demosthenes instead to accuse him of *kinaidia* and effeminacy, he supports his charges with reference to the distinguished orator's clothing: 'If someone were to unravel you from those lovely draperies of yours and the soft little chitons underneath, the clothes you wear when writing speeches against your friends, and if he were to take them round and let the jurors hold them in their hands, I think they would be quite unable to tell whether they had taken the clothing of a man or of a woman.' In the fifth century the *katapugōn* too seems to have been noted for his attire. This is why one comic character, in a splendid piece of metaphor-mixing, compares Euripides' tragedies to dishes over-dressed with spices and condiments, 'all this is *katapugosunē*', he says 'compared to a real piece of meat'. Another tragedian, the exquisite Agathon, has taken overdressing a stage further and appears in Aristophanes' *Thesmophoriazusae* in women's clothing. Euripides in trouble for his misogyny begs him to infiltrate the women-only festival of Thesmophoria and assuage the women's anger with a speech in his defence. His polite refusal earns a harsh rebuke from Euripides' relative Mnesilochus who calls him *katapugōn*.[49]

As with the *opsophagos*, it was easier to recognize a *katapugōn* than to define precisely what it was that made him one; but there is no explicit debate on the meaning of *katapugosunē* to match the ancient debate on *opsophagia*. This obscurity has not made recent students of antiquity correspondingly shy of deciding the issue among themselves, however. The *katapugōn / kinaidos* is that strange beast, 'the passive homosexual'. The consensus derives originally from some circumstantial ancient evidence together with some lingering modern preconceptions perhaps about the sexual behaviour of effeminate men, but it has been considerably reinforced by the representation of Athens in recent scholarship as an overwhelmingly 'phallocratic' society. Under this regime, this 'Reign of the Phallus', there was no sexuality as such, only what one scholar describes as a 'more generalized ethos of penetration and domination, a socio-sexual discourse structured by the presence or absence of its central term: the phallus'. People were sexually typecast not according to the gender of the persons to whom they were attracted but by the role they assumed in the act of intercourse, for sex in the ancient world did not bring people together, it kept them apart. Lovers, in the act of making love, looked distantly at each other across a great unbridgeable divide:

'the "active" and dominant role was always assigned positive values,' claimed Michel Foucault, 'but on the other hand, it was necessary to attribute to one of the partners in the sexual act, the passive, dominated, and inferior position.' Penetration is thus represented as an absolutely central concern, governing not just the zone of sexual relations, but the whole of ancient Athenian, or ancient Greek society. The *katapugones / kinaidoi* according to this theory were 'automatically assumed, according to the protocols that polarized penetrators and penetrateds, to desire to be penetrated by other men, which assimilates them to the feminine role'. This sexual predilection had severe repercussions outside the sexual context: 'Since sexual activity is symbolic of (or constructed as) zero-sum competition and the relentless conjunction of winners with losers, the *kinaidos* is a man who desires to lose.' [50] No wonder such characters inspired horror.

It is not too much to say this theory has been overstated, and presents a model of Athenian society which is not only simplistic and overschematic but quite misleading. Power was often described in gender terms and of course sex was linked to power in more profound ways, but this was a subtle and complex relationship, an intricate nexus of exchanged values involving love, gifts, desirability and favours, not a rigid 'zero-sum game' that the penetrator always won. In fact it is remarkable how little evidence there is for the language of sexual aggression and domination in the classical period. There are one or two examples of graffiti which might be taken to use penetration as a threat, but these are rare and often rather ambiguous. The contrast with other periods and cultures, even one as close as the Roman, is striking.[51] The Athenians did not rebuke each other with 'Fuck you's and 'Up yours's and it was almost unheard of for a losing competitor or a defeated army or a worsted trader to claim they had been 'buggered' or 'screwed'. In the absence of textual attestation, much of the evidence to support the theory is derived from the visual arts, especially vase-paintings, which though silent can be cajoled by expert hands into revealing tales of sexual oppression. Kenneth Dover started this particular ball rolling in his work on Greek homosexuality: 'The woman is almost invariably in a "subordinate" position, the man "dominant"; the woman bent over or lying back or supported, the man upright or on top.' Dover cites evidence from anthropology, Norse sagas, the use in Italy of the term 'inculato' (buggered) to describe a defeated football team, John Boorman's film *Deliverance*, and the behaviour of primates to back up his reading of the images, showing that penetration, especially penetration from the rear, is universally interpreted in this fashion. For others even this comparative material is not considered necessary. The symbolism of power and domination is inherent in the arrangement of bodies: 'Certainly the rear-entry stance allows the painter to show women being used impersonally, as mere sexual tools whose response and emotional reaction is of no concern to their male lovers.'[52]

The bent-over rear-entry posture they are talking about, of course, is *kubda*, the three-obol position at the bottom-end of a prostitute's price-range. There are several references to this position in literature which might have helped to throw light on its significance. Apart from cheap sex they indicate that it is associated with sex outdoors (what used to be called in Britain a 'knee-trembler') or pleasure quickly snatched in adultery while the husband sleeps, not domination. These hints from literature seem to illuminate some of the details present in the rear-entry scenes on vases. That the men are often shown still wearing shoes, for instance, in some versions, with walking-sticks and cloaks ready to hand, could easily be taken as an allusion to the hastiness of the back-alley or the brothel.

There is one vase, however, which seems to demonstrate unequivocally a connection between penetration and power. It is the so-called Eurymedon vase, a black-glazed, red-figured wine-jug of probably the second quarter of the fifth century. It has two figures, one on either side, and some writing in the space between them. One of the figures, naked but for a cloak, is holding his half-erect penis in his hand and striding towards the man on the other side who is dressed in an oriental bodysuit with a quiver hanging from his arm. This other figure is bending over and turns his bushy-bearded face full-frontal towards the viewer, his hands spread on either side of his head as if he were surrendering. Under the oinochoe's spout there is an inscription, running from the head of the strider to the foot of the other. It is not perfectly intelligible, but it seems to say 'I AM EURYMEDON I STAND BENT OVER'. Almost as soon as the vase was brought to scholarly attention this was interpreted as a reference to the battle of Eurymedon in the early 460s, when drink-loving Cimon got his faculties together for long enough to lead the Athenians to a famous victory over the Persians. The vase, it is said, represents 'eine spezielle Form des Triumphus' or, in Dover's more down-to-earth formulation, 'it proclaims "We've buggered the Persians."'[53] The theory has been very widely accepted by classicists – the name Eurymedon, the Asiatic costume and the approximate date are, for many, too much of a coincidence – but it does not really stand up to close examination. There can be no doubt, as Gloria Ferrari Pinney concluded in her examination of the vase, that the 'case for the patriotic interpretation is weak'. The context, for a start, is rather strange. What is this scene doing on a wine-jug? Then again, this man with his manhood in his hand looks most like a traveller. He is not a typical representative of the Athenian army. He is not even a soldier. The man on the other side need not be a Persian. It is strange also that the artist has left so much space between the two figures. If this is a triumph, why not show the moment of penetration, the triumphant act? As it is, the most the vase can claim is, 'We have high hopes of buggering the Persians'. Most damning of all, however, is the name Eurymedon itself. The battle was named after a river, and rivers for the Greeks were deities. It is very strange that the site of a battle should have been singled out for abuse. It is quite inexplicable when the site is a god. All in all, although there are numerous ancient representations of power and battles and conquest in painting and sculpture this vase remains quite unique. Interpreted like this it has no parallels, no symbolic context, and therefore leaves plenty of opportunity for the prejudices of the late twentieth century to creep into the decipherment.[54] The Eurymedon vase is a classic case of an ancient artefact which looks at first sight quite transparent, but which turns out upon close examination to be something rather more complex and mysterious. It has been misplaced, I think, as testimony to the association of penetration and power, but it has much to say about the *katapugōn*.

Although there is some evidence that some *katapugones* liked being penetrated – Agathon in the *Thesmophoriazusae*, for instance, is so suspected – there is no evidence that this unknowable predilection is what defined them. Dover tries to demonstrate the connection with a rather strange passage from Aristophanes' *Knights*, where the Sausage-seller thinks it a good omen for his political initiation when 'a *katapugōn* man' farts on his lucky right. Dover thinks this clinches it: 'The anatomy of the anus is altered by habitual buggery, and there are modern jokes which imply (rightly or wrongly) that the sound of farts is affected by these changes.' There might be some slight reason for this extraordinary conclusion if Aristophanes had attributed to the *katapugōn's* flatulence some peculiar revealing timbre, but there is no hint in the text that he is hidden from view and such men were known first and foremost from their appearance. Moreover, in response to the lucky omen, the Sausage-seller immediately bends over and alludes to himself being buggered. The most obvious candidate for the 'active, positive, masculine penetrating role' here would be the effeminate *katapugōn* himself.[55]

In fact, the term *katapugōn* seems to have a very broad frame of reference. It is often used of women and of certain kinds of animals like mice, even of fish like the wrasse. Dover is well aware of this, but argues that the word had become a meaningless insult, as if all that was left of the original penetratee was his humiliation: 'at least by Aristophanes' time, and perhaps by a much earlier date, the words had no more specific denotation than colloquial English "bugger"[.] "Louse" and "bitch" are perhaps the best current equivalents.' For those who find it hard to understand why comic characters should cast meaningless insults at fish and small mammals, there was, according to Liddell and Scott's Greek Lexicon, another meaning for *katapugōn* which Dover has ignored: 'lecherous, lewd'. Neither as specific as 'man who submits to anal penetration' nor as general as 'louse', it has the additional advantage in many passages of making sense. In *Lysistrata*, for instance, the resourceful and eponymous heroine, faced with a revolt by the other women, who would rather 'go through fire' than do without sex, turns on them angrily: 'O how wholly-*katapugōn* is our whole species!' According to the penetration/oppression theory this becomes either 'What a thoroughly buggered race we are!' or, in Dover's version, 'What a miserable bloody lot we women are!' If we forget about phallocentrism, however, and look to our Greek dictionary, the meaning is suddenly clear, fitting in perfectly with the theme of female sexual incontinence: 'What an absolute race of nymphomaniacs we are, the lot of us!' as Alan Sommerstein renders it.[56]

It seems quite clear, also, that the animals described as *katapugōn* are not being generally insulted nor are they being distinguished for their desire to be anally penetrated. They are being singled out for their lustfulness and promiscuity. Mice were the most lascivious of creatures, claimed Aelian, citing Cratinus as a witness to their '*katapugosunē*', and wrasse apparently didn't even cease from intercourse when they were caught, according to Apollodorus (not the orator), so that they became 'for the ancients' models of 'incontinence' and 'degeneracy'.[57] A *katapugōn*, then, is usually some creature, animal or human, male or female, that has sex without restraint. Sometimes, however, it is used even more broadly than this to refer to a comprehensive *akolasia*, or lack of self-control. *The Banqueters*, Aristophanes' first play, for instance, extant only in fragments, dealt with the contrasting fortunes of two brothers, one of them *sōphrōn* or self-controlled, the other *katapugōn*, not a 'louse' or a 'bugger' but 'a complete degenerate'. It is always difficult to say anything secure about plays which exist only in tatters, but it seems clear that the *katapugōn* son revealed his *katapugosunē* not in passive sodomy but in a more generally decadent lifestyle, skipping his classes and learning instead all about 'drinking and singing bad songs, and Syracusan feasting, and Sybaritic sumptuousness and Chian wine from Spartan cups'. This broad interpretation of *katapugosunē* helps to make sense of a passage from the *Acharnians* which has often perplexed commentators. An effeminate envoy reporting back from Persia remarks that 'the Persians consider only those who gobble up and drink up the most to be men of account', and Dicaeopolis comments, 'And we [consider such prodigious consumers] cock-suckers and *katapugones*'.[58]

Kinaidos seems to have supplanted *katapugōn* some time in the early fourth century. Although the term was to have a long posterity among the Romans and in the European Renaissance, it is much rarer than *katapugōn* in the classical period, not because it took a long time to catch on, but because the rhetorical and philosophical works which predominate among the surviving literature of the fourth century chose their words more carefully than Aristophanes whose plays probably predated the new terminology. From what we can see, however, the two terms referred to a familiar nexus: effeminacy, nymphomania and complete surrender to pleasure. Plato's *Gorgias* is perhaps the earliest extant text in which the word appears. Socrates is discussing with Callicles the nature of desire and its fulfilment. Callicles has adopted a position defending the pursuit of pleasure. Socrates is trying to get him to change his mind and to this end he compares the pleasure-zone inside the pleasure-lover to a jar that is always leaking. Callicles is not persuaded. Socrates elaborates, comparing the life of the self-controlled to that of the unrestrained: the former has sound casks, which he fills from the scanty resources available to him, with milk and honey and wine. The latter, however, has leaky vessels and is compelled night and day always to be filling them and to suffer agonies if he ever lets up. Which of the two leads the happier life? Callicles still does not give a satisfactory answer. The man whose vessels are filled has no more pleasure, he says, and lives the life of a stone. For a life of great pleasure there must also be a great influx. In that case says Socrates, getting nasty, you will need a correspondingly large outflow, not the life of a stone, perhaps, but the life of a stone-curlew, the 'ravine-bird' that eats and shits at the same time. He adduces some more examples; the life of a man who spends his life being hungry and eating, and that of a man who spends his life being thirsty and drinking, and 'one who itches and scratches, being able to scratch to his heart's content, and spends his life continually scratching; tell me if it can be said that he is happy'. Callicles is unmoved. Socrates moves in for the kill: 'What, then, of the supreme example of such things, the life of the *kinaidoi*, is this not a frightening and shameful affliction?' Commentators have argued over the passage, but it seems clear that Plato means what he says. The *kinaidos* is the paradigm of insatiability, of desire never-to-be-fulfilled, desire like that of the man who is always itching and scratching, a desire which dominates not only his sex-life but his daily existence. The life of the *kinaidoi* is *to kephalaion*, 'the paradigm' of the life of endless pleasure, the leaky vessel, the supreme example of appetite unbridled.[59]

Various scholars have made some attempt to reconcile a morality in which the most important thing is to avoid penetration with a morality centred on the necessity for self-control. Foucault, who was often accused in his work on the history of mentalities of not paying enough attention to the 'experts', seems on this occasion to have paid them much more attention than they deserved. Throughout his work on ancient Greece he stresses the importance of *enkrateia*, of self-mastery in the construction of gender at Athens, and masterfully charts the territory that connects it to the discourse of truth and meaning. Unfortunately, he attempted to reconcile this model with the penetration–power schema, which he had inherited from distinguished classicists like Kenneth Dover and Paul Veyne, coming up with the bizarre notion of ethical passivity: 'for the Greeks it was the opposition between activity and passivity that was essential, pervading the domain of sexual behaviours and that of moral attitudes as well . . . what constituted ethical negativity par excellence was clearly not the loving of both sexes, nor was it the preferring of one's own sex over the other; it consisted in being passive with regard to the pleasures.' Thus although the adulterer assumes a sexually active role, penetrating and masculine, this is cancelled out by his passivity with regard to pleasures, which marks him out as effeminate. We might be prepared to swallow this piece of sophistry, forgetting all the claims made for penetration itself and conceding that some metaphorical penetration might in the end be more important, if the Greeks really talked of being 'penetrated by pleasure', but as far as we know, they didn't. Moreover, in order to keep the phallocratic theory in play, Foucault is forced to seek a reconciliation between two quite different ethical models, the one an essentially lonely struggle of the Self or the Soul against the pleasures of the World and the Flesh, the other an intrinsically bipolar structure, in which the passive role is dependent on an active desiring subject, in which the subordinate role with its ethical negativity, the 1+, is created by the dominant, the 1+, in that 'zero-sum game' which is the act of sex.[60] So what plays the role of penetrating active subject that makes the *moichos* effeminate? The wives and daughters he seduces? The radish? And what active subject wields its symbolic phallus to make the *opsophagos* passive with regard to pleasure? The tuna-fish, the sea-bream, the fishmonger? Before they venture further into these absurdities the fans of phallocentrism should re-examine their premises. The notches on his bedpost earned the *moichos* no fillip whatsoever for his fragile masculinity. The Greeks did not award points for penetration. They did not see a gulf between a desire to penetrate and a desire to be penetrated and they certainly did not structure the whole of society let alone the entire world according to a coital schema. The whole theory is simply a projection of our own gender nightmares on to the screen of a very different culture.

Plato's *kinaidos*, then, is incontinent all on his own. He does not need some active penetrator to make him passive or effeminate. It's not a role he plays, it's a life he leads. It's the way he is constituted. He could theoretically be a virgin stranded on a desert island, and still be a *kinaidos*. If there is a connection between effeminacy and sex it lies not in passivity but in insatiability. The rear-entry position, as we have seen, is presented in literature as a quick, cheap and easy position, a *pornikon schēma* suitable for adulteresses and prostitutes. When men put themselves in this position it means the same thing, marking someone down as an easy lay, a male version of the nympho-maniac, desperate always for sexual gratification. Later in the early Hellenistic period this position can be read in physiological terms. Problem number twenty-six in book four of the book of Queries ascribed to Aristotle, the *Problemata*, turns to the question of those who are 'female-like' in nature, producing a model which looks like the exact opposite of Plato's leaky vessel, but which arrives at essentially the same conclusion. The author explains how sexual desire arises in those pelvic areas which are swollen with moisture and semen.[61] With ejaculation these fluids find release, but in some men the passages to the testicles are blocked, and the moisture flows instead into the bottom. This can happen to some extent to those who overindulge in sexual intercourse but with those who are by nature effeminate all moisture is secreted in this region. Unable to find release, their desire can never be properly assuaged 'wherefore they too are insatiable [*aplēstoi*, lit. "unfillable"], just like women'. The product of abnormal compulsions from nature or habituation, the effeminate man of the *Problemata* looks like the closest thing yet to a modern addict.[62]

Other words for these sexual degenerates can be decoded in the same terms. A common one is *lakkos*, cistern, or *lakkopr̄oktos*, cistern-arse, someone compared to a tank of water, endlessly filled from drainpipes and drains, a paradigm of 'bottomless debt' when used of the spendthrift son in *Clouds* and of indiscriminate promiscuity when used of the politician Timarchus soon to be accused of living as a common prostitute. *Molgos*, too, a wine-skin made from a whole ox, was another term of abuse found in comedy. With a certain amount of ingenuity the phallocrats suggest this was because the skin of one repeatedly penetrated came to resemble leather, but according to Pollux, an ancient commentator, it was because of its bottomless capacity (*to aplēston*). Another term, one of the favourites for those who think the only important thing in ancient sex was penetration, is *euruprōktos*, 'wide-arse'. But this, like all these other terms, is used to refer to a very general decadence or effeteness, particularly applicable to fashionable long-haired young men like Alcibiades with a reputation as womanizers. In the *Clouds* Aristophanes plays on the literal and the conventional understandings of the term. Badlogic is boasting that his sophistry could get even an adulterer excused: if Zeus must submit to Eros, how can a mere mortal resist? His rival demands to know with what argument he will prevent his degenerate students being 'wide-arsed' when they are 'given the radish' for following his advice. 'I'll show instead,' says Badlogic, 'that there's nothing wrong with being wide-arsed,' and goes on to assign tragedians, advocates and demagogues and then the whole Athenian audience to the class of *euruprōktoi*. Betterargument surveys the spectators and realizes the truth of Badlogic's argument. He surrenders and leaves the stage. There are probably connotations here of passive homosexuality as well as adultery, effeminacy, gullibility and greed, although it is surely not merely penetration that is at issue, but habitual penetration symptomatic of sexual insatiability. Even here we must be careful to avoid anachronistic conclusions. Not even the *euruprōktos*, it seems, is a passive object. 'I can make the people dilate and contract' ('wide' or 'narrow'), boasts one of the *euruprōktoi* demagogues, the Paphlagonian, in *Knights*. 'My arse knows that trick too', is his sausage-selling rival's coarse reply.[63] The 'passive' partner in ancient sex was certainly not inactive. He or she was not an object or a tool of someone else's enjoyment, a seamless body ready to be tunnelled, but a participant, opening up too readily to pleasure.

This brings us to the very heart of the misunderstanding on which the power–penetration theory is founded. The modern way of looking at sex, which chooses, out of all possible points of view, to zoom in on penetration, which divides sexual partners into penetrator and penetrated and which decodes the sexual act as domination, aggression and subjugation, is not a natural, inevitable and universal understanding of sex but a very specific, peculiar conception, the endpoint of a long meandering Western tradition about making love. Sex has been a major field of interest and anxiety and knowledge and reform since the classical period. It would be astonishing if all this ideological activity had not altered profoundly the way we look at sex today. This is not the place to go into this history in any detail, but some of the more significant developments might include: the growing importance of the notion of bodily integrity in the first centuries of our era, culminating in the Christian apotheosis of the virginity of the Virgin Mary, which helped to construct an image of the intact body as a blank whiteness or a seamless cloth waiting to receive marks, tearings and perforations; the invigilation of orifices that is a correlative of the juridical movement to define previously rather nebulous sexual crimes like sodomy, buggery and rape in the early modern period; the promulgation of the missionary position (an ideological intervention in sex if ever there was one) which tries to distinguish human sex from bestiality and civilized sex from barbarity, emphasizing and encoding in practice the activity of the active partner and the passivity of the 'passive'; the dominant Victorian view of sex that cast all penetrated bodies in the role of pleasure object enjoying no pleasure themselves, and viewing even the wife as a sexual martyr, lying back while her husband did unspeakable things to her for the sake of England. After all these revolutions in our sexual perspectives it would indeed be quite remarkable if the language of an Italian football fan or a scene from a Hollywood film could be used as a model for the sexual views of fifth-century Greeks.

Just one of these changes, the view of sex as one-sided enjoyment, has been crucial in helping to construct penetration as power, in making of the passive partner an inert object used for the other's sexual pleasure. Since the nineteenth century, of course, the clitoris (a Greek word) and the female orgasm have been rediscovered or republicized, but sodomy, in contrast with vaginal intercourse, is still presented as one-sided pleasure intrinsically sadistic and humiliating. It is small wonder that classicists have interpreted rear-entry penetration in the classical world in terms of aggression and power. But in classical Athens the penetrated were not seen as the inert objects of someone else's gratification. Women certainly did not lie back (or bend forwards) and wait for things to be done to them. They participated in full. The rear-entry position was not bestial or humiliating, but lewd. Even passive sodomites are shown joining in at every level, like the sausage-seller making his arse wide, and experiencing pleasure, as the *Problemata* show, not in sexual domination but in sex itself, a pleasure even greater than that of the penetrating partner, a pleasure like that of women: an itching kind of pleasure without end. The *kinaidos / katapugōn* is not a sexual pathic, humiliated and made effeminate by repeated domination, he is a nymphomaniac, full of womanish desire, who dresses up to attract men and has sex at the drop of a hat. This is the point of Aristophanes' description of 'Cleisthenes' boy' among the tombs of the Ceramicus, bent over and plucking his arse, and it is certainly the message of Timaeus' description of Agathocles the future tyrant of Syracuse: 'In his first youth he was a common prostitute [*pornos*] available to the most dissolute, a jackdaw, a buzzard, putting his rear parts in front of anyone who wanted.' Although, then, this has been used before now as evidence for ancient phallocratic thinking, Timaeus is drawing attention quite clearly to Agathocles' promiscuity. It is not his desire to be penetrated/dominated/turned into a sex object which is at issue but simply his boundless unending womanish sexuality. 'Passive' sodomy may be symptomatic of the *kinaidos'* promiscuity and insatiability, but it is insatiability and not passivity that defines him. For ultimately, as the philosopher Arcesilaus remarked on seeing some 'adulterous and intemperate' men, 'it makes no difference whether you are a *kinaidos* in front or behind'.[64]

The boundlessness that characterizes the sexuality of the effeminate was readily transposed to the other appetites, so that 'wide-arse', 'cistern-arse', can denote a general kind of decadence with no sexual connotations. The 'life of the *kinaidoi*' was paradigmatic long before

Plato of the life of endless pleasure. Instead of the passive object penetrated by desire, the predominant image of appetite in classical texts is that of a vessel, a full jar, a leaky jar, a bottomless well, a ravening stomach, an ox-hide wine-skin. Desire is capacity; to fulfil it is to fill. Through its mouth or its mouths the vessel engages with the world. It is not penetrated by the world, it absorbs it. It devours it; it fills itself from the world's pleasure streams. The image of the bottomless vessel or the damaged vessel enables desire to be derived from emptiness, from lack, from need, making the *kinaidos* a precursor of the modern addict. Both are defined not by extra pleasure but by diminishing satisfaction. Both suffer from errant appetites and damaged needs.

This image was applied to all kinds of appetite, to thirst, to greed, to sexuality, producing a conflation of different sensual pleasures. Prostitutes and banquet-lovers are both called 'cisterns', because they absorb what flows into them without discrimination; the *katapug ōn* son in Aristophanes' *Banqueters* shows his *katapugosunē* not in sex but in drinking, knocking back 'Spartan cups of Chian wine'; and those 'who drink the most and eat the most are cock-suckers and *katapugones*' in the *Acharnians'* memorable phrase. Even men's desire for women, the sexual itch that is assuaged in ejaculation, can be viewed as a sexual hunger relieved by consumption: 'My cock is a veritable Heracles invited to dinner,' says the sexually ravenous husband in *Lysistrata*, constantly frustrated by his wife. He would not have got much sympathy from Diogenes the Cynic, a great fan of masturbation whenever and wherever the need arose: 'If only one could satisfy one's hunger', he said, 'by rubbing one's stomach.'[65]

We have rather more of a context now for the Eurymedon vase and we can begin to make a little more sense of it. We note first of all that sex in the bent-over position, *kubda*, seems to be taking place (as in comedy and other vase-paintings) out of doors, symbolic of promiscuity. Secondly it should be quite clear that the distance between the two figures is not an awkward space to be ignored, but of central importance to any decoding. In those inches of black emptiness the artist has painted the decadence of the Asiatic. That he offers himself so easily is the point, a point that would be obscured if the act itself were shown in consummation. Like Agathocles he puts his rear parts in front of all and sundry, a sign of his sexual insatiability. He may well be represented as effeminate, weak and cowardly, but it is not the penetrating act to come that subordinates and womanizes him proleptically, he long ago surrendered not to the Greeks but to his desires. It is his leaky constitution, his evident nymphomania, that makes him womanish.

But what is this image doing on a wine-jug? As we have seen, a bent-over *katapugōn* can be emblematic of all kinds of consumption. The French student of vase-images, François Lissarrague, has noted that men dressed as Scythians on drinking cups seem to represent symposiasts who drink their wine Scythian-style, i.e. strong. A bent-over Scythian could easily represent one of Dicaeopolis' *katapugones* 'who drink the most', a joke directed at those in the company who might be tempted to vinous overindulgence, or those who drank from the jug, or those who started drinking too early: 'Whoever invented early drinking,' says one of Eupolis' characters, 'is responsible for much cistern-arseness' (*lakkoprōktia*).[66]

Then who is Eurymedon? This is not as much of a problem as it seems. Eurymedon was indeed the name of a river in Turkey where a famous battle was fought, but it was also the name of several historical figures and more than one character from mythology. The name might belong to another member of the drinking company in friendly or not so friendly jest. Alternatively the allusion might be literary. The vase looks like a spoof of the common scene of a hero and his Scythian squire, and the name Eurymedon was in fact given to the squires of both Nestor and Agamemnon. The fragments of Hipponax, an Ionian poet of the sixth century, provide another tempting point of reference, combining the effeminacy and bottomless appetite of the *katapugōn* with savage mock-Homeric satire: 'Tell me, muse, of that Eurymedontiad Charybdis of the deep, she who swallows whole [literally: keeps the cutting for her stomach], who eats in no kind of order. Tell how he'll die an awful death by stoning, by the people's decree, by the shore of the unharvested sea.' Is this a reference to a son of some unknown Eurymedon, or a joke patronymic in pseudo-Homeric style attacking Eurymedon himself?

Any of these unknown and half-known Eurymedons is a possibility. Possibly we will never know who he really was. However, if we put the vase in context and think about the jug moving around the circle of drinkers in some early classical symposium, Eurymedons begin to proliferate. As the wine-pourer pours in the wine the drinker sees the strange runner on the jug. He is intrigued. He notices the words seeming to come from his mouth. He follows the text round, reading, as usual in the ancient world, aloud. As he leans forward to read the end of the line he catches himself saying to the rest of the company 'I am Eurymedon, I stand bent over'. At the end of the text he finds himself by someone's foot. He looks up and sees the Asiatic archer staring back at him. *He*'s Eurymedon and he's been had.[67]

VI

ECONOMIES

THE VORACIOUS BODY did not, of course, exist in a vacuum and while philosophers agonized about the effects of errant appetites on the self-sufficiency of Body and Soul, for most Athenians the danger of excessive consumption was crystallized more immediately as a threat to House and Home.

THE *OIKOS*

Between the citizen and the state lay the *oikos*, variously translated as 'the family', 'the estate', 'the household', 'the House'. In Athens it found itself in a rather precarious position, squeezed between the stronger claims of the individual and the polis. For the special relationship between city and citizen which is such a defining feature of classical Greece in general and of democratic Athens in particular could only be achieved by damping down other affiliations that might get in the way. Links with tribal associations, family-cult, and ancestral domain had been deliberately undermined by the founders of democracy at the end of the sixth century and a whole host of polis-organizations erected in their place. As a result, there seems to have been no great emotional attachment to particular estates which were typically very small or composed of disparate little plots. There were no Taras in the Attic countryside, no Bridesheads, and unlike the great estates of the English aristocrats which tended to pass intact into the hands of the eldest son, while his younger brothers went into army, clergy or trade, the Athenian *oikos* often split apart on the death of its owner as it was divided among the surviving heirs, built up, disassembled and rebuilt in the space of a couple of generations. The *oikos* was not so much a sentimental homeland as an economic necessity, 'a machine for drawing an income from', as one modern historian puts it.[1]

The property a man inherited then was a fluid entity, rather like the proverbial talent of Matthew 25. People watched closely to see if the heirs increased or diminished their estates and were able to pass on more or less than they received. 'As a money-maker I hold a place somewhere between my grandfather and my father,' says the wealthy metic Cephalus, father of the orator Lysias, at the beginning of Plato's *Republic*. 'For my grandfather inherited about as much as I now possess and multiplied it many times, my father Lysanias reduced it below the present amount, and I'll be happy if I shall leave to these boys a little more and no less than I inherited.' The experience of Cephalus' family seems to have been quite typical in the classical period, and fortunes came and went with alarming rapidity. By tracing the family connections of those citizens who were on record as performing 'liturgies' (public services, such as financing a ship or a religious festival that were imposed on the richest few hundred citizens, with property usually of at least 18,000 drachmas), the historian John Davies was able to calculate approximately the rate of change among the upper echelons of Athenian society. He came up with only one family that was attested in the wealthiest class over five generations and three hundred and fifty-seven families that seemed to pass from 'rags' to riches and back to rags in the space of just one generation. The figures are not complete and not being rich does not, of course, mean being poor, but the gaps in the evidence probably only exaggerate the impression of instability rather than completely misrepresent it: 'It is not usual for the majority of citizens', says one reluctant tax-payer pleading poverty, 'to maintain a continuous level of material prosperity.'[2]

There were some spectacular examples of fortunes vanishing. Most conspicuous of all was the evaporation of the fortune inherited by Callias at the end of the fifth century. In the 420s, on succeeding to his father Hipponicus' fortune he was reputedly the richest man in Greece. Thirty or forty years later people were describing him as *penēs*, penniless. His enemies, of course, exaggerated his later poverty, but even with more precise figures the change is startling: 'his grandfather, they say, valued his property at 200 talents (1,200,000 drachmas), but today his property is valued at less than two (12,000 drachmas).' In modern accounts Callias' 'poverty' is ascribed to the Peloponnesian War, and in particular the occupation of Attica by Spartan forces in the last decade of the fifth century. This had the effect of severing Athens from the surrounding countryside and Callias from his concessions in the silver-mines which seem to have been the foundation of the family's wealth. Ancient observers, however, were less understanding. Callias had reduced his grandfather's estate to less than one per cent of what it had been through extravagance on a heroic scale. For in the ancient imagination the greatest threat to prosperity was not war so much as profligacy:

Perhaps you remember a time [says Andocides, in his speech *On the Mysteries*] when Athens dominated Greece and was at the height of her prosperity and Hipponicus was the richest man in Greece. But then, as is common knowledge, women and children started muttering ominously that Hipponicus' house was haunted, harbouring an evil spirit that 'upsets his table'. You remember this, men of Athens. So how do you think the omen has been fulfilled? Hipponicus thought he was rearing a son. In fact he was harbouring a curse, a poltergeist who has indeed spilled his fortune and kicked over the bounds of restraint and upset every other aspect of his life. That's who Callias is, not a scion of Hipponicus' house, but a jinx upon it.[3]

There were several ways for a prodigal son to work his way through a property. Gambling, for instance, in its various forms, dicing, cock-fighting or 'quail-tapping' (a circle was drawn around the bird, the bird was rapped on the head, bets were taken on whether it would stand its ground or back out of the ring), was sometimes implicated in financial ruin. Horse-breeding was also dangerous. In Aristophanes' *Clouds*, Strepsiades' *oikos* has been plunged into financial catastrophe by his son's passion for fast horses. He arranges for him to study with Socrates so he can argue his way out of debt; if sophists could argue that black was white they should have little difficulty putting the right spin on an account that had plunged into the red. Callias himself, however, was believed to have succumbed to more mundane vices and is satirized in comedy for lavishing money on two things in particular, women and dinner-parties. He was not the only one. When great estates disappeared the culprits most often implicated were the stomach and the heart.

FOOD AND DRINK

Fish-consumption, for instance, was not only considered hedonistic and self-indulgent but also a massive drain on financial resources. One comic character has a go at the fishmongers because they 'steal away our entire property every day'. 'Alive or dead', says another, 'the fish are at war with us', for anyone who falls overboard will be eaten, and even when dead 'they cost us our property and whoever pays the price runs off to instant beggary'. It seems quite clear from comedy that the price of fresh fish was generally high at Athens, a major source of anxious consideration for a fish-loving population. One talks of the fishmongers exacting 'royal tributes' for their produce. Others turned to heroic bathos. One character describes how he had to pay for a fish with its weight in silver, like Priam ransoming Hector's body from Achilles, another claims that he has to look away when he shops for fish, like Perseus avoiding the gaze of the Gorgon, for if he sees for how small a fish they are charging so much, he would be frozen solid![4]

It is more difficult to come up with actual prices for fish in classical Athens to set against the general impression of exorbitance, but there are some figures preserved in the comedies themselves. To put them in perspective, it is worth remembering that a good wage for a skilled labourer around the end of the fifth century was one drachma (six obols) a day. In the same period five obols a day was considered a ridiculous overestimate for the *opson*-allowance of an adolescent and two children. When Aristophanes, then, in *Acharnians* mentions a single eel priced at three drachmas some commentators have found it rather hard to swallow. On the other hand, eels did stand at the top of the list of fine foods in classical Athens and Aristophanes was describing a war situation. In a play of the next century we hear of eels for at least twelve drachmas. Other figures are slightly more reasonable. We hear of an octopus offered at four obols and a barracuda for eight. A character in a play of Alexis considers ten obols too much for two grey-mullets, although the same sum is accepted by the purchaser as the price of a single sea-bass in Diphilus' *Busybody* until the crafty fishmonger points out that he was of course talking not of the Attic but the higher Aeginetan standard. Finally, in Eupolis' *Flatterers*, someone, almost certainly Callias himself or his agent, is preparing a great feast with eight sea-bass and twelve gilt-heads: the cost, 100 drachmas. We must assume that the list of fishes continues beyond the end of the fragment, and that the purchaser got more for his money than that.[5]

Prices quoted in comedy are often vulnerable to exaggeration, of course, and should not be accepted uncritically. Fortunately, however, an inscription excavated from the site of Acraephia in Boeotia earlier this century offers the prospect of some external control. It contains a list of prices for fish, probably upper limits, designed to stop exploitation of the crowds who gathered in the city at the festival season. There are some difficulties in comparing the data from the inscription with the evidence of comedy. The prices at Acraephia, for instance, are all quoted by weight, whereas all the prices in Attic comedy are for whole fish or pieces of fish, whose size and weight we can only guess at. Despite the problems, however, comparisons have been attempted, and tend to vindicate the comic evidence: 'the congruence is surely noteworthy, and strongly suggests that there was nothing intrinsically inflationary about the dialogue of Attic comedy.'[6] If these little pieces of information are put together we can draw some conclusions about the price of fish at Athens. Small fishes and despised species were not particularly expensive and might add flavour and variety to the diet of many who lived in the city. Even the best fish would not be totally beyond the wage of an Athenian worker, but would take a large slice out of his weekly income. A dinner-party with fish-dishes served to several guests, however, would be out of the question for any but the most wealthy. A bottle of champagne, perhaps, provides a useful modern parallel.

It may seem surprising that a city so close to the sea should treat fish as a luxury but there is no mystery involved. Apart from the difficulty of preserving it and transporting it, the Mediterranean, unlike the North Sea or the Red Sea or the Atlantic, simply does not have a great abundance of good-tasting, decent-sized fish and probably never has. Later Arab chroniclers who had the opportunity to compare it with other stretches of water, considered it a particularly poor sea, cursed by Allah with lifelessness as a punishment for taking the lives of so many men.[7] Moreover, with the exception of the tuna which was available only during seasonal migrations and the smaller cheaper species like anchovy, the kind of fish the Greeks favoured were anti-social and did not generally flock together in shoals, so that Greek fishermen, themselves proverbially destitute, had to scrape a living by taking solitary fish one by one from coastal waters. Sometimes, they got lucky and hauled in a substantial specimen of a particularly prized variety. Most often they came up with very little. Fish was generally expensive because it was generally rare.

The inscription at Acraephia raises the question of government intervention in the market for fish. There were certainly market-supervisors, *agoranomoi*, appointed at Athens, who were supposed to keep an eye on all traders. One character in a fourth-century comedy proposes making his friend *agoranomos* just so he can intercept the *opsophagos* Callimedon at the fish-stalls before he can work his way through the catch, another calls for a board of three *opsonomoi* to be set up with a special remit to oversee the fishmongers. There is an amusing account in Apuleius' *Golden Ass* of what this kind of intervention might look like in practice, describing a quite different era, of course, but the same preoccupations (a love of fish is one of the great continuities in the pagan civilization of antiquity):

> Then I went towards the baths, first visiting the market to buy something for dinner. There was plenty of fish for sale, and though at first the fishmonger wanted two hundred drachmas for the basket, I eventually beat him down to twenty. Having paid I walked off with my purchase. [The hero bumps into a fellow-student from his days in Athens, Pythias, who now happened to be market inspector.]
> '. . . if I can be of any service in helping you shop for dinner, don't hesitate to call on me.'

'That's very kind, but I have already bought some fish!'

'Let me have a look at them,' he said and took the basket from me. He shook the fish about so that he could inspect them more closely and asked, 'How much did you pay for this rubbish? If you don't mind me asking.'

'I managed to beat the fishmonger down to twenty drachmas, but it took a long time.'

'Which fishmonger was it? Show me!' I pointed back at the little old man seated in the corner of the market. Pythias at once started abusing him in his most severe and official voice: 'You there! Is this the way to treat the Inspector's friends? Is this the way to treat anyone, for that matter, who comes to buy fish in the market? Asking no less than twenty drachmas, forsooth, for these ridiculous little tiddlers! Hypata is the most prosperous town in all Thessaly, but with people like you forcing up prices to such absurd levels we might as well be living in a desert. And don't think you are going to escape with a reprimand. By Heaven, I intend to keep you villains in check, so long as I am Inspector of Markets.'

With that he emptied the basket on the ground, ordering one of his officers to jump on the fish and squash them into fish-paste on the pavement. Beaming moral satisfaction with his own severity, he advised me to go home. 'All is well now, Lucius,' he said cheerfully. 'You need say no more. I am satisfied that the little wretch has been humiliated enough.'

Flabbergasted at having lost both my money and my dinner thanks to his kind intervention, I went to the baths, where I spent the afternoon resting.[8]

The Athenian *agoranomoi*, then, kept their eyes on the fishmongers along with all the other traders. But there are in addition some indications of more specific regulations dealing with the fish trade directly. We have already mentioned the law (probably fictitious) forbidding fishmongers to drench their fish with water to make them seem fresher than they were (the imagined consequence in all probability of some fantastic scenario, a water shortage caused by clouds on strike, perhaps). Then there are some laws ascribed to one Aristonicus in a play of Alexis in the second half of the fourth century. One of his laws apparently tried to enforce stable prices with a ban on bargaining. Another forced fishmongers to serve customers standing up. These may seem bizarre, but the target of the satire, Aristonicus, was a real figure in fourth-century politics and there are parallels. In fact, one of his ideas bears a striking resemblance to one of the measures proposed in the *Laws* of Plato: 'He that sells any article whatsoever in the market shall in no case put two prices on his wares. He shall ask one price and if he do not get it, he will do right to take his goods away again, and shall not, that same day, set a higher or lower price on them.' Because of the similarities some have thought the comedian was parodying the philosopher, although the reference seems too obscure for a general audience. On the other hand, very similar laws were actually enforced in Athens, like the ban on haggling for flute-girls. With prices fluctuating with every catch it would have been difficult to fix prices too rigidly. A ban on haggling is one way round it. This law at least could well be genuine.[9]

Fish was the most notorious drain on resources, but drinking too was implicated in financial ruin. Critias' right-wing encomium of Spartan drinking cups (from which, remember, they drank only water) was just a part of his hymn to the general excellence of Spartan habits of drinking. This characteristic self-denial benefited not only bodily health and judgement, but also 'property'. In contrast, the excessive Athenian way of drinking was the source of all kinds of problems: 'the body becomes enfeebled . . . reason wanders completely away; the slaves have undisciplined habits; and estate-wasting expenditure descends upon them.' Xenophon makes a similar comparison between the Spartan and the Athenian way of drinking that emphasizes the interests of the household as well as the Body: 'With their common messes organized according to these principles, what opportunity was there for someone to destroy himself or his estate through greediness or vinous over-indulgence?' (*oinophlugia*). Dionysius tyrant of Syracuse preferred less disciplined dining-companions, according to Theopompus, and deliberately surrounded himself with 'those who had thrown away their properties on drunken revels and dicing and suchlike incontinence; for he wanted all to be in a wretched state of ruin'. He might, in that case, have taken to Nausimachus and Xenopeithes, orphaned sons of a wealthy merchant, who on coming of age sued their guardian for their father's property and then fourteen years later sued him again for more. The guardian's own heirs counter-sued. The reason for the brothers' new claim, they argued, was not a sense of injustice at the first settlement, but simply that they had run out of money, having squandered their original inheritance 'in eating and wine abuse [*paroinountas*], in the company of Aristocrates and Diognetus and others of that ilk'. It was not only young men who were susceptible to this drain on resources. Aristophanes thought women's drinking posed a similar threat to the household. In *Thesmophoriazusae*, Euripides' agent, infiltrating the women's festival in drag, discovers a woman nursing a bottle wrapped up as a baby. This leads to a series of apostrophes on the subject of women's propensity to drink and the disasters that it precipitates: 'O feverish women, ever ready for a drink, inventors of all kinds of schemes to get at the bottle! O great blessing for the wine-merchants, and a curse in turn for us! And what a curse again for the household utensils and the weaving!'[10]

The most straightforward connection between drinking and financial ruin, of course, is the cost of wine itself. Precise information about the economics of drinking is, again, a rather problematic exercise which can produce no more than tentative conclusions. There is some evidence, for instance, that Chian wine, which was ranked topmost for most of the classical period, was appropriately expensive. A late anecdote about Socrates, told by Plutarch, describes one of his friends complaining to him about the high price of things in the city, illustrating his point by quoting some prices, including 'Chian wine for one mina (one hundred drachmas) . . .' But the passage cannot be taken seriously as evidence for the price of (an amphora of?) Chian wine in the classical period. Comedy is slightly more helpful. A fragment of Alexis refers to the price of wine as ten obols a *chous* (six pints), and in Menander's *Arbitration*, Smicrines reveals a little more in the course of a complaint about his son-in-law, Charisius', lifestyle: 'I am not talking about his getting drunk. For what's almost impossible to believe is this – how anyone can force himself to drink wine that he has bought at one obol the half-pint,' i.e. twelve obols or two drachmas a *chous*. Commentators have long debated whether this price is supposed to be low or high, satirizing Smicrines' stinginess or his son-in-law's extravagance. The latter is more probable, since this is in fact three times higher than the cheapest wine, the *trikotylos* which sold at a rate of one obol for a pint and a half, but the main target of Smicrines' scorn seems to be not the cost of Charisius' drinking, but the manner of it. Instead of sipping some nice wine with some nice friends at a nice symposium, he is drowning his sorrows in vulgar taverns and other houses of ill-repute where wine is sold by the glass.[11]

These extremely meagre statistics can be supplemented by archaeological evidence. Some of the amphoras found in the agora and elsewhere have numerical markings on them, and although some of these markings seem to be references to weight, others, including one written on a vase of Mendaean wine, and several written on jars of Chian, are very probably prices. The results of these studies are described by D. A. Amyx:

> A lot of six Chian amphoras was found in a fifth-century well in the Athenian Agora, all of approximately uniform size (about 22 liters), suggesting a possible standard of seven choes to an amphora. If the figures scratched on them have been correctly read and interpreted, the price of the wine in them would have come regularly, to one stater, or two drachmai, per chous. This is just three times the traditional retail price for Attic *trikotylos oinos* at 4 obols per chous, a price which agrees well with the premium quality of Chian wine.

It also happens to agree well with Menander's evidence. Charisius must have been drinking Chian wine! In his own survey of evidence for prices, including papyrological documents, François Salviat found a slightly higher factor with the 'grands crus' selling for four or five times the price of 'vin ordinaire'. Older wines, he notes, might be even more expensive. All these calculations are severely hampered by a failure on the part of commentators and archaeologists to differentiate between wine sold by the half-pint and wine sold by the jar. Moreover, one detects a slight sense of disappointment among French scholars that the price of wines that were used to evoke images of luxury were not higher, although wine does not have to reach the astronomical prices of a Petrus, an Yquem or La Tâche to be considered extravagant. Twelve pounds is still for most people a ridiculous amount of money to pay for a bottle of wine that is not champagne and a factor of four or five could take you in England today from a bottle of cheap Sauvignon Blanc to a good Sancerre, or in a wine-producing country like Spain, a more relevant comparison, from an ordinary red to a top-class Rioja. At the other end of the social scale, there are references to those vulgar enough to drink in bars getting through a *chous* of wine in a single session, an amount which might easily cost a worker more than a whole day's wages.[12]

We must bear in mind, however, the possibility that the authors who connect drinking and financial ruin are not thinking about the cost of wine at all. As we have seen, one of a drink-lover's characteristic features was carelessness, *ameleia*, and this had consequences for management of private estates as much as for public affairs. In these cases it is drunkenness from wine rather than expenditure on wine which is the main problem. In Critias' account of the evils of Attic drinking, *oikos*-wasting expenditure descends on the house hot on the heels of unreasoning behaviour and unruly slaves, out of a general atmosphere of alcoholic disruption caused by those decadent Attic toasts. It is drunken misbehaviour, *paroinia*, not simply extravagant consumption, which is responsible for the disappearance of the inheritance of the brothers Nausimachus and Xenopeithes. Because of drink women neglect their weaving, comic poets like Cratinus forget their comic craft and the master loses control of his estate.

We must remember also that these are not solitary vices. It would take a long time for Callias to work his way through one talent even if he spent a lifetime eating nothing but eels washed down with nothing but Chian wine. Luxurious eating really becomes ruinous when you begin throwing extravagant dinner-parties (*poluteleia deipnōn*) followed by protracted symposia afterwards. This is when expenditure really begins to mount. This is when we begin to reach sums that could make a dent in anyone's personal fortune. Menander mentions a party that cost a talent and two sources mention that Alexander set a limit on dinner expenditure at 100 minas – 10,000 drachmas or more than one and a half talents.[13]

SEX AND EXPENDITURE

Most ancient authors seem to agree that notwithstanding the temptations of fish-eating, horse-riding and quail-tapping, by far the biggest danger to the estate was women and boys. 'Many who are able to control their spending before love hits them, cannot restrain themselves when it does,' says Xenophon. Plato in the *Republic* takes only a few lines to get from love-affairs to asset-stripping: Love (for a hetaera or a boy, it seems) is a despotic spirit which takes over the 'tyrannic man': '"And many terrible appetites sprout up alongside love, making many demands on him every day and every night. Is that not so?" "Quite so, Socrates, yes." "And whatever income he has is soon being spent." "Clearly!" "And after this come mortgages and sell-offs." "Yes. Yes, they do indeed."'

Women, as we have seen, were deeply implicated in the disappearance of the largest private estate of the fifth century, the property of Callias. Andocides too, Callias' great enemy and purveyor of much malicious gossip about him, had himself sustained losses from lust. His own father Leogoras had been a famous wastrel and was attacked by the comic poets for having thrown away his property on a hetaera called Myrrhina. Falling in love with a hetaera in fact became a classic example of desiring something that was bad for you: 'A hetaera is a disaster for the man who feeds her; indeed he is overjoyed to keep a catastrophe at home.' Isocrates saw parallels with gung-ho imperialists: those who are enamoured of imperial power lose their reason, just like those who fall in love with courtesans, who make men love them and then ruin those who get involved with them. Socrates in Xenophon's *Oeconomicus* uses the same example to show that money need not always be an asset: '"If someone uses money to buy a hetaera and on her account harms his body, his soul and his estate, then in what way has money been of benefit to him?" "In no sense," says his interlocutor, "no more than you could call deadly nightshade, which causes madness in those who eat it, an asset."'[14]

Homosexual relations are less frequently cited but they could be just as dangerous. In his *Memoirs of Socrates*, Xenophon recalls the philosopher lecturing him about boys: ' "Poor thing. Do you have no idea what will happen to you once you have kissed a handsome boy? Without a doubt you'll become an instant slave instead of a free man, you'll spend large sums on harmful pleasures, you'll have no time for the business of a decent gentleman and be forced into pursuits even a madman would eschew." "Hercules!" said Xenophon, "What terrible power you ascribe to a kiss." ' It's hardly surprising after such a speech that, when older, Xenophon was rather homosceptic. One outraged speaker in a property dispute felt moved to come up with an alarming infinitive to describe the economic effect of homosexual liaisons. *Katapepaiderastēkenai* means 'to have wasted an estate in affairs with boys'. This was what his opponent had done with his own property and this is what he would do with the property at issue if he was allowed to get his hands on it.[15]

Many and various were the paths that led from infatuation to ruination. The philosophers seem to have been thinking of a general befuddling of the faculties under the influence of love, leading to all kinds of financial carelessness and expenditure on all kinds of foolish things. In this respect the economic consequences of love are rather like the economic consequences of drinking. Both lover and drinker become less able to concern themselves with what they should and to restrain themselves from what they shouldn't, claims Xenophon. This involves not only paying for the jewels and clothes that enabled Olympiodorus' mistress, to take one example, to make her splendid exoduses, but less predictable losses too. An anecdote about Alcibiades tells how on one occasion he burst into the home of his rich lover Anytus and decided to undertake a little wealth redistribution, toasting him with half the wine-cups (apparently of silver and gold), and then ordering his attendants to take them away to the house of his friend Thrasyllus who lived in more straitened circumstances. Some objected that Alcibiades' behaviour had been inconsiderate, but Anytus replied, 'not at all! It was in his power to take all of them, and it was very considerate of him to leave half behind.'[16]

Expenditure on love-affairs took as many different forms as the relationships themselves. In fact, as I argued in an earlier chapter, the nature of the economic transaction was crucial in defining the character of an amorous relationship in the first place. A fixed-price cash payment identified the anonymous promiscuity of the brothel. A gift denoted a more long-term arrangement of uncertain returns.

For the sexual act itself, the cheapest price attested for men and women was one obol. This is low. Too low, for some commentators, who think it a merely proverbial figure that might, in fact, take you no further in the Ceramicus than 'two bits' would on Forty-Second Street. It is attested by comic writers, philosophers and vase-painters, however, from the early fifth to the late fourth century and prostitutes in Athens must have been cheap enough even for slaves to afford, since slaves are known to have used them. 'Two-obols worth' (*diobolaria*), on the other hand, is an epithet for a cheap prostitute in Roman comedy and three obols is the price used to illustrate the low point hetaeras sink to when they are old. One drachma is what the tragedian Euripides charges the Scythian for sex with the flute-girl in *Thesmophoriazusae*. Two drachmas was what Didrachmon charged and what Lais' visitors hopefully offered her, a sum she turned down angrily in her youth, but accepted greedily in her dotage. This was also, not coincidentally, the maximum fee set by the Astynomoi for hiring a flute-girl. The playwright Theopompus thinks women who can be had for two drachmas are the middle-range (*mesas*) hetaeras.

At the other end of the scale, the highest fee we hear of is 1000 drachmas, charged by Gnathaena for a night with her daughter Gnathaenium. The client, a rich old 'satrap', wants to pay only 500. It makes no difference Gnathaena concedes. 'I'm confident you will give it to her tonight twice over.' This kind of money is, of course, quite exceptional. Elsewhere Gnathaena is said to have charged one mina (100 drachmas) for her daughter's services. When one client keeps coming back without paying more she reminds him the mina was for one night only, not a subscription for the whole course. The same sum of one mina is cited as the price of a night with Phryne.[17]

Slightly at variance with this discourse of pricing women is the evidence for pricing different sexual acts. Cited in two places at the rate of three obols, *kubda* the bent-over rear-entry position was whorish and cheap. The next in price (one drachma according to Plato Comicus) was *lordō*, rear-entry with the woman leaning back, and at the top of the range was *kelēs*, the racehorse. We are given no prices for this, but it was considered the height of luxury within the sex industry, only being performed if the client was prepared to spend a large amount of money. Machon tells the story of one bronzesmith who spent a fortune on the hetaera Gnathaenium in order to be accorded this privilege. The atmosphere of luxury invoked by this particular position is reflected in some Hellenistic epigrams which purport to be poems of dedication made by hetaeras as they metaphorically hang up their spurs: 'Lysidice dedicated to you, Cyprian Aphrodite, the golden goad of her shapely foot, with which she has exercised many a stallion lying on his back while her own thigh was never reddened, so lightly did she bounce. For she would finish the course without applying the spur. So she hung this her weapon of gold on the gate (of your temple).' A similar dedication from the pen of Posidippus, purporting to be in gratitude for victory in some sexual Grand National run against another hetaera is of a purple whip and polished reins. The epigrammatists of the Hellenistic period loved to compose their own arch and highly polished versions of the ordinary epitaphs and dedications that were found everywhere in this epigraphic culture. We have already come across their ironic and obscene versions of the wool-workers' dedications on turning to prostitution and even Lysidice's extraordinary gift to Aphrodite of her spurs seems to have had more humble models in the real world. An inscription found in Athens is an actual dedication (of what we do not know) by 'a certain woman' for 'many ridings' (*pollois keletismois*). It was customary for all kinds of traders to make dedications to Hermes for luck and to other deities seeking divine favour for their business, often with small clay tablets, *pinakes*, illustrating their line of work. There is no reason why workers in Aphrodite's guild should have been any different. Perhaps the tablets with erotic scenes in Oxford's Ashmolean Museum had the same function. If such dedications also served as advertisements, no one was complaining.[18]

It is with the 'hired' hetaeras, the *misthamousai*, who charged not for a sexual act but for the evening that we start to get consistently high prices. Most of them were musiciennes who were supposed to charge no more than two drachmas a night, but Menander talks of ten drachmas for running off to a symposium, and Charisius in the *Arbitration* pays for the harpist Habrotonon twelve drachmas a day.

Perhaps after the democracy was dissolved the lottery for music-girls was abolished too and flute-girls could charge more. Twelve drachmas was a large amount of money, but these sums are completely outclassed by a girl in another play of Menander, *The Flatterer*, whose fee is 300 drachmas a day. 'Such a rate seems fantastically high,' claim Gomme and Sandbach writing in 1973, 'yet even modern experience shows that huge sums may be spent for a woman's favours.' With hire-fees as high as these, women and boys made a substantial contribution to the costliness of dinner-parties.

For the longer periods laid down in contracts, the sums would have been correspondingly higher, although Simon, according to Lysias, claimed to have paid only 300 drachmas for an unknown stretch of the Plataean boy's time. Exclusive rights to Philaenium's company for a year, on the other hand, are valued at 2000 drachmas in Plautus' *Ass-dealer*. The disparity may simply reflect the difference between comic exaggeration and reality.[19]

When it comes actually to buying a lover and his or her freedom, naturally, even larger sums are involved. The hetaera Antigone needs only 300 drachmas to buy a slave-girl, a sum she receives as commission for arranging Epicrates' disastrous purchase of the perfume business; Demosthenes claims his father's factory slaves (skilled metal-workers) were worth 500 or 600 drachmas each; and it seems clear from a discussion of the different value of different slaves in Xenophon's *Memoirs of Socrates*, that 1000 drachmas was normally the highest price anyone would ever expect to pay for a slave (although there was a rumour that Nicias had paid much more for the manager of his silver-mine). When slaves are lovers, however, such enormous sums are not uncommon. Neaera, for instance, was sold by Nicarete for 3000 drachmas, and Epicrates was prepared to pay 4000 drachmas for the perfume-seller's son, with his brother and father thrown in for good measure. In the plays of Plautus sums of between 2000 and 6000 drachmas (one talent) are exchanged, the latter, part of a scam to cheat a whoreherder.[20]

These are truly significant sums we are talking about now, enough to make a dent in all but the largest fortunes. It takes two men to raise the 3000 needed to buy Neaera off Nicarete. And when Neaera herself is trying to raise two-thirds of that sum for her freedom she has to call on a wide circle of people to make contributions, placing herself under unwelcome obligation to some disreputable characters. Epicrates too has to go around visiting his friends to raise money to buy his lover and his family. It is rather naive, then, for the speaker to argue that there could have been no contract between Simon and Theodotus, because Simon simply could not afford the sum involved. If the price of possessing your lover was more than you had in the bank, the residue would have to be begged, borrowed or stolen. Freeing a hetaera was widely considered an act of reckless extravagance, not only because hetaeras cost a lot of money, but because young men would gladly ruin themselves to raise it.

However, even the sums paid for buying lovers body and soul are dwarfed by another kind of sexual extravagance, adultery. It was this rather than hetaeras that apparently led to Callias being 'plucked' of his wealth. Caught with the wife of one Phocus, he was forced to pay the enormous sum of three talents to escape the penalties for adultery. Three talents is 18,000 drachmas, enough to catapult a penniless man into the ranks of the few hundred richest citizens, but since the penalty for being caught *in flagrante* with an Athenian woman who was not your wife might be death, someone like Callias might consider it a cheap price to pay. Payments to cuckolded husbands are attested elsewhere, and seem to have been quite a common occurrence. One philosopher talks familiarly of those men who seduce their neighbours' wives 'on the basis of payment' and there are several examples of such extortions in Greek and Roman comedies. The wealthy adulterer escaping justice by paying a large sum became a proverbial example of money facilitating misdemeanours, a useful counter-example to the stereotype of the criminal poor pushed into error by dire necessity. Aristophanes' list of those who are kept in business by the god Wealth includes the adulterer who 'because of you gets off with a plucking when he is caught', 'for the rich were let go if they came up with some money,' an ancient commentator explains to a later readership. When Euphiletus and several others, all carrying torches to illuminate the scene, burst in upon Eratosthenes having sex with Euphiletus' wife, his first reaction is to offer the husband money. Especially after Callias' indiscretion, any husband who found his wife had managed to ensnare a rich lover might think he had won the lottery. In fact husbands were suspected of deliberately engineering their wives' adultery to make a profit. On trial now for murder Euphiletus has to prove that the whole deadly episode was not simply enacted 'for the sake of money, in order to raise myself from poverty to wealth'.[21]

It is in this context that we should place the story told by Apollodorus, that Neaera put her fees up when she moved into Stephanus' house 'on the grounds that she was by now enjoying a degree of respectability and sharing a home with a man. And this man here helped her in denunciations and blackmail. If she had as one of her lovers some rich and unworldly foreigner and he caught him *in flagrante*, he would lock him up indoors with her as a *moichos*, taking the opportunity to extort a large sum of money.' Apollodorus seems almost to conflate the adulterer's ransom money with the hetaera's increased fee. We have already seen how the hetaera is closer to an adulterous wife than the common prostitute in terms of her manipulation of the scopic economy, playing games with seeing and being seen, with the possibilities of possession. We have seen also how their long-term lovers talk about them as if married and refer to other men they have sex with as adulterers. It seems now that there are also close similarities in the kind of money which men pay to have sex with them. How much difference is there between what happens in Phocus' house when Callias is in there with Phocus' wife, what happens in Pyrrhus' house when Phile's mother is in residence and neighbours observe signs of debauchery and what happens in Stephanus' house when Neaera comes to stay? What is the difference between the higher fee Neaera regularly charges to her clients now she is living with Stephanus and the sums extorted from unwitting foreigners imprisoned as adulterers? The bronzesmith can still get Gnathaenium into bed, although she lives with Andronicus, has 'given up being an escort (*hetairein*)' and is 'unwilling to receive a fee', but it costs him a very large amount of gold and a great deal of persuasion.[22]

THE GRASPING HETAERA

The idea that Gnathaena's daughter or even Phryne could be had by anyone if the price was right is designed to subvert the hetaera's claim to be a lover and a friend. By giving the great and famous courtesans a standard price, they are seen to be the same as *pornai*, participating in the same kind of cash transaction, only on a grander scale, one mina instead of one obol, quantitatively not qualitatively different from a whore. It fits well into that misrepresentation of hetaeras by authors clearly hostile to them, like Theopompus of Chios, attempting to pin them down to common prostitution by claiming these elusive women could in fact be had by 'whoever wanted' 'at the same price for all'. On the other hand, Gnathaenium's '1000 drachmas for one night', like the one million dollars envisaged in hypothetical dares and Hollywood movies, is the kind of magically excessive figure that makes exceptions, a one-off, more akin to the adulterer's blood-money than the whore's fee.

At this level the relationships between price, demand and availability become rather confused. High prices are not just a reflection of availability, they symbolize exclusivity. Simmel's observations from turn-of-the-century Vienna seem appropriate once more:

> The abhorrence that modern 'good' society entertains towards the prostitute is more pronounced the more miserable and the poorer she is, and it declines with the increase in the price for her services, to the point at which even the actress whom everyone knows is kept by a millionaire is considered presentable in their salons, although she may be much more extortionate, fraudulent and depraved than many a streetwalker . . . the exorbitant price saves the object for sale from the degradation that would otherwise be part of the fact of being offered for sale . . . The courtesan who sells herself for a very high price thereby acquires a 'scarcity value' . . . As with many other commodities, the favours of some courtesans are greatly appreciated and in great demand only because they have the courage to ask quite extraordinary prices.[23]

A high price works in tandem with the scopic economy. It ought to mark a woman as sexually available but in fact it serves to keep her out of reach. She can be purchased by anyone, but only at an impossible price. Instead of a straightforward sequence of desire–payment–satisfaction, the nature of the payment determines the potential of satisfaction; the potential of satisfaction affects desire itself. The high fee, like the gift, maintains the hetaera's exciting oscillation on the threshold of availability, constructing an indecent seclusion. The hetaera locks herself away with her ill-gotten gains like a rich satrap, like Pharnabazus: 'It seems to me that Wealth is blind,' says a character in Amphis' *Grooming-technician*. 'He does not come to visit this girl, but sits indoors, paralysed, with Sinope and Lyca and Nannio and other such traps of livelihood and doesn't even step out of doors.' 'I fell in love with Phryne . . .' claims a character in Timocles' *Neaera*, 'when she didn't have what she has today; by spending large sums on each visit I've got myself excluded from her door.' 'The houses of the hetaeras are forbidden zones', says Aristophon, 'to those who cannot pay.' Aristodemus builds a parallel between the shields of modesty and the hurdles of price in a story about some clients of Gnathaena's daughter, reduced to penury and therefore excluded from the premises. The anecdote plays on the semantic range of '*peiraō*'. Instead of being metaphorically 'made trial of' like some chaste wife, Gnathaenium is literally 'laid siege to'. The men have brought tools with them, mattocks and picks, with which they threaten to pull the house down. 'If the tools actually belong to you,' said Gnathaena, 'you could pawn them and settle your bill.'[24]

However, the hetaera was rarely caught offering sex for a specific fee. As a result, money spent on hetaeras is not really money spent on sex. It is, as the philosophers point out, affiliated expenditure, costs that spring up *around* love, open-ended outlay on hopeful presents that may or may not result in fulfilment, para-extravagance. This is a difficult game for the women involved. On the one hand they must make sure their lovers do not become complacent and take their favours for granted. On the other hand, they must not be too obvious. If they are too specific about what they want or threaten to withdraw their favours unless they get it, friendship is transformed into a more explicit transaction: this for that. The hetaera must resort to hints and innuendo, the two-faced speech for which she was famous. Some fragments from lost plays of Menander illustrate well the techniques involved. From *Babe* (*Paidion*): 'You got me a gold one. If only it had been set with precious stones. That would have been so fine.' From the same scene, probably, with a little less tact: 'These should have been an emerald and some carnelians.' In *The Downpayment* a different girl tries a little petulance: 'You did well, I suppose, to buy me the serpent bangles.' This was clearly a subtle art and required a certain amount of training. One fragment seems to come from just such a tutorial: 'Let him put a necklace around your throat.' In the *Memoirs*, Xenophon shows Socrates himself working out this science of gift extraction with Theodote. The cycle of reciprocation, he suggests, is best initiated with a very small favour; the process of involvement should be gradual: 'First then you must ask your protectors for such favours as they can perform with a minimum effort . . .' Six hundred years later Athenaeus' guests were shocked at this image of the philosopher acting out the role of a procuress 'recommending lures for desire that were never envisaged by either Nico of Samos or Callistrate of Lesbos or Philaenis of Leucas (sic) or even Pythonicus of Athens'. Athenaeus shows in the course of his indignation that for those without a Socrates there were plenty of Teach Yourself books on the subject of seduction apart from Philaenis' well-known text and we can be sure they addressed themselves not only to *ton peirōnta*, the tempter, but also *tēn peirōsan*, the temptress.

The comic poet Anaxilas in his play *The Chick* manages to get all the complexity of the hetaera's strategy into a single metaphor, blending her notorious euphemistic language, her ballooning demands, the ambiguity of the gift and a sense of great danger in a version of the riddle famously answered by Oedipus:

And all the whores can be labelled Theban Sphinx; nothing they babble is straightforward, but it's all in riddles, of how they love 'to love', and 'be friends' and 'go with' someone. And then it's 'If only I could have something with four feet, . . . a chair perhaps.' And then it's 'what about something three-legged, a tripod table?', and then 'a maidservant, with two legs'. At this point if he has understood what's happening he gets well away, just like Oedipus, pretending not even to have seen her. It took some effort, but at least he is safe. Those on the other hand, who fall under the impression that the women are in love with them, lose in that instant all contact with the ground; they get carried away, tossed high into the air.[25]

There is no riddle in what Anaxilas was trying to say. The hetaeras' victims are drawn into a web of ambiguous two-faced words, they gradually get involved in a semblance of friendship and seduction, until they are ensnared and ruined. By solving the riddle, by seeing through the gift, by realizing that the women are faking friendship for material gain the men can escape, but if they take their words at face-value, they are lost. The speech is an excellent example of how language, desire and the gift work together to maintain the ambivalence of the hetaera. Spending is not just a sign of desires satisfied, but is itself involved in the construction of desires. Different structures of spending on pleasure – the purchase at fixed price, haggling, buying at auction, and giving hopefully in expectation of return – create a different relationship between the one desiring and the object desired, different probabilities of hitting the target, different degrees of deferral before satisfaction is guaranteed.

The greedy and cynical courtesan who pretends to be in love, but really is only interested in material gain is a stock character in comedy. The prologue of Menander's *Thais* began in mock-epic form: 'So sing me, goddess, of such a woman, brazen, but beautiful, persuasive too. Sing me of a woman who behaves badly, slams her door in your face; of a woman *whose demands come thick and fast*, whose love comes never, but ever instead its simulation.' This is what Epicrates was talking about in his play *Anti-Laïs* when, according to Athenaeus, he contrasted the ordinary flute-girls with 'the high-fee hetaeras': 'You see that the other flute-girls play Apollo's theme . . . and Zeus' theme; but these women only play the "Grasping Hawk".' This greed has a biological dimension. Hetaeras, like all women from Pandora onwards, are 'stomachs', gluttonous, bibulous and insatiable (*aplēstos*), a word that has the same sexual connotations in Greek as it does in English.[26] These human vultures are a particular feature of the Roman plays of Terence. His *Eunuch*, based explicitly on Menander's lost play of the same name, is centred on rival claims to the attentions of the hetaera Thais, who is represented as trying to get as much as she can out of Phaedria and Thraso. The opening of his *Hecyra* (*The Mother-in-law*) contains the most shameless example of the plundering hetaera, but with some understanding of the hetaera's point of view. An old prostitute, Syra, is teaching another how to survive. Cynicism is the only realistic strategy in a man's world. Men will always try to get something for nothing and will always prove faithless. Women have to look after themselves: 'That's precisely why I am always so busy warning you and encouraging you to feel no pity for anyone. If you manage to get hold of someone, strip him, plunder him, skin him alive!' Such stereotypes were not confined to comedy. Because she had 'devoured' Thallus (= 'leafy branch') her lover, the hetaera Nico earned the sobriquet 'she-goat'. Orators in particular were keen on this image of greedy women and were ready to put the blame for a whole range of misdemeanours on the demands of a scheming hetaera. We have already come across Antigone, who manipulated Epicrates into buying a whole family of perfume-sellers, and Olympiodorus' hetaera who drove him to all kinds of extravagant madness just so she could be seen about town in splendour. In addition we hear of a second Phryne, not to be confused with the famous woman of Thespiae, who, according to Herodicus in the sixth book of his *People Satirized in Comedy*, was nicknamed Sestos or 'Sifter' by the orators because she sifted the men who went with her.

Since imprecision is the whole point of money spent on gifts for hetaeras we rarely get a chance to compare this kind of expenditure with the exact and overexact figures we are given for other kinds of sexual commodity. Aeschines, however, as always, is ready to oblige. Timarchus, he claims, having made 2000 drachmas by extorting money from the brother-in-law of a citizen he accused of being a slave, spent it all on his hetaera Philoxene.[27]

MONEY AND MORALITY

Timarchus, in fact, provides a classic example of the process by which the unbridled body could work its way through the estate, a dramatic demonstration of the possibilities of economic self-destruction as understood by the Athenians:

> His father had left him a very large property which he has squandered ... but he was not a free agent; he was a slave, a slave to the most shameful pleasures: to *opsophagia*, expensive dinner-parties, flute-girls, hetaeras, dice, and all those other things to which no decent man should submit ...
>
> His father left him property which any other man could have used to support state-liturgies, but this man couldn't even preserve for himself. There was a house behind the Acropolis, an estate in the foothills at Sphettus, another piece of land at Alopece. More-over there were nine or ten slaves, skilled shoemakers, each of whom gave him two obols a day, and the manager of the workshop who gave him three; in addition, there was a woman skilled in weaving fine cloth who produced delicate goods for the market, and a man skilled in embroidery; there were outstanding debts, some moveable property ...
>
> The house in the city he sold to Nausicrates the comic poet (it was later sold to Cleaenetus for twenty minas), the foothill property he sold to Mnesitheus of Myrrhinusa, a large estate, but left to run wild thanks to this man. The place at Alopece, scarcely eleven or twelve stades from the city-wall, his mother, I have learned, asked him not to sell, begging him to keep his hands off it, to leave her, at the very least, a plot to be buried in. But not even this property was left alone. He sold it for two thousand drachmas. Of the slaves and slave-girls he hasn't left one. They've all been sold off.
>
> [As a result] He has nothing left, no house, no apartments, no plot of land, no slaves, no loans, nothing on which a decent man might live. He has exchanged his patrimony for lewdness, *sykophantia*, brazenness, degeneracy, cowardice, cheek, shamelessness over what should make anybody blush.[28]

This looks at first sight like a more systematic and carefully argued attempt to disqualify Timarchus from political responsibility, to set some facts and figures and reasonable argument against all the sexual innuendo, gossip and scandal that is always Aeschines' first resort, and it is indeed tempting when cataloguing the constant references to cost in Athenian accounts of pleasure to take the importance of expenditure at face value. It looks quite rational to worry about money. These economic anxieties, after all, were not frivolous. If we discount the comic high points, the banquet that cost one talent, the girl that cost the same, the night of passion with a neighbour's wife that sets Callias back three times that amount, there are still well-attested expenditures that might make a difference to anyone's means. There is no reason to disbelieve that the pleasures of the flesh often presented real problems to balance against the more nebulous and intangible problematic of the Self. But it would be wrong, I think, to keep the financial and moral or spiritual concerns apart. Rational economic thinking is not the sole or even the major force behind this economic discourse. There is much more to the Athenian preoccupation with expenditure than mere calculation of expense.

First, to give something a monetary value already makes it exchangeable and fluid. The Athenians made a distinction between two kinds of property: visible and invisible, *phanera* and *aphanēs ousia*. By liquidizing estates, by 'cashing them in' (*exargurizein*), real property could be made to disappear. It entered the field of exchange where it could easily evaporate. It became consumable, edible. A monetary evaluation in and of itself already points to spending, squandering, loss.

Second, money provides a general gauge with which to measure all kinds of vices. Greek morality has been characterized as fundamentally relative in contrast to the absolute proscriptions of the Judaeo-Christian tradition. In contrast with the Dos and Don'ts of the Bible, Greek ethics might be summed up with one short phrase, *mēden agan*, nothing too much. In a morality based on degree, money provides an essential gauge for measuring the extent and intensity of desire and pleasure. It is also, thanks to its interchangeability, a general gauge, which enables diverse appetites to be compared and associated with each other, as representatives of a general prodigality or lack of self-control rather than examples of particular predilections. In contrast, then, with a modern understanding of prices, which we might summarize as a reflection of both supply and demand (how *many* want something), expenditure and value in classical Athens are usually seen as indicative of the desires of purchasers, of *how much* someone wants something, of how much they are prepared to pay. Just as ancient morality is concentrated on the figure of the desiring subject, the discourse of the Athenian elite discusses the economy as something moved and directed by a mass of subjectivities, by consumers, by themselves. Plato in *Protagoras* blames the men who hire them for the high price of flute-girls. The comic character in Timocles' *Neaera* blames his own earlier expenditure for the high price of Phryne now. The disappointed *opsophagoi* blame other fish-eaters for allowing the price of fish to get so high.

The emphasis on expenditure, then, is not so much a rational reflection on the real problems of excessive eating, drinking and fornicating, but a measure of the degree of self-control. Anxiety about expenditure is anxiety about appetite itself. It is not rational so much as rationalizing, providing a reasonable justification for concerns which derive their main impetus from elsewhere, perhaps not unlike our recourse to arguments about health when we get worried about people taking drugs or having too much sex. There can be dangers to health in both these activities, as there were economic dangers in fish-dishes and courtesans, but it would be wrong, I think, to see the moralists' major concern residing in the financial or physical well-being of their targets. Indeed, it would have been interesting to see the reaction when in the middle of the third century Demetrius, grandson of Demetrius of Phalerum, called the moralists' bluff: 'When the members of the Areopagus summoned him and ordered him to live a better life, he replied, ". . . I do keep one of the most beautiful hetaeras and do no wrong to anyone, I do drink Chian wine and maintain myself in other respects very nicely, paying for it out of my private income, and I do not depend, as some of you do, on bribes and adultery." '[29]

EATING THE LAND

The profligate consumes his estate in the same way as he consumes a plate of fish. Indeed, the Greeks commonly refer to 'eating up the estate' (*katesthiō*) or 'gobbling it down' (*katabrōchthizō*). Puns and jokes keep the metaphor vivid. Cooks in New Comedy love to work for young men who are already 'eating up' their estates for the sake of some girl. One has even designed a special menu, mostly molluscs and other 'fish of the rocks' to fit their distracted appetites. Another surveys the audience and notes that he recognizes many among them who have 'eaten up' their estates on his account. Ctesippus, the son of the great general Chabrias, presented marvellous opportunities for such jokes, when he spent on his own vices money for his father's monument, or, as some said, actually sold the stones themselves, inspiring an old man in Menander's first play, *Anger*, of 321 to tardy emulation: 'Look, wife, I, too, was once a youth, although I didn't in those days bathe five times a day; as I now do. Nor did I wear a fine cloak; as I now do. Nor perfume, as I now do; and in addition I will dye my hair and depilate, by Zeus, and it won't be long before I'll shed my human form and become a Ctesippus gobbling up stones one by one and not merely my land.' Menander suggests a suitable punishment for such characters in the form of a prayer: 'Dearest Mother Earth, how very sacred you are, how valuable a possession to men of good sense! How we should have made provision for those who eat up the land they've inherited, forcing them to sail the seas for ever and never to even set foot on the earth, to make them appreciate what a good thing it was they inherited, what a good thing it was they failed to preserve!'[30]

Although a rational reader, then, might wonder why in a speech concerned above all with prostitution, so much emphasis is given to the sale of estates, Aeschines knows what he is doing. '[Demosthenes], therefore goes up and down the market-place expressing his wonder and amazement that one and the same man should have prostituted himself and also have consumed his patrimony.' But Aeschines is not talking of an economic logic in which prostitution would provide enough funds to save Timarchus the need to squander his patrimony, or *vice versa*. Instead, the real economy mirrors an internal libidinal economy. When Aeschines remarks that Timarchus not only 'gobbled up his estate, but actually drank it down' (*katepien*), he is alluding not to Timarchus' drinking habits but to *how* he spent his estate: he 'not only ate up his property, he "downed it in one"'. The impression is of the addict desperate for a fix: 'He sold off each property for something less than what it was worth. He couldn't hang around for a better price, or even for a decent price. He sold it for what he could get at the time. This is how desperate he was to indulge his pleasures.' It is not hard to see how this kind of metaphor enables spending and consuming to be fused into one image. The metaphor of eating or drinking property equates the appetite that needs to be sated with the process of raising the money that is needed to sate it. Timarchus' liquidization of his assets is not a decent citizen's attempt to afford what he wants, but a conspicuous demonstration of the desires that boil in secret underneath his skin, a spectacular hole in his patrimony, a Ctesippian anti-monument to his appetite.[31]

It is no surprise, then, to find that the incontinent and the prodigal, the *akratēs* and the *asōtos* are often fused into one, that the *katapugōn*, a figure who encapsulates lack of self-control is often depicted as a paragon of profligacy. We have already come across the *katapugōn* son in Aristophanes' *Banqueters* who is learning systematically how to live extravagantly and Strepsiades' horse-mad son is attacked in similar terms for bankrupting his estate: 'O foul destroyer of your father, burglar . . . *cistern-arse*.' Dover thinks these are 'very general words of abuse and contempt' but it seems perverse to deny they have a very specific reference to Pheidippides' effect on his father's estate. *Lakkoprōktos*, cistern-arse, refers to his prodigal ways, a direct inversion of the adjective used to describe the bottomless reserves of wealth held by Callias' family before Callias came along, *lakkoploutos*, cistern-rich. What Aeschines is doing, then, with his careful accounting of Timarchus' estates is to construct a vivid image of a profligate body, a body so given over to extravagant pleasures that its desires must be sated immediately: 'Look how Timarchus cashed in his property,' he is saying, 'just as he cashed in himself.'[32]

PART IV

THE CITY

VII

POLITICS AND SOCIETY

WE ARE QUITE ACCUSTOMED, now, to reading about the sex lives of public figures scrupulously investigated for us by unscrupulous newspapers in the name of 'public interest'. The Athenians too linked pleasure with politics, although the pervasiveness of these connections and the ingenuity with which they were pursued can seem to us quite bizarre. In fact to introduce the polis at the end of a book like this is a little dishonest, since so much of the material we have already discussed was produced because of politics in the first place: remarks made about political enemies in speeches before the Assembly of the People, or in front of the popular courts, aspersions cast against public figures in comedies performed at the public festivals, diatribes from the political treatises of the philosophers. All I intend to do in this final section is to put the evidence back where it belongs and to explain how it came to be there in the first place.

A CITY OF WITNESSES

From the overthrow of the dictator Hippias and the reforms of Cleisthenes at the end of the sixth century until Alexander's successors imposed an oligarchic regime in 322, and with only the briefest of interruptions in between, Athens was a democracy. It was not a representative democracy like almost all the modern exemplars, but a direct democracy. What this meant in practice was that the city was ruled by a sovereign Assembly, the *Ecclesia*, to which all adult male citizens were admitted. The Assembly met early in the morning several times a month to decide policy. Business was prepared for the Assembly by the Council of 500, a randomly, annually selected cross-section of citizens, who managed by rotation the day-to-day running of the state. In the Assembly anybody could propose a law or speak out against it. If it was passed by a majority it would be inscribed on stone and set up in a public place. In fact there were so many of these documents on display that they must have come in time to resemble overcrowded cemeteries, but thanks to this eccentric practice several thousand of the democracy's public documents have survived into the twentieth century, enabling historians to know the workings of the Athenian democracy in much more detail than those of many more recent regimes.

The more mature sections of the citizenry, those over thirty, were also eligible to sit on judge-and-jury-panels usually composed of a few hundred members, but occasionally numbering over one thousand. In the fourth century these older citizens also examined the laws passed by the Assembly to make sure they were not illegal or contradictory. The jury-panels, the Council and numerous other committees and magistrates were selected by lottery, which the Athenians considered the foundation of a democratic system. To ensure fairness elaborate lottery-machines, *klērōtēria*, were constructed. Several of these monuments to Athenian equity survive and their workings are described for us in a section of the Aristotelian *Constitution of Athens*, rediscovered on a papyrus at the end of the last century. The lottery-machines were a kind of bulwark against the constant threat of anti-democratic forces such as political parties or charismatic individuals who stood by waiting for any opportunity to overthrow the state and set up some kind of 'tyranny' or dictatorship in its stead. Since the democracy made such efforts not only to maintain the People's sovereignty, but to ensure massive participation in the day-to-day running of the government and the courts it is hardly surprising that Athenian life and Athenian culture were saturated with politics.

Athens was not only politically very open, but the population lived with very little state supervision, something that could not be taken for granted elsewhere in Greece. There was no police force as such (the famous Scythian archers seem to have been no more than bouncers at public meetings), no censors, no curfews, no personal files. In fact, in contrast to the monumental stone-inscriptions recording the accounts of public bodies, personal records were very limited in scope and often incomplete. In a city so jealous of its citizenship, there was no central registry of citizens. There was not even a land register, leaving ownership to be settled by the testimony of neighbours. Athens was not only a model democracy, in many ways it was also a paradigm of the minimalist state vaunted by today's extreme libertarians.

Such a society was not at first sight a promising arena for professional politicians. The system of selection by lottery made any attempt at a career in government literally haphazard. There were a few elected positions, the generalship, for instance, or membership of certain financial committees, which did indeed provide a power-base for some, but the majority of ambitious men, feeling uncomfortable both in the counting-house and the mess, need not despair. It was perfectly possible to carve out a position of power and patronage in the Athenian democracy, provided you were good at prose composition.

According to tradition, the art of speaking (*rhētorikē*) was dramatically revealed to the Athenians in 427, when one Gorgias arrived in Athens from Leontini in Sicily to secure Athens' assistance against his city's powerful neighbour Syracuse. There had been effective speakers before 'rhetoric', of course – Pericles, for instance, had hardly been tongue-tied in anticipation – but Gorgias brought all the self-consciousness of a new discipline as it had been elaborated over decades of post-tyranny property disputes in his native Sicily, as well as his own idiosyncratic version of the new patterning and style. Modern students of Greek find Gorgias' way of writing not the least bit seducing and his influence on Thucydides is an important part of what makes the historian so hard to understand, but there is little doubt that his impact on Athens was extensive. Not only did the city send help, fatefully, to Leontini, but rhetoric found in Athens its true home, with the democracy providing many opportunities for students of speaking to exercise their new voices. Gorgias compared the art of persuasion to charms and spells and there did seem something magical in the way that money and power began to gather around gifted speakers thenceforth. The most honest as well as the least honourable way of making a profit was to sell speeches to clients who would then use someone else's words to make their case in court (typically, the Athenians insisted that those involved in law-suits should represent themselves). Demosthenes started out in this way and Lysias, for centuries acknowledged as the master of the pure classic ('Attic') style, did little else, unable to pursue a public career because of his foreign (Sicilian) origins. It was much more profitable, however, if one was able, to use one's talents for oneself. Demosthenes deployed his speaking skills to recover some of the inheritance his guardians had pocketed during his minority. More typically Timarchus, a very effective 'speaker', was said to have extorted money by accusing someone falsely of being an ex-slave. The very fact that someone had trained at a rhetorical school could be used as evidence against them . . . by well-trained rhetoricians. 'I've got nothing against men who give money to Isocrates' (one of the most popular teachers), says a certain Androcles in a speech written for him by Demosthenes, 'but by Zeus I do not think that men should use their speaking-ability to slap claims on other people's property even taking it away from them in some cases, imagining they are superior to other men and clever.' This unscrupulous use of legal procedure was very common according to many sources, and the *sykophant*, the professional denouncer, was a figure of hatred and contempt. It did not help that Athens not only had no police force but even lacked a public prosecution service, relying instead on 'anyone who wanted to' (*ho boulomenos*) to bring infringements of the law to the city's attention often in return for a substantial reward.[1]

The greatest prizes, however, lay in the area of politics, where you could use your skill at speaking to swing the whole Assembly behind you. These public speakers (*rhētores*) were of a higher status than *sykophants* and speechwriters, although the boundaries between these groups were often blurred. They were effectively the cream of the oratorical crop and the closest thing the Athenians had to politicians and statesmen. This kind of power undoubtedly carried its own rewards, but it was also lucrative, and sometimes very lucrative indeed. Foreign governments would pay huge amounts of money to get the most influential speakers on their side. Money paid for Philip of Macedon's peace with Athens in 346, according to Demosthenes, but Demosthenes himself was not averse to enriching himself (as well as his cause) when the opportunity arose. His opposition to the Macedonians was subsidized with frequent gifts from the King of Persia and he made a mint when Alexander's renegade treasurer, Harpalus, arrived in Athens in urgent need of a safe haven for the vast sums of money he had embezzled from his king. Few orators retired penniless.

On the other hand, public speaking also carried very great risks and political enemies would seize any opportunity to prosecute careless or unlucky speakers for making illegal or ill-starred proposals. The penalty was frequently death. Some avoided exposure by paying others, the ever-ready *sykophants*, to put forward measures for them which they would then enthusiastically support. Apollodorus accuses Stephanus, Neaera's lover, of making his living like this. It is probably because he was perceived as an agent of some more shadowy figure that the *sykophant* becomes our 'sycophant' and he is closely linked in Old Comedy with other crawlers, like the parasite and the flatterer (*kolax*).[2]

If a rival did not slip up in the Assembly some other charge could be dug up in order to bankrupt him or remove him from the arena with penalties of exile, disenfranchisement or death. Politics regularly spilled over into the law-courts and Athenian politicians were very creative in using the law to pursue their own vendettas. Some of these suits seem terribly trivial to us. We hear of public impeachment for paying more than two drachmas for flute-girls, suits against men for calling themselves by the wrong name and a mysterious case against one Erasistratus 'concerning pea-fowl'. There were even indictments for excessive litigation, *graphai sykophantias*. For the social historian this creative use of the law has had unexpected benefits. It is to politics, for instance, that we owe so much of what we (think we) know about ancient prostitution. The speech *Against Timarchus* was Aeschines' retaliation against the allies of Demosthenes for accusing him of treason in arranging the treaty with Philip. The speech *Against Neaera* is Apollodorus' revenge on Stephanus who had attacked him for making illegal proposals before the Assembly and had even charged him with homicide.

The absence of a police force, therefore, did not mean that Athens was unpoliced. If anything she was overpoliced since each and every inhabitant was a potential agent of the polis. In the absence of proper records and files the courts relied more heavily on witnesses who were called on to testify to a wide range of facts and events: which of two brothers was older, whether someone was a citizen or not, whether someone was a slave, whether someone had been married or not, how rich someone was, how poor. Particularly valuable in this regard were domestic servants who often provided the only way of knowing what went on behind the blank walls of an Athenian house. It was domestic servants who revealed to an outraged population that the Eleusinian Mysteries had been profaned in private houses. Unfortunately, however, the testimony of slaves was considered viable only if they had been tortured. Consequently the rivals in an Athenian law-suit are often to be found demanding their enemies' household slaves or offering up their own so that they could have the truth tortured out of them. Anyone who refused might be suspected not of compassion but of having something to hide. Those who find this disturbing may comfort themselves with the fact that the torture-challenge was frequently made, but almost always rejected. On only two out of the forty-two occasions we know of was the challenge accepted, but in neither case was the torture actually carried out. It would be a reckless scholar, however, who claimed torturing slaves for information never actually occurred and although the challenge contained a great deal of bluff, it never seems to have become a mere ritual. Of course slaves (and foreigners and even very, very occasionally citizens) are known to have been tortured if they were thought to have been themselves involved in some crime.

In practical terms, a slave's knowledge was perhaps most dangerous in the case of disputes within the *oikos*. It is his wife's maidservant who under threat of torture reveals to Euphiletus the details of his wife's infidelity with Eratosthenes and so enables him and his friends to surprise the guilty couple one fatal night. We can see why Astyanassa, a maidservant of Helen of Troy, was made the mythical founder of the genre of sex manuals and why the women of Aristophanes' *Women in Power* are so grateful for the discretion of the lamp.[3]

Even if the house kept its mouth shut, the streets were ready to blab. Athens was too big to fall into the category of the 'face-to-face societies' studied by anthropologists of village life, where everyone knows each other, but public figures were frequently observed about town. As soon as they stepped out of doors they exposed themselves to a forest of eyes, often revealing much more about their personal habits or their foreign policy-affiliations than they suspected. Demosthenes hardly needs to remind his audience what Aeschines looks like 'parading through the market-place with his cloak let down to his ankles, puffing out his cheeks, there he goes, a close friend of Philip of Macedon at your service'. Apollodorus advises his jurors to listen to the arguments and the laws and then simply to turn their gaze on Neaera to see if she is guilty or not. He had learned this trick, perhaps, from Demosthenes. You only had to meet Apollodorus on the street, Demosthenes had once claimed, to see that he 'was living a licentious life', a charge Apollodorus, having by now secured Demosthenes' clever tongue for himself, vigorously denied: 'I can see for myself that I am unlucky in the way I look, my loud chatter, my fast walk . . . but thanks to the moderation I exercise with regard to my personal expenditure, it is also quite obvious how much more disciplined I am in my lifestyle in comparison with my opponent and men like him.' Even a shopping expedition could furnish damaging information, as Timarchus and his friend Hegesander were to find out: 'That this is true you all know', claims Aeschines, alleging conspiracy and immorality, 'for who hasn't arrived at the fish-stall and seen the sums of money they spend?' Timarchus' very flesh contained a record of his morals: 'only recently he threw off his cloak in the People's Assembly and his body was in such an appalling and shameful condition thanks to his drunkenness and his vices that decent men had to look away.'[4]

If the citizens could not quite recall waiting behind Timarchus and Hegesander in the queue for tuna-steaks or had not been able to read all his vices on bumping into Apollodorus in the street, the speakers could always resort to 'hearsay' instead. Aeschines makes great use of this public amenity to 'prove' that Timarchus had been a common prostitute. In particular he recalls a recent meeting of the Council of 500 at which Timarchus' banal speech about the maintenance of the city's defences was transformed, thanks to the power of innuendo, into a highly amusing allusion to his life as a street-walker. Aeschines reminds his audience that the goddess Rumour, an associate of the messenger-god Hermes, actually enjoyed a cult at Athens and despite his special pleading, it does seem as if hearsay enjoyed much higher status in ancient societies than it does today: 'word about the way a man lives his life and what he gets up to living it, wanders through the city of its own honest accord, broadcasting private deeds to the public and often even prophesying what will be.' The Athenian cult of Rumour seems to have been inaugurated to commemorate the fact that news of the great victory at the river Eurymedon in the 460s somehow crossed the Aegean to reach Athens on the very same day. In this context the scandalous implication that the audience discovered in Timarchus' unfortunate discourse on the state of the city walls represents a sudden supernatural eruption of truth like the window on the future that unexpectedly opens up in words of omen (*klēdōn*) rather than mere tittle-tattle. Andocides was appealing to the same kind of mechanism when he interpreted superstitious rumours about bad spirits in the house of Hipponicus as forebodings of Callias' profligate life. In this context giggling in the Council chamber moves far beyond nudge-nudge-wink-wink. Using words that have two meanings, one innocent, the other sexual, Timarchus seems like a hetaera, with her treacherous talk, her obscene innuendo and bendable words. But the *klēdōn* is the polar opposite of the *double-entente*. The hetaera is knowing. She feeds the other meaning into her words like a trap. Timarchus on the other hand is unwitting, ambushed by the truth. 'We know we should not be laughing . . .' say the Athenians when told to shut up, 'but the truth is such a powerful thing that it overwhelms all human calculations.' The *klēdōn* is smoke seen in the very heart of the city, warning of dangerous fires.[5]

The most common factories for gossip were barbershops and perfumeries which were such centres for interaction that someone who did not go there risked being labelled a misanthropist. A rumour really knew it had hit the big time, however, when it made an appearance on stage. Aristophanes, as we have seen, begins the *Wasps* by casting aspersions at various members of the audience for their fondness for gambling, drinking and attending sacrifices and there are numerous other examples of gossip and slander in his oeuvre and that of his contemporaries. This kind of scurrilous defamation had a role in several religious festivals and might often be taken in good spirit. Socrates famously stood up during the *Clouds*, so that the audience could see for themselves the target of the satire. His pupil Plato reacted more bitterly and considered the comic poets partly responsible for the false image of his master that led to his trial and death. There were occasional attempts to silence comedy or to prosecute comedians, but in the time of Timarchus the theatre was still a very dangerous place for public reputations. There are other young men called Timarchus, says Aeschines, 'but when the comedies were being played in Collytus, and . . . some people were said to be "great big Timarchian whores" . . . everyone thought it a reference to you'. Someone has only to hear the name Timarchus and he asks, 'Which Timarchus are you talking about? Timarchus the whore?'[6]

None of Timarchus' speeches survives, but anyone who got as far as he did in Athenian politics would have developed a very thick skin and his own phial of venomous accusations. So many of the slanderers are themselves slandered elsewhere in the corpus of Attic oratory that it is tempting to put all of this gossip and innuendo and vilification down to the 'robust nature' of Athenian politics. Isocrates even saw *sykophants* as perpetrating a form of wealth redistribution by targeting inarticulate men with sufficient cash, but not enough commonsense to hire a good speechwriter. However, there were undoubtedly times when powerful speakers used their influence to victimize those without the power or resources to answer back, and other occasions when innocent associates became caught up like Neaera in the crossfire of political rivalries. Such people did not make speeches worth immortalizing, or because of their status were prevented from speaking at all. Perhaps these are the kind of men and women who resorted to witchcraft instead, leaving behind not exemplary pieces of prose, but curse-tablets written in lead and posted to Hermes and Persephone, the Underworld, asking them to bind the tongues of their accusers so that when they laid their claims before the court they may 'seem to be of no account, either in word or deed'. The disempowered, on the other hand, do not have a monopoly on magic.[7]

The Athenian democracy was a great achievement. It gave real power to ordinary people over a considerable period of time, but the openness of the system was a double-edged sword. The deficiency of records and files meant, perhaps, that slaves could occasionally slip into the citizen-body, but it also meant that unpopular citizens were vulnerable to accusations that they had usurped their status. It meant that some women could elude attempts to pin them and their sexuality down. It also meant that people could claim that legitimate wives had been no more than courtesans or even that one's mother was a whore. Athens was very successful in frustrating accumulations of power in the hands of dictators and parties, but very few positive measures, on the other hand, were taken to protect the rights of individuals. In comedy and philosophy Demos, a personification of the People, is sometimes compared to a monarch. Athens was never an authoritarian state, but from some angles it could take on the appearance of a totalitarian one.

RICHES AND DIFFERENCE

This is the political context for the revelations we find in our sources concerning the eating, drinking and copulating habits of public figures. Most modern historians tend to dismiss such accusations as mere vindictive commonplaces, trivial attempts by unimaginative politicians to insult their opponents in a rather unfocused fashion. Those who have devoted a little more attention to the matter see class antagonism as the key. Josiah Ober in a study of the Athenian elite provides a fair summary of this approach: 'A litigant's portrayal of his rich opponents was often intended to inflame to the point of open resentment the envy of a poor man who had previously observed the life of the leisure classes only from a distance.'[8]

At first sight this emphasis on class seems able to account for a large part of our material. Drinking is the most obvious example. Wine *is* property, and cellars were sometimes listed in the inventory of an estate. Wine features, for instance, in the property confiscated from those wealthy men who were condemned to death for vandalizing the images of Hermes, just as it had probably featured in the evening that got them into trouble in the first place. Love of drinking (or drinking-parties) in general is said to be a disease of 'worthy men' (*chrēstoi*) at the beginning of *Wasps*, a tag which sometimes carries class overtones, although, as we have seen, it was usually not how much you drank, but how you drank, and above all where you drank that provided the important criteria. Because of their associations with different classes, emptying one's cup in a *kapēleion* and in a symposium had very different connotations, the former, according to Isocrates and the comic poets, a hang-out of slaves and the uncouth, the kind of institution, according to Theopompus, that flourished in cities where the common people had taken control; the latter, according to Aristophanes, a place where rich young men exchanged witty anecdotes about the luxuries of Sybaris and took it in turns to sing songs about the aristocratic 'tyrant-slayers' Harmodius and Aristogiton. The clash of cultures is perhaps best illustrated by a scene towards the end of the *Wasps*, where the vulgar old father Philocleon has a lesson in how to behave like a gentleman from his sophisticated son: 'Come recline on the couch and I'll teach you how to behave in sympotic company.' 'So how am I to recline, pray tell?' 'Gracefully.' 'Like this you mean?' 'No! Not like that' 'Well, how then?' 'Extend the knees, and pour yourself out among the throws liquidly, like a gymnast. Next, praise one of the ornaments and turning your gaze to the ceiling gasp at the "tapestried" hangings of the chamber . . . the flute-girl blows her flute . . .' The symposium with all its abstruse rituals, its learnt songs and learned conversation must have seemed a terribly alien environment, designed to insulate the participants not from the world in general but from the city's plebeian masses in particular and some of these official and unofficial dining-societies seem to have deliberately courted public notoriety. In a lost speech of Lysias, a man was attacked for belonging to a group called the *kakodaimonistai* (the 'wicked devils') who, it was claimed, held feasts on days of ill-omen. One historian has even argued that the witch-hunt that followed the vandalizing of the statues of Hermes and rumours that the Eleusinian Mysteries had been profaned in private houses, should really be seen as reflecting the people's mistrust of the symposium, an aristocratic institution within their midst, revealing 'the potential existence of a true class struggle in Athens' centred on the drinking-group.'[9]

The practice of drinking from Spartan cups, the notorious *kōthōones*, carried more specific implications. Already in Aristophanes' first play of 427, we find that 'drinking Chian wine from Spartan cups' is associated with the decadent sympotic 'gentlemanly' world of the *katapugōn* son, and it is still seen as typical of a particular kind of young man almost a century later in Demosthenes' harangues. The practice seems to have reached its apogee, however, at the end of the fifth century at around the time of Athens' defeat in the Peloponnesian War. At this time the cup figures prominently in the pro-Spartan propaganda of Critias, an aristocrat, a relative of Plato, and a leading figure in the oligarchic junta that used the defeat as an opportunity briefly to bring the police state to Athens. We also hear of men putting this ideology into practice, 'playing the Spartan' (*lakōnizein*) in their habits and dress, wearing their hair long, etc. It is surely not a coincidence that archaeologists have dated to this same period, the end of the fifth century and the beginning of the fourth, a large proportion of actual *kōthōns* discovered in the area of the Agora.[10]

Half a century after the profanation of the Mysteries, the symposium could still be a source of 'gentlemanly' misbehaviour, as one Ariston found out when he was spotted by an old enemy taking an evening stroll. The man himself was too drunk to do any damage on his own, but unfortunately his father and friends happened to be drinking at a house nearby and Ariston's *passeggiata* was brought to a rapid and violent conclusion as the whole party left the *andrōn* to teach him a lesson. A charge of assault followed and we are back in the courts once more. Ariston knows very well the kind of defence the father will make: 'That there are many men in Athens, sons of "gentlemen [*kalōn k'agathōn*], who give themselves nicknames, as a joke, the way that young people do", nicknames like the Ithyphalli [Sacred Erections] or Autolekythoi [Self-abusers?], that "among them are men who are in love with hetaeras", that his own son is one of these, and that "often they get into fights over the women, as young men do".' Ariston moves easily from drunken violence to affairs with hetaeras, and indeed, 'men who get involved in fights over hetaeras' are a group regularly featured in our sources. These were the kind of men who most appreciated the comedies of Antiphanes, as the playwright explained to Alexander the Great, who did not. From Ariston's speech it appears that this ribald group might think they were behaving in an upper-class kind of way and that the world of sex was also bifurcated by class distinctions.[11]

Indeed, it does seem indisputable that the language of commodity and gift which is used to distinguish between the hetaera and the *pornē* contains a strong class element. The 'working-girls' (*ergazomenai*) of the 'workshop' (*ergastērion*) or the 'hired women' (*mistharnousai*) who decorate symposia are given names that taint them with the low status of slaves and the labouring classes. *Hetairēsis* (companionship), on the other hand, is a more aristocratic kind of relationship, appropriate to women who belong to the world of friendship and gifts. If class is involved in the distinctions between women, class also divides their clients. The hetaeras and the musiciennes (though they might be labelled 'hired women' by their enemies) belonged very much to the world of the symposium. In her early years, Neaera travelled with Nicarete and Metaneira on the international festival circuit, drinking with distinguished men from all over Greece, Thessalian potentates and wealthy Athenian metics. Such women, like the *semnotatas* ('unapproachable' – and lethal) 'ladies' booked to entertain the pro-Spartan junta in Thebes in 379, added a bit of class to such gatherings and got a little reflected glory from the distinguished company in turn. Such women might easily turn their noses up at the *pornai*, 'the two-obol sluts of dirty little slaves' in the hetaera Adelphasium's succinct and snobbish appraisal, who belonged, instead to the commoditized world of inns and brothels and bars.[12]

The Athenians were able to joke about sex and sex-objects as goods that could be distributed more, or less, fairly. Aristophanes' *Women in Power* include sex in their new communistic system, making sure that wizened old hags have an opportunity to sample a young man's charms first while his young girlfriend must wait her turn. Gnathaena's *Nomos Syssitikos* which outlined principles of equality and fairness for all, and Phryne's new god Sharing (Isodaites), who led to her indictment for blasphemy, reveal that the sympotic principle of equal participation might be applied to a hetaera's favours too.

Socrates shows a similar kind of reasoning at the beginning of the dialogue *Phaedrus*. Learning that the orator Lysias has written a clever essay on love arguing that boys should grant favours to those who are not in love with them rather than to those who are, the impoverished old philosopher wishes he had suggested they give their favours to poor men rather than the wealthy, and to the old rather than to the young, and generally to ordinary people like him. If he had, he concludes, his essay would have been democratic as well as clever.[13]

It is at the fishmonger's stall, however, that the gap between rich and poor gapes most widely. In one play, Timocles describes the gate-crasher known as Lark cruising the market-place: 'an agora well-stocked with fish is a joy to behold if you can afford it, but beyond endurance if you're of meagre means.' With no prospect of a dinner invitation and only four pieces of bronze, Lark wanders forlornly around the fish-stalls staring helplessly at the mouth-watering eels, the tuna, the rays and crayfish. Having discovered the price of each, he scuttles off towards the cheap sprats. In Aristophanes' *Frogs* Dionysus describes a wealthy man who avoids paying taxes by dressing in rags, but who reveals his true worth when he is seen buying fish at the fish-stalls. There are even a couple of passages which seem to treat fish-consumption as a jealously guarded privilege of the rich. A fragment of Alexis' *Heiress* has one character suggesting that if a man, who in other regards is clearly short of money, is seen buying eels, he should be arrested and taken off to prison. Another poet, Diphilus, in his play *The Merchant*, has a Corinthian claim: '[In Corinth] if we see someone buying fish conspicuously, we ask where he lives and what he does. And if he prove to have an estate whose revenues can pay his expenses, we let him enjoy this lifestyle. But if it happens that he is spending beyond his means, they forbid him to do it again. And if anyone disobeys, they are fined . . .' Class is an obvious ingredient likewise in Antiphanes' description in *Rich Men* of two 'veteran fish-consumers' who, seeing one Euthynus 'with sandals and a ring and drenched in perfume' settling some kind of *opson*-deal, get into a panic that the market for fish has been cornered by a few rich men. They gather crowds around them and denounce the perpetrators, ending their complaints: 'It's not democratic for him to do this and chomp on so many fish.' In this context we should not be surprised to find that fish-slices figure in the list of things which will at last be available to all in the revolutionary redistribution of property envisioned by Aristophanes' communally-minded *Women in Power* (*Ecclesiazusae*).[14]

There seems plenty of evidence, therefore, that the pleasures of the flesh could be related to different classes within Athenian society, providing opportunities for comedians and orators to mark out their enemies as members of an elite group practising an elitist lifestyle, easy targets for envy and class antagonism. Unfortunately, however, it is not as simple as that. As soon as we try to apply these class distinctions to actual socio-economic groups in Athenian society we come unstuck.

CLASS

In sharp contrast with the very rigorous differentiation that separated Greek and barbarian, man and woman, free man and slave, social and economic distinctions within the citizen population are rather hard to pin down. The problem is not that there are two few possibilities for classification, but too many.[15]

In the archaic period Athens had been ruled by an aristocracy called the Eupatrids and although a number of reformers from Solon onwards took measures to weaken its power and influence, many of the great men of the fifth-century democracy could demonstrate aristocratic connections. Pericles, for example, was attached to the Alcmaeonids, one of the most important of these families, as was Alcibiades. Callias was not only the richest man in Greece, he also belonged to the distinguished family of the Kerykes, guardians of the Mysteries of Eleusis. By the fourth century, however, aristocrats have faded almost entirely from the political scene. A mere shadow of their former glory, however, they were still around, clinging to their identity through famous names, hereditary priesthoods, ancestral tombs, and in some cases (e.g. descendants of the tyrant-slayers Harmodius and Aristogiton) special privileges. Just when one might have thought they had disappeared from the political stage for ever in the age of Alexander, one of the very grandest of these families, the Eteobutadae, threw up a leader of the democracy for the last time in the person of Lycurgus.

In the course of undermining the power of the Eupatrids in the early sixth century, Solon the lawgiver had instituted a new class system based on property. At the top were the 'five-hundred-bushel men', then the Knights, the Zeugitai (Hoplites or 'Yoke-men') and on the bottom rung, the thetes. These formal categories survived into the democracy, but are rarely referred to and played little or no part in the main democratic institutions. Those the lot had selected for magistracies, for instance, had to state their property class late in the fourth century just as they had early in the fifth, it was just that by that time no one made himself ineligible by admitting to be a thete and no one made himself unpopular by challenging him.

Political philosophers applied a more straightforward binary structure when analysing different constitutions throughout the Greek world, talking of 'the few' and 'the many', or the 'notables' (gnōrimoi) and 'the people'. The history of the constitution ascribed to Aristotle sees Athenian political development as a constant struggle between these two groups ending with the triumph of the latter. Elsewhere we find a number of labels that seem to refer to class. There are the 'gentlemen' (kaloi k'agathoi, lit. 'the beautiful and good'), the 'favoured' (eudaimones), the 'worthy' (chrēstoi), the 'refined' (charientes) and of course 'the rich' and 'the poor'. The last two categories are almost always found without any intervening middle class between them, and any study of their usage quickly reveals confusion and inconsistency. Callias, remember, is described as a 'poor man', when he still has two talents. They are best seen as relative terms.

Modern studies of Athenian society, based on models derived from similar but much better known economies, and fed with what little information we have about Athenian peculiarities – for example, inheritance law, extent of ownership, size of farms, type of crops, amount of imported food, average yields, weather etc – have reached a broad consensus that the Athenian citizen-body covered a wide range of economic positions from poverty to great wealth, with the vast majority of the population, at least 80 per cent, being peasants who worked their own land and whose well-being varied considerably from year to year thanks to the vagaries of the Attic climate. Problems begin when attempts are made to identify a few significant gradations along this continuum. Some have taken their cue from Solon's quasi-military categories, dividing the citizenry according to their military role: the horsemen who could afford horses, the hoplites, a reassuring 'middle class' who could afford armour and weapons and the rowers who could afford nothing. Thus, when Thucydides describes the huge numbers wiped out by the plague in the early years of the Peloponnesian War, he counts casualties among the knights, hoplites and 'mob' separately. However, this attempt to divide up the Athenians also has its failings. The military classes were not the exclusive preserve of particular groups. There is evidence for poor hoplites, who must have borrowed their equipment, as early as the fifth century and both rowing and hoplite warfare are considered the common experience of comedy's audience, part and parcel of war. Moreover, military categories are rarely referred to in civilian life and with the singular exception of the young men of aristocratic pretensions and long hair who formed the cavalry, military categories do not seem to fit any coherent or consistent social or political grouping.[16]

Another division popular among modern historians lies between those who performed state-services, called *leitourgiai* 'liturgies' (which only become specifically religious services in later Greek) and those who did not. The liturgical class was itself divided for much of the fourth century, with the heaviest burden falling on a core group of about three hundred very rich men with property of at least three (?) talents. These were backed up by a larger group of twelve hundred to two thousand men with property of at least one (?) talent and a rather lighter share of the city's financial burdens. However, although services to the state were naturally invoked on many occasions in public speeches, it was properties not people who were *defined* by their ability to support liturgies and there is little evidence for the tax-payers forming a self-conscious class. It is true that Demosthenes describes one member of this elite, a certain Meidias, reminding his audience at every opportunity, 'We are the performers of liturgies, we are the tax-payers, we are the rich', but this is probably a pompous 'we' singular and the statement is designed to characterize Meidias' exceptional arrogance and hypocrisy. In fact, says Demosthenes, Meidias had a rather mediocre record as far as his services to the state were concerned, especially in comparison with himself, for Demosthenes was among the wealthiest of this very wealthy group although he shows no sign here or elsewhere of class solidarity.

In the absence of any obvious cleavage in Athenian treatments of the citizenship and in the face of these competing and often conflicting categorizations, some historians have started talking about a 'leisure class'. This is the group of people with enough property to free them from having to earn a living. The leisure class has one advantage over other groupings, inasmuch as it is treated as a natural and automatic class which needs no ancient label or tag to call it into existence. Because of their 'leisure lifestyle' these men just are different whether or not this difference is acknowledged by themselves and their fellow-citizens. They might be identified with those who are called the 'rich' and with the broader group of the liturgy-payers, those twelve hundred to two thousand men with property of at least one talent. The remainder of the population can be called 'poor' because they do not fall into this category.

This view of Athenian society shows the influence of the sociologist Thorstein Veblen, whose *Theory of the Leisure Class* was published in 1899. Veblen is most famous for his notion of 'conspicuous consumption' and much of his work concerns the semiotics of elitism, the signs by which aristocrats mark themselves out from the rest of the population. Veblen thought leisure the most crucial element in the formation of social hierarchies, providing a key to the language of aristocratic display. Only the elite could afford to do no work and to sustain wastefulness. It was not enough, however, to be useless in private. They needed to advertise the fact constantly. They had to do nothing conspicuously.

The Greeks themselves were not unaware of this kind of logic. Aristotle, for instance, notes that wearing the hair long like the Spartans and their admirers 'is the mark of a free man [*eleutherou*] for it is not easy to do any menial [*thētikon*] work with long hair'. Long hair, however, was rare in Athens and, as we have seen, there is not much sign of the ostentation we find among elites in other societies. Demosthenes thought that this was beginning to change in his time with politicians building more lavish houses, but in truth his account of one of the worst of these offenders, Meidias, shows how pathetic the Athenians were at showing off even towards the end of the classical period: 'He has built a house in Eleusis big enough to over-shadow his neighbours, he drives his wife to the Mysteries and any-where else he wishes, with a pair of white Sicyonian horses, he swaggers about the agora with three or four attendants, reeling off his deep cups, his drinking-horns, his saucers.' Demosthenes may have exaggerated a little but even so Meidias, one of the most con-spicuous consumers of his time, would not have caused the slightest stir among the elites of other societies, 'Only three or four servants? Only one house? Not in Athens but in Eleusis? With neighbours!' Among the rich and nouveaux-riches of Athens there were some show-offs who built bigger houses, some even with a couple of pillars outside the front door, but as I have tried to show throughout this book Athenian energies were not generally absorbed in splendour at all.[17]

It could be argued that expenditure on more ephemeral things like food, drink and sex is even more appropriate for Veblenian analysis, a pleasure class rather than a leisure class. The money Callias spent on one of his parties for all his flatterers, philosophers and friends, with all the fish-dishes and kraters of wine, the flute-girls and harp-pluckers and acrobats, was money he would never see again. Callias, perhaps, thought he was just being generous, but this was also a way of displaying his wealth to other rich Athenians and to visitors from all over Greece. We hear very little about his house, by contrast, which was so small that in *Protagoras* (315d) he has to clear out a storeroom to make room for all the sophists he has staying with him, but his parties made such an impression on contemporaries that Plato and Xenophon were still writing about them half a century after the tables had been cleared. Equally splendid dinners were still being held at the end of the fourth century, one of which, given by the orator Xenocles, was immortalized in Matro's Homeric parody *The Attic Dinner* 'Threw I to the floor prickle-tressed sea-urchins, which echoed as they rolled between the feet of slaves and on to the open floor ... many were the spines I pulled out, roots and all'; 'And having tasted I wept that I would see such things no more tomorrow, but must make do with cheese and barley-bread roll, ever-at-hand.'[18]

There are, however, just as many problems with the notion of the leisure class as there are with other attempts to classify Athenians. An ideological divide concerning work is to be found not at the top of the scale but at the bottom. The Athenian elite held on to their lands but did not share the abhorrence of business and trade in general that characterize many landed aristocracies. On the other hand there seems plenty of evidence that the cycle of agricultural labour gave very many poor Athenians leisure enough to participate in the democracy and that they shared with the rich a distaste for certain kinds of paid service or workshop labour of a 'slavish' nature. Among the manuscripts of Demosthenes is a speech written for one Euxitheus whose mother had worked as a wet-nurse and sold ribbons in the market-place, evidence enough it seems for his fellow-demesmen to have deprived him of his citizen status. He appeals to the jury: 'Poverty often forces free men to do slavish things, but it would be fairer to pity them than to destroy them. For I have heard of many women, citizen women, who became wet-nurses and loom-workers and grape-pickers because of the disasters suffered by the city in those times, and many of them are rich now, having left poverty behind.' We are more justified in identifying a 'menial class', who made themselves conspicuous by working alongside slaves, at the bottom of the pile than a 'leisure class' at the top. Even the 'pleasure class' with its lavish banquets and wastefulness, at first sight the least objectionable category of all, begins to look a rather fragile grouping if we stare at it for any length of time. Indeed its very obviousness is a fault. For what is it other than the product of a meaningless tautology: that those who enjoy expensive things must belong to the class of those who can afford them? For most Athenians, as we will see, that begs a lot of questions, and there is more surely to class-consciousness than this. Although a rich man may be able to afford more eels than other Athenians, more and better wine, and more and more exclusive women, there is no indication that these relative advantages add up to an absolute distinction that separates him from the rest of the population. There is no sign that these quantitative differences ever amount to a qualitative rift.[19]

It is second nature to modern historians, as it was second nature to ancient philosophers, to see social structure as the key to every society, a corollary, perhaps, of the automatic importance granted to economic factors in historical causation, but what this brief survey demonstrates at the very least is that there is little agreement about how to divide the Athenians into socio-economic groups and even less agreement about how particular individuals might be assigned to them. Other historians, historians of the city-states of Renaissance Italy or Britain in any period, not to speak of Roman historians, have little difficulty identifying elites and can spend their scholarly energies investigating how they maintained their pre-eminence in the face of new situations. Greek historians, in contrast, are still stuck on the starting-line. However, the difficulty involved in getting a fix on class in Athens should not be seen as a problem; it is an important feature of Athenian culture.

We can divide this characteristic 'class confusion' into three parts. First, it seems undeniable that our sources make a contribution, operating a kind of deliberate, even ideological class blindness. The threat of *stasis* (civil strife of any kind) terrified the Greeks in all periods and much political philosophy and many laws were devoted to avoiding it. The Athenians were no different. They were hostile to the very notion of a divided citizenry and in the law-courts and on stage they talk and act as if their audience is a homogeneous group of well-to-do citizens, whose minor differences are overwhelmed by the great gulf that separates them from women, slaves and foreigners. Aristophanes, for instance, often puts in one family characters who seem to belong to quite separate socio-economic groups and creates single characters, like Dicaeopolis in *Acharnians* or Trygaeus in *Peace* who seem to belong to several classes at once. Demosthenes, too, one of the richest men of his time, identifies unself-consciously with the masses whom he refers to as 'us'. At another level, it seems clear that many Athenians played along with this ideology in practical terms, the rich (with one or two exceptions) accepting limits on their ostentation, eschewing too grandiose houses and too conspicuous clothes, the thetes, similarly, refusing to acknowledge their thetic status when allotted a magistracy, taking it out on those among them whose lifestyle approached that of slaves and when allotted to the archonship or a jury loyally forswearing any redistribution of property, a measure against political factionalism as well as class antagonism: 'The first thing the archon does on entering upon his office is to proclaim that each man shall keep until the end of his term whatever he possessed before it.' Finally, however, it seems undeniable that this ideological class blindness had a practical effect in lowering class-consciousness among the Athenians. Economic disparity may have been what family counsellors call 'an elephant in the living room' of this citizen family, a big matter that is never addressed directly, but this reticence seems to have been quite a successful strategy and Athens managed to avoid serious civil strife and class war.[20]

The Athenians were assisted in their indifference by some structural factors that prevented the gap between rich and poor becoming apparent too often. Like species in nature, groups in a society can be recognized both by their internal homogeneity and by differences that keep them apart from other groups. Thanks in part to the democratic revolution, Athenians were not identified by family (*genos*) name at all, but by their father's name and the deme or diocese in which they were registered. Names were often passed down within a family, but the omission of a *genos*-label must have made it much more difficult to recognize family relationships between rich men and to identify wealthy families rather than wealthy individuals. Even if blood-relationships had been more transparent, it is not certain that a common lifestyle would have materialized with it. In fact, there is evidence that many Athenians had relatives by blood or marriage who were much richer or poorer than themselves. The man Timarchus accuses of being a former slave, for instance, is too poor to pay the orator off himself (a fact that may have persuaded his fellow-demesmen to disfranchise him in the first place) but he has a brother-in-law who can pay thirty minas and Timarchus himself has an uncle so poor he has to receive state welfare. Moreover, as mentioned in the last chapter, there is evidence for a high turnover in the ranks of the wealthy exacerbated by the vicissitudes of war. The result is that in Athens from the time of the Peloponnesian War onwards, there seems to have been a rather loose relationship (and getting looser all the time) between hierarchies of wealth, status and power, rather feeble links within those hierarchies and a rather inefficient perpetuation of these advantages from one generation to another. What homogeneity there was might be obscured by the democracy's insistence on identifying each citizen as an individual. Under these circumstances, it is not surprising if there was a rather unstable sense of elite identity at Athens.[21]

Moreover, thanks to the large numbers of slaves and the high proportion of small-holders who owned and farmed their own land (*autourgoi*), disputes between citizen factory-workers and citizen proprietors, say, or between citizen landowners and their citizen tenants or labourers, which are such an important source of class-consciousness in other periods, were rare in Athens. The citizens were not economically very integrated, but formed a series of discrete, highly autarkic economies in parallel throughout the countryside, an economic self-sufficiency that provides the background for the emphasis in Greek morality on being master of oneself. There were few ruptures along this socio-economic continuum, few points where differences became hierarchies. The exceptions, again, were those citizens who worked for others in the city, but they were few in number and despised by the independent peasant farmers of the countryside, whose poverty they shared. The polis itself stood between rich and poor, almost monopolizing relations between the two groups. It was the polis that took money from the former in the form of liturgies. It was the city that eased the misfortunes of the latter by means of various subsidies (Assembly-pay, jury-pay, payment for attendance at festivals) and occasional public banquets.

Many of the references to class in comedy and oratory turn out, on closer examination, to refer to something much more vague or to something quite different. Class antagonism was displaced by (or transposed on to) safer divisions. The main lines of distinction in the Athenian citizen-body, if comic poets and orators are to be believed, were drawn between younger and older generations, the countryman and the city-dweller and, above all, the speakers and the spoken to. One speaker talks as if there is an unspoken contract at Athens between the young and the old: You are like a family, he says, of different generations and different interests.

The younger members of the family try at least to be modest and discreet in what they do, while the older generation if they see them spending too much or drinking too much or taking fun too far, pretend not to notice . . . It's the same with you, men of Athens, you live together in a generous familial community. Sometimes you observe the activities of men who get into trouble, and as the saying goes, though you see, you don't see, though you hear, you don't hear.[22]

Often these various divisions are conveniently amalgamated. A number of comedies pitch extravagant and/or sophisticated and sophistic young men against their rude crude penny-pinching fathers, including Aristophanes' *Clouds*, *Wasps* and perhaps the *Banqueters*. The greed and pretensions of political leaders and the gullibility of the led provide the theme for many others. By the late fifth century references to 'gentlemen', 'noble men' (*gennaioi*) and 'worthies' identify particular modes of behaviour more often than they label particular groups. It is a matter of being respectable, of avoiding what is slavish (including 'slavishness with regard to one's appetites') or uncouth, of 'classiness' rather than 'class'. It is always dangerous to read too much into Aristophanes' images, but it is interesting that in both the *Banqueters* and *Wasps*, we find lessons in airs and graces as if they are things one can be taught rather than things one is born to. Gentility is no longer the prerogative of the aristocracy. Anyone can learn to be effete.

The emphasis in Athenian comedy on eating, drinking and sex can be seen as part and parcel of this blindness to social and economic divisions, this class-unconsciousness. Far from pointing up divisions in Athenian society, references to the pleasures of the flesh most often serve to remind the audience how much they have in common. Instead of dwelling on the fact that some may only be able to afford fish once or twice in a good year, while others have sea bass every day for breakfast, the Athenians focused on the shared moment of pleasure. These are animal passions shared by all mankind, a common denominator of baser instincts, enticements which all need to resist, temptations to which anyone may succumb. Poor men liked to drink as much as Alcibiades or Alexander and knew as well as them the pain of the morning after. Some might drink in bars and some in well-appointed *andrōn*s, but all knew the pleasures of wine and the dangers when it was not mixed with water. Hetaeras feature in the lives of ordinary Athenians like Trygaeus in Aristophanes' *Peace* as well as in the complicated ménages of men like Hyperides and Alcibiades, but sex, at any rate, is the same whether it's with flute-girls, Thracian servants, or the women in the brothel at the city gate. When fish are paraded on the Attic stage, the whole audience is assumed to be slavering over them and even slaves could be accused of *opsophagia*. It is the simplicity of these pleasures that is the important thing. On the comic stage men are motivated by the petty objectives of mundane appetites. Pericles gets worked up over some whores, issues decrees that sound like drinking-songs and starts the Peloponnesian War. Cleon can barely tear himself away from a nice plate of squid when he is called to speak before the Assembly. Lysander is persuaded to join an alliance by a bigger cup of wine. Behind high-minded principles and high-flown words lie base gluttony and simple lust. In comedy's perspective, the assemblies of the world are moved by bodily functions common to all mankind.[23]

Moreover, reversing the formula that expensive things are the prerogative of those rich enough to afford them, we must remember how cheap it could be to participate in the world of pleasure. Anybody could save up his state-payments for a nice piece of fresh fish, a *kotylē* of imported wine, a quickie with a flute-girl down on her luck, a few minutes in a cubicle with a philosophical aristocrat from Elis unhappily enslaved in war. The market-place was viewed as a demotic space, a zone of participation. The market for sex, for wine, for fine foods was a complex system with a range of prices from very low to very high and something for everyone in between. If sea bass was too expensive, you could still be a consumer of sprats. If flute-girls were beyond you, at two drachmas, you could always go to a cheap brothel and pay one obol instead. What separated you from the better 'goods' was merely a few coins you happened to be lacking that day, not your status. Moreover, apart from these numerous qualitative distinctions there was also the quantitative element, which is so apparent particularly in the discourse of food. This is one reason why long lists are such a feature of comic descriptions of the lavish banquet. A skilful novelist of the 'sex and shopping' genre of novel popular in the 1980s could suggest an opulent dinner-party in just a few words: Krug, beluga, lobster, foie gras. An Athenian like Matro trying to do the same thing needs forty or fifty lines to count out the costliness, item by item. Proper extravagance can only be represented in the proliferation of detail. If the rich are different in Athens, the difference is one of degree. What this means is that there is a continuum of consumption that parallels the socio-economic continuum. There are few ruptures to break it up into distinctive lifestyles. According to the same logic, the individual consumer is safe eating one slice of tuna or drinking one glass of wine. The danger lies in losing control, but that was a danger that applied to all men, rich or poor.

In fact, in the Greek obsession with self-control we can see the relationship between class and consumption completely inverted. The true gentleman manages his appetites. He is in charge of himself. Unlike Timarchus who is enslaved to vices 'that no free or noble man should ever submit to', or vulgar Cleon who wolfs his food and downs his wine in one, the man of refinement takes time to sip and intersperses his drinking with water and conversation. It was one of the great themes of philosophers and orators that though rich men seem to have nothing to do with the servants who surround them, in reality those who consume immoderately are the true slaves, being slaves to their appetites. It is the profligate and the incontinent who really engage in menial tasks as they are for ever running back and forth trying to fill their leaky jars of desire. The life of *kinaidoi* may seem to be given over to pleasure and self-indulgence, but it is not only 'terrible and shameful', it is also 'a struggle' (*athlios*).[24]

WHERE MONEY LIES

When the Athenians did connect pleasure with property the sources reveal a very different logic from Veblen's displays of wealth. The kind of consumption that went on in the men's room may have been supremely wasteful, but it failed for that reason to be conspicuous for any length of time. When all the fish-bones had been cleared from

the floor, when the flute-girls had gone home, there was little to
show for all the money that had been spent and not everyone could
rely on a Plato, a Xenophon, a Eupolis or a Matro to immortalize
the evening in poetry or prose. The important thing about the famous
and much-copied work called the *Unswept Hall*, by the Hellenistic
mosaicist Sosos, is not only that it represents a triumph of art over
nature, but that it preserves an ephemeral residue for posterity,
making a monument out of the inconsequential, a triumph of art
over time. As well as being short-lived, the symposium was also a
rather secret display to a limited group of invited guests in the closed
world of the *andrōn*. For a Veblenian aristocrat such invisible waste
was a waste. For an Athenian, however, concealment was its main
attraction. This was a discreet way of spending money, inconspicuous
consumption, for it did not pay to advertise your wealth in Athens.

The Athenians had a very simple and direct way of managing
public finance. Those rich enough to be eligible were obliged to pay
taxes when the state needed the money and to support the costs of
performances at religious festivals (*chorēgiai*) and ships of war (*trierarchies*) on a regular basis. There were numerous such burdens, about
one hundred festival liturgies a year and a fleet of several hundred
ships. To sponsor a dithyrambic chorus or a group of pyrrhic war-
dancers might cost no more than a few hundred drachmas, a trilogy
of tragedies at the great festival of Dionysus considerably more, while
a single trierarchy could reduce by as much as one talent a rich man's
estate. No one had to undertake more than one liturgy a year, but
there were so many that they came around with great regularity and
anyone who curried favour with the people was obliged to do more
than the technical requirement. The city rewarded with crowns and
honorary decrees liturgists who performed their services to the state
with distinction. Victories in the dramatic competitions should be
looked at in the same light. Those who worry that some excellent
classical dramas came last in competition (Euripides' *Medea*, for
instance, or Aristophanes' *Clouds*) should remember that it might
be the sponsor who was being penalized for cost-cutting on the
costumes, not the playwright for the play.

An account of their liturgies was a useful source of credit for rich
men who became involved in court-cases. Demosthenes himself, of

course, was far too modest to remind his audience of 'the trieremes I have subsidised, the choruses I have sponsored, the taxes I have paid, the prisoners-of-war I have ransomed and other such acts of generosity I have performed', but others were not so reticent. Among the speeches of Lysias is a peroration he wrote at the end of the fifth century for a man defending himself from a completely unrelated charge, who lists everything he has done for the city, seemingly from the time he received his inheritance: 3000 drachmas on tragedy, 2000 for a chorus at the festival of Apollo and Artemis for which he won a victory, 800 drachmas on pyrrhic war-dancers at the Great Panathenaea, 5000 on a victorious male chorus at the Dionysia, 300 on a dithyrambic chorus at the Little Panathenaea, six talents on trierarchies, plus 1200 drachmas on games for the festival of Prometheus, 1500 on a children's chorus, 1600 on a comedy by Cephisodorus who won the competition in 404/3 and 700 on a chorus of beardless pyrrhic dancers. Moreover, he performed his trierarchies zealously:

> . . . and I will tell you the surest proof of the fact: Alcibiades was on board my ship, initially at least . . . Now I am sure you must know that because he was general he could do whatever he wished and would never have gone on any but the best ship afloat . . . and when you removed the generals from office . . . it was my ship their replacements wanted to sail on . . . How much money, I ask you, do you think so well-equipped a ship must have cost? How much damage must she have done to the enemy? How much benefit did she render the city?

Our friend Apollodorus seems to have performed his trierarchies particularly extravagantly, offering the highest rates of pay and equipping the ship 'as beautifully and splendidly' as possible, even making sure he paid all his war taxes before he left. His successor in the job asked whether he had gilded the rigging as well (I wonder if this was the ship recorded in dockyard accounts with the name *Truphōsa*, 'Decadent'). As the son of a slave who made a great fortune from banking, Apollodorus thought he had something to prove.[25]

Of course there were many who did not perform so enthusiastically and tried to dodge the responsibilities of wealth. They might find their lack of generosity equally well advertised by their enemies. Dicaeogenes, a descendant of Harmodius the tyrant-slayer, but falling far short of his ancestor in his value to the state, had been awarded a property by the people in a court-case, but did not do his bit for them in return: 'He sponsored a chorus for his tribe at the Dionysia and came fourth; he sponsored a set of tragedies and pyrrhic dancers and came last. These were the only liturgies he undertook – was forced to undertake, and this is how well he performed them, despite his large income.' In 392 Dicaeogenes' meanness became a matter of public record when 'his name was on a list set up in front of the statues of the tribal heroes, the list of men who did not keep their promise to contribute to the war effort, the list headed: "These are the men who promised the people they would make a voluntary contribution for the salvation of the city and paid nothing." '[26]

The liturgies gave the Athenian people an interest in private property that landowners or would-be landowners encouraged. Rivals for an estate often focus their arguments on how well they will manage the estate for the city, how many liturgies they will undertake and how few their opponents will support (thanks to their vices) if granted the title, as much as on any technical right:

[Thrasyllus] served as a trierarch year after year without intermission, not simply going through the motions, but making the best provision possible and you, in return, remembered what he had done, voting honours to him and rescuing his son when his property was being taken away from him . . . Apollodorus himself [Thrasyllus' son, not Neaera's scourge] did not register a low value for his property, as Pronapes did [the husband of the rival claimant] . . . in the belief that you deserved to get nothing out of it, but he organized his assets without subterfuge [phanera] and performed whatever services you assigned to him . . . thinking he should spend on himself only moderate amounts and preserve the rest for the city, so that it might have sufficient for its expenses.

Athens rejected the revolutionary redistribution of property that was often vaunted and occasionally carried out in other Greek cities and wholesale confiscations were rare, but on the other hand the liturgic system combined with endless property cases judged before popular courts made the Athenians think that they were not only the ultimate arbiters of ownership, but in some way remote owners of these estates as well, with a right to feel aggrieved if their assets were being mismanaged. There was in fact a law against dissipation of patrimony, the *graphē argias* and perhaps the *graphē paranoias*. We do not find many references to its actual use, but Lysias wrote two speeches for such suits at the turn of the fifth century and Euxitheus uses the existence of the law to attack those who attack market-traders, thus proving that the law was still considered in use in the second half of the fourth century. Athenians of the classical period thought the law a very ancient one. In one of his speeches Lysias claimed that Draco at the end of the seventh century had laid down the death penalty for such negligence, which Solon at the beginning of the sixth had commuted to a heavy fine. Plutarch must be thinking of this when he claims that Solon ordered the Areopagus to establish a regular inquisition into 'how each man afforded his lifestyle and to punish the idle', reminding us of the close link between 'dissipation' and 'laziness'.[27]

Despite the importance of the contribution the rich made to the state, the state did very little to assess property accurately or even to record who owned what. There was no land registry and taxation seems to have been based on self-assessment, giving opportunities for cheating as the speaker observes of Pronapes in the speech above. Those selected to pay for festivals and trierarchies could object that it was not their turn or nominate someone else to do it, threatening an exchange of properties (*antidosis*) if he refused. This extraordinary procedure seems to be another example of the eccentricity of the Athenian constitution, but its logic was impeccable, effectively calling the bluff of someone who claimed they were too poor to help the people. As with the torture of slaves for information, the threat was usually sufficient in itself and we don't know of any exchanges that were definitely completed, although some were definitely initiated. The very fact that such an extreme measure could be contemplated underlines the strange separation of the wealthy from their wealth in Athens and reminds us that it was properties and not people that really constituted the 'liturgical class'.[28]

This typically Athenian combination of great public interest and a great dearth of public information is what puts wealth under scrutiny in the first place. How wealthy you *seemed* was the most significant factor in determining whether you would be taxed, whether your self-assessment would be contested, whether the archon would ask you to perform liturgies, whether someone might challenge you to an exchange of properties. Aristophanes gives a striking example of what it was like to be so closely scrutinized in his fourth-century satire *Wealth*. The god Wealth has at last recovered his sight and begun to bestow his favours on those who truly deserve them, transforming the fortunes of just men. Immediately a *sykophant* comes sniffing around a good man newly enriched: 'Where did you get this cloak from?' he asks intimating law-suits for theft. 'Yesterday I saw you wearing a poor man's tunic.' Isocrates, whose success as a teacher of rhetoric had not gone unnoticed and who inevitably found himself challenged to a property exchange, claimed that 'Now a man must defend himself from a charge of being rich as if it were the greatest felony . . . it has become much more dreadful to be suspected of being well-off than to be caught red-handed doing wrong.' The people's gaze was directed towards the private lives of citizens in the first place not to show how the other half lived and to provoke envy, but simply to see where money was. As Dionysus observes in *Frogs*, the man who dresses in rags and refuses to pay taxes reveals his true worth at the fish-stalls, making purchases that belie his poverty.[29]

Despite the emphasis on signs therefore we are far from Veblen's conspicuous ostentation. The rich are not displaying their status through spending, it is their uncontrolled appetites that accidentally give them away, a rather different balance in the relationship between signs and signified: instead of Veblen's semiotics of elitism, we have the epistemology of wealth. This epistemological priority is reflected in the way the Athenians distinguished between different classes of property, talking normally not of movable and immovable or real and personal property but of 'visible and invisible' property, the latter category treated with great suspicion as presenting opportunities to defraud the people. Sharing out the land is straightforward, says Blepyrus, contemplating the communist state of Aristophanes' *Women in Power*, but what about 'silver and Persian coins, the invisible wealth?' Archaeologists have lots of evidence for this kind of property.

Almost all the ancient coins to be found in modern museums and private collections come from deposits deliberately hidden away in antiquity, making this ancient tax-dodger's conjuring trick the very foundation of the modern discipline of numismatics. The god Wealth is terribly nervous of going into a stranger's house thanks to bitter experience: 'If I happened to enter the house of a skinflint he dug a hole straightaway and buried me in it; and if some worthy friend came up to him and asked for a little bit of money he'd deny he'd ever even seen me.' There were large numbers of such hoards throughout the Greek world, buried to avoid the attention of invading armies or the covetous city as well as unfortunate friends, and the secret 'pot of gold' plays a role in the plots of several ancient comedies. The fact that all this vanished wealth is only now, thousands of years later, seeing the light of day shows how effective hoarding could be, although the fact that it is archaeologists and not the owners who are digging it up means that the strategy must to some extent have backfired.[30]

Again, this lack of proper information was a double-edged sword. Some rich men successfully feigned poverty and were able to keep their money to themselves. Others could not shake off a reputation earned during a rare and exceptional visit to the fish-stall or from being seen with an expensive girlfriend or an expensive philosopher in tow, and found themselves faced with taxes they could not possibly afford: 'I don't think it is right, men of the jury . . . to ruin us unjustly. I have been told by my father and others of the older generation that on many previous occasions you have been deceived in a question of property, not only in this case. Men you thought were rich while they were alive were shown to be quite the opposite at their deaths.' This still small voice of reason, however, seems to have fallen on deaf ears. In the absence of any better information the inexact science of snooping on people's private life was bound to be a major part of wealth-assessment in Athens, giving gossip and prejudice a free rein.[31]

We must bear in mind, however, that property was considered very fluid in democratic Athens and the vicissitudes of financial fortunes were acknowledged by many men who got up to speak before the people. Scrutiny of the private lives of citizens revealed where money was, but more importantly it played a role in charting money's course, showing where it had come from, where it was going. The orators tend to calculate a man's wealth by narrating what had happened to it over several generations, using a series of snap-shots taken on those occasions when it briefly surfaced in wills, liturgical services, sales and court-cases. Aeschines goes back as far as Timarchus' grandfather when telling the tale of his property. A citizen's wealth is but a frozen moment at the end of a long sequence of events. Consumption plays a role in these narratives sometimes by making invisible money briefly visible but more importantly in making property disappear. Consumption is not just a sign of wealth, but an important event in wealth's history, usually the grand finale. Estates are spirited away in self-indulgence. They are *opsophaged* away, drunk away, consumed in passions for boys, as we saw in the previous chapter. This kind of thinking which ends up linking consumption not with wealth at all, but with *impoverishment*, imagines appetites working directly on patrimony, eating up estates, a curiously inert view of property or a curiously exaggerated view of appetite or, most often, a curious blend of both. In a speech of Demosthenes, for instance, Mantitheus denies having sold his share in the family house to Crito, because Crito could not have bought it: 'and you will easily see that his evidence is false. In the first place he does not live with sufficient moderation to buy someone's house, quite the contrary. His way of life is so extravagant and profligate that he uses up not only his own property but those of others too.' The same argument appears in reverse, that if someone inherited a large property and does not have any expensive vices they must have converted it into cash and hidden it. The speaker of Isaeus 5, for instance, uses the fact that Dicaeogenes does not have a mad passion for horses as evidence that he is stingy rather than poor and has simply rendered his visibles invisible and salted them away.[32]

Much of the discourse of private consumption, therefore, plays not on class antagonism, but on a more direct conflict between public and private uses of private wealth. An inheritance dissipated in vices is not only lost to the individual and to his family, his heirs and rival claimants, it is also lost to the city. That banquet could have paid for a trireme. All the money wasted on hetaeras could have gone on festivals to honour the gods instead. 'You are a rich man, Demosthenes,' Aeschines jeers, 'and you perform liturgies – sponsoring the festival of your own pleasures.' 'The greatest liturgy one can perform for the city', says another speaker whose catalogue of services may have been rather short, 'is to live day by day a life of discipline and self-control.'[33]

APPETITE AND CRIME

Aeschines neglects none of these arguments when he places Timarchus' private life under public scrutiny. His inheritance was large enough to support liturgies but he spent it on private self-indulgence rather than on the state (and if people asked why, since the property was so valuable, his father had not performed liturgies himself, the answer is that his father of course had made his property invisible to avoid them). Secondly, because of his vices he prostituted himself and squandered his entire estate, reducing himself to poverty. Thirdly he made himself so poor that this man who inherited so much was forced to rely on corruption and embezzlement. The final part of this rake's progress linking profligacy to misconduct was not Aeschines' invention and is a very common theme in disputes over property. Numerous speakers stood up before the people to claim that their enemies, having got through their own resources, were now turning their attention to the property of others, pursuing unjust claims when they had no legitimate title or resorting to *sykophantia* and false testimony (*pseudomarturia*). The need to pay for his profligacy is what has led Crito falsely to claim to have bought Mantitheus' share in the house. It forces Neaera to extort money from unsuspecting foreigners. It leads Timarchus to accuse someone falsely of being a former slave. It causes the brothers Nausimachus and Xenopeithes to seek more money than is their due from their guardians' estate. In fact so common is this charge of funding one's incontinence through unjust claims that Thrasyllus thinks it an example of Apollodorus' public-spiritedness that he didn't.[34]

This linkage of errant appetite and criminality, reminiscent in many ways of the nineteenth century's view of the perils of drinking or our own view of pilfering, self-prostituting drug-addicts, was not confined to the particular context of property disputes or even to the law-courts and is part of a more general way of thinking that sees crime as the result of straitened circumstances. The strange anomaly that in a city ruled by the common people, the lowest class was officially barred from holding office derives most probably from this logic. Of course thetes should not hold office; the temptation to take bribes and steal money would be too great for a poor man. Many of those passages from comedy which seem to use consumption to mark out class distinctions turn out to depend on this understanding of the causes of crime. In Alexis' *Heiress* the poor man who is seen buying eels is arrested because he must be a 'cloak-snatcher' (an ancient version of mugging, usually taking place late at night and often involving violence). The summary arrest is the same penalty as if he had been caught red-handed actually committing the crime. The same reasoning lies behind the Corinthian law in Diphilus' *Merchant*: 'If someone has no property whatsoever, but does have an extravagant lifestyle, they hand him over to the public executioner . . . for his way of life must of necessity involve some crime, do you understand. He is bound to spend his nights cloak-snatching, or digging through walls [burglary], or he must be in league with those who do, or play the *sykophant* in the Agora, or give false testimony.' This is what worries Blepyrus about the revolution of Aristophanes' *Women in Power*. You won't get people to put their resources into a common pot, he says. They will lie about their wealth, even on oath, since bearing false witness is how they got the money in the first place. They will no longer have a motive, says Praxagora, the women's leader, in response; fish-slices, along with wine, cloaks and other things will be available to all from now on, so no one will have any cause to steal. That won't stop them, says Blepyrus. As it is, the men who enjoy those things are precisely the ones most inclined to theft.[35]

According to Herodotus, avoidance of crime was the motivation behind the Egyptian law on declaring one's means, a law he claimed Solon adopted into the Athenian law-code and which still remained in force under the democracy: 'this was the law that every man once a year should declare before the local governor the source of his livelihood. If he failed to do so, or was unable to prove that his living was an honest one, the penalty was death.' Amasis, the pharaoh who established the law, knew what he was talking about. As a private citizen he had been a typical jolly carefree drunk making his living from theft. When challenged by his victims he would take them off to the nearest oracle which sometimes convicted him and sometimes didn't. As a result when he found himself in control of Egypt he had little regard for the gods who had wrongly acquitted him, considering this measure a more effective means of preventing crime.[36]

This view of wealth as something changeable and fragile and rather separate from the men who owned it and this view of consumption as a warning of an individual's dangerous appetites rather than as a sign of elite membership, of imminent poverty in other words, rather than wealth, is clearly related to Athens' peculiar democratic system with its horror of internal division, its symbolic appropriations, its suspicion of riches, its weakened sense of family or clan identity. The democracy suffused Athenian society with politics but it also transformed it structurally, changing not only the composition of classes, but undermining the visibility and the very significance of socio-economic groups. Politics dominated social identity and social relations to a far greater degree than in other cultures. In Athens politics effectively was society.

The democracy, however, did not survive the coming of the Macedonians and in 318 its conquerors imposed an oligarchic regime, headed by Demetrius of Phalerum, a pupil of the Aristotelian philosopher Theophrastus. Among other measures Demetrius abolished the trierarchy and other liturgies and wealth suddenly became a less dangerous thing to have. In these new circumstances and surrounded by a new universe of kings and courtiers who favoured elites and used display to set themselves apart from commoners and each other, the artificial limits on ostentation were removed and we can see Athens falling more into line with other societies where consumption might be seen as something less hazardous, a mark of distinction, indicating not ruination and crime, but a large steady income, a source of pride even, rather than shame. It was a grandson of Demetrius of Phalerum, who stood before the Areopagus in the third century and refused to 'live a better life' on the grounds that he could pay for his extravagances very well out of his own revenues. When the Macedonian king heard what he had done, he rewarded his cheek by making him an archon. Demosthenes would have been turning in his urn.[37]

VIII

POLITICS AND POLITICIANS

TIMARCHUS ON QUEER STREET

THE GAZE OF the citizens was turned with even greater intensity on those among them who became public figures. On leaving a post, officials had to undergo *euthunai*, a review of their conduct in office, but there was also an automatic examination before the Council or a court of all those allotted to public positions before they were allowed to assume their responsibilities. The numbers involved were enormous. Each year, all five hundred members of the Council had to go through this process of scrutiny, known as *dokimasia*, as well as the nine archons and about seven hundred other officers. Needless to say most of these examinations were mere formalities. Each man was asked who his parents were, who his grandfathers were and from which deme or village they all came. He was also asked whether he was of higher than thete status in the property classification, whether he had done his military service and whether he was kind to his parents. He was obliged to support his answers with witnesses and evidence and anyone could challenge his candidacy. After hearing all the evidence and any objections, or even after hearing none, there was a vote and the candidate was accepted or rejected without any further action taken against him, but with no possibility of appeal.

One scholar has suggested that these examinations could be wide-ranging, designed to test the general character of candidates, but this view has not received much support. There is very little evidence that objections were any more common than they are at wedding ceremonies today and in consideration of the numbers involved, most candidates will have gone through on the nod. The purpose of the examination was to make sure candidates were eligible according to the most basic criteria, that they were the right age, that they were true Athenian citizens, that they were not disqualified for some reason. There might be exceptions, however, and the examination always had the potential to be a much more general scrutiny. Juries were not obliged to account for their decision against a candidate and were perfectly at liberty to reject someone they didn't like or whom they considered unworthy. In particular at the turn of the fifth century, in the aftermath of the oligarchic revolutions, these routine examinations seem to have become much more antagonistic. The speechwriter Lysias was working at precisely this period and among his works were no fewer than five written for public examinations, while in the remainder of the corpus of Attic oratory, examinations hardly feature at all. It seems clear that in all these cases suspicions of oligarchic sympathies were the main bone of contention and evidence was sought in all aspects of a man's life. One candidate has to work out a defence for his habit of wearing his hair aristocratically long.[1]

One group of citizens was automatically to be rejected. These were the *atimoi*, the disfranchised, men who were banned from participating in the democracy, unable to attend the Assembly, sit on juries, give evidence, initiate law-suits, or hold offices and who were also excluded even from entering the Agora and the temples. *Atimia* seems to have been a punishment reserved for those deemed to have transgressed their obligations as a citizen, deserters, for instance, or those who were in debt to the gods or the state for as long as they were indebted. It was also applied to magistrates convicted of misconduct, and those who had been condemned three times for giving false evidence or for dissipation (*argia*), a reminder of the public nature of private profligacy. Rejecting a candidate on the grounds of *atimia* is sometimes spoken of as a technical disqualification of narrow significance in contrast with the broader objections made against oligarchic sympathizers, for instance, and usually this was true. In most cases those deprived of their rights in this way had been through a trial and it was a straightforward matter to discover who they were, but there was a group of offenders who were deemed to incur automatic disfranchisement by their actions without any formal verdict needing to be pronounced. These included men who made illegal proposals in the Assembly, prostitutes and procurers, men who refused to divorce an adulteress and also (perhaps) those who had squandered their patrimony. A man undergoing scrutiny without any convictions or debts might still find all kinds of questions being raised about his private life.[2]

The haphazard appointments for which citizens underwent this scrutiny were not usually positions of great power in Athens. The real figures of authority, the real 'leaders' of the city were the *rhētores*, those who made speeches in the Assembly. Naturally such public figures should also be subject to public examination. There was a problem here, however. Although there was a recognizable body of citizens who were active in politics and regularly made speeches, it was not a formal group and technically any citizen could be a *rhētōr* and address the people. This was nothing less than a fundamental principle of the democracy. The *dokimasia* of the speakers, therefore, was rather different from the other examinations and everyone was assumed to be eligible unless challenged. Such challenges were issued very rarely. I know of only one certain example in the whole history of the democracy. Loss of political rights was a rather tame penalty in the battles fought between politicians, who preferred to seek exile, ruination or death for their enemies, and the grounds for disqualification were rather hard to prove. Nevertheless in 346/5 it seemed just the right kind of missile to fire at Timarchus whose exercise of his prerogatives had recently taken a most disagreeable form when he instigated a prosecution against Aeschines for misconduct on a recent peace mission to Philip.

Although speaking in the Assembly was simply another citizen privilege and was therefore already covered by the various laws on disfranchisement, it seems that there was a specific law referring to the examination of *rhētores* in particular, which clarified or emphasized the exclusion of certain kinds of miscreant. Aeschines does not hesitate to list its provisions in detail, providing his own running commentary on the significance of each. First on the list is a ban on 'the man who beats his father or his mother, or does not support them or house them'. Second is 'the man who has failed to perform his allocation of military service or has thrown away his shield in battle'.

Third is 'the man who has served as common prostitute or as an escort' (*hētairēkōs*), and finally 'the man who has squandered his patrimony or other inheritance'. Although the speech is often considered an indictment for prostitution, therefore, it is in fact a much more general demonstration that Timarchus is unfit to address the people. Aeschines devotes the largest part of his speech to the charge of *porneia*, but a substantial section and most of the actual evidence he provides, as we have seen, concerns Timarchus' squandering of his patrimony. All the way through the speech he refers to both charges and in his peroration, when he imagines the kind of men who will come forward to support Timarchus in the hope of an acquittal, he mentions not only the male prostitutes and their clients, but also the prodigal sons, listing them first. He tells the jury to dismiss each in turn: 'Tell those who have eaten up their patrimonies to go and get a job and to earn their living elsewhere', linking the charge of *argia* (laziness, dissipation) with the ban on profligate politicians.[3]

The trial of Timarchus and the *dokimasia rhētorōn* have been the subject of a great deal of scholarly interest recently. Kenneth Dover started the ball rolling when he made the indictment the starting-point for his investigation of the strange phenomenon of Greek homosexuality. Twenty or so years later it had a starring role in the work of Michel Foucault and his American followers, investigating the relationship between politics and sexuality in Athens. These studies tended to focus on the presumed sexual passivity of the male prostitute, a passivity which they connected with all kinds of negativity and Otherness:

[A]ny citizen male who became a prostitute positioned himself in a socially subordinate relation to his fellow-citizens: he lost his equal footing with them and joined instead the ranks of women, foreigners and slaves – those very bodies, receptive by definition to the administrative or pleasure-seeking projects of the masculine and the powerful, acknowledged the citizens of Athens as their rightful masters. For a male of citizen status, then, prostitution signified a refusal of the constitutional safeguards of his bodily integrity provided by the Athenian democracy; it represented a forfeiture of his birthright as an Athenian to share on an equal basis with his fellow-citizens in the government of the city. To be a prostitute meant, in effect, to surrender one's phallus – to discard the marker of one's socio-sexual precedence – and so it was, next to enslavement, the worst degradation a citizen could suffer, equivalent to voluntary effeminization.

Foucault has a slightly different variation on the same theme: what was wrong with Timarchus is that

> ... in the course of his youth [he] placed himself and showed himself to everyone in the inferior and humiliating position of a pleasure object for others; he wanted this role, he sought it, took pleasure in it, and profited from it ... What was hard for the Athenians to accept – and this is the feeling that Aeschines tries to play upon in the speech against Timarchus – was not that they might be governed by someone who loved boys, or who as a youth was loved by a man, but that they might come under the authority of a leader who once identified with the role of pleasure object for others.

These accounts depend on a very simplistic polarization of the population of Attica into adult male citizens and the Others, a polarization which is paralleled precisely in a sexual one between penetrators and penetratees. The logic is simple. The male prostitute, they assume, is a penetratee. Therefore he is Other. Therefore he cannot be a citizen.[4]

The problem with these accounts is that they completely ignore the charge of squandering patrimony (unless this is simply another form of being penetrated: 'being passive with regard to one's desires'), and base their entire argument on the precise details of sexual activity, something that Aeschines like most Athenian sources does not discuss explicitly at all. If the crucial issue in Athenian society was penetration and not prostitution, we would expect the law to say so. It is true that Aeschines does refer to someone calling Timarchus a woman, but women, according to common belief, had many vices and being penetrated was not normally considered the most important one. The normal route to effeminization in Athens lay through cowardice in battle or boldness in entering the women's quarters. It may be that there is a sub-text buried deeply beneath Aeschines' discourse about who possesses the phallus and who has lost theirs, and that this is where the real argument lies, but such a sub-text needs to be carefully uncovered, not simply assumed on the basis of observations about other societies, or Freud, or the behaviour of primates. Without that elucidation, this kind of analysis is mere guess-work.

If Aeschines had restricted himself to proving the technical grounds for disqualification without asking why, there might be some excuse to fill the gap and make occasional obscure innuendo the centrepiece of the speech, but in fact he makes a series of connections between politics, profligacy and prostitution that have received little attention. The power and effectiveness of Aeschines' argument comes from the repetition of a single powerful image, sustained throughout what is a very long speech. This is despite the fact that the two charges, of wasting his estate and of *porneia*, seem superficially quite unrelated. According to one modern account, Aeschines 'has taken a welter of stories and anecdotes reaching back to Timarchus's youth and made them fit three of the four rules set forth in the law on the scrutiny of rhetores'. Even Demosthenes thought it absurd to accuse the same man of both crimes and was going around the Agora outside the court telling everybody so. We have already seen, however, that extravagance and promiscuity can be closely connected in Greek thinking, and are embodied in degenerate figures like the *katapugōn* and the *kinaidos*. Far from taking haphazard pot-shots at Timarchus, Aeschines makes a great effort to bring the charges together, elaborating through the speech a coherent characterization of a man of unbridled appetite, a profligate body.[5]

It is Timarchus' uncontrollable self-indulgence that is the hero of Aeschines' narrative. This is what drives him to sell both himself and his property: when approached by the notorious lover of cithara-boys, Misgolas, who offered him a sum of money for moving in, 'Timarchus agreed without hesitation though he had plenty of money for a moderate lifestyle. His father had left him a large property, which he has eaten up as I will demonstrate in the course of my speech; but he behaved as he did because he was enslaved to the most shameful vices, to *opsophagia* and expensive dinner-parties and flute-girls and hetaeras and dice and those other vices that a free and noble man should not submit to.' Timarchus did not haggle over his virtue for long, of course, but that readiness is a direct consequence of his impatient desire for pleasure and finds a precise echo in the fact that he later sold his property off without waiting to realize its true value. In Aeschines' argument both prostitution and dissipation are merely side-effects of Timarchus' desperate attempts to satisfy other desires. Like the Corinthians who deduce that a poor man who buys fish must be a cloak-snatcher, Aeschines deduces Timarchus' prostitution from his extravagance:

> What must we say, when a young man of quite extraordinary looks leaves his father's house and spends the night at the homes of other men, when he dines out at lavish dinner-parties without making any contribution, when he keeps flute-girls and the most expensive hetaeras, and goes gambling, without paying anything for it, what must we think, when someone else picks up his tab? Do we need a seer to read the signs for us? Is it not as plain as day that a man with such expenses must, of necessity, be giving pleasures in return to those who pay them off?[6]

It is true that Aeschines alludes to what went on between Timarchus and his clients, implying he did not mind what he was paid to do and was only too ready to have 'the thing done to him', but there is no reason to add domination into the equation or some profound socio-sexual dichotomy. Aeschines emphasizes that Timarchus was simply careless of his body. Reflecting only on what he will spend the money on, he lies back and thinks of flute-girls. He even 'defiled' himself with a public slave, apparently quite a wealthy one, 'thinking only of getting him to sponsor his degeneracy'. If Aeschines sometimes hints that Timarchus enjoyed his job, he enjoyed sex itself, 'not being used as a sex-object'. He was whorish as well as a whore. Aeschines' innuendo about buggery or oral sex or whatever else he was trying to implant into his audience's mind simply contributes to the same consistent image of a profligate body, quite lacking control over its appetites and getting the money to feed them, by whatever means possible, with a hint that sometimes he was paying for one pleasure by indulging another. Such a bag of incontinent lust was a dangerous thing to have wandering around the city let alone striding around the Assembly and the Council chamber.[7]

It does not take Aeschines long to come to the political dimension of Timarchus' voracious appetites. This is the third stage of his rake's

progress, linked neatly to the other stages not by Otherness consequent upon penetration but by means of the same insistent incontinent appetites. First while he is still handsome and 'well-fleshed' he
wastes his own assets, his body, but then one day he found 'his
youthful beauty had faded and no one, as you would expect, was
any longer willing to pay, while on the other hand his lewd and
immoral nature kept on desiring the same things, and kept making
demands upon him one after the other without the slightest restraint,
so he was drawn back to that day-to-day way of living and that is
when finally he turned to gobbling up his patrimony.' Even his
ancestral estate does not supply enough to feed his appetites, however,
and we arrive at stage three. He turned on the city itself: 'Not only
did he eat up his patrimony, he consumed your property too, the
commonwealth.' By narrating Timarchus' crimes in this order,
Aeschines creates a neat image of his appetites exploding outwards,
feeding first off his own physical endowments, then off his ancestral
endowment and then off the city itself.[8]

How he made the city fund his pleasures is explained in the
next few paragraphs. Timarchus had been one of the Reckoners, the
Logistai, a review committee who examined the conduct of officials,
priests, trierarchs and so on at the end of their term of office. He
used the position, says Aeschines, to extort money from innocent
men and to receive bribes from the guilty. Next, he bought himself
the governorship of the island of Andros, a member of Athens'
maritime league, and proceeded to misuse the wives of the inhabitants, 'making of your allies an amenity for his lust' (*bdeluria*). Athens
was terribly fortunate, Aeschines continues, that no one tried to buy
the island while Timarchus was governor. Back home, he teamed
up with his degenerate associate Hegesander, already an accomplished
embezzler on his own account, to steal 1000 drachmas from the
Parthenon temple-fund. Finally he proceeded to steal money destined
to pay mercenaries at Eretria, on the island of Euboea. Aeschines
moves from his theme of selling patrimony to selling the state easily
and smoothly. One minute Timarchus is contemplating the sale of
his estate at Alopece, next it is the island of Andros, all in a vain
attempt to satisfy his decadent appetites.[9]

Aeschines has outlined for us the most straightforward path

between private consumption and the state. As the most direct route, it is also very well-trodden and there are many other examples in our speeches. In many ways it is simply the political corollary of the link between lust and crime. Private citizens pay for their insatiable desires by standing on street corners and snatching the cloaks of passersby or by initiating claims on property that isn't theirs. Profligate politicians mug the public instead. We have already seen this connection on a number of occasions. It is for the sake of 'whores and fish' that Philocrates, the main mover behind Aeschines' 'corrupt embassy', sold Athens to Philip. It plays a part in Demetrius' cheeky reply to the august Areopagus. He can afford Chian wine and beautiful hetaeras, but his judges must resort to adultery and corruption to get their pleasures. In a comedy of Timocles, two characters are discussing the corruption of various politicians, including Demosthenes and Hyperides: 'Well he will make the fishmongers rich,' says one, 'for Hyperides is an *opsophagos* so as to make Syrians of the sea-gulls' (Syrians were thought to eat no fish). In another play, the *Icarians*, the poet compares Hyperides to a noisy frothy river teeming with fish and ready to irrigate anyone's fields for a consideration. One modern study of bribery in Athens notes the evidence that 'curiously enough' the ultimate beneficiaries of corruption were often hetaeras and fishmongers.[10]

Aeschines' argument, then, connecting profligacy with corruption, was already well established. It is even found at the very beginning of the rhetorical tradition in the work of Gorgias. Demonstrating his skills as a speaker he constructs an imaginary defence of Palamedes who was stoned to death at Troy when a sum of gold (planted by Odysseus) was found in his tent. He couldn't have received bribes from Priam, claims mythical Palamedes. He had no motive. It is squanderers who need money, not moderate men like himself; those who are masters of their own pleasures have no need of bribes, but those enslaved by pleasure do. If an Athenian, then, had to account for the fact that profligates constituted one of only four groups of people named in the law on the behaviour of public speakers, it is likely he would turn to the same kind of reasoning. In fact, when the orator Isocrates explains the same law in the *Panathenaicus*, he does exactly that: 'men who have spent what they received from their fathers on shameful pleasures seek to remedy private poverty with public property.' Later in his career Aeschines returns to the theme and comes up with an even more succinct formula. A 'friend of the people' must be 'self-controlled and moderate in his way of life so that he won't take bribes to the detriment of the people, because of his indecent expenditure'.[11]

This last speech is interesting, because it leads to another set of dangers commonly ascribed to profligate politicians, this time in the area of foreign policy. The occasion is the award of a crown to Demosthenes. His vehement opposition to Philip had failed at Chaeronea in 338 and Philip's son Alexander was even now conquering Persia, but the people still hailed Demosthenes as a hero for trying his best. Aeschines, whose activities are looking more and more like appeasement in this atmosphere, does his best to put a stop to the honour-loaded bandwagon trundling in the direction of his bitterest rival. Demosthenes' hawkish policy was not for the benefit of the city, he says, it was simply designed to support his own pleasures. For Demosthenes is an abyss, a wastrel just like Timarchus fifteen years before. 'It is true that recently Persian gold has floated his extravagance, but even that won't be enough, for no fortune ever survived a bad character. In sum, he subsidises his way of life not from his own revenues but from putting you in danger.'[12]

Isocrates had made the same point in his speech *On the Peace* which also attacked hawkish imperialistic politicians who grew rich on war while the people suffered, but the most famous example of this kind of argument was in the debate on the great Sicilian expedition of 415. This mighty armada was originally conceived as a form of assistance to Athens' allies, but its ever-increasing size proved its avowed aim specious. In reality it was the first expedition of conquest the city had launched for many years and it provoked a great debate which Thucydides records in his history of the Peloponnesian War. One of the main issues was the personality of the general Alcibiades, a young and glamorous character of aristocratic background and long hair, who had been very successful in racing chariots at the Olympic games:

There may be someone here who is delighted to have been chosen for the command [says Nicias, one of the generals who opposed the expedition], someone who will urge you to make the expedition after careful consideration of his own selfish interests, not the least of them being that he is too young for the job. This someone wants to be admired for the horses he keeps in his stables, but stables are expensive and so he wants profit as well as admiration from the post. Don't hand him an opportunity to live in splendour at the city's risk. Bear in mind, that while they spend privately, it is the public that bears the cost of their misconduct.[13]

In their debates over foreign policy, both hawks and doves used the powerful image of the prodigal whose decadent desires bring disaster, warning Athens that it was squandering its patrimony by following the policy of their opponents. Isocrates compares the allure of empire to a seductive and destructive hetaera and claims the Athenians lack self-control in their greed for the pleasant words of flattering demagogues. Demosthenes, the master of this approach, makes the same point about the Athenians' decadent appetite for flattery and in numerous speeches in the Assembly he berates the Athenians for their degeneracy in order to rouse them to greater things. They have chosen the pleasure of the moment and a life of ease instead of future advantage. While politicians enrich themselves, Athens' estate is spent, for a city's wealth is measured in allies, trustworthiness, and goodwill. In one extraordinary metaphor he compares the damage inflicted on Greek states under the Athenian and then the Spartan empires to a son who wastes his patrimony through mismanagement. This is bad, he says, but at least it was their own flesh and blood. The damage Philip will do is more like an estate wasted by a supposititious bastard or a slave![14]

THE DISAPPEARANCE OF PHILIP

Philip, of course, was the big issue that Aeschines and Timarchus were fighting over. Timarchus had attempted to have Aeschines prosecuted for misconduct on a peace mission to Macedonia.

Aeschines indicted Timarchus for misconduct as a speaker to stop him. The embassy, on which Demosthenes himself had served, as well as Philocrates and Aeschines, had returned to Athens in 346 with a treaty of reconciliation. Although he had had a hand in framing the terms, Demosthenes nevertheless began to undermine the agreement almost immediately. He put the Athenians in a nervous mood and made them very suspicious of Philip's intentions, suggesting they were walking into a trap. He described the anxious atmosphere of the time in his own later indictment of Aeschines: 'Matters were in a state of suspension, it was quite unclear what the outcome would be and throughout the whole market-place there were arguments and discussions of all kinds.' By accusing one of the ambassadors of corruption at this time, Timarchus and Demosthenes were adding fuel to the fires of suspicion, implying the city had been sold out. This is the context also for Timarchus' recent speeches in the Council about 'the walls' and 'the tower'. In this nervous atmosphere this was a clear reference to preparing the city's defences in case of an attack. This is also the context for his excitable behaviour in the Assembly when he threw off his cloak and started leaping around like a gymnast. Timarchus had also proposed in the Council a measure forbidding any arms trade with Philip under pain of death. It was this in particular, says Demosthenes, that provoked Aeschines, Philip's friend.[15]

What is so remarkable about Aeschines' speech, of course, is the way this political context, the threat of Philip of Macedon, the fragile position of the city, has completely disappeared. This was a brilliant and highly effective strategy and *Against Timarchus* is even now seen as a useful document for the study of Greek homosexuality and little else. Thanks to Aeschines, for many people Timarchus is still 'Timarchus the prostitute' and some are surprised to find he was involved in politics at all. We do not have to peer very hard beneath the surface, however, to see foreign policy raising its head. By misusing the wives of the men of Andros, Timarchus was alienating Athens' allies. He did not actually betray the island for a bribe, but he would have done if an interested buyer had come along. The business in Eretria was even more serious, since it refers to an episode that led to the loss of almost the whole of Euboea, a very large island which lay right along Athens' east coast, separated from Attica only by the narrowest of channels. Without giving us too much detail, Aeschines makes a direct connection between the defendant's corruption and one of the greatest foreign policy disasters of recent years. Timarchus talks about security and defending the city, but thanks to his insatiable desires he has succeeded only in undermining it. Exactly the same pattern is found in the account of the activities of Hegesander, Timarchus' associate. He was treasurer to a general in the Hellespont, stole money from the troops' pay and then left the general to face banishment as a penalty for the (consequent) failure. The implication is that the main interest of Timarchus and his allies in fomenting war is the opportunities it will give them for pocketing more cash to feed their decadent appetites, an old charge, as we have seen, against hawkish politicians, and one that Aeschines was happy to roll out once again in an attempt to deprive Demosthenes of his crown.[16]

There are other more subtle ways in which Aeschines undermines his opponents. He is arguing that Timarchus and his associates should not be allowed to speak in public, but in the course of his speech he activates the gag himself, undermining their ability to be heard, or, if heard, to be understood. Disfranchisement is automatically applied to men who live like they do and their lifestyles have, in accordance with the law, automatically deprived them of the ability to speak. Without waiting for a court verdict, Aeschines through his speech retrospectively silences them himself. The way he does this is terribly clever. He does not ignore Timarchus' political activities, he actually puts them before our eyes. We see Timarchus speaking. We see him in the Assembly, but we cannot hear what he is saying. We are distracted by his flesh, only interested in reading signs there of drunkenness and debauchery. We see him talking in the Council, and this time we even hear fragments of his speech, but we don't understand them, interpreting these references to towers and walls as allusions not to the defence of the city but to his nights of shame. Aeschines imprisons Timarchus in an echo-chamber. He cannot make himself heard. People look at the way he dresses, the way he moves, the condition of his skin, oblivious to what emerges from his mouth. Every time he tries to get a word out it refers back to himself. His important discourse on national security and Athens' position in Greece turns into a confession of his own private sexual depravity. How can he be a speaker when his lifestyle makes his words so unstable and invites such ridicule?

One technique used by the orator here is to co-opt his audience by conjuring up mediating figures who observe Timarchus for us on these occasions. It is not merely Aeschines who sees the defendant's debauched flesh, so do many decent men in the audience who turn and look away. It is not Aeschines in the Council chamber, but the councillors who burst out laughing at this so-called 'time of crisis'. At the very end of the speech Aeschines uses this silencing trick once more distracting the jury with a game of reading visual signs instead of listening to the other side of the argument. Among the men who will come to testify in Timarchus' defence, he says, are whores, their clients, and profligates. He won't name names, but as each one comes forward, see if you can guess which one is which! It may seem risky for Aeschines to treat matters of national importance in this way, but his whole point is that there really is no great crisis. Thanks to the treaty, Philip presents no danger to Athens and men like Timarchus and Demosthenes are simply being hysterical and making themselves look ridiculous. The councillors who are relaxed enough to giggle when Timarchus is discussing repairs to the city walls have got the situation just about right.

In some ways, however, Timarchus had the last laugh. In the summer of 343 in the course of his own prosecution of Aeschines for ambassadorial misconduct, Demosthenes actually read out one of the measures the 'young man' had proposed to the Council in 346, forbidding trade in weapons or equipment with Philip on penalty of death. Aeschines, he claims, had only prosecuted Timarchus to put a stop to this thorn in the Macedonian side. After three years in which Athens' relationship with Philip had deteriorated dangerously, Timarchus' hysteria looks like amazing foresight. If they had ever been laughing in the first place, it is doubtful that anyone in the audience was laughing now.

THE BRAVERY OF BANQUETS

Trivializing the political situation is a strategy that Aeschines uses throughout the speech. The very fact that he has chosen to fight a foreign policy battle on the field of private life is tactical. Flute-girls and phalanxes, cuttlefish and cavalry, hoplites and hetaeras, wine and 'walls' simply do not go together. Oswyn Murray has argued that the culture of the banquet deliberately eschews the language of the city and politics. It has its own rules and regulations declaring UDI for the evening's duration. When these two opposed worlds are brought together the result is a subtle amalgam of irony and bathos. This is part of an old tradition, in which the world of home-life, peace and private pleasure is contrasted with the world of great affairs, deprivation and war ('[Sardanapalus'] sword is wine-casks, his spear a cup . . . His war-cry "Pour out perfume"' etc.). The two things simply do not mix. For Plutarch, we recall, it was quite impossible that someone who achieved as much as Alexander could have been drinking as much as was claimed. The theme can be traced as far back as the un-Homeric or anti-Homeric ethos of the Greek Lyric poets in the archaic age and it surfaces throughout the history of comedy. The premise of *Acharnians*, for instance, is that one particular citizen, Dicaeopolis, has made a private peace while the rest of the city is still fighting the Peloponnesian War. He enjoys a market-place full of embargoed merchandise and makes preparations for a feast while the general Lamachus gets ready for battle. In a long piece of dialogue each order to the slave for arming is answered by a cheeky order from Dicaeopolis to bring more food: 'Bring me my round gorgon-faced targe', 'Bring me my round gorgonzola-laced tart', etc. etc. etc.[17]

This clash is the key to the fragment of Antiphanes' *Rich Men* which describes the two 'veteran *opsophagoi*' using all the clichés of political discourse because they have got to the market and found no fish:

264

They gathered crowds around them and made a speech to the effect that they could not live with such a situation, that it was unendurable that some of you should be spending great sums of money to fight for marine ascendancy, while not even a bit of fish was making it into port. What was the point of having island-governors? It should be possible to pass laws to force compliance, a naval escort should be provided for the fish.

The politician Callimedon, apparently a minor figure in the 'pro-Macedonian' camp, attacked on one occasion by Demosthenes for oligarchic conspiracy, was constantly ridiculed in this way. His votes of honour come only from the fishmongers. His resolution is most apparent in his fighting at banquets for fish. Other men are prepared to die for their fatherland. Callimedon would die for a mother-pig's womb (apparently a great delicacy).[18]

THE ECONOMY OF WORDS

Of course there is sometimes a serious purpose to this linking of great affairs with little pleasures, suggesting that it is the politicians who trivialize politics by making it a mere subsidy for their enjoyment, not the orators and satirists who merely point this out. Demosthenes' jibe at Philocrates that he had sold the city and spent the money on whores and fish is part of this game, pitting the petty cravings of private life against the fate of nations. Aristophanes' juxtaposition of great debates in the Assembly with Cleon's plates of sea-food is designed to pop his self-righteous rhetoric. Timarchus' dangerous pleasures are also noticeably trivial. Andros might be sold for a gambling debt, Euboea lost for a flute-girl. The money Timarchus extorted by accusing someone falsely of being his former slave went straight on buying presents for his hetaera Philoxene. In all these cases the passions of private life reveal the true workings of the man of politics. Cleon's desperate political style is nicely illustrated by his greedy and vulgar way of eating and drinking.

Similarly, Timarchus' excessive political activity can itself be viewed as another example of his unrestrained character as well as a way of paying for it. His way of prancing around the Assembly half-naked is perfectly in tune with his immorality, exhibiting the same kind of recklessness that he shows in his impatience to satisfy his insatiable desires, revealing the same shamelessness he shows in the prostitution that pays for them. Both are examples of the general disorder of his life. Aeschines draws attention in particular to those political activities of Timarchus that led to his own indictment. Timarchus was a corrupt *Logistes*, a member of the review body that investigated magisterial misconduct, the same sub-committee, as it happens, that was to examine Aeschines' misconduct on the embassy, if Timarchus' indictment was allowed to go ahead.

The activities of the *rhētores*, speaking and even making laws, can be viewed in terms of dissipation. Words are seen as operating within a kind of economy of meaning, which is preserved through self-restraint or squandered like a patrimony. The roots of this idea go back to the fifth century where we often find an association between sophistry and degeneracy. The *katapugōn* son, it seems, in Aristophanes' *Banqueters* learnt how to use the decadent neologisms of orators like Alcibiades along with his other bad habits. His astonished father tries to identify the source of each. The poet uses the same trick in *Wasps*, where the son's lesson in sympotic behaviour includes not only the choreography of reclining, but an extraordinary vocabulary with which to praise the room. In fact, Aristophanes was ridiculed by his rival poets for being a bit of a sophist, rather like Euripides.[19]

One decadent politician of the early fourth century, Callistratus of Aphidna, is compared in a comic riddle to an arse-hole, blabbering on and farting out law upon law. Words and laws that are produced simply to pay for a politician's appetite for pleasure are produced in proportion to that appetite and share its excess. Laws are like coinage, says Demosthenes, and those who produce too many devalue and debase the currency of the city. In the same way, the veteran *opsophagoi* produce out of a hat the rostrum's clichés about national interest and taxes and security when they go down to the harbour and find no fish. Timarchus had been the proposer of one hundred laws and Aeschines places his political excesses, his sykophantic litigiousness, so perfectly exemplified in his attempt to prosecute Aeschines himself, side by side with all his other bodily excesses in a list of his vices: 'lewdness, sykophancy, brazenness, luxuriousness [*truphē*] . . .'[20]

It looks as if his opponents in the case were charging Aeschines with devaluing the laws by bringing such absurd charges as *porneia* against Timarchus. Aeschines takes pains to deny the charge. He himself does not engage in endless speeches and court-cases. He almost apologises at the beginning of *Against Timarchus* for bringing a prosecution at all, a reluctance that derives from his moderation. He elaborates this theme when he is trying to deny Demosthenes his crown. Unlike the great man, he doesn't talk all the time. He is a man who guards his words and preserves their value: 'The moderation of my way of life, Demosthenes, keeps me quiet. I don't need much and I don't want more. In fact I consider it shameful. I speak or I say nothing according to what I think is best. There is no pressure on me from a profligate nature. You, on the other hand, go rather quiet when somebody has paid you off, and when you have spent the money, that's when you start screeching.'[21]

PARTNERS IN PLEASURE

Individual appetite may have been the main factor in making the private lives of politicians a threat to the state, but there was another danger of a slightly different kind in all these expensive dinner-parties, these drunken symposia: conspiracy. It was characteristic of ancient pleasure-seekers that they sought pleasure in groups. Timarchus is a very sociable character. His vices – gambling, flute-girls, drinking and so on – are social vices. When he stands at the fish-stall he doesn't stand alone. Modern historians who study the symposium have emphasized the bonding that goes on in the *andrōn*, what anthropologists call commensality, the companionship of the table. It is a very real phenomenon for Catholic congregations or members of academic or legal colleges who may dine each night on a common 'High Table' resplendent with silver tankards, loving-cups, cruets and teaspoons given to them by past *commensales* of several centuries ago. In a very real way, the table itself provides the continuity over centuries, while the diners who eat off it are continually renewed. Commensality was also a very powerful institution in Athens. Aeschines seems to have charged Demosthenes with a great crime because he betrayed his fellow-ambassadors on their return, men he had dined with: 'He goes around like a tragic actor declaiming, "What about the salt we took together?", "Where now is the table we shared?", "What has happened to the wine we poured out together in offerings to the gods?"' Demosthenes repeats the charge, however, only because he thinks it will win Aeschines no points. In a society as nervous as Athens was of friendships between politicians, this commensality was not quaint so much as sinister, as Aeschines had himself demonstrated three years earlier.

Aeschines moves quickly over Timarchus' other associates, but dwells at some length on his affair with Hegesander. Flush with the money he had embezzled from the army chest, Hegesander goes gambling at the house of the public slave Pittalacus. There he sees the lovely Timarchus. He likes what he sees and wants to take him home, recognizing a man 'close to his own nature'. Pittalacus objects, but ever-ready Timarchus is persuaded instantly. The scene is set for a good old 'fight over a hetaera', except that in this case the hetaera is Timarchus himself. Pittalacus refuses to accept the new situation and follows the couple pathetically around. Sick of being pestered the two men decide to discourage his attentions. They break into his gambling-den and wreck it, even killing the man's beloved gambling quails, who normally suffered no more than a tap on the head. With Pittalacus out of the way, Timarchus is soon safely ensconced with Hegesander. The proof of this? They have been seen shopping together . . . at the fish-stall![22]

The very fact that nothing was known about what went on between Hegesander and Timarchus is made to appear sinister in Aeschines' assured hand. Why are there no witnesses? Because they were alone. 'What exotic lewdness didn't they indulge in, do you think, left alone together, drunk?' With such intimacy between two such profligate politicians, it is hardly surprising that they embezzle together too, stealing 1000 drachmas from the city; 'such terribly comradely behaviour', comments Aeschines of their collusion.[23]

The threat of conspiracy, then, must also be added to the list of dangers presented by the pleasures of the flesh. Men are bonded together in banquets and symposia. This is where political alliances are formed, creating factions to work against the state. We have heard of some of these groups already, the *Kakodaimonistai*, the 'wicked devils' mentioned in a speech of Lysias, the 'Erections' and 'Wankers' that crop up in the speech *Against Conon*. Perhaps the *hermokopidai*, who bashed up Athens' lucky herms on the eve of the Sicilian expedition, should also be included here. It need not be a formal group. All the men who happen to be drinking with Conon on the night of Ariston's stroll are happy to help him beat up his son's enemy.

Timarchus and Hegesander sometimes look very much like members of one of these rowdy gangs, going around and beating up poor Pittalacus, and, when he complains, getting together with their other gambling friends and claiming it was all just *paroinia*, drunken excitement. 'Who among you has not come across their fights and revelries [*kōmos*] and not felt aggrieved for the city?' asks Aeschines. The symposium, with its small space and its intense atmosphere, cut off from reality, is a perfect place to forge alliances. In particular there is that cup of friendship, the *philotēsia*, that pledged one drinker to another. Demosthenes illustrates Aeschines' treacherous complicity with Philip by referring to the *philotēsias* he made with the Macedonian king. The cup apparently could be pledged individually or as a group, but it is in the latter more conspiratorial context that it crops up most often in comedy. The women in Aristophanes' *Lysistrata* each hold the cup while they plot their sexual coup.[24]

An Athenian citizen has every right, therefore, to be extremely suspicious when he sees men active in politics supping together or queueing together in the market-place. Aristophanes has only to make a guest-list to hint at dangerous alliances: 'And your sympotic company will consist of Cleon, Theorus [one of Cleon's hangers-on, described in comedy as a flatterer, a false witness and a hero of the law-courts], Aeschines [another two-faced character of the fifth century] and Phanus [another friend of Cleon, apparently his *sykophant*, his "sub-editor of indictments"].' In fact, Philocleon ends up dining with a much less populist group of politicians, men of pretension, wealth, long hair and flattery, several of whom were later associated with the oligarchic conspiracies. These are perhaps the men least likely to put up with the old man's dreadful vulgarity.[25]

There are special implications quite apart from bonding if one of the guests is being paid for. The politics of the parasite is in fact a very large subject, and one that has received much less attention than it deserves. Men who dine for free are treated as apolitical creatures, mere gate-crashers, whereas in comedy they often appear as agents of other men, especially of politicians, helping them out with adultery, bearing false witness, fighting their battles for them in the street. Parasites are closely related to those *sykophants* who prosecute citizens on behalf of someone else. In Athens as elsewhere there was no such thing as a free lunch. A typical example of the parasitic breed is Amynias, pictured in *Wasps* dining greedily at Leogoras' table, and described as a boaster, a flatterer and a *sykophant*. He is therefore very probably one of the *sykophants* whom Leogoras is said to feed (*trephei*) in *Clouds*. Another example of this kind of character is one Smicython. He is listed in the *Wasps* along with other parasites, with invented or distorted names, Chremon ('Needy'), and Pheredeipnos ('Fetch-dinner'), as one of those 'who will be involved in law-suits in the coming year'. He pops up again at feeding-time in a fragment of Pherecrates where he is described as 'a throat-man, a professional guest I take everywhere with me'. In comedy, parasites are seen performing a whole range of services for their 'feeders', from assistance in seduction to assistance in brawls. Very often their help was sought in law-suits. Modern historians take great pains to draw a distinction between the litigious *sykophant* and the sycophantic parasite. An Athenian of the fifth century might think they had rather a lot in common. Timarchus' relationship with Hegesander, then, has many parallels in the annals of Greek comedy. He too, is a *parasitos*, someone who dines at other men's houses for free and does them favours in return. The word Aeschines uses to describe him, *asumbolos*, 'without contribution', is one of the parasite's most common epithets.[26]

At this point, of course, sex rears its head. When one Pamphilus discovers what Timarchus and Hegesander are up to, robbing the state of 1000 drachmas, he denounces them in the Assembly with sphinx-like obscurity: 'a man and a woman' are embezzling public money, he cries. The audience do not understand. Pamphilus explains: 'Don't you know what I mean? The man, as he is now, is Hegesander over there, but before he was Leodamas' wife; and the woman is Timarchus here.' These kinds of denunciations out of the blue against personal enemies were often to be heard in the Assembly. News of the profanation of Demeter's Mysteries first broke out in this way. Many of the denouncers will have been crackpots with a grudge but not enough evidence for a law-suit, serving only for a bit of light relief during the Assembly's tedious formalities. But who was this Leodamas and why was Hegesander his woman or wife? In his Loeb edition of Aeschines, first published in 1919, Charles Darwin Adam felt compelled to list Leodamas twice in his index: once for 'Leodamas, prostitute of Hegesander', and once for 'Leodamas of Acharnae, an Athenian friend of Thebes'. Kirchner, however, in his standard Attic Prosopography made them the same person and his example has been generally followed: a very distinguished politician who flourished in the second quarter of the fourth century, cited by Aristotle in his *Rhetoric* who describes him as the leader of opposition to law-farting Callistratus in the 360s, and placed among the foremost orators by both Demosthenes and Aeschines.[27]

The description of Timarchus as Hegesander's 'woman' or 'wife' has been seized on by the penetration people as a clear indication of sexual passivity. The audience, however, found the remark rather more difficult to understand, and it is unlikely that Pamphilus would risk scandalizing the Assembly with so definite a reference to sexual roles. There must be a primary reference which is not quite so obscene and since all three members of this ménage are prominent politicians, politics seems a good place to start looking. There are, in fact, some parallels. Other parasites and *sykophants* in fact are effeminized in comedy. In Aristophanes' *Knights* of 424, for instance, the Sausage-seller describes an oracle of his which foretells that Demos will pursue Smicythe and her 'husband' (*kurios*) through the courts. Modern commentators tend to agree with the ancient commentators here that a man is in fact being referred to despite the female name, and it seems very likely that it is our litigious parasitic friend, Smicythion. Amynias, too, known as a *sykophant* and parasite of Leogoras, gets a feminized version of his name in *Clouds*. Neither of these men has any aspersions cast on his preference for sexual role. Those aspersions might still be found in some new papyrus fragments of course, but they are not necessary. The change of gender derives from what we already know of their position of dependency.[28]

Studies of the Greek banquet often go out of their way to emphasize its equality, but there is no equality when Leogoras' 'Phasian' *sykophants* dine with him. There is no equality when Cleon dines with Theorus, or Timarchus with Hegesander. There is no equality between the feeder and the fed. In fact the verb *trephein*, 'to feed, rear, or keep', the Greek term used to identify the relationship between the parasite and his sponsor, describes a fundamentally unequal relationship. It is commonly used of the relationship between slaves and their owners (*trephōn*, 'keeper', is another term for 'master'). It is also a word which describes a husband's 'husbandry' of his wife. Feeding is a fundamental part of the married relationship. Persephone has been carried off to Hades' house, but it is only because she has eaten there that she is lost to Demeter and the daylight world and must marry her abductor. A kept man, like the drones in a hive, is rendered less masculine by his being kept. This fundamental principle of sexual relations is nicely illustrated in the case of hetaeras. For these rich women too had parasites feeding at their tables, producing a neat reversal of gender roles. Like a wife who moves into her husband's house and swells there with babies, the parasites swell with food. The subordination of women to men is blatantly an economic, a social and a political actuality in Athens, before it is a sexual one.[29]

Modern historians importing modern obsessions into ancient history automatically think of sexual intercourse as the primary referent when they find a man described as a woman or wife, but this is a mistake. Aeschines finds evidence for Timarchus being a prostitute in the fact that he left his father's home and dined with Hegesander for free. It seems quite likely that the same two factors are what led Pamphilus in the Assembly to denounce him as Hegesander's woman or wife. Cohabitation, *synoikein*, is a synonym for marriage itself. Aeschines calls Hegesander, like Timarchus, a 'whore', trying to get him to confess that there was the same relationship with Timarchus now as there had been with Leodamas previously. Pamphilus draws the same parallel between Timarchus' relationship with Hegesander and Hegesander's previous relationship with Leodamas, but uses the slightly more respectful language of a man and his wife to describe them. In both cases it is the visible relationship of intimacy and dependency, of dining at a patron's house, that accounts in the first place for the gender roles and sexual roles assigned to them, just as in the case of Amynias and of Smicythion in the fifth century. If a parasite is, like Timarchus, good-looking, says a character in Anaxandrides' play *Odysseus*, he gets nicknamed 'Holy Marriage'. Athenaeus cites the speech *Against Timarchus* itself, precisely to prove the point that those 'male whores' who dine for free pay later. He compares it to a fragment of Ephippus where a character on the comic stage notes knowingly that when you see a young man going into a house and laying a hand on the food without making a contribution, you must imagine he will be paying the bill during the night. A parasite hangs around his political friend so much that it's almost as if he has moved in with him. This is what the people can see. This is what they can know and this is the basis for insinuations of sexual subordination, 'prostitution' or marriage.

Some may wonder why it is necessary to unpack the tight bundle of ideas involved in the description of a man as a woman or a male whore – cohabitation, feeding, sex – giving some more importance than others. It is important, however, because it is the subordination implicit in being kept and being housed, in the visible relationships, that determines which roles are assigned, of man and wife, or whore and whore-keeper. The economic relationship and the fact of moving in should in fact be grounds enough for the charges. A politician is 'a prostitute' because he 'prostitutes himself' to another. The parasite sometimes pays for dinner with sexual services as well as political services, but the economic relationship of dependency on his *trephōn* (keeper) or *kurios* (husband or guardian) is the primary element. The sexual extrapolation is just icing on an invective cake.[30]

Timarchus does not stand alone. Politicians are often referred to in Athenian literature as if they were all *katapugones* and *pornoi*. Sometimes this is said to be a position they go through on the way to becoming a *rhētōr*. The Sausage-seller in *Knights* gets buggered by a *katapugōn* in the courts before he becomes a proper speaker, and

Paphlagonian Cleon boasts in the same play of stopping *tous binoumenous*, 'the fucked' (with a play perhaps on *tous boulomenous*, the prosecutors) by striking one Gryttus off the (citizen-) lists and making an example of him. The Sausage-seller answers that he only did it out of jealousy, to stop them becoming orators. We know nothing more of the disfranchisement of Gryttus, but it seems to have been a case very similar to Aeschines' prosecution of Timarchus ninety years later. As we have seen, allegations of *katapugosunē* may refer simply to an effete, decadent way of talking or of life, to degenerate (urbane) mannerisms and a dangerous lack of self-control, but it is also a way of representing political relationships. Sex and gender are being used to caricature political intimacies. Politicians are 'getting in bed together', forming dangerous collusions. There is something fundamentally undemocratic about politicians having friends.[31]

When Hegesander moves from being Leodamas' wife to Timarchus' man, he has not become more masculine, or decided to see what it is like to be 'on top', he has simply graduated from political client to political patron. The strange ménage described between Leodamas, Hegesander and Timarchus makes perfect sense in political terms. Together with Hegesander's influential brother Hegesippus, known as Crobylus, 'top-knot', because of his hairstyle, they seem to have formed a strong pro-Theban anti-Macedonian grouping of the 360s and 350s, which Demosthenes in the 340s found very useful. If the jurors had been privy to the nights that Hegesander and Timarchus spent alone they would probably not have heard or seen anything to satisfy their prurient itch. When the dinner-party had ended and everyone else had gone home, Timarchus and Hegesander were not drunkenly experimenting with exotic forms of lust. They were talking about politics.

We should not be too keen to draw a distinction, then, between *hetaireiai*, the dining societies and political clubs that undermined the fair workings of democracy through assistance in law-suits, and *hetairēsis*, sexual companionship. Aeschines himself fudges the distinction, when he describes the co-operation between the two men (Timarchus 'the prostitute' and Hegesander 'his client') in embezzling money from the state as *philetairōs*, 'like the best of friends'. The hetaera herself, of course, talks only of 'gifts' and 'favours' and 'friends', trying to place herself at a great distance from the 'buying and selling', the 'factories' and 'labour' of prostitutes. The same word, *misthameîn* ('work for hire'), is used both of politicians who work in another's interest for pay and of call-girls who are paid to run off to symposia. Aeschines and Demosthenes are particularly fond of invoking this imagery of the market-place when attacking each other and others for corruption. David Harvey, in his study of bribery in Athens, notes that orators can talk of selling 'truth', 'honour' and 'law-suits' as well as 'the city' in the course of their vituperations. Very often the charge is the more direct one of 'selling themselves', exactly the charge that Aeschines lays at Timarchus' door. The connection between the prostitute who sells himself and the corrupt politician who sells himself is not something for the audience or later students of the period to infer, however. Aeschines is quite explicit about it. Why does the law-giver ban prostitutes from speaking? 'Because the man who has sold the right to abuse [*eph'hubreî*] his own body would, he thought, be ready to sell the commonwealth as well.' Sometimes it is rather difficult to see whether an opponent has sexual or other services in mind. Aeschines finds it quite astonishing that he has been accused of corruption by Demosthenes of all people, a man 'who has not one single limb of his body left unsold'.[32]

This talk of prostitution and buying and selling and dining for free is worrying at a question absolutely central to Athenian politics and Greek society: the nature of friendship. When does obligation become submission? When does a favour become a service? When does a gift become a payment? When does a lover become a whore? These perennial anxieties became even more complicated in a political context. A defining moment in Athens' democratic revolution came in the middle of the fifth century, when Pericles decided to introduce pay (*misthos*) for jurors. It was said to be a direct response to the way Cimon, the careless, drink-loving general, was using the wealth he had accumulated from battling the Persians to buy influence with the people. According to Theopompus, he put no guard on his land and allowed whoever wanted to come and take what he needed. He also kept an open house where he entertained huge numbers of citizens, inviting poor Athenians to dine at his own table. By instituting the *misthos*, Pericles was deliberately attacking this system of patronage, putting citizens in the city's pay instead of in Cimon's pocket. At the same time the liturgy formalized the benefactions of the wealthy, turning 'gifts' into 'services', not only the sponsoring of triremes and choruses, but also the liturgy of *hestiasis*, feasting the people at festivals. The Athenians came to expect these donations from the rich; instead of feeling obligation when they received them they felt aggrieved when they did not. In this context, the *misthos*, paid out by a lottery-machine that emphasizes the anonymity of the transaction, is a pillar of democracy, standing for a clear, clean and utterly impersonal relationship in contrast to the cringing burdens of 'generosity'. Jury-service is a job and for that job jurors are paid. Even in the fourth century, when the state doles out payments for nothing, it is still treated as a wage for a specific service, for attending the Assembly, or for attending festivals. The unwelcome element of the *misthos*, that you have been hired out, or briefly sold, is obscured by the lottery-machines, because the paymaster is invisible, being the people or the city itself. The lottery makes wages more acceptable, bringing them closer to the portions of sacrifice. It is interesting that when Bdelycleon in the *Wasps* argues that jury-service is actually slavery, he personalizes the wage by invoking a paymaster instead of a machine, a *katapugōn* politician who can deny the jurors their three obols if they are late.[33]

If the democracy was hostile to friendships between politicians and voters, it was also suspicious of friendships between politicians themselves. Nobody was more suspicious of Greeks bearing gifts than the Athenians. Going one step further than Pericles, Cleon, the populist who dominated Athens during the turmoil of the early years of the Peloponnesian War, made a formal and public renunciation of his friends, implying that a good politician should have obligations only to the city. It seems likely that his vilification of poor Gryttus and other would-be speakers as 'those who are being fucked' is part of this disparagement of political rivals who began their political careers as friends of more senior politicians. Demosthenes, like Cleon, was accused of 'writing speeches against his friends' and of betraying his commensals on the embassy by denouncing them on his return. He answers the charge by acknowledging the companionship but denying the obligation: 'I am aware that the presiding committee of the

Council also share in sacrifice together, that they dine together, that they pour libations of wine together, but that does not mean that the good men amongst them are obliged to mimic the wicked ones. On the contrary, if they catch one of their number committing a crime they report him to the rest of the Council and to the People.' Camaraderie between citizens presented a challenge to the democracy that it tried to meet with a wide range of strategies, attempting to outlaw private associations like the *hetaireiai* and doling out fees for political service, trying to replace associations based on friendship with professional relationships based on the wage, fighting the cringing economy of the gift with commodities. At the same time, however, the city tried to substitute its own forms of sociality, inviting the citizens to public banquets or having them to dinner at its own expense, even offering prizes for being the 'people's friend'.[34]

Social relations between citizens and politicians present a complicated set of issues with no simple rules. It is not that friendship is a freer relationship than employment, that freely offered favours are good and wages are bad, or that payments are more democratic than gifts. All we can say is that these are the questions that are being argued over. A single relationship can be portrayed in very different ways by different writers, but the terms of the debate are constant. Although Foucault and his followers were right, therefore, to see charges of prostitution as political, they were quite wrong to emphasize the sexual act. What is happening is a problematization of political friendship in sexual terms, not the problematization of penetration in political terms. It seems very obvious and it is amazing that so many have overlooked it, but the crucial point about prostitutes is not what they get up to in bed, for ultimately that is mere speculation; it is that they are for sale.

TYRANNY AND REVOLUTION

WE HAVE ALMOST REACHED THE END of the political history of Athenian appetites, but there is a final stage to come. For although there were constant concerns about ordinary citizens with extraordinary desires, and real fears that the weaknesses of speakers might lead the city into danger and betrayal, the greatest anxiety was reserved for the spectre of revolution. An uncontrolled appetite had the power not only to disturb the just machinery of government, but to overthrow the government itself: 'If someone buys a grouper but turns his nose up at the sprats, straightaway the sprats-seller next to him declares, "This man here would appear to be on a spree for tyranny"', says Bdelycleon, the court-addict's son, in *Wasps*, describing an everyday shopping trip. His slave Xanthias has had similar experiences: 'Yes, I know. Only yesterday I went to the brothel and just because I told the whore to ride me like a racehorse she got all upset and asked if I was racing to reinstall the tyranny of Hippias.'[1]

POWER AND PLEASURE

We have, by now, seen so much, standing at the fish-stalls – rich men only pretending to be poor, cloak-snatchers about to be arrested, politicians colluding to embezzle money from the state, poor ineffectual Callimedon doing nothing of any consequence at all – that we can hardly be surprised to find it is a site for unmasking tyrants too. Some elements of Bdelycleon's narrative will already look rather familiar. The most obvious of these is the bathos. This is a satire on political discourse. The point is that, as Bdelycleon says, the cry of 'tyranny' and 'conspiracy' goes up all the time these days, even when you are shopping. The charge is made so often that it has become cheap. We can call to mind how readily the veteran *opsophagoi* in Antiphanes' play fall into rhetorical clichés when they see the sold-out sign at the fishmongers: it is not 'democratic to chomp on so many fish'. Similarly, when one comic character proposes that a market supervisor should stop Callimedon swooping on the fish-stall. the other complains that to do so would be the action of a tyrant. The point of the anecdote is to show how the Athenians have become profligate with political discourse, producing clichés at the drop of a hat that serve to cheapen the currency of the state, invoking the most serious charges when the most trivial interests are threatened.[2]

More seriously we can read the scene as an allusion to conspiracy. Aristophanes points out in the course of the *Wasps* two groups of politicians who feast together, one centred on Cleon, and one around Phrynichus, clearly insinuating the presence of populist or elitist but at any rate undemocratic factions, meeting around the dinner tables. One has only to talk of shopping and suppers are implied. One only has to hint at suppers to come up with collusion. In the same way, Aeschines only has to picture Hegesander and Timarchus at the fish-stalls to find evidence for conspiracy to defraud. If charges of 'conspiracy' are cheap at Athens, Aeschines and Aristophanes himself have just cheapened them further.

There is a further level here, however, which also needs exploring, since Bdelycleon's tyrannical shopping expedition seems to belong to a very strong current that connects power and pleasure. This is a familiar theme, for instance, in ancient thinking about conquest and empire. When the Greeks living on and off the coast of what is now Turkey sought help from the Greek mainland in their revolt from Persia in the late sixth century BCE, they presented their argument very much in material terms, talking of the precious metals that could be won from making war on Persia, the fancy clothes, beasts of burden and slaves. It was considered rather bemusing when, a generation later, the rich Persians invaded the meagre plains of Greece. In a scene rich in symbolism, Herodotus describes the Spartan king Pausanias inspecting the Persian camp at Plataea after the Greeks' final victory. He finds Xerxes' own tent, abandoned by the frightened monarch the year before. It is full of gold and soft furnishings. Pausanias asks the king's cooks to prepare for the victors a proper Persian banquet, which amazes all by its magnificence. At the same time he asks his own cooks to make a typical Spartan banquet as a joke and sends for the other Greek commanders. The contrast is truly remarkable. 'I called you here,' says the Spartan king, 'to show you how irrational the Persians are. This is the kind of life they have and yet they come over here to rob us of our wretched poverty.'[3]

Thanks to its defeat, Persia was indeed responsible for alleviating Greek poverty and in the wars that followed, up to and including the battle of Eurymedon in the 460s, Athens in particular grew rich. One episode, which must stand for many that have not left a trace, concerns the great general Cimon sorting out the spoils after the sack of Persian-held Byzantium. He took the Persian captives and stripped them, placing all their jewels and fancy robes on one side and asking the allied cities to choose either the adornments or the men. Seeing that the men were useless for labour and would not fetch anything as slaves, they chose the finery, thinking Cimon was a fool. Soon, however, the families of the captives arrived from Lydia and Phrygia with huge ransoms, giving Cimon enough money to pay his soldiers for a whole season and more. Cimon used the booty from the Persian wars to feast the poor citizens of Athens and to beautify the city itself, planting plane trees in the Agora, turning the Academy into a leafy grove of running-tracks and walks, and building the great south wall of the Acropolis. When Pericles added the other temples and statues, including the giant gold and ivory statue of Athena modelled by Pheidias, it was seen very much as a reflection of the city's empire, a material monument to material power, though some said it made the city look like a courtesan.[4]

This very straightforward connection between wealth, pleasure and conquest meant that imperialism could be considered a rather dangerous game. Decadence was imported into the city along with all the valuable trophies, bringing seeds of decline with the harvest of war. The classic example to Greeks of the fourth century was Sparta, which was destroyed at Leuctra in 371 after a hundred and eighty years of apparent invincibility. Responsibility for its decline was discovered in its success. Victory over Athens in the Peloponnesian War in 404 quickly led to the establishment of its own empire, ending a long period during which overseas dominion had been eschewed. The empire led to wealth. Wealth led to civil discord and decadence. Even a great lover of Sparta, like Xenophon, was disappointed. The penultimate chapter of his treatise on the Spartan system notes the way the Spartans of his own time have been corrupted by the flattery and gold that accompanies imperial power. At the end of another work, *The Education of Cyrus*, he sees the same pattern in Persian history. The Persians had not always been a pushover, luxurious and effeminate. Before their conquests they had been austere and tough, rather like the Spartans in fact.

Athens itself was not immune to such criticism, and Isocrates frames his attack on the imperialistic policies of the hawks in the 350s in terms of the necessity of controlling desires, translating the tenets of private morality on to the state. In the next century exactly the same misgivings were felt by the Romans as they embarked on their own imperial adventure. The bequest of the rich province of Asia Minor was seen as the point at which the republic started to decline and on several occasions before and after that the Senate actually refused to accept and exploit territories that were offered or were in their grasp as if frightened of doing themselves damage. We should take this ancient fear of empire seriously, if not quite as seriously as the usually more powerful impetus to conquer. Certainly the terrifying wealth of Egypt was one reason why Cleopatra VII still had a throne to sit on long after the other Hellenistic monarchs had fallen to Roman legions. Looking at what happened to Mark Antony, many Romans thought they should have kept more distance from such luxuriousness for longer.

The Greeks looked at individual monarchs in more or less the same way as they looked at imperial powers. Often when classicists study stories of decadent tyrants in Herodotus or other writers, they think it is simply a means of blackening their characters with commonplaces of vice, but as with empires, the benefits of power, the pleasures of power, describe something central and essential about monarchy. Xenophon opens his dialogue on kingship, *Hiero*, with the premise that 'tyrants' differ from private citizens primarily in the amount of sensual pleasure they have access to. The rest of the treatise is designed to demonstrate how much, on the contrary, they suffer thanks to their fear, a condition vividly re-created by Xenophon's contemporary Dionysius of Syracuse, who reputedly sat his friend Damocles under a sword suspended by a single hair. It is only by ruling selflessly and making his people prosperous that a monarch can be truly happy and secure. The fourth century produced a great efflorescence of theories of monarchy from apostate citizens of the Athenian democracy. Apart from Xenophon and Plato, Isocrates devoted several pamphlets and letters to the subject. Often he comes back to pleasure and extravagance. Private citizens cannot help learning self-control through the pressure of budgeting their daily necessities. Monarchs have no such education in means and so must rely instead on . . . Isocrates. A king must demonstrate self-mastery above all, because it makes him least like a slave and most like a ruler, because he must be an example of moderation to his people.

Monarchs like imperial nations can simply decline into effete ineffectiveness, corrupted by the abundance of good things that accumulates around them, but there is a more complicated mechanism connecting pleasure to a monarch's demise. If power is pleasure, then the way pleasure is managed has direct consequences on the nature of power itself. The difference between a good king and an evil tyrant lies in the exercise of self-control. Sometimes this link is straightforward. Theopompus compiled a catalogue of drink-loving monarchs and statesmen and, as the brave woman who appealed to 'sober Philip' over drunken Philip's head, pointed out, drunken rulers were bad rulers, careless and unpredictable. Lack of control over sexual desires was another charge commonly laid against tyrants. Incontinence led monarchs to make sexual misappropriations, commiting adultery and rape with citizens' wives and sons. When Aeschines alleges that, as governor of Andros, Timarchus had used the women of the island as a sexual facility, then, he is clearly painting him in the colours of a tyrant.

There are also some less direct connections between self-indulgence and despotism thanks to the large sums which are needed to feed such gross appetites. Taxes, confiscations and other oppressive exactions derive from a tyrant's profligacy. His profligacy is the direct result of his lack of self-control and assassination its bitter end. In the fourth century we find this element of oppression fed into the formula on the decline of nations. Thucydides refers to Athens at various points as a *polis tyrannos* and matches its history to a tyrant's increasing despotism. Xenophon includes Spartan disregard for their allies as part and parcel of their imperial decadence. In the speech *On the Peace*, Isocrates comes up with the most explicit and detailed analysis of the theory of kingship applied to a city: there are tyrannical empires and kingly ones, the latter founded on virtuous self-restraint, the former inevitably overthrown by oppressed subjects or subject-cities. According to Xenophon, Isocrates and a number of other contemporaries, contrary to appearances, Athens was not defeated by Sparta in the Peloponnesian War; Athens was a tyrant assassinated by its subject-cities 'because of her cruelty'.[5]

POWER BANQUETS

A spectacular aspect of this link between pleasure and power is the power banquet. Eating is a potent metaphor in all societies. We have our 'Fat-cats' controlling banks and utilities, our 'gravy-trains' packed with politicians, and we still argue over 'slices of the cake'. Ancient societies were no different, and often took the metaphor more literally. In *Wasps*, Bdelycleon finally gets through to his jury-loving pro-Cleon father that he is being had by the demagogues, with straightforward images of pleasure and food: the subject-cities keep the orators happy with wines and cheeses, honey and cushions, crowns and toasts, but don't give so much as a clove of garlic to the people. He proposes a more equitable distribution, where each city of the empire would be required to feast twenty Athenian citizens on simple peasant luxuries like beestings and hare.

As several scholars have pointed out, Bdelycleon is alluding to a Persian practice. The Persians seem to have used consumption as a major way of representing their power. Herodotus tells a story of Cyrus the Great making his people toil hard one day and feasting them lavishly the next, a graphic indication of the options open to them of being victors or vanquished. One of his successors, Xerxes, followed his example and used feasting to clarify his relationship with the rich island of Thasos during his invasion of Greece. The bill for feeding the army and entertaining the court itself came to 400 talents. One local wit ordered a thanksgiving for the great blessing the gods had bestowed on them, that King Xerxes did not eat breakfast as well. The 'King's Dinner' seems to have been quite a formal imposition. Theopompus compares it to a tax: 'Whenever the king visits any of his subjects twenty talents are spent on his dinner, sometimes thirty, in some cases more. For the dinner, like the tribute, has from ancient times been imposed on all cities in proportion to their size.' We see the system at work when Themistocles went over to the Persians after the Persian Wars. As a reward for his treachery, the emperor gave him three cities to supply his table, Lampsacus for his wine, Myus for his *opson* and Magnesia for his bread. Sometimes the cities of the Persian Empire were obliged to furnish other items. Plutarch cites sources who say Themistocles was also given a city for his bedding and one for his clothes and, in his survey of Egypt, Herodotus mentions a city that was taxed to supply the Persian queen with slippers. Pausanias' demonstration of the two dinners at Plataea, then, far from being 'a joke', goes right to the heart of what the Persian invasion was all about.[6]

Athens itself in its capacity as an imperial power made use of a similar symbolic mechanism. The Athenian Empire started out as the Delian League of Greek cities formed immediately after the Persian Wars to recapture territory from the Persians. It was centred on the sacred island of Delos in the Cyclades and placed under the protection of Apollo who had been born there. As father of the hero Ion, Apollo had long been the patron of the Ionians, a loose grouping of Greeks according to dialect and culture which included Athens. The huge sums raised from tribute and plunder were kept in his temple and meetings of the allies were held in his precinct. In 454–3, however, the centre of the League along with its treasury was moved to Athens and historians start calling it the Athenian Empire. As a reflection of Athena's coup against Apollo, each city of the League of Delos paid a portion of its tribute now to Athena's temples in Athens. This tithe was carefully recorded on stone, furnishing future historians with a detailed knowledge of the empire's finances. Moreover, we find evidence from now on of subject-cities being forced to supply sacrificial victims to the goddess as part of the great festival in which she was given a new dress, the Panathenaea. It is interesting to note that the festival in honour of Apollo at Delos was reinaugurated by the Athenians in 426, with proper competitions and even a chariot race. Thucydides the scientific historian tells us it was in response to some oracle, others imply the oracle was in response to the plague. Apollo had long been recognized as the god who sent pestilence – both the *Iliad* and *Oedipus Rex* start from this premise – and Athens was just recovering from a particularly devastating one that had numbered Pericles among its victims. The reinvented festival together with a new temple were clearly attempts to placate an angry god of whose lethal power they had recently been reminded. Watching, from Delos, Athena's festival wax with offerings from his Ionians, with new temples and glittering monuments and then turning to look at his own shoddy, half-built sanctuary and much diminished festival, Apollo perhaps thought he had a lot to be angry about. The Athenians, however, were not about to make the same mistake twice and provoke Athena's jealousy in turn. Just in case the new festival proved too popular with the empire's disgruntled subjects and began to damage the procession of Athena's new dress, a law was passed the next year on the motion of one Thudippus underlining the obligation to supply victims at the Panathenaea and making the duty a universal one applicable to all members of the empire (around one hundred and seventy cities). After the sacrifices this meat was taken from the Acropolis to the Ceramicus where it was distributed among the demes or dioceses and used to feed the people of Athena's city in great festival banquets. In this way the Athenians too had some idea of what a King's Dinner tasted like, not quite the same as a Persian banquet, perhaps, but better than a mere 'clove of garlic'.[7]

The 'King's Dinner' was not only a symbol of Persian supremacy in Egypt and the Near East, it was also a symbol of the king's superiority at home. The Greeks were not slow to mark how different it was from their own symposium: 'Of those who are invited to dine with the King, some have their dinner outside in full view of all who want to watch, and others inside with the King. Even these men, however, do not actually dine with him. Instead there are two rooms facing each other. In one of these the King has his meal, and in the other his guests. The King can see them through a curtain in the doorway, but they cannot see him.' On special occasions the king came out into the main banqueting hall, and sometimes after dinner he invited certain guests into his own room for a symposium, again significantly different from the Greek version: 'the symposiasts are summoned by one of the eunuchs. They enter and drink with him, but even they do not drink the same wine. They even sit on the floor, while the King alone reclines on a golden-footed couch.' Clearly the very structure of the banquet as well as the tribute food from the cities of the empire serve to underline the king's supremacy in a way quite antithetical to the collectivity of the Greek banquet.

Even in the fifth century, Persian banquets were famous in Athens. Aristophanes' *Acharnians* begins with the return from Persia of an effete ambassador who is accused of spinning out his mission deliberately so he can enjoy more King's Dinners, bringing with him only empty promises: 'They entertained us as guests, and often we were forced to drink sweet wine from cups of glass and cups of gold, neat wine! . . . The Barbarians, you know, consider only those who eat and drink in huge quantities to be men of account.' 'And here', replies Dicaeopolis, 'we consider them to be cocksuckers and *katapugones*.' The ambassador carries on obliviously, reaching the climax of his trip: 'Then the *King* entertained us, and set before us whole oxen pot-roasted.'[8]

The Macedonian successors to the Persian King's Dinners were not unfamiliar with its protocols. The Macedonian royal banquet looks like a strange hybrid, incorporating the commensality of the *andrōn*, with its peculiarly Greek emphasis on collectivity and sharing within a hierarchical environment centred on the king. This dangerous mixture of comradely equality and absolute power, of relaxed openness and glorification, produced tensions that were never fully resolved and the Macedonian symposium often seems to have provided the background for misunderstandings between the sovereign and his subject-pals, sometimes even for assassination and murder.

On the other hand, certain elements within the symposium, the 'first' position, the symposiarch and so on, provided a good basis for displays of symbolic power and had been so used by the Sicilian tyrants. Both Philip and Alexander used symposia as a major site of representations of pre-eminence. Here it was that Athenian ambassadors pledged loving-cups to the king of Macedon, allegedly. Here it was that Alexander experimented with the Persian custom of obeisance, getting his loyal comrades to bow down in front of him, a little coda to the normal loyal toast, a little prelude to the friendly embrace. Interestingly, it is a Greek guest, Callisthenes, pupil of Aristotle and the expedition's historian, who demurs, mindful perhaps of the Greek traditions of equality around the mixing-bowl. When told that without the bowing and scraping there would be no kiss, he replied that in that case he would have to stay kissless. It was not long before he lost his life as well. Even Plutarch, a great apologist, notes that Alexander's drinking-parties were occasions for flattery and sycophancy on the part of the guests and arrogance on the part of Alexander. Maybe Plutarch is right and Alexander wasn't a heavy drinker despite attending so many drinking-parties. Maybe he was addicted to admiration, not wine.

Alexander also made use of the normal prerogatives of the power banquet, the food itself manifesting his pre-eminence as it had the Persian king he supplanted. Choice fruits and the inevitable fish were sent to him from the coast. These prerogatives that set him apart, however, were used to forge loyalties and friendships with his courtiers, more in the fashion of the commensality of the Greek banquet. Plutarch says he shared these delicacies with his friends so generously that there was often nothing left for himself. The banquets seem to have been extravagant affairs with sixty or seventy guests and the cost of entertaining the king began to approach ruinous totals. A limit was imposed, but at 10,000 drachmas, i.e. more than one and a half talents, some might think it was hardly a limit at all. By Greek standards such banquets were extraordinarily lavish. On the other hand, Ephippus, a Greek critic of Alexander, notes that this was nothing in comparison with the Persian 'King's Dinners' where as many as fifteen thousand guests were entertained and the cost could rise to 400 talents. The difference perhaps is that at 'Alexander's' parties other individuals were often paying. For Alexander's power was reflected in a two-way system of giving and repaying favour, as well as giving hospitality and sharing out his privileges. The Diaries and other accounts of his death show that he was often entertained also as the honoured guest at other men's houses, rather like Autolycus in Xenophon's *Symposium* or the descendants of Harmodius and Aristogiton, who were permanently honoured guests of Athens itself. The Persian king, on the other hand, seems always to have been the entertainer. Even when he went abroad and was feasted by his subjects, it was still the 'King's Dinner' and if he wanted he could give these perquisites to his friends, who were under obligation to him, and not to the cities that fed them.

When Alexander went off to India, the banquets continued among those he left behind. His friend Harpalus, left looking after the treasure in Babylon, not only brought beautiful Pythionice all the way from Athens, a nice illustration of the sudden shift in power from the city to the court, but he also had a great multitude of fish sent to him from the Persian Gulf, a usurpation of Alexander's prerogatives, in the expectation that Alexander was not coming back.[9]

Fish very often features in these power banquets. The most famous example perhaps turns up five hundred years later, when the Roman satirist Juvenal describes the journey of a giant turbot to the emperor Domitian's table, a parody of his tyranny, but there were Greek precedents for this tale of fishy tribute. One of these concerns Polycrates, 'tyrant' of the island of Samos at the end of the sixth century and the dominant power in the Aegean. As Herodotus tells it, Amasis, his friend and ally, the wise, drink-loving King of Egypt, was worried that Polycrates was too prosperous, inviting the envy of the gods. He wrote to him suggesting that as a precaution he should get rid of the thing he prized most. Accordingly, Polycrates went through his jewellery collection and decided upon his favourite ring, an emerald set in gold, the work of one Theodorus son of Telecles from Samos. He mounted an expedition to nowhere in a great warship and discarded the ring in full view of everybody far out at sea. Then he went home and lamented his loss. Five days later a fisherman caught a huge fish which he presented to the tyrant. When his chefs cut it up, they found the ring inside and presented it triumphantly to Polycrates. Polycrates thought the gods were smiling on him and wrote to tell Amasis the good news. Amasis immediately broke off their alliance. It was impossible to save a man from his destiny and it was clear that Polycrates would die a miserable death, which would cause him less grief if he was no longer his friend. As soon as the Persians came on the scene, Amasis' prognostication was seen to be well-founded. Polycrates was betrayed by the satrap of Lydia and strung up on a cross. It is not known whether Amasis grieved less.

What is interesting for our purposes is the way the fateful fish finds its way to the dictator. The fisherman tells Polycrates that ordinarily he would have taken it straight to market, but since it was such a prodigious specimen he thought it 'a fish worthy of you and of your *archē* [rule]; and so I have brought the fish to you as a gift.' This is a neat way of making the tyrant's power the very mechanism that gets the fish back to his own table, but the idea of a fish 'worthy of your rule' is a perfectly plausible notion in Greek terms.

Another story was told to explain the fact that Syrians would not eat fish: 'whenever they eat fish, because of some loss of will-power, their feet and their stomachs swell up; then they put on sackcloth and go and sit in the road, on a dung-hill and supplicate the goddess by total self-abasement.' 'The goddess' is Atargatis of Syria, one of the most important deities in ancient Lebanon and all over the Near East. It is clear that fish figured prominently in her cult, inasmuch as real fish or golden representations of fish were offered to her, and there were some kind of limitations on her followers' consumption of fish. The Greeks, typically, interpreted this as an example of tyrannical *opsophagia*. In a tradition that probably goes back to the fifth-century historian Xanthus of Lydia, they refer to a historical Queen Atargatis, who was such a great *opsophagos* that she monopolized all the fish for herself, forbidding any of her subjects to have even a taste, and, as a result of this *hubris*, she and her son Ichthus 'were captured by Mopsus the Lydian and sunk in the lake of Ascalon to be gobbled up by the fish'.

From the Cyclades, rather closer to home, comes another strange tale of fish and power. It comes from the *Constitution of the Naxians*, a research pamphlet probably composed by one of Aristotle's students to help him with his work on political theory. A muddled account of some episode during the rise of tyranny on the island in the sixth century tells of a citizen called Telestagoras of the 'Pirate clan', very rich and of great reputation, whom the people honoured with gifts. When people tried to beat down the price of fish, the fishmongers would say they would rather give it to Telestagoras for free than sell it for so small a price, a clear reference I think, to tyrannical Polycratean privilege again, jumbled up with some fishmonger jokes from fourth-century comedy. Some youths try to purchase a large fish, and the fishmongers repeat their formula, saying they would rather give it to Telestagoras for free. This provokes the youths into a drunken attack on the good man and his daughters, which leads to a popular uprising in his defence, led by one Lygdamis, a friend of the Athenian tyrant Pisistratus and soon tyrant himself of Naxos.[10]

ATHENS

It may seem a little far-fetched to connect Bdelycleon's shopping expedition to these tyrannical goddesses and fishy despots, to see his simple request for a grouper in terms of symbolic power. There are, however, clear allusions to the Persian system in the *Wasps*, which make the link between tyranny and food more cogent. We have already seen that the notion of the 'King's Dinner' supplies the background for Bdelycleon's proposal that each city of Athens' empire adopt twenty citizens to entertain with beestings and hare and it is also a conspicuous element in his fraught shopping-spree. After he has been accused of plotting tyranny by the sprats-seller, the greengrocer joins in: 'Tell me then, so you're after a leek; I suppose it's with a view to tyranny, or maybe you think Athens should be taxed to supply you with relishes?', a clear reference to the 'King's Dinner'. The same idea crops up in other comedies, when, reversing the metaphor, the fishmongers are accused of demanding 'royal tributes' for their wares. The question remains, however, what's with the fish?

At this point it is useful to remind ourselves of the obsession with fairness that controls ancient sacrifice and renders the meat of cows, sheep and pigs into equal portions, randomly composed of meat and gristle and randomly distributed through the population, or the officials called *oinoptai*, who watched to make sure each citizen got an equal portion of wine at public festivals. The city seems to have used this notion of the sacrificial community as the basis for its own community of citizens reinforced through a great array of public banquets. At Athens there were huge sacrifices at religious festivals with hundreds of cattle slaughtered at one time, providing meat for all the citizens. In addition the presiding fifty members of the Council of 500 were fed each day of their presidency at the city's expense, and a few honoured citizens were maintained by the city for life. In fact, in the light of recent research, it is not too much to say that banqueting stands at the very heart of the polis: 'participation in the feast is synonymous with participation in the citizen-body.' There were even laws forcing people to eat the city's food.

This principle might be considered the true foundation of Athenian democracy, since we hear of *isonomia*, 'fair shares', some time before we start hearing the ideology of *dēmokratia*, 'people power'. *Isonomia* is a nexus of ideas deriving from *nemō* ('distribute') directly related to *kreanomia*, the distribution of meat at sacrifice, with a punning reference to another derivative of the verb, *nomos* (law). It is *isonomia*, not democracy, that the 'tyrant-slayers' Harmodius and Aristogiton brought to Athens when they 'ended the tyranny' at the end of the sixth century, according to the testimony of contemporary drinking-songs. Cleisthenes, the democracy's founder, is in fact much better seen as a fair and equal distributor than a people's revolutionary. It is very unclear that he gave any new powers to the people at all. He simply shifted the political structure from a vertical system of patronage into an Attica-wide horizontal arrangement, reorganizing the demes and tribes along isometric (and probably random) principles, breaking up regional loyalties and the power-bases of aristocrats, and elevating thereby the people, who became a force in their own right.[11]

It is not hard to see that the tyrant's special privilege of the best fish from the market has to be understood in this context. The point is nicely made by Polycrates' successor who, having seen how the old tyrant met his destiny on a cross, decides to give up the tyrannical power he has inherited. He inaugurates a cult of Zeus Liberator and summons the people together, offering a vivid illustration of his political programme at the communal sacrifice. He will share out rule (lit. 'putting the *archē* in the middle') and proclaims 'equal distribution' (*isonomia*) for the Samians, a marked contrast with Polycrates' monopolization of the big fish 'worthy of his rule'. A similar fishy image occurs in an early Athenian metaphor of power, in the political poems of Solon, almost a century before Cleisthenes' fair-shares democracy. Solon describes the kind of things his critics said to him when he was lawgiver, mocking him for not assuming the supreme power that was within his grasp: 'his nets teemed with fish', they murmur, 'but so astonished was he at his catch he could not pull it in.'[12]

It seems clear that the principle of 'fair shares' or 'equal chance at a share' embodied in sacrificial distributions could also be applied to the market-place which is viewed as a *meson*, a 'common place' in the middle of the city, in the heart of the community. On Naxos and in Samos, fish is not only given to the leading man as a gift or prerogative, it is also removed from sale by the fisherman or the fishmonger. Thus at the very beginning of the democratic tradition we can see hints of that marriage between political freedom and freedom of economic exchange, which is the most characteristic feature of modern Western liberal ideology. The same notion perhaps lies behind the law that later fixed the price of flute-girls and allotted them randomly to whoever wanted their services and to the democratic speech of the *opsophagoi* when they find the catch monopolized. This was not, however, a system that was supposed to benefit the traders. Often they were not even part of the citizen-body. This was a 'free market' for consumers only, a market of participation in which fixed prices might very easily find a role.

In the light of Greek insistence on the equality of the sacrificial community, then, an equality re-enacted in practice at every blood-sacrifice, the descriptions of politicians eating greedily has automatic overtones of a power-grab. When Aeschines describes Timarchus not only consuming his own property but also eating up the commonwealth, *ta koina ta humetera*, he is making a very neat connection between private appetite, the consumption of estates and the embezzlement of public funds, but thanks to this long tradition of a politics of eating there are unavoidable references to tyranny. This kind of imagery was very common in comedy and it features particularly in Aristophanes' portrayal of the demagogue Cleon in the 420s BCE. We have already seen him consuming tuna-slices and squid before making speeches in the Assembly. Aristophanes links this metaphorically to his corruption: Cleon is like a tuna-scout, looking out for silvery shoals of imperial tribute to swim into his nets. He was widely believed to have taken bribes from the Milesians to use his influence perhaps to lower the imperial dues they had to pay to Athens. Aristophanes refers to these bribes as 'Milesian sea-bass', after a speciality of the area. Cleon drinks up all the gravy of public affairs. He is a dog who snatches the *opson* from the table of the people and by night licks 'the plates and the islands clean'. It is not just that food here stands for bribes, Cleon is snatching food from the table where Athens' 'King's Dinner' is spread. His metaphorical gourmandise is turned on the tribute, on the subject-islands, on the Athenian Empire itself. With these images of eating, Aristophanes is painting the demagogue as nothing less than a usurper of the city's own *archē*. We see now the profound truth contained in the speech of the outraged *opsophagoi* in Antiphanes' *Rich Men*: 'It is not democratic to chomp on so many fish.'[13]

Coming to public notice a decade or so after Cleon, but cut from a very different kind of cloth, it was aristocratic, charismatic Alcibiades who crystallized this metaphorical sequence from banqueting to tyrannizing most vividly during the celebrations of his great victories at the chariot-races in Olympia in 416. He entered seven chariots and was placed first, second and fourth. Euripides wrote him a victory ode and his fame was celebrated throughout the Greek world. As Plutarch notes, he had done what no man had ever managed to achieve in the past, neither private citizens nor kings. Some aspects of his campaign, however, gave cause for concern. The essential problem was that he was subsidized by the cities of Athens' empire, the Ephesians supplying a Persian tent, the Chians providing provender for his horses, the Cyzicenes victims for the sacrifice and the Lesbians the wine and all his other daily needs. The similarities with the 'King's Dinner' and Themistocles' Persian prerogatives must have been obvious to everyone even without Bdelycleon's warning of eight years earlier. Yet again the sticky gift with all its unspoken obligations was threatening to undermine the democracy.[14]

TYRANNY

In 416 Alcibiades was not alone in his *hubris*. His extraordinary display at Olympia seemed to suit the national mood. Having survived ten years of war without losing any significant ground, and having since then enjoyed five years of a fragile peace which saw its enemy's enemies bring war to Sparta's door, Athens was starting to feel cocky again. In the same year Alcibiades went on an expedition to the Peloponnese to take prisoner Spartan sympathizers in Argos while another fleet went off to the little island of Melos in the Cyclades, a city which had somehow managed to avoid absorption into the Athenian Empire over the past half century, but whose luck had now run out. The city inevitably fell to Athens' massive superiority. Her men were mostly executed, her women and children sold into slavery, the island resettled with colonists from Attica. Next year even greater ambitions were revealed. An enormous expedition to Sicily was proposed, ostensibly to help Athens' beleaguered allies, but big enough to conquer the whole island for the Athenians and even, it was said, to make a start on Carthage too.

During the debate on the expedition, Alcibiades' success at Olympia came back to haunt him. The general Nicias, a cautious man opposed to the plan, warned that Alcibiades was using war simply to fund his own lavish lifestyle, deploying the image later used by Aeschines to account for Demosthenes' hostility to Philip, of the public figure whose private passions lead to risks and dangers and war. Thucydides himself, although a fan of the young general, seems to agree:

> [H]e had desires greater than what his property could sustain both with regard to horse-rearing and other expenditures. This, in fact, as it turned out had much to do with the city's downfall. For the masses were afraid both of the great unruliness he revealed in respect of his body [sic] and his lifestyle and of the great resourcefulness he

showed in his actions on all occasions. They thought he lusted after tyranny and so they turned against him.[15]

At the time of the debate, however, fears about Alcibiades were still latent, or rather any misgivings about the motivation of those who urged a vote in favour were overwhelmed by the people's greed for the legendary riches of Sicily and the West celebrated in anecdotes and tales of cities like Sybaris, Akragas, Siris and Tarentum. In the fifth century, *Sybaritikoi logoi*, 'stories about Sybaris', seem almost to have been a literary genre in their own right and, in a manner which should by now be quite familiar, the wealth of the West was above all visualized as food, for Southern Italy and Sicily were renowned for fertile fields, fat cheeses, cooks and cuisine. Judging from a Sicilian I met on a train to Syracuse in 1982 who showed me his fat stomach and made a speech repetitive enough even for me to understand about the island's fabulous productivity, two and a half millennia have done nothing to diminish the soil's special character. A Syracusan table is already famous enough to feature on the curriculum of the *katapugōn* son in *Banqueters* a decade or so before the expedition was debated, and Metagenes, a comic poet of the end of the fifth century, wrote the following description of the riches of the area in his *Thuriopersians*, blending the two things for which the West was most famous, sophisticated banquets and simple natural abundance, into an incongruous and slightly sinister image of the raw and the cooked: 'the other river [Sybaris] thrusts at us a wave of cheese-cakes and meats and ready-cooked rays wriggling over to us here, while these little tributaries flow with baked cuttle-fish, with sea-breams and crayfish ... Fish-slices stewed of their own accord come on down sweeping into our mouths.' As the citizens of Athens raised their hands to send the fleet on its disastrous journey a careful observer trying to fathom the citizens' motives might have noticed the sound of many stomachs rumbling. The rich cities of the West could provide much more than 'beestings and hare', a 'King's Dinner' fit for a king.[16]

The bubble of self-confidence was burst in dramatic fashion. First someone got up in the Assembly and claimed the Mysteries of Eleusis had been profaned in private houses, naming Alcibiades as one of the culprits. Then one morning, not long before the expedition was due to sail, the Athenians woke to find that a terrible act of vandalism had been perpetrated during the night. Their statues of Hermes had been disfigured and 'cut about'. Hermes was the god of travel and happy accidents, of thresholds and new ventures. His cult was small-scale and personal and extremely popular at Athens, sharing some similarities with cults like that of Ganesha the elephant god in India today. His unusual images, called in English herms, consisted of a handsome bearded head, an erect penis and a useful and informative text on a square-cut block of stone. They were a peculiarity of Athens, a distinctive feature of Athenian roads, doorways and entrances, informing travellers from country-villages they were half way to the city or advising them to 'think just thoughts' en route. An enormous number were dedicated at the entrance of the Agora in the Stoa of the Herms, an opportunity for traders, plaintiffs and politicians to start the day's business on the right footing and a useful platform to watch Athena's new dress go by, like a giant sail, during the Panathenaea. Among these herms was a group dedicated by the general Cimon after the first victory of the Delian League over the Persians in *c.* 476–5 marking the start of the Athenian half-century and therefore as good a place as any to situate the threshold of the classical age itself. Thucydides says their attackers had 'cut around' the statues' faces, and some of those excavated from the Agora do indeed seem to fit this description, as if their attackers wanted to trim their archaic-looking beards to a more modern classical style. Modern scholars, inevitably, have suggested the main targets were the herms' provocative penises, including one feminist historian who proposed the whole thing was organized by ancient women, protesting at the oppressions of a patriarchal regime. If the motives and sometimes even the identities of the Hermokopidai are still in question, however, there is no doubt of the effect of their actions on the general population. People panicked that the god's favour was now in jeopardy, that the expedition itself was jinxed. The mutilation of the herms in 415 stands in perfect symmetry to Cimon's dedication sixty years before. Instead of allowing the herms to inaugurate a second phase of imperial conquest, the mutilation marked the beginning of the end for the first.[17]

The fleet was allowed to sail as planned, but as soon as it had left the harbour the anxieties of those who remained behind reached hysterical proportions fed by a constant trickle of more and more alarming revelations. According to Thucydides thoughts were concentrated on a particular period in Athens' past, the tyranny of Pisistratus and his son Hippias, who ruled the city a hundred years before:

> . . . recalling everything they had heard about them, they were now in an angry mood and suspicious of those who had been accused in connection with the Mysteries; everything that had been done appeared part of some plot designed to install an oligarchy or a 'tyranny'. With feelings inflamed like this a number of prominent men were in the prison forthwith and there was no sign of any easing in the situation. On the contrary, they became more merciless by the day and more arrests were made.

According to Andocides who was himself heavily implicated, every time the Council met in the Agora, the market-place emptied, as people feared they would be next in line for denunciation and arrest. Eventually Andocides, the supergrass as hero, decided to put a stop to the suffering and tell all, securing the death penalty for many of those imprisoned, but getting himself and some others released. Now they had the Herm-vandals sorted out, the people turned with more confidence on the profaners of the Mysteries, part, they assumed, of the same conspiracy to overthrow the democracy. Convinced by now that Alcibiades had something to do with it they recalled him from Sicily, pushing into Sparta's arms the general most in favour of the expedition and initiating a sequence of events that, according to some contemporaries, led to Athens' ultimate defeat in the Peloponnesian War and, according to Thucydides and many later observers, led to the discrediting of democracy itself.[18]

The Athenians had long nurtured fears of tyrants. It is one of the most striking features of the democracy and of Greek political thinking in general. The dictatorship of Pisistratus and his sons had been ended as long ago as 510 BCE. The possibility of Hippias, the last tyrant, being reinstated, had been dashed in 490 when the old man saw his Persian backers defeated at Marathon, and most modern commentators consider the prospect of a coup after that very remote indeed. Nevertheless, almost a century after the ending of the tyranny the charge of tyrant was still bandied about in the Assembly and on stage, where it was used to attack prominent figures like Pericles. When Aristophanes claims in *Wasps* that the charge of tyranny was cheaper than salt-fish in Athens he was probably only exaggerating a little. Most of his contemporaries, however, considered it much more than a rhetorical topos handed out like a special offer by politicians. There may have been no tyranny in Athens for over eighty years but, as Thucydides observes, the Athenians still took the threat very seriously indeed.

Cleisthenes or his successors had built into the Athenian constitution a mechanism for getting rid of possible tyrants before it was too late. A vote was taken on whether the city needed to expel some prominent citizen for a limited period. If the result was in favour, a further vote was taken to determine who it should be. The names of nominees were written on pieces of pottery called *ostraka* and deposited in urns. The 'winner' was ostracized, which meant exile for ten years, after which he was allowed back with full citizen rights to reclaim his property. It was an attempt to manage and control the damaging cycle that had destabilized Athens before the tyranny and which continued to destabilize other cities even now, a cycle in which a faction pushed its rival into exile from where it would plot return and bitter revenge, including the exile of its enemies in turn. The recent history of Rwanda provides perhaps a modern parallel. Pisistratus himself had seized tyranny on the rebound in just this way. Some have objected that ostracism cannot have been a defence against tyranny since the greatest threat was posed by populists who would for that reason be impossible to vote out, but this is applying a modern idea of dictatorship to a very different culture. In Athens a potential tyrant made himself known by qualities that had nothing to do with popularity or policy and much more to do with personality and lifestyle.

The reason why Alcibiades was suspected of involvement in a conspiracy to overthrow the state was not that he was especially popular, or had made speeches against democracy or had been seen hoarding weapons for a coup. His accusers, says Thucydides, 'found evidence in the unruly and undemocratic nature of the way he lived his life'. This could be interpreted in different ways. Alcibiades certainly displayed *paranomia*, unruliness, disdain for the law, and there are numerous stories told about him which seem to illustrate this element of his character. Most vivid perhaps is Plato's account of him bursting in upon Agathon's hitherto well-ordered symposium quite drunk, leaning on a flute-girl with a huge wreath falling over his eyes. He elects himself leader of the drinking and tries to get everyone as intoxicated as he is. He doesn't even wait for the wine to be mixed safely with water but drinks it straight from the cooler. Others might point to his sexual activities, his affairs with married and unmarried women, even with an illegitimate daughter. This kind of disregard for norms might be considered dangerous in any society and was considered typical of tyrants. Alcibiades' behaviour at Olympia certainly seemed to show a desire for greater prerogatives than were his due as a mere citizen in the city of fair shares. This *paranomia*, however, is not mere delinquency, some general disregard for all laws or authority, it is a disregard for the limits of appetite, for the laws and protocols that control desire, particularly in Alcibiades' case, the rules that govern sex and drinking.

It was not just that a man of 'tyrannical lifestyle' seemed to covet the king-sized pleasures reputedly enjoyed by the monarchs and satraps of Persia and the Greek dictators of long ago. Rather, a tyrannical man's desires were already outpacing the resources of a private citizen and forcing him into extremity. He needed to overthrow the system to get himself out of debt. It was not so much a tyranny of aspiration as a tyranny of desperation. Thucydides spells this out: '[Alcibiades] had desires greater than what his property could sustain.' The people 'thought he desired tyranny and so they turned against him'. Alcibiades was thought to need a revolution because he couldn't control his desires and his expenses outpaced his resources. According to this analysis then, the suspicion of tyranny that got him recalled from the Sicilian expedition was based on the same quality in his character that, according to Nicias, made him so eager to conquer Sicily (and Carthage) in the first place, his extravagance.[19]

There was in fact an oligarchic coup in Athens in 411, but far from showing that Athenian fears in 415 or 422 (when *Wasps* was performed) were well-founded, the coup was a consequence of measures taken to defend the city on that occasion. For the revolution followed directly on the chaos and demoralization brought by the Sicilian disaster, itself the consequence of recalling the general most in favour of the campaign and leaving Nicias, the general most opposed to it, as sole commander in his place. This was not only a bad idea in itself, but seemed to confirm to many that the democracy was capable of putting political rivalry before national interest and was quite unable to rule coherently and consistently. As Thucydides observes, reflecting on Athens' eventual defeat, the city did not really lose to Sparta, nor was it assassinated by its own allies. Athens lost the Peloponnesian War because it defeated itself. Indeed, among the demagogues who made such a fuss about the Mysteries and the herms and the threat that had been revealed to democracy were some characters who later turned up as ringleaders of the oligarchic tyranny. Like a character in tragedy, therefore, the action the city took to avoid its fate, the recall of Alcibiades, was responsible for bringing that fate about. In this tragedy, as Thucydides notes, extreme anxieties about appetite, extravagance and spending certainly played their part.[20]

The classic account of the origins of *coups d'état* occurs in Plato's description in the *Republic* of the way constitutions succeed one another and evolve. The tyrannical man has himself a tyrant inside, love, which dominates other desires. His way of life is all 'feasts and *kōmos* and revels and hetaeras'; this leads to 'debts and mortgages' and this in turn to mistreatment of parents who resist his demands for more money. He beats up his mother for the sake of a hetaera, or 'rains blows on his . . . father for the sake of a handsome new friend'. Soon short of money again, but afflicted by the same swarm of pleasures buzzing like bees in his head, he turns to crime: 'will he not then for the first time put his hand to the wall of some house or to the cloak of someone taking a walk late at night.' Sometimes there is an outlet for such characters in mercenary armies or in the ranks of a foreign tyrant's henchmen, but, if not, these dangerous characters stay in the city engaged in petty crime: 'they steal, they break into houses, they cut purses, they snatch cloaks, they plunder temples, and kidnap people for the slave-trade and some, if they are good at speaking, become sykophants, false witnesses, takers of bribes.' When there are enough of such characters in a city they realize their strength in numbers and with the help of the people's stupidity find a leader to be tyrant of all. If there is any resistance, then with the help of his comrades (*hetairoi*) he will enslave his motherland as he once mistreated his mother. 'Would this not be the final outcome of the desire of such a man?' 'This would indeed.'[21]

THE END OF CIVILIZATION

If this pattern looks familiar, it is because we have already seen extracts from the tyrant's history in Aeschines' indictment of Timarchus. The star of Plato's tale of the tyrannical man is the same as the star of Aeschines' biography of Timarchus, desire. The orator has already accused the defendant of *sykophantia*, bribes and temple-robbing, but he doesn't stop at that, following Plato right up to the punch-line: 'You'll find many men of his sort who have overthrown cities, and fallen themselves amidst the very greatest calamities . . . The body's reckless indulgence in pleasures, taking no limit as the limit, this is what fills the robbers' bands, this is what pipes pirates aboard the pirate-ship, this is for each man his Fury, bidding him cut the throat of his fellow-citizens, to become a tyrant's henchman, to help overthrow the democracy.' Tyranny it seems will be the *telos* (and Demosthenes, it is implied, the tyrant), the final outcome of Timarchus' fondness for flute-girls, dice-games and fish, unless he is stopped now. If the eighteenth-century 'Rake's Progress' ended up in Bedlam, the march of the classical spendthrift was headed for the citadel, threatening to bring Bedlam to the city itself.[22]

Aeschines' image of pleasure-seekers as murderers, law-breakers, pirates and plunderers, linking the pleasures of the flesh to savagery and barbarism, shares a great deal with Plato's desire-driven profligates who haunt the streets at night, snatching cloaks, breaking into houses, cutting purses and end up wandering the world in mercenary armies. A similar picture of savage degenerates occurs in Theopompus' picture of the core of Philip's Macedonian army, the *hetairoi* or Companions of the King:

Philip generally spurned those who lived an orderly life and budgeted according to their means. He preferred and promoted bigspenders, men who never left the gambling tables, men who were always drunk . . . Some of them used to shave and kept themselves smooth, although they were grown men . . . They took around with them two or three male prostitutes and they served others in the same capacity, so that we would be justified in calling them not hetairoi but hetaeras, not marchers, but streetwalkers, for they were man killers by nature, but man thrillers [*andropornoi*] in their way of life . . . Careless of what they had, they desired what they had not, despite the fact that they possessed a good part of Europe . . .

In short . . . I think that those called Philip's friends and companions were worse brutes and of a more beastly disposition than the Centaurs who established themselves on Pelium, or the Laestrygones who lived on the plain of Leontini.

The Laestrygones were man-eaters, encountered by Odysseus on his long journey back to Ithaca. They came down to the shore and threw huge rocks at the fleet, sinking the ships and 'spearing their crews like fish', before taking their catch off home for supper. The Centaurs feature in several myths. One story provides the background for one of the most popular subjects in Greek art, the Centauromachy, shown on countless Athenian cups and wine-jars, on the splendid pediment of the temple of Zeus at Olympia, on the lost painted friezes of the Theseum in Athens dedicated by Cimon, on surviving stone friezes of the Hephasteion, on the temple of Apollo on the remote hilltop at Bassae in Arcadia, on the Parthenon itself. The Centaurs had been invited to the wedding of Pirithous, king of their civilized neighbours, the Lapiths. Unaccustomed to wine, the Centaurs get wildly intoxicated and run riot through the wedding banquet, attempting to carry off the Lapith women (we know of no lady centaurs) and even the bride Hippodamia herself. Another story concerns a visit by Heracles. As a guest of the Centaurs, he wonders why their hospitality does not extend to offering him a cup of wine, especially since he can see an unopened amphora lying inside the cave. His host tells him this was a present from Dionysus to all the tribe of Centaurs, who forbade them to open the vessel until the appropriate time. Heracles persuades them that the time has now come, but as soon as the Centaurs smell the vinous aroma, they gather round, get quickly drunk and go wild. Heracles has no choice but to slaughter them with arrows dipped in the venomous blood of the Hydra. Even his host is killed as he examines one of the arrows in disbelief, amazed that so small a dart could bring such powerful beasts to the ground.[23]

The battle of Lapiths and Centaurs was a great one to depict, full of movement and life, drunken horse-men, desperate women, and tables overturned, but it is given such prominence on temples of such major significance, that it would be naïve not to see it as symbolic of other struggles, of Greeks against Persians, of civilization against barbarism, of the inner struggle of rules and regulations against the anarchy presented by animal passions, of civilization versus chaos. The opposition of Dionysus to Apollo, representing inspiration versus intellect, dissolution versus form, drunkenness versus the dream, is mostly a modern invention, but it does have some ancient foundation and seems central to any account of the Centauromachy: the savage drunken horse-men represent the violence which will afflict anyone who doesn't know how to drink Dionysus' wine; the Lapiths, on the other hand, are assisted by Apollo, who stands serenely above the chaos in the pediment at Olympia, guarantor of the order that will return.[24]

It is often said that though both savagery and self-indulgence are characteristics of barbarians in Greek thinking, they are rarely seen combined. It is also true that there was a persistent strand in Greek thinking that considered it impossible for the same man to be both pleasure-indulging and warlike. Polybius objects to Theopompus' portrayal of the Macedonian Companions on precisely these grounds. On the other hand, it was a commonplace to see power reflected in pleasures, to portray conquest and empire in terms of the 'good things' they supplied for the victorious city or the successful tyrant. It is hardly a large step to view the violence and war which is needed to win a King's Dinner as an intrinsic part of the King's Dinner itself, to see the violence necessary to win these imperial pleasures as a reflection of some violence inherent in desire itself. Theopompus is a step ahead of Polybius in his portrait of the Macedonians, his opposites go very well together, exposing the savagery which lies under the patina of pleasurable refinement. The comparisons with which he concludes already encapsulate this incongruous mixture. It is not just that the Centaurs and the Laestrygones are wild and barbarous. Like the Macedonian Companions, they show their barbarity in the way they sate their appetites, in cannibalism, in drunken madness, in rape at a wedding banquet.

The Laestrygones who haul the Greeks from the sea like fish, bring to mind another people encountered by the Greeks at the margins of the world. The year is 325 BCE. Nearchus of Crete, an intimate of Alexander the Great, is sailing back from India, shadowing at an incommunicable distance the Conqueror's gruelling land-route through the Gadrosian desert of Iran, chosen deliberately, it was said, to punish his men for prevailing upon him to go back. Nearchus had been charged with surveying the northern coast of the Persian Gulf, its peoples and their customs and presenting a full account to Alexander. The report was eagerly awaited, and as soon as there were rumours that the explorers had been sighted, a search-party was sent out to meet them coming from the coast. The voyage, however, had left the voyagers unrecognizable, long-haired and briny, pale and sleepless. The search-party did not at first realize who they were and answered their request for assistance with directions. Their story was worth the wait, however, and they had many wonders to report. They had seen whales for the first time, shooting water into the sky. At first they had dropped their oars in surprise, but instead of fleeing they had rowed towards them, making a great din, splashing the sea with their oars, blowing trumpets, shouting, and had frightened the creatures into the depths of the sea. Afterwards, relieved, they had clapped. Even this natural wonder was eclipsed, however, by their account of a strange tribe who inhabited a long stretch of the northern coast of the Arabian Sea, perhaps in the area of Baluchistan. Stories had been told of *Ichthyophagoi* or Fish-eaters by the earliest geographers and ethnographers. The name was bestowed generously in antiquity to a number of different tribes inhabiting the coasts of the Persian Gulf and the Red Sea. Herodotus in the earliest reference to them talks of Fish-eaters living around Aswan in Egypt and tells of how in the sixth century the Persian king Cambyses had made use of their ability to survive on limited provisions by sending some of them to reconnoitre the distant and legendary kingdom of the Ethiopians at the southern extremity of the world. Until Nearchus, however, little was known of this way of life apart from their names. What he found at the edges of the known world was something rather close to home, a grotesque inversion of the highest refinements of Greek civilization:

> For these Fish-Eaters, fish is the staple, hence their name. Few of them, however, actually go fishing, for few of them have any fishing-boats or have discovered the art of hunting them. For the most part it is the ebbing sea that keeps them supplied ... At low tide the land is exposed again. There are virtually no fish to be found where the land is dry, but where there are hollows and some water has been left behind the fish are abundant ... The most tender of them they eat raw, pulled straight from the water; larger and tougher specimens are laid out to dry in the sun until they are quite desiccated, then ground into flour to make loaves and, in some cases, cakes. Even their herds are fed on this dried fish, for the country has no pasture not even any grass ... In fact there are some who live in desert regions without trees or crops; their entire diet consists of fish. A few, however, manage to cultivate a little land which provides them with corn they can add to the fish as a relish. For fish is their staple.[25]

Here at the ends of the earth was a grotesque image of Greek appetites, reflected in the lifestyle of poor savages, a kind of 'Mirror of the *Opsophagos*', a people who really did use fish as a mainstay of existence, and bread as a relish to relieve the monotony, a people who knew neither hooks, nor boats, nor fire. Discovered a little too late for Theopompus, the *Ichthyophagoi* provide a perfect example of the savage and bestial image of unrestrained pleasures, enjoying a level of gourmandise the greatest *opsophagos* could only dream about in the context of the very lowest level of civilization known to man.

Fundamentally, the pleasures of the flesh, eating and drinking and sex, are also animal passions, and for all the connoisseurship a degenerate man shows around the dinner-table, he is really giving in to desires he shares with the meanest of creatures. He is exhibiting the beastly side of his being. He is a dog like Cleon, licking the plates clean. As the Centaurs and Laestrygonians show, hunger, thirst and lust if uncontrolled are capable of bursting through the bounds of custom and law, destroying institutions of society like marriage and hospitality and replacing them with cannibalism, riot and rape. Civilization itself is built on the containment of animal passions within the boundaries of rules and protocols: mixing the wine properly with water, letting it pass in good order round the company, keeping the bread in the left hand and the *opson* a mere embellishment on the right. If these rules are broken or inverted, even with too much refinement, then civilization itself is in jeopardy and a '*daimōn*' is loose in the *oikos* who will turn the table over.

At various points throughout his indictment of Timarchus, Aeschines places bleak little images of destruction and devastation. Most vivid is a picture of an anti-Athens conjured up in the speech Autolycus makes in the Assembly, where harmless and banal references to different parts of the city are suddenly seen as references to the places streetwalkers like Timarchus take their clients. This other Athens, the Athens conjured up in innuendo, is desolate and disturbing. This city is filled not with households, but *oikopeda*, 'derelict buildings', like 'building Z' perhaps, the brothel whose ruins had been lying within the shadow of the Sacred Gate for fifty years, or the 'place of the horse and the girl', a ruin so called, says Aeschines, because an Athenian of olden times, with an old-fashioned sense of virtue, had locked his unchaste daughter up in it together with a horse which devoured her before succumbing itself to starvation, a little centauromachy in the very heart of Athens, a little piece of savagery in the *oikos* to subsidize chastity and good order. In this anti-Athens of *double-entente* the hill of the Pnyx is no longer the central point of Athenian government, the meeting-place of the Assembly of citizens, but 'a wasteland' where street-girls take their clients. 'You must not be surprised, fellow-citizens,' Autolycus began, in a speech to the Athenians delivered on that very hill, 'if Timarchus is better acquainted with this desolate place [*erēmia*] and the area on top of the Pnyx'; '. . . perhaps,' he continues when the laughter has temporarily died down, 'Timarchus thought that in this quiet spot [*hēsuchia*] there is little expense for each of you.' This area of the Pnyx does not seem to have been occupied by houses or homes at all, but 'settlements', the main concern of Timarchus' proposal. 'Settlements', *oikēseis*, is a strange word to use of residences of Athenian citizens. It was a word used of barbarian cultures that had not yet reached the level of urban civilization and sometimes even of animal lairs. Perhaps it was an ancient version of a shanty town colonized by the destitute, immigrants or even refugees from the countryside who were taking the threat of Philip seriously.

Plato's tyrannical man driven by uncontrolled desires is rather like a nomad, pursued endlessly by 'the gadfly' of his itching lusts, looking for a place in a mercenary army or in the bodyguard of a foreign tyrant. The image recalls the archetypal wanderer, the poor cow Io who was pursued by Hera's gadfly from Argos up the Adriatic coast, giving the name Ionian to the islands round Corfu, past Prometheus in northern Europe (she passes through Aeschylus' *Prometheus Bound*), across the Bosphorus (Ox-ford) which she also casually christened, eventually arriving in Egypt where she gave birth. Aeschines paints Timarchus too as a nomad, selling off his property, and pursued endlessly by the 'Fury of his desires', not so much Io as Orestes, who was harried all over Greece for murdering his mother, until he finally arrived at Athena's just city. Timarchus, of course, had not left Athens, but having sold off his own homes and the soil that bore him, as fast as his Fury demands, he ends up on Queer Street. The wastrel is resourceless, *aporos*, forced to wander over a wasteland of promiscuity, finding refuge in other men's houses, in other men's arms, on the streets and in abandoned buildings. He is a tramp in every sense of the word: 'wherever he lays his hat' is home. But Timarchus is also a speaker whose words are listened to, the proposer of one hundred laws, and so, as a whore at the heart of the city, he threatens not only to turn the homes he has sat in into brothels, but to make the city he wanders a wasteland, making the centre of Athens a marginal space, the stamping-ground of streetwalkers and turning the Assembly over to the Assembly's strange hinterland, turning the polis itself inside out through innuendo.

The context of the speech is relevant here too. Timarchus has been spreading panic, pacing the speaker's platform with his cloak hanging off, placing a ban on selling arms, proposing urgent measures to repair the city walls and its defensive towers, as if the city was about to be sacked by Theopompus' savage, drunken, ever-marching, overspending, pleasure-loving, streetwalking bestial Macedonians. Aeschines simply counters his opponents' attempt to frighten the Athenians with imminent assault from barbarians outside with another image of a city devastated from within by consuming passions, by the beast that lurks inside. The Athens Timarchus inhabits with its hollow zones, its derelict buildings, its bottomless wells, barbaric settlements and wasteland is already within the city walls, waiting to take over. This anti-Athens has been there for a long time; the polis was built on its repression. But it never finally disappeared and lurks still in the city's crevices and on its margins and between the lines of Timarchus' speeches. It is the space of the streetwalker and the wastrel, of unbridled appetites and animal passions, waiting like abysmal Charybdis to swallow Athens down.[26]

Conclusion

I BEGAN THIS BOOK by observing that the Greeks were fond of fish. I ended by suggesting that fish played a significant role in the invention of ideas of freedom and democracy and that the concept of fishcakes holds a clue to the ancient understanding of civilization itself. Historians often end up concluding that their chosen subject is of absolutely central importance and shamefully neglected by the rest of the profession. Perhaps when the subject relates to such basic human activities as eating, drinking and sex, this claim is more forgivable, although what is interesting is not the hunger, nor the lust, nor any of the other appetites in themselves, but what happened to those universal cravings in the particular context of classical Athenian culture; the wide range of regulations and representations used to grasp them, the symbolic significance they thereby acquired.

Some of this context is broadly Greek. The difference between sacrificial meat and foods that were consumed outside a ritual context, the perceived dangers of wine, the difficult distinctions drawn between commodities and gifts, were features of Greek civilization in general and helped to construct similar environments for pleasure elsewhere. In the city of Athens, however, there was a further element. Athenian appetites acted on subjects who participated in a democracy of a very radical nature. This peculiar political configuration produced peculiar attitudes to wealth and spending and, most importantly, a peculiar atmosphere for the production of knowledge of appetites and for public representation of appetites. Unless some mosaic artist chose to capture for posterity the moment before the floor was swept and the refuse carried away, these appetites produced no monuments and few artefacts, leaving the impression that Athens was a rather austere place, where the only extravagance was to be found in public buildings and on the Acropolis: '*On voit l'extrême pauvreté de cette civilisation si ingénieuse,*' noted the French historian Paul Veyne, comparing Athens to Rome, '*son pauvre luxe, son luxe de pauvres*'. But as a counterpoint to the poverty of material signs, we have rich seams of discourse, which enable us to recapture something of this lost world of consuming in its images, arguments and hesitations. This is not a fortuitous compensation, but derives from the same anxiety about the dissipation of resources, an attempt to make the evanescence of property visible, to problematize the liquidization of substance. It is not an accident that we know more about the pleasures of the flesh in Athens, and more from Athenians of the pleasures of the flesh in other Greek cities. The fact that this information exists is a political fact. The importance granted to the ephemeral in Athens is itself revealing about the nature of spending in such a society. Moreover, this knowledge comes from public texts, from the theatre, the Assembly and the law-courts. It is not information that was confined within some secluded royal court or an isolated symposium of aristocrats or some marginal theatre of the disfranchised. This is a discourse that sits 'in the middle', at the political centre of the democracy, at the heart of the community of citizens.

In other ancient societies, it is true, as in many more modern cultures, we can see very similar examples of a concern with expenditure on food and sex and drink, but it has a rather different significance. A passion for fish along with other vices spread from Greece to other parts of the ancient world. In Rome too, for instance, fish consumption was a great luxury, but in this very different political culture, oligarchic and hierarchical, there is a rather different emphasis. Unlike the fish consumers of the Athenian democracy who queue up in the market-place in disguise, the wealthiest Romans are, in Cicero's memorable phrase, *piscinarii*. They have their own pools, their own fish-farms to feed from. In this context, *opsophagia* has been transformed into a sign of landed wealth, the ephemeral has become material, real, a discreet pleasure has become a way of showing off. Descriptions of the Athenian banquet are overwhelmingly concerned with the food and drink that were consumed, the 'hired' flute-girls and kithara-boys who sang songs and entertained for the evening. In most cases the *andrōn* was tiny and dark, and though some might be proud of their furniture, their tapestries, their cups and cushions, the emphasis was always on the food itself and the sex and entertainment that accompanied it, on things that lasted only for the evening's duration. A seventeenth-century traveller to Moghul India, observing his hosts' lack of splendid furniture and the magnificence of their carpets, noted that, 'All their bravery is upon their floors'. The bravery of the classical Athenians, by contrast, was all on their tables, in their wine-cups, or in the air.

Outside Athens and after the classical period, the banquet realized its potential to be something much more spectacular and monumental. There was much more emphasis on property, on gold and silver utensils, the marble of splendid surroundings, valuable furniture, like the tables cut from a single tree that were so prized at Rome. Petronius' satire on the dinner of Trimalchio in the *Satyricon* illustrates this shift nicely. Apart from the obvious nouveau-riche luxury of the banqueting-hall itself, and all the valuable cups and plates, it is stressed that all the food has been produced on his own estates. It is a sign of property, of territorial wealth, rather like the banquets of the Persian king, Themistocles or Alexander. The preparation too is astonishingly elaborate, indicative of the number of slaves available to work in the kitchen, and indeed there are numerous slaves in attendance throughout the evening, many of them specializing in ludicrously narrow and trivial tasks. No longer a machine that accelerates the evaporation of resources, in the Roman context the banquet becomes a theatre of wealth and property, of social distinction, or social-climbing.

Some of these ancient appetites look very odd from our perspective. It seems very strange that the Greeks got so worked up about fish. It is almost unbelievable that they did not recognize the addictive qualities of alcohol. In contrast to our simple sexuality and our straightforward recognition of the salience of sex, their erotic world seems unnecessarily complicated and terribly difficult to pin down. Many historians and cultural critics would conclude from this (and some, with regard to Greek sexuality, already have) that these appetites and desires are not simply being constructed in particular ways, bent and altered and distorted by the cultural context, but actually forged. Thirst, lust, gluttony were not the same as what we recognize today under those names. Ancient appetites were fundamentally different. Those who emphasize biology, however, or those who are attached to the notion of human universals may argue that a fish is a fish is a fish, and tastes the same no matter whether it is caught in 425 BCE or 1997.

I have argued throughout this book for the importance of language and discourse and cultural context in understanding the pleasures of the past, but I do not think that culture monopolizes or creates experiences. It is true that when we enjoy a fried slice of tuna, or a fine fillet of sea-bass, when we enjoy wine or find ourselves attracted to men and women, our enjoyment is situated in a particular historical, social, economic, cultural, intellectual, ideological, etc. context which lends it specific connotations and values that are quite different from those of the ancient Athenians. These contexts are hugely important, but they are not absolute or fixed or uniform. While researching this book I have at different times imagined strong resemblances between the world of Athenians and of the Tamils of South India, of the Athenians and of fundamentalist Muslims of Afghanistan, of the Athenians and of modern Americans. The Victorians probably understood much better than we do what a hetaera was. And while the English are amazed at the Athenian preoccupation with sea-food, some Spaniards I have spoken to wonder why I am making such a fuss about something so natural as a love of eels. The recent re-establishment of democracy, even such a compromised version as our own, has made us suddenly sympathetic to the Athenian political system after two and a half millennia of disdain and it is quite certain that our descendants will find some aspects of the ancient world more obvious than they are to us, and some more strange. While the liberation of women has made it much more difficult to understand the sexual charge of female bareheadedness, the extraordinary disrobing we have experienced in the twentieth century after two millennia of covering up, has put us back in touch with the Greek appreciation of gym-toned male flesh.

The world is full of pleasures. Not all cultures discover all of them, but just because they are not discovered does not mean they do not exist. The world we inhabit and the bodies we inherit and the experiences that are provoked at the points where they meet are 'found objects'. We can make our own thing out of these experiences but cannot make whatever we want of them. There are limits to our virtual realities, occasions when the real world imposes itself, when we knock against the limitations to our ideologies, when the world forces itself on us, when we get drunk, when our mouths water, when we get hot and bothered at the sight of human beauty. On these occasions the differences between us momentarily vanish and we realize that we too are part of the world, somewhat bestial, somewhat part of humankind.

Other cultures have reacted quite violently to such appetites, putting them under interdiction or subjecting the body to strict controls. The Greeks imposed few rules from outside, but felt a civic responsibility to manage all appetites, to train themselves to deal with them, without trying to conquer them absolutely. There is little sign in Greece of the metaphysical ascetic tradition we find in the cults of Christianity, Islam, Shiva and Buddha. The Greeks never went so far as to renounce the world, by opening monasteries, espousing virginity, practising yoga or fasting for long periods of time, in an attempt to gain psychic power. They were in fact rather suspicious of complete abstention, as the story of the Centaurs reveals. Socrates sometimes gets close to that position, but he seems to have backed off from it, renouncing the world only when the hemlock gave him no other choice.

Following Nietzsche, Foucault concluded from this that the pecularity of Greek morality lay in the freedom it granted citizens to make their own rules, a kind of DIY morality which today's religious leaders so publicly abhor. The major constraints on this freedom were aesthetic, the life one led had to be beautiful and fine. There were no imposed limitations, but only what he called a 'stylization' of freedom instead. The only true problematic concerned sexual penetration and to account for this Foucault invented the strange notion of 'ethical passivity/activity' which he made the key to his understanding of the Greeks and his starting-point for the genealogy of the Western sexual subject. How he came to settle on this particular unspoken-of intimacy and why he was so enthusiastically believed is more a question for his biographers and our sexual philosophers, I think, than students of antiquity.

From the perspective of Athens, this aesthetic view of Greek morality looks astonishingly naïve. Looking for power everywhere, Foucault missed it where it was most obvious, in politics. Private appetites were a matter of enormous public interest and often found themselves being discussed in law-courts and regulated in laws. If there were few absolute prohibitions there was nevertheless a great deal of monitoring in the interests of the community. This morality might be described as basically economic rather than absolute. This does not mean that money was the bottom line, although it was a valuable gauge of personal and political consequences, rather that morality was seen as a total system rather than as a series of discrete activities, a matter of degrees rather than rights and wrongs. Appetites were managed constantly and minutely through a series of ubiquitous practices. Each cup should contain more water than wine, each mouthful more bread than meat. The subject was a vessel that existed in an intermediate zone between incomings and outgoings, in the decent pause between taking from the world and giving back to it, between feeling the urge and satisfying it, in resisting the pressure to become the world's commodity, to become erased.

It is a long time since the Greeks were viewed as guiltless pagan pleasure-seekers and I would not like to propose their approach to appetite as an alternative to our own. It may have been less dogmatic, but it was also more totalitarian and at times much more intense. On the other hand, it does throw our modern attitudes into perspective. The Greeks gave full recognition to pleasures in themselves. We, on the other hand, are tending more and more to ascribe lack of self-control over appetites to some agent of compulsion within the object consumed, or to some disguised psychical damage sustained in childhood, babyhood or even in the womb. The Greek notion of addiction may have been too innocent, but by denying that people consume too much of something because they enjoy it, we are also making a mistake. If we ignore pleasure then we cannot really claim to know the true dangers of the sensual world and are leaving ourselves and our children open to ambush.

Despite or because of its politicization, the Greek approach to pleasure was vigorously rationalistic and humane, talking appetites down, engaging with the present world and its urges without waiting for the next, confident enough to insist on personal responsibility in managing appetites, never so frightened of pleasures as to flee them in panic. While Buddha is commemorated as a skeletal figure meditating under a Bo tree and Jesus is monumentalized in triumph over the flesh on a cross, Socrates is best remembered in conversation at a lavish symposium, fretting that another guest is being greedy with the *opson*, or arguing gently in favour of the small cups.

Notes

CHAPTER I · EATING

1. Xen. *Mem.* 3.14. The best discussion of the term is J. Kalitsunakis ''Οψον und ὀψάριον' in *Festschrift für Paul W. Kretschmer: Beiträge zur griechischen und lateinischen Sprachforschung*, (Vienna etc., 1926), pp. 96–106.

2. Plu. *Mor.* 667ff. It seems that it was customary in many Greek cities to announce the arrival of the catch with a bell, a fact on which an anecdote from the geographer Strabo depends: 'A cithara-player was giving a demonstration of his art. Everybody was listening, until at a certain point the fish-bell rang and they abandoned him and went off to the fish-stalls, except for one man, who happened to be rather deaf. So the citharode went up to him and said, "I must express my gratitude, sir, for your courtesy and appreciation; all the others disappeared the moment they heard the bell." To which the other responded, "What's that? Has the bell rung already?" and when the citharode said that it had, bade him "Goodbye" got up and went to join the others' (14.2.21, p. 658, Iasus).

3. Archestratus 15 and 21.

4. Phylarchus *FGrHist* 81 F45; DS 8.19; Theoph. (or Chamaeleon of Pontus) *On Pleasure ap.* Ath. 6.273c.

5. Clearchus F59 (Wehrli), *ap.* Ath. 12.518c; Ath. 8.341a, 3.105c, 7.282a and 325f; Plato *Gorgias* 518b with Dodds ad loc.

6. Dem. 19.229; Aeschin. 1.42, 65 and 95.

7. Ar. *Wasps* 491; Ath. 3.116ad.

8. Ar. *Wasps* 495; Timocles 11 K-A; Alexis 200, 159 K-A; Chrysippus, *On things to be chosen for their own sake* (*ap.* Ath. 7.285d); Antiphanes 69 K-A. Other fish that crop up in this desultory category are the crow-fish, or corbs, and the picarel. Some of these attitudes are found elsewhere. Alan Davidson quotes G. L. Faber, a British consul at Fiume in the nineteenth century, on Venetian attitudes to the picarel: 'it is a common mode of derision to accuse a person of eating this class of fish', *Mediterranean Seafood* (London, 1981), p. 90.

9. Archestratus 8; Anaxand. 40 K-A; Antiphanes 145 K-A.

10. Anaxand. 34 K-A lines 5ff. (the last few lines are somewhat corrupt). 'Fish-fingers' is a rather loose translation of *phryktos*, which is glossed by

317

Hesychius, the ancient lexicographer *s.v.* as 'cheap little dried fish'. Lynceus of Samos *ap.* Ath. 7.295ab. For Apuleius and the fish-magic nexus in general see Adam Abt, *Die Apologie des Apuleius von Madaura und die antike Zauberei* [= Albrecht Dietrich and Richard Wünsch, eds, *Religionsgeschichtliche Versuche und Vorarbeiten*, Heft II] (Gießen, 1908; repr. Berlin, 1967), pp. 135–6 and 140–44. The vases are *ARV* 101.3 and Eduard Gerhard, *Auserlesene Griechische Vasenbilder*, I, plate LXV.

11. Ath. 13.586ab; Ar. *Ach.* 885 cf. 894, *Peace* 1013–14; cf. also Eubulus 34 and 36 K-A, Archippus 27 K-A and Antiphanes 27 K-A with the editors' comments ad loc. The goddess of Madurai in Tamil Nadu who seduces Shiva and becomes his bride is known there as Meenakshi, the Fish-eyed goddess.

12. Ar. *Knights* 927ff.; *Ach.* 1156–61; Antiphanes 77 K-A; *SVF* III, 167 #667.

13. Eubulus 118 K-A; Plato *Rep.* 404b–405a.

14. See the introduction to J. Wilkins and S. Hill's edition of Archestratus, *The Life of Luxury* (Totnes, 1994), pp. 11–15, and R. L. Hunter's remarks in his commentary on Eubulus 37 K (Cambridge, 1983).

15. Euphro 1.6 K-A; Eriphus 3 K-A; Men. 264 (Koerte). A Hellenistic inscription from the city of Thera records that the heroes must have their ration of three fishes, *Griechische Dialekt-Inschriften*, III, 4706, ed. F. Blass, 191–3.

16. G. Berthiaume, *Les Rôles du Mageiros* (Leiden, 1982), p. 63. For the distribution by lottery, see [Xen.] *Ath. Pol.* 2.9, Plu. *Mor.* 642ef, and in general on Greek techniques of butchery, Berthiaume, p. 50.

17. Homer *Iliad* 16.747, 406ff., 24.80ff., cf. 5.487, cf. M. Schmidt, *Die Erklärungen zum Weltbild Homers und zur Kultur der Heroenzeit in den b-T Scholien zur Ilias* (Munich, 1976), pp. 182–5.

18. *Odyssey* 12.329–32, cf. 4.368–9. In Leiden and other Dutch cities, for instance, a special meal of bread and herring commemorates the deprivation of the Spanish siege raised in 1574, for which see Simon Schama, *The Embarrassment of Riches* (London, 1987), pp. 26–8; cf. Mikhail Bakhtin, *Rabelais and his World* (Bloomington, 1984), p. 298 on Molinet's 'Dispute of Fish with Meat'. N. Purcell argues that sea-food never really lost its negative connotations, 'Eating Fish: the Paradoxes of Seafood', in J. Wilkins, D. Harvey and M. Dobson, eds, *Food in Antiquity* (Exeter, 1995), pp. 132–49.

19. Pauline Schmitt Pantel, *La cité au banquet* (École Française de Rome, 1992), pp. 53–105 and for the Hellenistic period, pp. 359–420.

20. Antiphanes 217 K-A; Xenarchus 7 K-A; Ath. 7.313f.

21. Antiphanes 69 K-A, cf. 127; Ar. 402 K-A.

22. Ar. *Clouds* 982–3; Xen. *Mem.* 3.13,4; Thuc. 1.138.

23. Plu. *Mor.* 439f, 99d, 5a; M. M. Ahsan, *Social Life under the Abbasids* (London, 1979), p. 158; Xen. *Cyr.* 8.5,3; cf. Dicaearchus 51 (Wehrli) *ap.* Varro *Rerum Rustic.* 1.2,15, Alexis 57 K-A, since the Greeks seem to have avoided images

of people eating, the imagined monument was perhaps designed to offend the audience's sensibilities. We should also note that the gourmand Philoxenus dips only one hand in hot water to accustom himself to eating hot *opson* straight from the pan, Chrysippus *ap*. Ath. 1.5e.

24. These codes of orientation need not be simple, however, and can reach enormous sophistication, as Pierre Bourdieu demonstrates in his essay on the Kabyle house, printed as an appendix to *The Logic of Practice* (Cambridge, 1990). In the case of *opson*, a simple left = bad / right = good formula leads to quite opposite conclusions about the respective values of right-hand food and left-hand food.

25. Cf. Ar. *Wasps* 300ff. and Lysias 32.20.

26. Plato *Rep*. 372ae.

27. Xen. *Mem*., 1.3,5.

28. A. N. Wilson, *Jesus* (London, 1992), p. 49.

29. I wonder if there is any significance to be drawn from the importance of casting nets on the right-hand side, since this is of course where a Greek would reach out for *opson*.

30. D.S. 11.57,7; Kurt Hubert, 'Zur indirekten Überlieferung der Tischgespräche Plutarchs', *Hermes* 73 (1938), 326–7; Ingemar Düring, 'Athenaios och Plutarchos', *Eranos* 34 (1936), 8f.

31. Sidney I. Landau, *Dictionaries: The Art and Craft of Lexicography* (New York, 1984), p. 98; cf. Thomas Pyles, *The Origins and Development of the English Language* (New York, 1964), p. 305.

32. A glance at today's (17.11.94) *Times*' leader produces the following suspect remark: 'popular taste is by definition vulgar.'

33. Derek Attridge, 'Language as History/History as Language: Saussure and the Romance of Etymology', in Derek Attridge, Geoff Bennington and Robert Young, eds, *Post-structuralism and the Question of History* (Cambridge, 1987), pp. 183–211. Etymology does indeed seem to hold a particular fascination for popular writers of the right-wing like William Safire, for whose misplaced use of etymology as an indication of true meaning see Landau, *Dictionaries*, p. 99.

34. See in general, R. J. Hankinson, 'Usage and Abusage: Galen on Language', in S. Everson, ed., *Language* (Cambridge, 1994). The German philosopher Heidegger thought Greek itself was the *Logos*, this special language where words and what they named were as one.

35. Wilhelm Schulze, *Quaestiones Epicae* (Gütesloh, 1892), pp. 498f.; Friedrich Bechtel, *Lexilogus zu Homer* (Halle, 1914), pp. 202–3; Émile Boisacq, *Dictionnaire Étymologique de la Langue Grecque* (Paris, 1923); cf. J. B. Hofman, *Etymologisches Wörterbuch des Griechischen* (Munich, 1949), *s.v.*, *opson*. Hjalmar Frisk, *Griechisches Etymologisches Wörterbuch* (Heidelberg, 1970); Philippe Chantraine, *Dictionnaire Étymologique de la langue Grecque* III (Paris, 1974), *s.v.* ὄψον.

36. It would be too simplistic to say such etymologically derived meanings are actually wrong. In a world before dictionaries and Academies, idiosyncratic usage was unpoliced. Even today, false etymologies have their own impetus, and if they attain enough popularity and transparency they can start to affect meaning and to make their definitions retrospectively right, albeit for the wrong reasons. *Outrage* has begun to adopt some of *rage*'s foreign overtones, for instance, and Plato's etymology of *opson* from *hepso* meant that the smell of cooking was from now on more often to be found around that word.

37. Plu. *Mor.* 667f.

38. Hegesander *ap.* Ath. 8.343d.

39. The same double-ban occurs in Athenaeus' own dialogue; at least it happens to be a noted abstainer, Ulpian, 'a Syrian when it came to fish' who denies that *opsarion* means fish (8.346c; cf. 9.385b). Philosophers in general seem to have been famous for their abstention from the pleasures of the fish. Antiphanes 132 has probably a Cynic philosopher announcing 'we always have one item of sea-food . . . salt'.

40. Xen. *Mem.* 3.14,7.

41. This still happens even in today's invigilated language. In my mother's family, for instance, the word 'fornicator' was used quite freely to mean 'liar'.

CHAPTER II · DRINKING

1. Ch. Baudelaire, *Du vin et du haschisch comparés comme moyens de multiplication de l'individualité*, in Claude Pichois' edn of *Les Paradis artificiels* (Paris, 1961), esp. pp. 77–8; Roland Barthes, 'Lecture de Brillat-Savarin', introduction to *Brillat-Savarin: Physiologie du goût* (Paris, 1975), trans. in M. Blonsky, ed., *On Signs* (Oxford, 1985), pp. 63–4.

2. See the introduction to Susanna Barrows and Robin Room's collection *Drinking: Behavior and Belief in Modern History* (Berkeley, 1991); Mary Douglas, *Constructive Drinking. Perspectives on Drink from Anthropology* (Cambridge, 1987), p. 4: 'Drinking is essentially a social act, performed in a recognized social context. If the focus is to be on alcohol abuse, then the anthropologists' work suggests that the most effective way of controlling it will be through socialization.'

3. Mnesitheus ap. Ath. 11.483f–484b. For the *Problemata*, see Pierre Louis' new edn (Paris, 1991), pp. 51–6. Louis considers most of it written towards the end of the third century BCE within the tradition and under the influence of medical writing. For Theopompus' list, Ath. 10.435d = *FGrHist* 115 F283a – probably a resumé to draw together the allusions to drinking-habits found throughout his work. Significantly, Aelian who cites Theopompus' researches on the subject includes just such a list (*VH* 2.41).

4. Arist. F96 (Rose); Mnesitheus *ap.* Ath. 1.32d; Hippocrates *Regimen* 2.5; Theoph. *De Odor.* 51f. The best recent and accessible survey of wine and wine-making in Greece is found in Roger Brock's contributions to Jancis Robinson, ed., *The Oxford Companion to Wine* (Oxford, 1994), *s. v.* Greece, Symposium.

5. Fernand Braudel, *Capitalism and Material Life*, Eng. transl. (London, 1973), pp. 164–5; Archestratus 59–60 (Ribbeck) (the connoisseur seems to have made a mistake. The city of Byblos located in the north of modern Lebanon was famous for exports of papyrus, so giving the Greeks their word for book and the English a word for Bible, but Bybline wine probably came from Thrace); Eubulus 122 K-A; cf. Alexis 280 K-A. Fine wines especially are supposed to be drunk aged, cf. Eubulus 121 K-A, Clearchus 5 K-A, Epinicus 1 K-A, Cratinus 195 K-A. For the notion of 'bloom', see François Salviat, 'Le vin de Thasos, amphores, vin et sources écrites', in J.-Y. Empereur and Y. Garlan, eds, *Recherches sur les Amphores Grecques* (École Française d'Athènes, 1986), p. 179.

6. Hermippus 77 K-A ll. 1–5, with editors' notes ad loc.; cf. F. Salviat, 'Le vin de Thasos . . .' pp. 187–93; Pliny *NH* 14.73; cf. Philyllius 23 K-A. Isaac Casaubon thought the gods wet their beds because they drank so much of it, *Animadversiones in Athenaei Dipnosophistas*[2] (Lyons, 1621), pp. 68, 40.

7. Virginia Grace, *Amphoras and the Ancient Wine Trade* (Athens, 1961); Ath. 1.32f; Pollux 6.15; F. Salviat, 'Le vin de Thasos . . .' pp. 188–9 and note 95.

8. F. Salviat, 'Le vin de Thasos . . .', pp. 147–154 and 173ff.; Robin Osborne, *Classical Landscape with Figures* (London, 1987), pp. 105–7. The author overemphasizes, however, the conflict of interest between town and country. It is too much of a coincidence that such vigorous state control over the production of wine should be observed in a well-known wine-exporting polis. The farmers, too, benefited from tight quality control.

9. Plato's *Symposium*, ed. K. J. Dover (Cambridge, 1980), p. 11. At Agathon's dinner-party, Phaedrus lies in the 'first' position, and Agathon the host 'last' (177d and 175c). The inherent hierarchy might be used by a king or a tyrant to give and take away favour, cf. Hegesander *ap.* Athenaeus 12.544c. Pauline Schmitt Pantel in her analysis of public banqueting contrasts dining in the prytaneum, an oblong structure imitating sympotic space and the world of archaic aristocracy, with being fed in the *tholos*, a completely circular structure with strong democratic credentials; *La cité au banquet* (École Française de Rome, 1992), pp. 147–77, esp. p. 169, note 69. O. Murray, ed., *Sympotica. A Symposium on the Symposion* (Oxford, 1992) presents a series of articles on the phenomenon, with a good introduction to the issues by the editor.

10. François Lissarrague, *The Aesthetics of the Greek Banquet*, Eng. transl. (Princeton, 1990), pp. 19–20.

11. Timaeus *FGrHist* 566 F149. This is the main gist of Lissarrague's treatment of the episode. The drinkers are taking a common metaphor seriously, and confusing fantasy and reality, see *The Aesthetics of the Greek Banquet*, pp. 108–10. For marine metaphors see M. Davies, 'Sailing, Rowing and Sporting in One's Cup on the Wine-Dark Sea', in *Athens Comes of Age: from Solon to Salamis* (Princeton, 1978), pp. 72–90; and W. Slater, 'Symposion at Sea', *HSCP* 80 (1976).

12. Xen. *Symp.* 2.1; Plato *Symp.* 176a; Philochorus *FGrHist* 328 F5; Ath. 11.486f–487b; Xen. *Anab.* 6.1,30 has an election, but Eryximachus in Plato's *Symposium* just seems to assume his position.

13. Xen. *Mem.* 3.13,3 and 2.1,30; Plato *Rep.* 4.437d, Ath. 3.123a–125d, cf. 8.352b (it seems that cold drinks were considered especially appropriate for toasts); Machon 270 (Gow), with the editor's note ad loc. and ad 259; Theophrastus *ap.* Ath. 11.782ab.

14. Sophilus 3 K-A; Anacreon 11 (Page); Diocles 7 K-A; cf. Ath. 10.426de; Anaxilas 23 K-A; cf. Ion of Chios *FGrHist* 392 F2; Hermippus 24 K-A; Eupolis 6 K-A; Ameipsias 4 K-A; Nicochares 2 K-A; Hippolochus *ap.* Ath.4.129ef. Not all wines were equal, however. Some were thought to bear dilution better than others, as is suggested by terms like *polyphoros* in Ar. *Wealth* 853 and *autokras* in Pollux 6.24 etc. Cratinus 196 K-A: 'this wine can take half and half' must be a joke. A heavy drinker is so impressed by the strength of a wine he considers adding what most would think of as much too little water.

15. Eubulus 94 K-A; see Kassel-Austin ad Ar. F 540; F. Jacoby ad Philochorus *FGrHist* 328 F87 (IIIb [Suppl.], p. 371); F. Lissarrague, *The Aesthetics of the Greek Banquet*, p. 26, 'Un Rituel du Vin: la libation' in *In Vino Veritas*, O. Murray and M. Tecuşan, eds, (British School at Rome, 1995), pp. 126– 144; J. Rudhardt, *Notions fondamentales de la pensée religieuse et actes constitutifs du culte dans la Grèce classique* (2nd ed, Paris, 1992), p. 242; M. P. Nilsson, 'Die Götter des Symposions', in *Opuscula Selecta* I (Lund, 1951), pp. 428– 42. Jacoby's remarks on the subject (loc. cit.) should be borne in mind: 'the tradition about the number, sequence, and the recipients of the official libations at symposia shows wide differences.' A Hellenistic site in Corinth turned up the remnants of a tavern with many other possible drink-demons, including Stop-hangover, Sweet-drinking, and Painless; O. Broneer, 'Investigations at Corinth in 1946–7', *Hesperia* 16 (1947), 239–41.

16. Theoph. *Char.* 13.4, 10.3; Plato *Symp.* 176be; cf. Critias D-K 88 F6 ll.6– 9, 23–4; Alexis 21 K-A; Xen. *Resp. Lac.* 5.4; *Symp.* 2.26 cf. 25, the contrast made by Socrates in a metaphor of drinking between plants that are flooded with water, and plants that drink only as much as they enjoy, Ath. 10.425ab; P. Schmitt Pantel, *La cité au banquet*, pp. 85–6, cf. Theoph. *Char.* 10.3.

17. Eubulus 94.6–11 K-A; cf. R. L. Hunter, *Eubulus: The Fragments* (Cambridge, 1983), pp. 185–9; Com. Adesp. 101 ll.11–13 K-A.

18. Antiphanes 112–13 K-A; Plato 192 K-A; Alexis 9 K-A; Men. 443 (Koerte); cf. Pollux 6.99. *Akratos* ought to mean 'unmixed' but often means simply 'strong'. This explains why Demosthenes can complain of men drinking wine 'more unmixed' in Hyperides *In Dem.* Frag. b = p. 24 Jensen, and Xenophon can talk of 'very unmixed' *Anab.* 4.5,27; cf. also Antiphanes 25 K-A and Alexis 246 K-A.

19. Plato *Symp.* 213e, 223bc.

20. Artemidorus 1.66; Critias F 6 (West); Ar. *Ach.* 978–86.

21. Ar. *Knights* 1288–9; cf. Robert Parker, *Miasma* (Oxford, 1983), p. 99 with note 101, Ar. *Ach.* 959ff. E. *IT* 947ff. H. W. Parke, *Festivals of the Athenians* (London, 1977), p. 113; Richard Hamilton, *Choes and Anthesteria Athenian Iconography and Ritual* (Ann Arbor, 1992), pp. 113–15. Some have suggested wine at Choes was poured out as normal into a cup, since Plutarch (*Mor.* 643a), claims that this was how Orestes was served. There is no mention, however, of cups in the other sources and no cups appear alongside the *chous* in the vases that commemorate the festival. Most cogent, however, is Dicaeopolis' boast in *Acharnians* 1203 and 1228–9 that he drank his *chous* without a breath. By conjuring up cups for the Choes, scholars are missing what was most transgressive about drinking at the festival.

22. Plu. *Mor.* 679a and 716a.

23. Ath. 11.781d; Xen. *Symp.* 2.26; Antiphanes 205 K-A (following Kock's text); Alexis 9 K-A 11.8–10, 183 K-A 11.3–4 *ap.* Ath 10. 421d; cf. 228 K-A, Satyrus *ap.* Ath. 4.168cd.

24. Alexis 285 K-A; Ar. *Wasps* 79–80, 1251–61; cf. *Frogs* 739–40: 'He must be well-bred if all he knows how to do is drink and fuck.'

25. Oswyn Murray, 'The Affair of the Mysteries: Democracy and the Drinking Group', in *Sympotica*, pp. 149–50.

26. Cf. Hug, *RE* 10, 1888–9: 'Am häufigsten versteht man unter einem κάπηλος, einem der Getränke, Wein oder Weinessig im einzelnen verkauft oder ausschenkt.'

27. Nicostratus 80 K-A; Ar. *Ecc.* 49 (it seems probable that wine sold by the *kotylē* necessarily refers to wine drunk in a *kapēleion*; in that case Smikrines in Menander's *Epitrepontes* 127–31 is complaining not about the cost of Charisius' drinking but about where he chooses to do it); Plato *Gorgias* 518b; Pollux 7.193; Arist. *Rhet.* 3.10,4, 1411a.24; and in general see my article 'A Ban on Public Bars in Thasos' *CQ* (forthcoming).

28. Ar. *Wealth* 435, F285 K-A; Antiphanes 25 K-A; Nicostratus 22 K-A; Eubulus 80 K-A; Lysias 1.24. *IG* 3.3, ed. R. Wuensch, *Appendix: Defixionum tabellae* no. 87, index s.v. *kapēl*-. D. R. Jordan, 'A Survey of Greek Defixiones Not Included in the Special Corpora', *GRBS* 26 (1985), 151–97 no. 11, with curses directed against two women each described as *graus kapēlis*, 'old barmaid'; *IG* 2.2.773A; Alexis 9.5 K-A; Ar. *Ecc.* 154–5.

29. T. Leslie Shear Jr., 'The Athenian Agora: Excavations of 1973–4', *Hesperia*

44 (1975), 357–8; for a later tavern in Hellenistic Corinth, see O. Broneer, 'Investigations at Corinth in 1946–7', *Hesperia* 16 (1947), 239–41.

30. Theopompus 66 K-A *ap.* Plu. *Lys.* 13.5; Plato *Leg.* 11.918bd and the references collected by Hug *RE* 10, 1888; Ar. *Wealth* 436; *Thesm.* 347–8; cf. *Ecc.* 154–5, where the women want to ban water-tanks from the *kapēleia*, a joke about the taverners diluting wine, or about the women wanting their wine served neat; Antiphanes 25 K-A, and perhaps Plato's Sarambus, *Gorgias* 518b.

31. Theopompus *FGrHist* 115 F62; Phylarchus *FGrHist* 81 F7, cf. Ath.10.442c, *IG* MXII suppl. 347, II 11.12–15.

32. Isoc. *Areop.* 49; *Antid.* 286–7.

33. Hyp. 138 (Jensen) *ap.* Ath. 13. 566f; cf. Ar. *Ecc.* 134, where the women accuse the men of attending the Assembly in a state of inebriation, Ar. *Knights* 353–5.

34. Eubulus 80 K-A; Ar. F 699 K-A; cf. *Wasps* 656ff. esp. 698–702; P. Schmitt Pantel, *La cité au banquet*, p. 11, Plato *Symp.* 223bc; Hesychius s.v. *trikotylos*; Men. *Epitrep.* 130–1; and possibly Eubulus 80 K-A 11.4–5.

35. Antiphanes 25 K-A; Paul Millett, *Lending and Borrowing in Ancient Athens* (Cambridge, 1991), p. 220. For this phenomenon see Hermippus 78 K-A *ap.* Pollux 7.193; and Lysias F 1.3 (Thalheim) 38 (Gernet-Bizos), *ap.* Ath. 13.612c. Also relevant is Ar. *Lys.* 113–14, where there seems to be a reference to a cloak put down as surety for drinking; see Henderson's commentary ad loc. and perhaps Adespota 807 K-A a parody of Sophocles' *Phineus* 711 (Radt), if we assume that the reason why the tavern-doors are tightly shut is because the subject, like Aeschines Socraticus (and countless clients of the hetaeras), has not paid his drinking debts.

36. Critias D-K 88 B34. It was once thought that the Spartans drank no wine, but this is demonstrably untrue, see O. Murray, 'War and the Symposium', in W. J. Slater, ed., *Dining in a Classical Context* (Ann Arbor, 1991), pp. 83–104; N. R. E. Fisher, 'Drink, *Hybris* and the Promotion of Harmony', in Anton Powell, ed., *Classical Sparta: Techniques Behind Her Success* (London, 1989), pp. 26–50, although I am much more pessimistic than the author that much can be said with certainty about actual drinking practices at Sparta.

37. Xen. *Resp. Lac.* 11.3; Arist. F 542 (Rose), *Rhet.* 1.9, 26. Plu. *Mor.* 238 F cf. Aelian *VH* 6.6, Val. Max. 2.6,2.

38. Ar. *Wasps* 1157–8; the red dye is sometimes described as 'Sardian', thus emphasizing its connotations of Lydian luxury, Plato Com. 230 K-A; Ar. *Peace* 1172–6, cf. Xen. *Cyr.* 8.3,3, where the *phoinikis* is included in a list of especially rich and fine costumes.

39. Ar. 225 K-A. Athenaeus (11.484f) thinks this passage is evidence for another Spartan cup. However, as Critias testifies, the *kōthōn* is *the* Spartan cup already by the end of the fifth century. It seems unnecessary to postulate

a second 'Spartan cup' which shares the *kōthōn*'s decadent associations. The two are one and the same. Athenaeus seems to have been distracted by the fact that Aristophanes describes this Spartan cup as a *kylix*. This can be used to specify a shallow saucer-like vessel quite unlike a *kōthōn*, but is often used also as a general term for any cup, even deep cups like those manufactured by the bibulous women in Pherecrates 152 K-A 1.4. It is notable that Critias' explanation of the Spartan use of the *kōthōn* is framed in the same terms as Aristotle's defence of their red cloaks. The bloody colour of the *phoinikis* functions like the dark mud-disguising interior of the *kōthōn* to render invisible to the soldiers the inconveniences of military life.

40. DL 1.104; Xen. *Symp.* 2.23–6; Alexis 9 K-A 1.9; Sophilus 9 K-A; Timocles 22 K-A (often the people rejecting the small cups and taking up the bigger ones are women, cf. Eubulus 42 K-A, Ar. *Lys.* 200–1); Pherecrates 75 K-A.

41. Pherecrates 152 K-A; Epigenes 4 K-A.

42. Xenarchus 10 K-A; Eubulus 80 K-A; Alexis 120 K-A, cf. Plautus' *Persa* 821: 'bibere da usque plenis cantharis.' T. Carpenter, *Dionysian Imagery in Archaic Greek Art* (Oxford, 1986), p. 1, note 1. For the origin of the shape and its association with the god see Michel Gras, 'Canthare, société étrusque et monde grec', *Opus* 3 (1984), 325–39, who argues that it stands as a trophy indicating Dionysus' victory over the Etruscan pirates and the Giant Kantharos, depicted in the North frieze of the Siphnian treasury at Delphi, see esp. pp. 329–30.

43. Epinicus 2 K-A; Damoxenus 1 K-A; Ath. 11.476ae; Hermippus 44 K-A; Diphilus 5 K-A; F. Lissarrague, *The Aesthetics of the Greek Banquet*, pp. 32–3, 58 and 90–1. The verb *skythizein*, literally 'to make like a Scythian', meant 'to drink immoderately'.

44. Chamaeleon 9 (Wehrli). Chamaeleon is part of the Peripatetic tradition defending the ancients from the charge of heavy drinking, cf. Theoph. F 571 (Fortenbaugh et al.) *ap.* Ath. 11.782ab.

45. Ephippus 9 and 16 K-A; Anaxand. 33 K-A (cf. Ath. 11. 482bd); Pherecrates 101 K-A; Ath. 11.485a; Theopompus 41 and 42 K-A; Antiphanes 47 K-A; Philyllius 5 K-A; Theopompus 31 K-A; Ameipsias 21 K-A. The *amystis* is described by Pollux as 'a large cup', 6.97.

46. Alexis 181 K-A; Polemon, *ap.* Ath. 11.484bc; Theopompus 55 K-A (women are rarely abstainers in comedy so this is more likely to be a statement than a question, cf. M. Whittaker, 'a woman expresses her readiness to endure hardships [sic] in much the same strain as *Lysistrata* v. 113–4 . . .' 'The Comic fragments in their relation to the structure of Old Attic Comedy', *CQ* 29 [1935], 182 and note 1); Ar. *Thesm.* 620 cf. 630–3; Archilochus F 4 (West); Ar. *Knights* 599; O. Broneer, 'Excavations at Isthmia' *Hesperia* 28 (1959), 335, no. 9 and Plate 70i; Bert Kaeser,

'Griechisches Vasen-Trinkgeschirr', in Bert Kaeser and Klaus Vierniesel, eds, *Kunst der Schale. Kultur des Trinkens* (Munich, 1990), p. 188 and figs 30.4 and 30.5, the latter vase is illustrated with hoplites, referring back to its original military function; Peter E. Corbett, 'Attic Pottery of the Later Fifth Century', *Hesperia* 18 (1949) nos. 78–81 and p. 333. On drinking in the army, Oswyn Murray, 'War and the Symposium.'

47. The one illustrated by Kaeser loc. cit. fig. 30.5, for instance, and dated to about 490, is decorated in red-figure and looks rather too elegant for the campaigns it evokes.

48. Eubulus 126 K-A and Mnesitheus F 45 (Bertier) *ap*. Ath. 11.483f–484b; cf. J. Bertier, *Mnésithée et Dieuchès = Philosophia Antiqua, A Series of Monographs on Ancient Philosophy* XX (Leiden, 1972), pp. 85–6; for his probable dates see pp. 9–10 and 147.

49. Hyp. *In Dem*. Fa = p. 24 (Jensen); Lynceus of Samos *ap*. Ath. 6.245f–246a; Mnesitheus F 25 (Bertier) *ap*. Ath. 11.483f–484a; Gow ad Machon 442; Chrysippus *ap*. Ath. 1.8cd, for Lycon Ath. 12.547d.

50. Theophrastus (*ap*. Ath. 11.782ab) makes the same point rather more literally, suggesting that one of the reasons why the ancients did not drink so much was because they used to play *kottabos*, which involved tossing wine at targets, F. Lissarrague, *The Aesthetics of the Greek Banquet*, pp. 80–6. Originally, perhaps, deep cups were associated with strong wine because they were used for toasts, cf. Theopompus 41 and 42 K-A; Sophilus 4 K-A; Anaxand. 3 K-A; Men. 275 (Koerte); Cratinus 322 K-A.

CHAPTER III · WOMEN AND BOYS

1. [Dem.] 59.122. The passage has been much analysed and debated, see e.g. J.-P. Vernant, *Myth and Society in Ancient Greece* Eng. transl. (London, 1980), pp. 47–8: 'It is a purely rhetorical distinction which has no meaning in terms of the existing institutions.' Cf. H. J. Wolff, 'Marriage Law and Family Organisation in Ancient Athens', *Traditio* 2 (1944), 74; Roger Just, *Women in Athenian Law and Life* (London, 1989), p. 52; P. G. Mc C. Brown, 'Plots and Prostitutes in Greek New Comedy', *Papers of the Leeds International Latin Seminar, Sixth Volume* (Leeds, 1990), 248 and note 35; W. K. Lacey, *The Family in Ancient Greece* (London, 1968), p. 113; Eva Cantarella, 'Donne di casa e donne sole in Grecia: sedotte e seduttrici?', in Renato Uglione, ed., *Atti del II Convegno nazionale di studi su La Donna nel mondo antico Torino 18–19–20 Aprile 1988* (Turin, 1989), p. 45.

2. Ath. 12. 521b = Phylarchus *FGrHist* 81 F45.

3. Cf. J.-P. Vernant, *Myth and Society in Ancient Greece*, p. 47.

4. Charles Seltman, *Women in Greek Society* (London, 1953), pp. 115ff. The distinction between *pornai* and *hetairai* parallels very closely the division made by 'Hans Licht', the grandfather of ancient studies of sex and sexuality,

in his *Sittengeschichte Griechenlands* (Dresden/Zurich, 1925), cf. II, p. 53: 'Auf ungleich höherer Stufe stehen und nehmen im griechischen Privat-leben eine viel wichtigere Stellung ein die Hetären. Von den Bord-ellmädchen unterschieden sie sich zumal durch ihre gesellschaftliche Achtung und ihre Bildung.' For a critique of Hans Licht and other earlier approaches to the hetaera, see now Carola Reinsberg, *Ehe, Hetärentum und Knabenliebe im antiken Griechenland* (Munich, 1989), pp. 80–6.

5. A good recent example of this phenomenon taken to extremes is found in the account of Pericles' marriages by Charles W. Fornara and Loren J. Samons II, from which Aspasia emerges merely as Pericles' wife, with all the evidence for her being a *pallakē* or *hetaira*, or manager of a brothel, ascribed to 'the assumption of her lubricity coupled with her low civic status'. In fact, 'her harlots had solidified out of the empty air', *Athens from Cleisthenes to Pericles* (Berkeley, 1991), p. 164.

6. Eva Keuls, *The Reign of the Phallus* (New York, 1985), p. 204.

7. R. Just, *Women in Athenian Law and Life*, p. 141. If anything, attitudes are hardening. The most recent treatment stresses 'the absoluteness of the disjunction between the roles of the *hetaira* and the wife', D. Ogden, *Greek Bastardy* (Oxford, 1996), p. 105.

8. C. Reinsberg, *Ehe, Hetärentum und Knabenliebe . . .*, p. 87.

9. R. Just, *Women in Athenian Law and Life*, p. 5; cf. Peter Brown, 'Plots and Prostitutes in Greek New Comedy', *Papers of the Leeds International Latin Seminar, Sixth Volume* (Leeds 1990), pp. 248–9.

10. See for instance, Dem. 39.26, with 40.8 and .27; Isaeus 3.10–17 and .39; Antiphanes 210 K-A; Plu. *Alc.* 8.3; Porphyr 260;F11; Ath.577cd, acknowl-edged by Lipsius and Wyse; J. H. Lipsius, *Das Attische Recht und Rechtsver-fahren* II (Leipzig, 1912), pp. 480f.; Wyse ad Isaeus 3.5.' An unnecessary and unwarranted modern dogma is being created by which an Athenian woman cannot *by definition* be a hetaera: 'any *hetaira* who took up residence with a man could be referred to as a *pallakē*. The question, however, is whether in the classical period there were also *pallakai* who were not *hetairai*, but Athenian women, *astai*' (R. Just, *Women in Athenian Law and Life*, p. 52, cf. pp. 140, 151). For Daniel Ogden in the most recent treatment of the subject, these Athenian hetaeras are only pseudo-hetaeras, *Greek Bastardy*, p. 161. The debate is already an old one, and claims that there are no examples of Athenian *hetairai* have on more than one occasion been answered by citations from the relevant passages; cf. Rudolf Hirzel, *Der Name. Ein Beitrag zu seiner Geschichte im Altertum und Besonders bei den Griechen – Abhandlungen der Philologische-Historischen Klasse der Sächsischen Akademie der Wissenschaften* 36,2 (1918; 2nd edn Amsterdam, 1962), p. 71, note 1, responding to Schömann's denial.

11. [Dem.] 59.28; Men. *Samia*, 390ff.

12. Draco's code was traditionally dated to 621 BCE. The aggrieved husband

was considered no more culpable than a man who killed someone accidentally at an athletics contest [Dem.] 23.53.

13. [Dem.] 59.67; cf. Lys. 10.19; Plu. *Solon* 23,1. The phrase seems to have been a formula since it is found in whole or in part in at least two separate laws; E. Ruschenbusch, *Solōnos Nomoi* [*Historia Einzelschriften* Bd. 9], (Wiesbaden, 1966), Frr. 29 and 30; cf. M. Hillgruber, *Die zehnte Rede des Lysias* [= *Untersuchungen zur antiken Literatur und Geschichte* Bd. 29], (Berlin/ New York, 1988), pp. 77–9.

14. Cf. J.-P. Vernant, 'Hestia-Hermes', in *Myth and Thought among the Greeks* (London, 1983), pp. 127–75; Susan Walker, 'Women and Housing in Classical Greece', in Averil Cameron and Amélie Kuhrt, eds, *Images of Women in Antiquity* (Beckenham, Kent, 1983), pp. 81–91.

15. Hesych. s.v. *gephuris*; Phrynichus Com. 34 K-A; Com. Adesp. 1352 K; Theopompus, *FGrHist* 115 F225 and 213; Timocles 24, 1–2 K-A.

16. Xen. *Mem.* 2.2,4.

17. Aeschin. 1.80–5. For *lakkos* (cistern, well or reservoir) cf. Aristodemus *ap.* Ath. 13 585a; Machon 281–4 (Gow).

18. Ar. *Knights* 1397ff. R. A. Neil in his commentary ad loc. reviews the evidence for Greeks eating ass-meat (rare) and dog-meat (very rare) and recalls that Jerome Cardan served the Archbishop of St Andrews with a dish of whelps as late as 1553. It is very likely, however, that some obscene allusion to prostitution (male or female) lies not far below the surface of this phrase. For the Ceramicus and its reputation see R. E. Wycherley, *The Athenian Agora* III, pp. 222ff. (Princeton, 1957); Knigge, *Der Kerameikos von Athen* (Athens, 1988).

19. *Frogs* 422ff. Cleisthenes was notorious for his effeminacy. The reference is perhaps to his son or his lover.

20. *Peace* 11.164ff.

21. For the *aulos*, see M. L. West, *Ancient Greek Music* (Oxford, 1992), pp. 105f. I am grateful to Peter Wilson for showing me his unpublished paper on the *aulos* in Athens.

22. Metagenes 4 K-A; cf. Theopompus *FGrHist* 115 F290; Ar. *Ach.* 551; Adespota 1025.1 K-A. In general, see H. Herter, 'Die Soziologie . . .', *JbAC* 3(1960), 86, note 290.

23. Another element in the military metaphor of the prostitute infantry, Plato 170 K-A, with editors' comments ad loc. The flute accompanied all kinds of activity, from kneading dough to pulling down walls, see M. L. West, *Ancient Greek Music*, pp. 28ff.

24. Dio Chrysost. 1.1–2; Arist. fr. 583 (Rose). The earliest version of this story is told of the people of Cardia whose enemies learn the correct tunes by buying a flute-girl from there, Charon of Lampsacus *FGrHist* 262 F1.

25. 'Hippocrates' *Epidemics* 5.81. For the mystic power of the *aulos* and the importance of flute-girls in the *kōmos*, see F. Lissarague and F. Frontisi-

Ducroux, 'From Ambiguity to Ambivalence', in D. Halperin, J. J. Winkler and F. Zeitlin, eds; *Before Sexuality* (Princeton, 1990): pp. 220ff.

26. Isoc. *Antid.* 287; Plato *Symp.* 215c; H. Herter, 'Die Soziologie . . .', 97–8, Gomme-Sandbach ad Menander *Perikeiromene* 340. A comic fragment found on papyrus refers to a girl (probably) as αυλ]ητριδιου γαρ συμπο[-τικου, Adespota 1007 K-A 1.34, as if a distinction was drawn between sympotic and non-sympotic flute-girls.

27. cf. Men. *Perikeiromene* 337ff.: Moschion wants to know why Glycera fights shy of him and Daos reminds him that she is no flute-girl and will require a certain amount of getting to know, see A. W. Gomme and F. H. Sandbach, *Menander: A Commentary* (Oxford, 1973). In Epicrates *Anti-Lais* 2 K-A, flute-girls are contrasted with the rapacious 'high-priced hetaeras', see Athen. 13.570b. *Aulētris* is sometimes paired with hetaera instead of *pornē* to denote the full range of sexually available women, so Phylarchus *FGrHist* 81 F42 claims that in Ceos 'there were no hetaeras or flute-girls to be seen'. Cf. Theopompus *FGrHist* 115 F213.

28. Xen. *Hell.* 2.2.27.

29. Dem. 21.36; Ar. *Wasps* 1353ff; *Ach.* 524ff. (this makes better sense of the joke than looking for arcane parallels with Herodotus, as D. M. McDowell has noted recently, *Aristophanes and Athens* [Oxford, 1996], pp. 62–3), cf. Lysias 3.43, 4.7; K. J. Dover, *Greek Homosexuality* (London, 1978), p. 57: 'the mauling and pulling of a slave-girl, with the imminent intervention of someone who wants to take her to a different destination, is not an infrequent motif in late archaic and early classical vase-painting, and the end which the energetic males in these pictures are pursuing is not philosophical discussion.' Athenaeus (13.555a) has a story which illustrates the centrality of such disputes in ordinary life. The comic poet Antiphanes was not surprised at Alexander's cool response to a recital of one of his plays: 'To appreciate this kind of stuff', he replied, 'it is necessary to have dined out often at bring-your-own dinners, and to have exchanged blows over a hetaera even more often.'

30. [Arist.] *Ath. Pol.* 50.2, who also mentions harp- and cithara-players, and Adespota 1025 K-A, where the conversation seems to be concerned with flute-girls at cross-roads, Astynomoi and wings being clipped.

31. Hyp. *Eux.* 3; cf. Suid. Δ 528, an *eisangelia*, perhaps because the Astynomoi were considered public arbitrators.

32. Anacreon *PMG* 346.12 [=fr1(b)]. Harpocration 63,3 (Dindorf) collapses those supervised by the Astynomoi into one category: 'they were in charge of the flute-girls and the harp-girls and the shit-collectors and suchlike.' An obscure joke by the hetaera Gnathaena illustrates this conception of the 'passive' partner as a mere receptacle: 'Two men, a soldier and a brigand, hired her. The soldier made a coarse remark, calling her *lakkos* [cistern]. She replied, "Is that because two rivers are flowing into me: the

Scavenger and the Freed?"', Aristodemus *ap*. Ath. 13 585a; cf. Machon 281–4 (Gow). Parent-Duchatelet made a similar connection with the women of Paris's streets and brothels: 'Prostitutes are as inevitable where men live together in large communities, as drains and refuse dumps', Dr. Alex. J. B. Parent-Duchatelet, *De la prostitution dans la ville de Paris* (Paris, 1836), II, 513. His idea that good management of prostitution is an intrinsic part of city government finds echoes in the comic poets who ascribe the provision of cheap prostitutes to the law-giver, Solon, himself.

33. Artemid. 1.78. Although Artemidorus was writing a long time after the classical period, in the second century CE, the connection he is making had deep roots in colloquial language and in the space of the Ceramicus and its equivalents on the periphery of other ancient cities.

34. *Poenulus* 268; cf. *Pseudolus* 178; 214ff.; 229ff.

35. Some time afterwards the wife of the friend was accused of having plotted the whole thing to take revenge on her unfaithful husband, tricking the slave into believing that the poison was in fact a potion to rekindle her master's love. We cannot, of course, be sure what actually happened, although the case against the wife looks unconvincing, but if the prospect of being moved to a brothel did not in fact drive the slave-girl to murder Philoneos, it was certainly considered a plausible motive by the Athenians who executed her and/or by the woman who framed her.

36. Xenarchus 4 K-A; Eubulus 67 and 82 K-A.

37. Alexis 206 K-A.

38. Eupolis 99.27 K-A; Philemon 3 K-A.

39. The best survey of the evidence is H. Lind, 'Ein Hetärenhaus am Heiligen Tor?' *MusHelv* 45 (1988), 158–69, with U. Knigge, *Der Kerameikos*, pp. 88–94. For the link between inns and brothels, see Hans Licht, *Sexual Life in Ancient Greece* (London, 1932), pp. 175–9.

40. Aeschines 1.80–5; cf. Aristodemus *ap*. Ath. 13 585a; Machon 281–4 (Gow). In *c.* 355 in his work on revenues *Poroi* (2.6), Xenophon pointed to a number of derelict buildings within the city walls and, in an early scheme for urban renewal, suggested they should be used for housing, to encourage 'more and better people' to live in Athens. It would be ironic if his suggestion led to the brothel's revival at this time.

41. Alexis 206 K-A; U. Knigge, *AM* 97 (1982), 153–70. The courtesan Laïs was devoted to a Corinthian cult of Aphrodite 'the Dark', who appeared to her at night and told her of the approach of wealthy men, Ath.13. 588c.

42. *ARV* 101.3; Alfred Brueckner, *Lebensregeln auf athenischen Hochzeitsgeschenken* [*Winckelmanns-programm der Archäologischen Gesellschaft zu Berlin* 62 1907], pp. 4–7, pl. 1. Carl Robert, *Archaeologische Hermeneutik* (Berlin, 1919), pp. 125–9.

43. Arnold von Salis, *Theseus und Ariadne* (Berlin, 1930), p. 5, cf. Robert Zahn, 'Kleinigkeiten aus Alt-Athen', *Antike I* (1925), 282: 'Ihresgleichen lieben

ja bisweilen auch mit den Tugenden der züchtigen Penelope zu kokett-ieren.' J. Beazley, Review of *CVA* Athens, Greece, fasc. 1, in *JHS* 51 (1931), 121; G. Rodenwaldt, 'Spinnende Hetären', *AA* 47 (1932), 21; Johann Friedrich Crome, 'Spinnende Hetairen?', *Gymnasium* 73 (1966), 245; C. Reinsberg, *Ehe, Hetärentum und Knabenliebe.* . . pp. 122–5; E. Keuls, *The Reign of the Phallus*, pp. 258–9.

44. Xenophon (*Mem.* 2.7) records a story of Socrates telling Aristarchus, who has many female relatives to support and no source of income, to put them to work at the loom. But this is another example of the philosopher applying logical solutions in the teeth of common convention. Aristarchus at first assumes that only slaves work like this and needs to be reminded that weaving is in itself a suitable occupation for women.

45. *Anthologia Palatina* 6.48, 285, 284 and 283.

46. 8.6,20. More literally, 'I've taken down three masts [or loom-beams] already in this short time' – a reference perhaps to entertaining ships' captains, putting in at Corinth.

47. *ARV* 795, 10294–7. For the naked spinning *hetaira* (Copenhagen, Nat. Mus. 153, = *ARV* 1131, 161), see Dyfri Williams, 'Women on Athenian Vases', in A. Cameron and A. Kuhrt, eds, *Images of Women in Antiquity*, (London, 1983), pp. 94–7; C. Reinsberg, *Ehe, Hetärentum und Knabenliebe* . . . , p. 124.

48. D. Williams, Women on Athenian Vases', pp. 96–7. The vase is Munich, Zanker: Münzen und Medaillen AG, *Auktion* 51 (Basel, 1975).

49. e.g. *ARV* 275, 50; *ARV* 189, 72, 1632.

50. Apart from Strabo, some fragments of Roman poetry place prostitutes, especially the cheapest and most despised prostitutes, next to the wool-basket, [Tibullus] 3.16 + 4.10, Petronius *Satyricon* 132. A fourth-century inscription recording grants of freedom to professional women includes many wool-workers but no prostitutes although these form the vast major-ity of such freedwomen known to us from literary sources (only prostitution made sufficient funds or sufficient patrons available). One or two hetaeras can be supplied from the ranks of the musicians on the inscription – there is one flute-girl and a harpist – but some should be drawn too perhaps from the ranks of the poorly-paid spinsters, especially those like 'Malthace' with hetaera-like names, another example perhaps of the subterfuge, or at least the avoidance of explicit labels characteristic of hetaeras; David Lewis, 'Attic Manumissions', *Hesperia* 28 (1959), 208–38.

51. See Ar. *Thesm.* 300–1; Xen. *Mem.* 3.11, 6–7 and 11; Theophilus 11 K-A, Gow ad Theocritus II.2. According to Artemidorus, in the second century CE, dreaming about woollen garlands indicates love-potions and bewitch-ment, *Oneirocrit* 1.77.

52. See Wankel ad Dem. 18.129 (694f.); cf. Xenarchus 4.17 K-A; Ar. *Wasps* 500.

53. *ARV* 795, 102; Theophilus 11 K-A.

54. *ARV* 432,60.

55. Aeschin. 1.74. I know of no *porneion* for men and when Aeschines talks of a *porneion* he refers only to female prostitutes and their pimp (124), even though his target is a man. *Oikēmata*, on the other hand, are attested for women too. When Antisthenes wishes to attack Pericles' son Xanthippus, he claims he lived with a man who was in the same trade as *the girls* stationed in the small *oikēmata*, implying that even this kind of prostitution was more familiar with female occupants, Antisthenes ap. Ath. 5.220d. In Isaeus 6.19, Euctemon's property apparently included girls stationed in *oikēmata*, and we hear of someone being prosecuted for setting up an Olynthian girl in one after her city had fallen to Philip of Macedon, but these are described as *paidiskai* ('girls'), a more respectful term than *pornai*, perhaps reflecting a more respectable kind of prostitution; one of the girls, Alce, achieves a degree of renown which would have been rather difficult for an anonymous slave in a *porneion*; cf. Wyse ad loc.; Dinarchus 1.23, [Dem.] 59.18; Theopompus *FGrHist* 115 F114.

56. D. L. 2.105. He grew his hair long perhaps to distinguish himself from the slave-prostitute he had once been and to recall his aristocratic background, or perhaps it had been for his clients' benefit.

57. Plato *Charm.* 163b; Aeschines 1.158; Ar. *Frogs*: 148: the *pais* referred to could be male or female.

58. A letter of the later third century from Egypt records a complaint against one Demo, 'the hetaera' (*hē kai mistharnei*), P. *Magd.* 14.3.

59. Epicrates 2 K-A. For Charixene, Ar. *Thesm.* 943, *Etym. Magn.* 367.12, Hesychius 5413 and see my comments on Gnesippus and the *paignion* in F. D. Harvey and J. Wilkins, eds, *The Rivals of Aristophanes* (forthcoming). For Glauce see Gow ad Theocritus 4.31.

60. See Kassel-Austin ad Eupolis 184.

61. Xen. *Hell.* 5.4,4.

62. Men. *Samia* 390ff. The sixth of Lucian's *Dialogues of the Courtesans* which look back to fourth-century comedy present a quite different pressure on the *mistharnousa* to eat only with her finger-tips, to take only little sips of wine, and to keep her gaze fixed only on the man who hired her.

63. Aeschin. 1.188; [Dem.] 59.30; cf. Theoph. *Char.* 6.5; Arist. *EN* 1121b.

64. Men., *Epitrep.*. 136-7, and 436ff.; Plautus, *Asin.* 746ff.

65. Xen. *Symp.* 2.1, 9.2ff.

66. Xen. *Symp.* 4.53-4; Aeschines 1.41 and the comic fragments cited by Athenaeus 8.339ac.

67. Aeschin. 1.160-5.

68. Lysias 3.21-6, with Carey's notes ad loc.

69. Plautus, *Asin.* 746ff., cf. *Mercator* 536ff., *Bacchides* fr. X and 896f., Turpilius com. fr. 112 Ribbeck *Leucadia*; cf. Hans-Peter Schonbeck, [*Sprach- und Literaturwissenschaften: Klassische Philologie*] *Beiträge zur Interpretation der plauti-*

nischen 'Bacchides' (Düsseldorf, 1981), pp. 150–1 and 203, note 77 and in general H. Herter, 'Die Soziologie . . .', 81, notes 193 and 194.

70. [Dem.] 59.29. Sharing a mistress was not a particularly unusual arrangement in the ancient world. Often as in this case a slave might be too expensive for one man to afford on his own. Other *ménages* are the result of a compromise enforced between two men fighting over the same woman, cf. ibid. 47; Lysias 4.

71. Ar. *Peace* 1138–9; Lysias 1.12.

72. [Dem.] 59.22, [And.] 4.14, cf. D. Ogden, *Greek Bastardy*, pp. 100–6.

73. Hyp. *In Athenog.* 5–6; Antiphanes 236 K-A; Ar. *Wasps* 1345–59; cf. E. Fantham, 'Sex, Status and Survival in Hellenistic Athens', *Phoenix* 29 (1972), 63–4: '[freeing a slave] is both a symbol of their infatuated folly and a mark of the escapism and pie-in-the-sky of this type of comedy. Terence allows his boys to keep but not liberate their slave-mistresses.'

74. [Dem.] 59.30–48. It is possible that Phrynion, like the defendant in Lysias 4, claimed that Neaera was not a freedwoman but a slave, see Carey ad 40.

75. Even he seems to acknowledge that 'hetaera' is normally used of a woman in a permanent relationship, by using the qualification *misthamousa* (hired) whenever she isn't, and referring to Neaera as Stephanus' hetaera or his *pallakē*, apparently interchangeably, [Dem.] 59.118–19. Likewise, Chrysis in Menander's *Samia* is referred to both as Demeas' hetaera (170) and his *pallakē* (508). We hear of citizen women 'given' as *pallakai* on specific terms, Isaeus 3.39, but hetaeras too had their contracts and this does not mean that *pallakē* is therefore a 'technical' term or was once a more officially defined status; see G. Busolt and H. Swoboda, *Griechische Staatskunde*[3] (Munich, 1926), p. 941, note 3; Wyse ad Isaeus 3.5; and Carey ad [Dem.] 59.122. For men too *hetairein* implies monogamy: according to Aeschines, if Timarchus had stayed with Misgolas the cithara-boy fancier, he would have accused him only of that, 'For the man who does this with one person and does it for pay seems to me to be liable to precisely this charge', 1.51.

76. Ar. *Peace* 439–40; Lycurgus, *In Leo.* 19 and 55; Hyp. *In Athenog.* 18; Dem. 48, 53–5; Plu. *Alc.* 39. Athenaeus has numerous stories about famous men associated with and often living with hetaeras in book 13.

77. Plu. *Per.* c.24.

78. Isaeus 6.21; Dem. 36.45; cf 40.51, Letters 3.31.

79. Idomeneus *FGrHist* 338 F14; cf. Hyp. *In defence of Phryne* fr. 124 (Blass).

80. Isaeus 6, Dem. 48.53–5.

81. Amphis 1 K-A; Plato *Rep.* 420a; Xen. *Anab.* 4.3,19; cf. Theopompus *FGrHist* 115 F213.

82. Polybius 14.11, 3–4; Machon 11.252, 258, 262–84 (Gow); cf. 175, Callimachus fr. 433 Pfeiffer; Ar. *Clouds* 996; Amphis 23 K-A; [Dem.] 59.37, 42; Xen. Mem. 3.11, 4; Ath. 13.591d.

83. David M. Schaps, *Economic Rights of Women in Ancient Greece* (Edinburgh, 1979), pp. 15–17; [Dem.] 59.46 and 41; Ath. 13.574e.

84. Lynceus of Samos *ap.* Ath. 13.584b, 6.246b; Machon frr. 6 and 7 (Gow); Ath. 13.591de. A couple of papyri from the military colony of Elephantine concerning payments by a woman called Elaphion may throw some light on the phenomenon. A. E. Samuel viewed the documents as records of a hetaera hiring a 'lord and master': 'The sum she pays as *tropheia* is to accomplish two purposes. The man to whom she pays it is to serve as her *kurios*, so that she will have someone to fulfill these duties when she has occasion to have legal documents drawn up. At the same time, he is to provide her with such material support as she may need', *Ptolemaic Chronology* (Munich, 1962), p. 23; cf. E. Grzybek, 'Die griechische Konkubine und ihre Mitgift (P. Eleph.3 and 4)', *ZPE* 76 (1989), 206–12.

85. Crates *ap.* Plu. Mor. 401a; Ath. 13 591b; Theopompus *FGrHist* 115 248 and 253; Dicaearchus 21 (Wehrli) *ap.* Ath. 13.595f (even a work on divination provides opportunities for moralizing); Philemon 15 K-A.

86. Lysias 365 (Thalheim).

CHAPTER IV · A PURCHASE ON THE HETAERA

1. Aristophanes *Wealth*, 149–59. For this opposition between gift-exchange and commodity-exchange, see the broad definition provided by C. A. Gregory from the insights of Mauss and Marx, *Gifts and Commodities* (London, 1982), 19. The relationship between gift-exchange and seduction and between commodity-exchange and the promiscuous quest for orgasmic pleasure is nicely drawn out by Jean Baudrillard, *Seduction* Eng. transl. (London, 1990), p. 38. Baudrillard sees these two dynamics as exclusive alternatives, but the case of Athens seems to show how they can function in the same place at the same time, as self-consciously opposed terms, dependent on each other for meaning. Georg Simmel's reflections on prostitution are similarly perceptive and relevant although they precede Mauss's essay by several decades, *Philosophie des Geldes* (2nd edn Berlin, 1907; Eng. transl. London, 1978), pp. 370ff. esp. 376–8.

2. Philemon 3 K-A.

3. Isaeus 3.13–15; [Dem] 59.67.

4. Aeschin. 1.123–4.

5. Aeschin. 40 and 70; Ath. 13.588f.

6. *SVF* 1 fr. 451; Antigonus of Carystus 117 (Wilamowitz); Aeschin. 1.40; Dem. 19.229.

7. [Dem.] 59.108, cf. 30, 32, 39, 41, 49, 108; Asclepiades, *FGrHist* 157 F1. There must be a possibility that Clepsydra was a fictional character.

8. Xenarchus 4 K-A: [Dem.] 59.22, 36: Aeschin. 1.52, 31, 39, 55, 40.

9. *Wasps* 1353, *Ach.* 764–96. For this episode and a thorough exegesis of the

word-play involved, see K. J. Dover, *Aristophanic Comedy* (Berkeley, 1972), pp. 63–5. Cf. J. Henderson, *The Maculate Muse* (New Haven, 1975), pp. 131ff. Henderson cites also Aristophanes 589 K-A, but Pollux, who preserves the fragment, gives no indication that the 'piglet-sellers' referred to are prostitutes or pimps.

10. Aeschin. 1.15 cf. 137, Arist. *Politics* 1311b. Eubulus 67.9 K-A contrasts it with *pothos* (something like 'sentimental longing') and connects it with adulterers. D. M. MacDowell, 'Hubris in Athens', *Greece and Rome* 23 (1976), 14–31, esp. 17–19; cf. J. Henderson, *The Maculate Muse*, p. 159, no. 249 with note 40; D. Cohen, 'Law, Society, and Homosexuality in Classical Athens', *P and P* 117 (1987), 7; N.R.E. Fisher has provided a comprehensive survey of the term in his *Hybris* (Warminster, 1992). I do not agree with him on the importance of the 'dishonouring' of hubris' victims. There can be hubris without victims, cf. most recently D. L. Cairns, 'Hybris, Dishonour and Thinking Big', *JHS* 106 (1996), 1–32.

11. Suda s.v. *pernatai*; Eupolis 99.27 K-A; Ar. *Frogs* 1327, with schol., cf. Plato 143 K-A; 188 K-A; *Wasps* 500–3 puts *kelēs* in the same context as a luxurious fish, the *orphōs*. *SEG* xviii.93 looks like a prostitute's dedication after the performance of 'many jockeyings', Machon 300–10. Note also the early Attic red-figure pinax fragments with erotic scenes in the Ashmolean Museum, dated to late sixth/early fifth centuries, see A. Greifenhagen, 'Fragmente eines rotfigurigen Pinax', in L. Bonafante and H. von Heintze, eds, *In Memoriam Otto J. Brendel. Essays in Archaeology and the Humanities* (Mainz, 1976), pp. 43–8. *Pinakes* are often dedications depicting the labours of a particular profession. For the sex manuals, see Holt N. Parker, 'Love's Body Anatomized: the Ancient Erotic Handbooks and the Rhetoric of Sexuality', in Amy Richlin, ed., *Pornography and Representation in Greece and Rome* (Oxford, 1992), pp. 90–111.

12. Theopompus *FGrHist* 115 F253; Gorgias *ap.* Ath.13.596f.

13. Georg Simmel, *Die Philosophie des Geldes* (2nd edn Berlin, 1907), transl. as *The Philosophy of Money* (London, 1978), pp. 376–7; Artemidorus *Oneiroc.* 1.78; Epicrates 3 K-A.

14. For some interesting observations on the terminology of sex-work, see the letter from Tracy Quan, published in *The New York Review of Books* 5 November 1992, vol. 39, no. 18, p. 61; cf. Cecilie Høigård and Liv Finstad, *Backstreets, Prostitution, Money and Love* (London, 1992), p. 52.

15. Xen. *Mem.* 3.11,4 and 12, cf. 1.2,52.

16. Ar. *Thesm.* 344–5; Pausanias 1.20,1–2; 9.27,3–5; Strabo 9.2,25; Ath. 13.591a, cf. *AP Planudean Appendix* 204. Perhaps the famous passage from Plato's *Phaedrus* (255ce), where desire is described in terms of the creation of a replica of love in the image of the other's love, throws light on the epigram's logic here. The complex ramifications of the gift were not lost on later epigrammatists *AP Planudean Appendix*, 203–6. What is especially

interesting is the way that Praxiteles' gift to Phryne is seen as discharging an obligation and thus liberating himself. Leonidas of Alexandria (?) calls the statue 'a ransom of his desires', 206.

17. Theopompus *FGrHist* 115 F248.

18. Netta Zagagi, *Tradition and Originality in Plautus* [=*Hypomnemata 62*] (Göttingen, 1980), p. 118; P. Oxy 3533 = Menander, *Misoumenos* A 37–40; cf. E. G. Turner, 'The Lost Beginning of Menander, *Misoumenos*, *Proceedings of the British Academy* 73 (1977), 315–31; A. Borgogno, 'Sul nuovissimo *Misumenos* di Menandro', *QUCC* n.s. 30 (1988), 87–97; Men. *Theophoroumene* 16–22; E. W. Handley, 'Notes on the *Theophoroumene* of Menander', *BICS* 16 (1969), 88–101.

19. Xen. *Mem.* 3.11,10–11, 13, cf. 14; Machon 429–32 (Gow), cf. 327–32, 226–30; the punchline is an adaptation of Sophocles' *Electra* 1.2, see Gow ad loc. Philemon 3.15 K-A, cf. Men., *Samia* 392. Pierre Bourdieu, *Outline of a Theory of Practice* Eng transl. (Cambridge, 1977), pp. 5–6; Socrates got into trouble for his cynical attitude to friendships, according to Xenophon's account of his trial, *Mem.* 1.2,52.

20. For Philaenis see K. Tsantsanoglou, 'Memoirs of a Lady from Samos', *ZPE* 12 (1973), 183–95. I think it highly likely that fr. 3, col. ii, which contains the flattering epithets for various kinds of ladies is still part of this section of *peirasmoi*. Xen. *Mem.* 3.11,1, 1.16,3; [Dem.] 59.20 cf. 23; Isaeus 3.16, cf. 13; Theopompus *FGrHist* 115 F253; Aeschin. 1,52; cf. Didrachmon who would visit 'whoever wanted' for two drachmas.

21. Pierre Bourdieu, *The Logic of Practice* Eng. transl. (Cambridge, 1990), p. 99; Machon 450–5 and 349–75 (Gow); Ath. 13.588e. There could be dangers however in leaving behind the certainties of Clepsydra's clock and Two-drachma's pricing policy. Men too could work uncertainty to their advantage: 'Sometime afterwards, they say, Gnathaenium refused to show her usual affection to Andronicus when they were drinking together. She was angry because she was receiving nothing from him.' He complains to Gnathaena, who reproaches her daughter: 'But mother', she replies, 'is it likely that I would be a friend to someone who brings me no benefit but wants the whole of "hollow Argos" under his roof as a free gift (*dōcrea*)', Machon (Gow) 376–86. The punchline is rather obscure, but presumably 'hollow Argos' refers to her lap.

22. Timocles 24 K-A.

23. The classic study remains John Gould's article, 'Law, Custom and Myth: Aspects of the Social Position of Women in Classical Athens', *JHS* 100 (1980), 38–59. More recent is Lisa Nevett's study of the archaeological evidence: 'The Organization of Space in Classical and Hellenistic Houses', in Nigel Spencer, ed., *Time, Tradition and Society in Greek Archaeology* (London, 1995), pp. 89–108.

24. Luce Irigaray, *Ce sexe qui n'est pas une* (Paris, 1977), Eng. transl. (Ithaca NY, 1985), pp. 25–6; Ar. *Peace* 978–86; *Thesm.* 790 and 797–9.

25. Xen. *Mem.* 3.11,1–3.

26. *Ecc.* 1–13; Xen. *Mem.* 3.11,10; Ath. 13.585c; cf. J. Henderson, *The Maculate Muse*, pp. 137ff.

27. Eubulus 67.3–4 K-A, 82.3 K-A; Xenarchus 4.6, 4, 18–23 K-A, with Ath. 13.569a; Philemon 3.10–12 K-A.

28. Dem. 23.53. D. Cohen, 'The Athenian Law of Adultery', *RIDA* 31 (1984), 147–65; 'The Social Context of Adultery at Athens', in Paul Cartledge, Paul Millett and Stephen Todd, eds, *Nomos. Essays in Athenian Law, Politics and Society* (Cambridge, 1990), p. 147. The problem lies in the search for a single Athenian law on adultery when, in fact, the penalties and definitions of the crime were probably an amalgamation of provisions in different laws, not only the Draconian law on justifiable homicide, but also the Solonian law referred to by the speaker of Lysias, *Against Theomnestus* I, 10.19. Xenarchus indicates and Lysias 1 assumes, that the law of Draco was treated as a law on *moicheia*; cf. Stephen Todd, *The Shape of Athenian Law* (Oxford, 1993), p. 278: 'to speak of one statute dealing with the subject may be to import misleadingly substantivist notions into the organization of Athenian law.' Cf. M. H. Hansen's comments on the class of *kakourgoi*, which included *moichoi*, *Apagoge, Endeixis and Ephegesis against Kakourgoi, Atimoi and Pheugontes* (Odense, 1976), p. 47: 'Since there were no professional lawyers in Athens, the interpretation of the law was left to the parties in the case, to the Eleven and, most of all, to the jurors. They decided what was Athenian law, at least on that particular day. Practice may have changed not only from generation to generation but from year to year, and even from case to case. As precedent was an almost unknown phenomenon in Athenian law, it must have been impossible to arrive at any fixed interpretation of the law. The magistrates who accepted the written accusation and imprisoned the arrested person varied from year to year, and the jurors from day to day. Accordingly, even if our source material had been perfect, it would have been impossible to draw up a definitive and comprehensive list of *kakourgoi* in the legal sense of the word.'

29. Glycera in the *Perikeiromene* 1.478, 357, 370, and 390 (cf. 986) with Gomme-Sandbach ad loc., the new fragment of *Misoumenòs* A 37–40, Machon 1.218–25 (Gow). Also relevant is the passage from the *Misoumenos* (11.216–21) in which Getas, Thrasonides' servant, finding Cratia in the arms of Demeas, in fact her father, treats him like a *moichos* caught *in flagrante*, using language which would identify the old man as one of that very specific group of criminals called *kakourgoi*, see M. H. Hansen, *Apagoge, Endeixis and Ephegesis against Kakourgoi, Atimoi and Pheugontes*, pp. 48–9. Ugo Paoli cites a parallel passage from Plautus' *Miles gloriosus* (461–2, cf. 146). He concludes: 'la norma che consente di uccidere l'adultero sorpreso in casa con la concubina è così chiaramente attestata dalle fonti che la conferma offerta da una concreta fattispecie non è necessaria.' 'Il reato di

adulterio in diritto Attico', in *Altri Studi di Diritto Greco e Romano* (Milan, 1976) 253ff [=*SDHI* 16 (1950), 123ff.], 263. Daniel Ogden in the most recent treatment of the subject considers the use of terms like 'married' when used of hetaeras merely 'affectionate' and paradoxical, *Greek Bastardy*, pp. 105–6.

30. For Gnesippus, see Chionides 4 K-A; Eupolis 148 K-A; Telecleides 36 K-A; Cratinus 17, 104 and 276 K-A; and my forthcoming article in F. D. Harvey and J. Wilkins, eds, *The Rivals of Aristophanes*. For Philaenis see K. Tsantsanoglou, 'Memoirs of a Lady from Samos', 183–95.

31. Aristophon 4 K-A. Epicrates 3.11–13 and 16 K-A; Ath. 13.588c; Machon, 337–8 (Gow); Xen. *Hell.* 5.4,4; Philemon 3.10 K-A; Antiphanes *ap.* Ath. 13.587b; Alexis 103.7–15 and 19 K-A; cf. Guy Oakes (transl.), *Georg Simmel: On Women, Sexuality, and Love* (New Haven, 1984), pp. 136–7, 'Die Koketterie': 'In contemporary ethnography, it is regarded as certain that the covering of the sexual organs, and clothing in general, originally had nothing at all to do with the feeling of shame. Rather, it served only the need for ornamentation and the closely related intention of exercising sexual attraction by means of concealment. Among peoples who go naked there are cases in which only prostitutes wear clothing! . . . refusal and the withdrawal of the self are fused with the phenomenon of drawing attention to the self and presenting the self in one indivisible act. By ornamenting ourselves or a part of ourselves, we conceal what is adorned. And by concealing it, we draw attention to it and its attractions.'

32. Hermippus 68aI (Wehrli) *ap.* Ath. 590ef.; Ath. 13. 590de, 591f; cf. [Plut.] *Hyperides* 849e; Harpocration s.v. Euthias; Anon. *de sublimitate* 34.3; Quint. 10.5,2. The trial is also referred to in tne third century comic playwright Posidippus 13 K-A. He does not refer directly to Phryne's exposure of herself, but should not be considered to present a contradictory account. In general, see A. Farina, *Il processo di Frine* (Naples, 1959). The fascination with the story has not been confined to antiquity. As late as the nineteenth century Phryne could be a subject for painters, see J. Whitely, 'The Revival in Painting of Themes Inspired by Antiquity in Mid-Nineteenth Century France' (D.Phil thesis, Oxford University 1972), pp. 238ff., cited by T. J. Clark, *The Painting of Modern Life* (London, 1985), p. 294, note 117, who discusses the theme himself and reproduces some of the representations, pp. 111–14.

33. Plautus, *Asin.* 792; Anaxilas 22.22–24 K-A; *Anth. Pal.* 5.2. Plutarch records the following story of the wise eighth-century Pharaoh Bocchoris: A man had been smitten with love for the hetaera Thonis. Unfortunately she charged too much, but then he had a dream in which he enjoyed her favours and was released from his desires. Thonis was wise to the concept of intellectual property and sued for payment. The pharaoh resolved the dispute by ordering the man to bring the sum demanded into court,

allowing Thonis to grasp at its shadow. The hetaera Lamia at the end of the fourth century, however, argued that Bocchoris had got it wrong, since Thonis' desire for money was not sated by the shadow of gold, while her client's desire for her had been sated by the dream. Plu. *Dem.* c. 27.

CHAPTER V · BODIES

1. Harry Gene Levine, 'The Discovery of Addiction. Changing Conceptions of Habitual Drunkenness in America', *Journal of Studies on Alcohol* 39.1 (1978), 143–74.
2. For a critique of the addiction model in drinking see Nick Heather and Ian Robertson, *Problem Drinking* 2nd edn (Oxford, 1989).
3. Antiphanes 188 K-A.
4. Euphanes 1 K-A.
5. Ar. *Peace* 801–812; Archippus 28 K-A; cf. *Peace* 1009–115; Eupolis 178 K-A; Callias 14 K-A; Leuco 3 K-A; Pherecrates 148 K-A. Clearchus 55 (Wehrli) *ap.* Ath. 1.6c.
6. Antiphanes 77 K-A.
7. Alexis 57 K-A, Eubulus 8 K-A, with editors' notes ad loc.
8. Machon IX, X (Gow). Philoxenus was enslaved in his youth by the Athenians when they captured Cythera during the Peloponnesian War. He seems to have ended his days at the court of Dionysius, tyrant of Syracuse – see Gow ad loc.
9. *Knights* 353–5 and 928ff.
10. Anaxand. 34 K-A.
11. Chrysippus *ap.* Ath. 1.5df; Clearchus 54 (Wehrli) *ap.* Ath.1.6c, a story perhaps remembered from comedy cf. Crobylus 8 K-A.
12. H. G. Levine, 'The Discovery of Addiction', 143; Dwight Heath, 'A Critical Review of Ethnographic Studies of Alcohol Use', in R. Gibbons, Y. Israel, H. Kalant, R. Popham, W. Schmidt, and R. Smart, eds, *Research Advances in Alcohol and Drug Problems* Vol. 2 (New York, 1975), p. 57.
13. See for instance Oswyn Murray's introduction to the collection of articles on the Greek symposium, 'Sympotic History', in *Sympotica: a Symposium on the Symposion* (Oxford, 1990), pp. 3–13, esp. pp. 5ff. and now 'Histories of Pleasure', in id. and M. Tecuşan, eds, *In Vino Veritas* (London, 1995), pp. 4–5. For older alcoholist treatments cf. W. L. Brown, 'Inebriety and its "Cures" among the Ancients', *Proceedings of the Society for the Study of Inebriety* 55 (1898); J. D. Rolleston, 'Alcoholism in Classical Antiquity', *British Journal of Inebriety* 24 (1927), 101–20; A. P. McKinlay, 'Attic Temperance', *Quarterly Journal of Studies on Alcohol* 11 (1950), 230–46.
14. *FGrHist* 115 FF185 and 143 cf. F121 = Ath. 10.444e–445a and the other anecdotes in 10. 435f–436c.
15. F20 cf. his comic namesake Theopompus 31 K-A.

16. Crates, T 2a K-A; Philemon 104 K-A. For a useful survey of wine in comedy, see E. L. Bowie's article in O. Murray and M. Tecuşan, eds, *In Vino Veritas*, pp. 113–25.

17. *Knights* 104ff. and 354–5; Cratinus 203 K-A; for *Putinē*, see Kassel-Austin ad fab. and Bowie loc. cit., pp. 116, note 12 and 121–2. For the vase, see A. Greifenhagen, '*Philopotēs*', *Gymnasium* 82 (1975), 26–32.

18. Hyp., *In Dem.* p. 24 (Jensen); Lynceus of Samos *ap.* Ath. 6.245f–246a.

19. J.-C. Sournia, *A History of Alcoholism* (Oxford, 1990), pp. 10–11.

20. Antiphon, B 87 F 76 D-K.

21. Athenaeus 10.433b tries to distinguish between a wine-lover, who is eager for wine, a drink-lover who is eager for drinking-sessions and a *kōthōnistēs* who drinks to intoxication, but the latter does not seem to have been a classical category.

22. Philemon 104.3 K-A. This is not to say that there weren't drinkers in ancient Greece who would have found it difficult to stop if so required – I have no doubt that there were – simply that without a Temperance Movement to test them their compulsion was invisible to their neighbours and perhaps to themselves.

23. Arist. *Hist. Anim.* 559b; [Arist.] *Prob.* 3.5, 871a.

24. For Alcibiades, see Eupolis 385 K-A. For Philip, D.S. 16.86,6–87,2; Theopompus *FGrHist* 115 FF163, 236, 282; Duris *FGrHist* 76 F37b; and Val. Max. 6.2 ext.1.

25. Men. *Kolax* F2 (Koerte).

26. *FGrHist* 117 F2a *ap.* Aelian *VH* 3.23. It is hard to say whether the sarcastic tone revealed in this extract is original or Aelian's own.

27. The best review of the question is in P. A. Brunt's introduction to the Loeb edition of Arrian, I, pp. xxiv–vi cf. II, 288–93 nn. A. B. Bosworth, *From Arrian to Alexander* (Oxford, 1988), c. 7 comes back to the theory that the diaries are designed to refute a charge of poisoning.

28. The modern example that springs most readily to mind is the vicar's wife in Alan Bennett's *Talking Heads* monologue.

29. Her. 2.174,1, Theopompus *FGrHist* 115 FF139, 227.

30. Theopompus *FGrHist* 115 F20; Plutarch *Alexander* c. 23.

31. Dem. 6.30, 19.46; Lucian *Dem. Encom.* c. 15. Comedy was generally in agreement with the unsympathetic treatment of water-drinkers, cf. Baton 2 K-A, Phrynichus 74 K-A.

32. *Knights* 344ff.

33. [Hippocrates] *Airs, Waters, Places* c. 1.

34. Cf. R. Joris, 'Le vin comme médicament dans l'Antiquité', in *Proceedings of the 29th International Conference in the History of Medicine* (Cairo, December 1984). In the Roman period, some doctors were famous for their alcoholic prescriptions, see John D'Arms, 'Heavy Drinking and Drunkenness', in O. Murray and M. Teçusan, eds, *In Vino Veritas*, pp. 304–17.

35. The ancient lifespan was normally too short for chronic health problems to make themselves manifest.

36. For Cleomenes of Sparta, Her. 6.84. Athenaeus 10.434d claims to have found the story about Callisthenes in three authors including the normally reliable Aristobulus; for Hephaestion, Plu. *Alexander* 72, cf. [Hipp.] *Epid*, 3.1є', 17ι', ιϛ', Mnesitheus *ap*. Ath. 10.483f–484b.

37. Ephippus *FGrHist* 126 F3, DS 17.117,1–2 cf. Arrian 7.25,1–26,3, Plutarch, *Alexander* 76.

38. *Iliad* 14.294, Euripides *TGF* 438.

39. *Rep.* 3.403a; *Laws* 6.783ab; Prodicus D-K 84 F7.

40. Plato *Charm.* 154c; Xen. *Mem.* 1.3,13.

41. Antiphanes 101 K-A; Ar. *Frogs* 428–30; *Birds* 285–6 with schol., Kassel-Austin ad Eupolis *Kolakes*, T iv; Cratinus 81 K-A; And. 1.124–9 with the introduction to MacDowell's edition, pp. 10–11.

42. Plu., *Alcibiades* 23; Lysias, p. 346 (Thalheim); Antisthenes *ap*. Ath. 5.220c; Arist. *Rhet.* 2.6,4. The story of Sophocles' joke against Euripides that while he might be a misogynist in his tragedies he was a 'gynophile' in bed, has more satirical point if we see it as a reference to adultery, Hieronymus of Rhodes *ap*. Ath. 13.557e and 604ef.

43. For the legal penalties of adultery, see S. Todd, *The Shape of Athenian Law* (Oxford, 1993), pp. 276–9; cf. Dover ad Ar. *Clouds* 981.

44. Arist. *On Sophistic Refutations* c. 5 (167b 9); *Rhet.* 1.12,5, 3.15,5; Phylarchus *FGrHist* 81 F45.

45. Aeschylus, *Ag.* 1625–6; K. J. Dover, *Greek Homosexuality* (London, 1978), pp. 105–6.

46. Callisthenes, *FGrHist* 124 F34, and see A. B. Bosworth, *A Historical Commentary on Arrian's History of Alexander I* (Oxford, 1980), ad II.5. The account of Arbaces' visit seems to come from the fourth-century historian of Persia, Ctesias of Cnidus, and is listed among his fragments by Jacoby, *FGrHist* 688 F1p. There are some twentieth-century parallels for this attitude, perhaps inevitable in societies where men and women are seen to occupy separate worlds. Apart from the allusions to effeminacy contained in terms like 'womanizer' and 'ladies' man', it is thought that 'puff' may originally have come from 'powder puff', military slang for a womanizer.

47. For Misgolas, see Aeschines 1.41 and the comic fragments cited by Athenaeus 8.339ac. For Sophocles see Ion of Chios *ap*. Ath. 13.603e–604d.

48. Dicaearchus *ap*. Ath. 13.603ab.

49. Aeschin. 1.131,; Ar. *Thesm.* 130ff. esp. 200, F128 K-A.

50. There is a rather large bibliography on this subject now, but some of the highlights might include, Kenneth Dover's *Greek Homosexuality*, esp. pp. 100–9; M. Foucault, *The Use of Pleasure* (Paris, 1984) Eng. transl. (New York, 1985), esp. p. 220; D. Halperin, *One Hundred Years of Homosexuality* (New York, 1990), esp. pp. 34–5; J. J. Winkler, *The Constraints of Desire*

(New York, 1990), esp. pp. 52 n. and 54; and Eva Keuls, *The Reign of the Phallus* (New York, 1985). Much of this is dressed up in the language of modern cultural theory, but it is impossible to ignore its similarities with more old-fashioned assumptions. Benjamin Bickley Rogers, for instance, in his edition of *Ecclesiazusae* had little problem with line 103 that referred to the politician Agyrrhius as 'previously a woman': 'The expression . . . refers *of course* to unnatural crimes in which Agyrrhius as a youth was supposed to have participated.' In his study of obscenity in Aristophanes, Jeffery Henderson provided a list of forty-two 'individuals attacked by comic poets as pathics', several of whom are identified as such by nothing more graphic than a female version of their name, *The Maculate Muse* (New Haven, 1975); cf. M. Poster, 'Foucault and the Tyranny of Greece' in D. Couzens Hoy, ed., *Foucault: A Critical Reader* (Oxford, 1986), p. 213: 'It appears that Foucault assumes that a sexual relation in which one partner is required *exclusively* to play an active role and the other partner *exclusively* to play a passive role is possible, as if the fact of "activity" and "passivity" were not ambiguous from the start, as if the Greek *interpretation* can be noted as an observation by the historian and left at that.'

51. The graffiti often state no more than x will/did bugger y, or x is *katapugōn*. On one frequently cited vase the writer says he will bugger the reader, but this is a joke about sexual frustration if the girl he loves goes off with another man; O. Masson and J. Taillardat, *ZPE* 59 (1985), 137–40. There are more examples of these graffiti in a Roman context.

52. K. J. Dover, *Greek Homosexuality*, pp. 100–5, esp. p. 101; R. F. Sutton Jnr., 'Pornography and Persuasion on Attic Pottery', in A. Richlin, ed., *Pornography and Representation in Greece and Rome* (Oxford, 1992), p. 11. Dover goes to great lengths to determine whether anal or vaginal penetration is indicated by dorsal sex, but few of his followers have pursued this line of enquiry.

53. K. Schauenburg, *AthMitt.* 90 (1975), 97–121; K. J. Dover, *Greek Homosexuality*, p. 105.

54. 'If the point of the scene is the triumph of one country over another, the national traits of either man should be stressed, or at least clearly expressed. Instead the characterization is remarkably ambiguous . . . It is also odd that the site of Athens' victory should be singled out for abuse.' G. Ferrari Pinney, 'For the Heroes are at Hand', *JHS* 104 (1984), 181.

55. Ar. *Knights* 638–42; cf. K. J. Dover, *Greek Homosexuality*, p. 142.

56. Ar. *Lys.* 137 cf. 776; Roger Just, *Women in Athenian Law and Life* (London, 1989), p. 160; K. J. Dover, pp. 113–4 and 142–3; Marjorie J. Milne and Dietrich von Bothmer, 'Καταπύγων, Καταπύγαινα, *Hesperia* 22 (1953), 215–24; E. Fraenkel, 'Neues Griechisch in Graffiti (I) Katapugaina', *Glotta* 34 (1955), 42–5; J. and L. Robert, *REG* 71 (1958), 294, note 377.

57. Aelian, *Hist. Anim.* 12.10; Cratinus 58 K-A; Sophron 63 (Kaibel); Apollo-

dorus *ap*. Ath. 7.281ef. Cf. *Et. genuin.* s.v. *alphēstai*, Suidas, Photius s.v. *katapugōn*.

58. Ar. *Clouds* 529 and F225 K-A; *Ach.* 77–9. In the past, most commentators and translators have rendered this as a paradox 'And we consider the only real men are fellators and buggers', but as the detailed study of the passage by Jocelyn has shown, the most natural reading is 'We consider those able to consume and drink the most to be fellators and *katapugones*', H. D. Jocelyn, 'A Greek Indecency and its Students. *Laikazein*', *PCPhS* 26 (1980), 41–2.

59. Plato *Gorgias* 493a–494e; cf. W. H. Thompson, *The Gorgias of Plato* (London 1905), p. 193; E. R. Dodds, *Plato Gorgias* (Oxford, 1959) ad 494e 3–4; cf. Martha Nussbaum, *The Fragility of Goodness* (Cambridge, 1986), p. 460, note 27.

60. M. Foucault, *The Use of Pleasure*, pp. 85–6, cf. 47, 220.

61. The most recent edition of the *Problemata* is the Budé, ed. Pierre Louis (Paris, 1991). He dates book four to the third century, locating it in the circle of Straton of Lampsacus, p. 79.

62. The idea that women are sexually insatiable and display a general lack of self-control is well documented, see for instance, Aeschylus fr. 243 Nauck; Sophocles fr. 932; Ar. *Thesm.* 504ff; *Ecc.* 468–70, 616–20; *Clouds* 553ff.; Aris. *EN* 7.7.1150b6. Alciphron characterizes female sexual voracity as a 'Charybdis (1.6,2) and warns another man that his hetaera will gobble him up whole (3.33). For this discourse about women, and its relationship to theories of wetness and leakiness, see Anne Carson, 'Putting Her in Her Place: Women, Dirt and Desire', in D. Halperin et al., eds, *Before Sexuality*, pp. 135–69.

63. Aeschin. 1.84; Ar. *Clouds* 1330 (*lakkoproktos*) and 1083–104 (*euruprōktoi*). For the *molgos*, see Pollux 10.187. For *euruproktia*, *Knights* 720–1, cf. 640–2; *Ecc.* 364 schol. ad *Knights* 78. When Aristophanes talks of the 'yawning-arsed Ionians' in *Acharnians* 106–7, it seems to be an obscene version of 'open-mouthed', indicating that they are gullible and greedy for Persian money, cf. Pollux 3.112.

64. Ar. *Frogs* 422–7 (Dover); Timaeus *FGrHist* 566 F124b; Plu. *Mor.* 126a and 705e.

65. Aristodemus *ap*. Ath. 13.585a; Lynceus of Samos *ap*. Ath. 13.584b; Aeschin. 1.84; Ar. *Lys.* 928; Plu. *Mor.* 1044b; D.L. 6.2, 69, cf. J. C. B. Gosling and C. C. W. Taylor, *The Greeks on Pleasure* (Oxford, 1982), pp. 71 and 80.

66. F. Lissarrague, *The Aesthetics of the Greek Banquet* Eng. transl. (Princeton, 1990), pp. 90–1; Eupolis 385 K-A.

67. G. F. Pinney, 'For the Heroes are at Hand', 182; Homer *Od.* 7.58ff., *Iliad* 8.114, 11.620, scholiast ad *Iliad* 4.228; Pausanias 2.16, 6; Hipponax 128 (West). For the first-person inscription, see J. Svenbro, *Phrasikleia* (London, 1993), esp. cc. 2 and 10.

CHAPTER VI · ECONOMIES

1. J. K. Davies, *Wealth and the Power of Wealth in Classical Athens* (Salem NH, 1984), p. 76. Continuity was preserved in some families not by maintaining links with ancestral estates, but in their guardianship of cults and family tombs.

2. Plato *Rep.* 1.330b; J. K. Davies, *Wealth*, p. 86; [Dem.] 42.4; cf. K. J. Dover, *Greek Popular Morality* (Oxford, 1974), pp. 74−5.

3. Lysias 19.48; Andocides *On the Mysteries* 131; Ar. *Ecc.* 810−11; Arist. *Rhet.* 1405a; cf. J. K. Davies, *Athenian Propertied Families, 600−300 BC* (Oxford, 1971), p. 260.

4. Alexis 204.3−6 K-A, 76.7−8 K-A; Diphilus 32 K-A; Antiphanes 164 K-A.

5. Lysias 32.20; Ar. *Ach.* 962, with W. J. M. Starkie's notes, ad loc.; cf. A. Boeckh and E. Oder *RE* I col.3; Antiphanes 145 K-A; Amphis 30 K-A; Diphilus 67 K-A; Eupolis 160 K-A; and in general see A. Boeckh and Max Fränkel, *Die Staatshaushaltung der Athener* (Berlin, 1886), p. 129.

6. Michel Feyel, 'Nouvelles inscriptions d'Akraiphia', *BCH* 60 (1936), 27−36; F. Salviat and C. Vatin, *Inscriptions de Grèce Centrale* (Paris, 1971), pp. 95−109; D. M. Schaps, 'Comic Inflation in the Market-place', *Scripta Classica Israelica* 8−9 (1985−8), 66−73, esp. 68−70. See also T. W. Gallant, *A Fisherman's Tale* (Ghent, 1985), pp. 39−40, who provides much useful information on the economics of fishing in the Mediterranean.

7. Cf. Nicholas Purcell, 'Eating Fish: the Paradoxes of Seafood', in J. Wilkins, D. Harvey and M. Dobson, eds, *Food in Antiquity* (Exeter, 1995), p. 135 and T. W. Gallant, *A Fisherman's Tale*, esp. pp. 39−40.

8. Apuleius, *Golden Ass* (based on Robert Graves' transl.), 1.24−5; Alexis 249 K-A; Sophilus 2 K-A.

9. Xenarchus 7 K-A; Alexis 130−1 K-A; Plato *Laws* 11.917bc. The evidence for laws concerning fishing and the sale of fish is collected with a none-too-critical eye by Diedrich Bohlen, *Die Bedeutung der Fischerei für die antike Wirtschaft*, thesis (Hamburg, 1937), pp. 23ff. Caution is necessary because imaginary laws and treaties are a favourite theme of comedy, teasing out on a day-to-day basis the consequences of some fantastic situation, women in power, a pantheon of birds, a truce with the fish, etc. On the other hand, there was nothing to stop the people of Athens passing decrees on anything they felt strongly about, whether or not the measure was enforceable; cf. P. Millett, 'Sale, Credit and Exchange in Athenian Law and Society', in P. Cartledge, P. Millett and S. Todd, eds, *Nomos. Essays in Athenian Law, Politics and Society* (Cambridge, 1990), pp. 172, note 13 and 192, note 53. W. G. Arnott, 'Towards an Edition of the Fragments of Alexis', *PCPhS* N.S. 16 (1970), 6, note 2; and on Aristonicus, M. H.

Hansen, 'Rhetores and Strategoi in Fourth-century Athens', *GRBS* 24 (1983), 161.

10. Critias F6 West, 11.17−18 and 9−13; Xen. *Resp. Lac.* 5.4; Theopompus *FGrHist* 115 F134; Dem. 38.27; *Thesm.* 735−8. The scholiast thinks the household utensils are in danger of being pawned to pay the barman.

11. Plu. *Mor.* 470f. (the anecdote about Socrates seems to have been a detachable one, and is very similar to stories told of Diogenes the Cynic with slightly different lists of products); Alexis 15.19 K-A; Men. *Epitrep.* 127−31; cf. W. Pritchett, 'The Attic Stelai II', *Hesperia* 25 (1956), 201.

12. Mabel Lang, 'Numerical Notation on Greek Vases', *Hesperia* 25 (1956), 1−24, esp. 13−16; D. A. Amyx, 'The Attic Stelai III', *Hesperia* 27 (1958), 176 with Hesychius s.v. *trikotylos*; François Salviat, 'Le vin de Thasos amphores, vin et sources écrites', in J.-Y. Empereur and Y. Garlan, eds, *Recherches sur les Amphores Grecques* (École Française d'Athènes, 1986), pp. 180−1. Interpretation of the prices takes much for granted. In his article on the Attic Stelai, W. Pritchett notes that many things apart from wine were kept in amphoras, including oil, milk and pickled slices of dolphin! 'The Attic Stelai II', note 192, pp. 202−3.

13. Men. 264 (Koerte); Ephippus *ap.* Ath. 4.146c; Plut. *Alex.* c.23.

14. Xen. *Mem.* 1.2.22; Plato, *Rep.* 9.573d cf. 574bc; schol. ad Ar. *Clouds* 109d; cf. Kassel-Austin ad Eupolis 50 K-A; Antiphanes *Agroikos* 2 K-A; Isocrates 8.103; Xen. *Oec.* 1.13.

15. Xen. *Mem.* 1.3.11−12.

16. Xen. *Mem.* 1.2.22; Ath. 12.534f.

17. Antisthenes 182 (Caizzi); Philemon 3.13 K-A; Epicrates 3 11.12 and 18 K-A; Theopompus 22 K-A; Machon 333−48, 451 (Gow); Lynceus of Samos *ap.* Ath. 13.584c; and in general D. Halperin, *One Hundred Years of Homosexuality* (New York, 1990), pp. 107−12.

18. Machon 11. 308 and 362 (Gow); Asclepiades (c.320 BCE) *AP* V.203 = *HE* Asclepiades VI. The translation is from Alan Cameron, who neatly resolves the unnecessary difficulties earlier editors had found with the poem: Alan Cameron, 'Asclepiades' Girlfriends', in Helene P. Foley, ed., *Reflections of Women in Antiquity* (New York, 1981), pp. 294−5, *Anth.Pal.* V.202, *SEG* xviii.93. For the paintings see A. Greifenhagen, 'Fragmente eines rotfigurigen Pinax', in L. Bonafante and H. von Heintze, eds, *In Memoriam Otto J. Brendel. Essays in Archaeology and the Humanities* (Mainz, 1976), pp. 43−8.

19. Men. *Epitrep.* 136; *Kolax* 129, with Gomme-Sandbach ad loc., Lysias 3.22.

20. Dem. 27.9; Hyp., *In Athenog.* 2 and 5; [Dem.] 59.29, Gomme-Sandbach ad Men *Epitrep.* 136.

21. Cratinus 81 K-A; [Plato] *Eryxias* 396e; Callias 1 K-A, with the editors' comments; Laon 2 K-A *ap.* Heraclides *On the Cities in Greece* 1.22 (On the Boeotians); Plautus, *Bacchides* 850ff. cf. 1096ff., *Miles Gloriosus* 1394ff.

The former is probably, the latter possibly, a version of a play by Menander and the legal language used in both cases is Greek. Interestingly, the women in question are not in fact wives, but courtesans, see A. W. Gomme and F. H. Sandbach, *Menander: A Commentary* (Oxford, 1973), pp. 7–8 and 118ff.; Ar. *Wealth* 168 with schol. (there is some uncertainty as to whether the *moichos* pays for the privilege of being merely plucked painfully rather than despatched, or whether a metaphorical plucking is also entailed. The latter seems most plausible, given the frequent use of the metaphor in precisely this context with regard to Callias Ar. (*Av.* 286–7), Lysias 1.25, 4 cf. D. Cohen, *Law, Sexuality, and Society* (Cambridge, 1991), pp. 127–30. The women of Baluch tribes in Pakistan are campaigning to stop a religious law which is abused by some husbands who kill their wives for adultery in order to make money out of the accused adulterer.

22. [Dem.] 59.41; Machon 349 ff. (Gow); cf. Georg Simmel on the old English system of compensation for cuckolded husbands, *The Philosophy of Money* Eng. transl. (London, 1978), p. 384.

23. G. Simmel, *The Philosophy of Money*, pp. 383–4.

24. Amphis 23 K-A; Timocles 25 K-A; Aristophon 4 K-A; Aristodemus *ap.* Ath. 13.585a; cf. Socrates, who points out to Theodote that her soul teaches her that it is necessary to keep the prodigal locked out, Xen. *Mem.* 3.11,10.

25. Men. 314 (Koerte hardly needs to comment, 'Videtur meretrix loqui dono amatoris non contenta') 315, 329, 224 (Koerte); 'Docet lena puellam, quomodo amatorem emungere argento debeat', says Kock; Xen, *Mem.* 3.11,12 with Ath. 5.220e, Anaxilas 22 K-A 11.22–6. The image of being carried up into the air probably alludes to the Sphinx's habit of carrying off her victims.

26. Men. 185 (Koerte), cf. Aristophanes' hetaera in *Thesm.* 345 who accepts the gifts, but betrays her friend; Epicrates 2 K-A; cf. Ath. 13.570b. For gluttony, etc. cf. Epicrates 3.1–3 K-A; Philippides 5 K-A; Timocles 16 K-A; J.-P. Vernant, 'At Man's Table', in M. Detienne et al. *The Cuisine of Sacrifice* (London, 1989), p. 60. Sometimes hetaeras are unwilling to wait for things to be given to them: 'The other night I brought a girl Nicostrate, with a very hooked nose, nicknamed Skotodine (Dark spin, Swoon) because she had once lifted a silver *dinos* in the darkness' (Archedicus 1 K-A). Sappho herself provides a template for this female stereotype in her representation of Rhodopis, whom she calls Doricha (gift-holder? Dorian?) as having appropriated much of her brother Charaxus' property; Ath. 13.596bc, cf. Her. 2.134.

27. Terence *Hecyra* 11.63–5; cf. Dwora Gilula, 'The Concept of the *bona meretrix*. A Study of Terence's Courtesans', *RFIC* 108 (1980), 162ff; Machon 422ff. (Gow); cf. the woman known as Mare (Hippe), who consumed her lover the Keeper of Provender, Machon 439ff (Gow); Ath. 13.591c; Aeschin. 1.115.

28. Aeschin. 1.42, 97–9, 105.
29. Hegesander of Delphi *ap.* Ath. 4.167e.
30. Anaxippus 1.31–35 K-A, Men. 303, 287 (Koerte).
31. Aeschin. 1.94, 96.
32. Ar. *Clouds* 1327–30; K. J. Dover, *Greek Homosexuality* (London, 1978), p. 143.

CHAPTER VII · POLITICS AND SOCIETY

1. Dem. 35.39–40. The most up-to-date book on the Athenian legal system is Stephen Todd's *The Shape of Athenian Law* (Oxford, 1993); the political system is described most thoroughly by M. H. Hansen, *The Athenian Democracy in the Age of Demosthenes* (Oxford, 1991); a more disturbing perspective is provided by V. Hunter's *Policing Athens* (Princeton, 1994).
2. [Dem.] 59.43; cf. M. H. Hansen, *The Sovereignty of the People's Court in Athens in the Fourth Century and the Public Action Against Unconstitutional Proposals* (Odense, 1974), 28; and id., *The Athenian Assembly* (Oxford, 1987), 59–60. Amynias is one Old Comedy figure who combines the roles of sycophant parasite and flatterer of Leogoras (?), *Wasps* 1267ff.; Cratinus 227 K-A Schol. ad Ar. *Wasps* 74b. On risks for politicians, see S. Todd, *The Shape of Athenian Law*, pp. 300–7.
3. Thuc. 6.28,1; Lysias 1.16–20; Ar. *Ecc.* 1–13, *Suda s.v. Astyanassa*, S. Todd, 'The Purpose of Evidence in Athenian Courts', in Paul Cartledge, Paul Millett and Stephen Todd, eds., *Nomos. Essays in Athenian Law, Politics and Society* (Cambridge, 1990), pp. 32–6; *contra* V. Hunter, *Policing Athens*, pp. 90–1.
4. Dem. 19.314, 36.45, 45.77; Aeschin.1.26 and 65; cf. Dem; *Ep.* 4.12.
5. Aeschin. 1.127 and 84; the logic of the *klēdōn* still has power: I know of one person who ended a relationship after an assignation in Paris, because as he was finding his way back to his hotel a Metro official informed him 'il faut changer'.
6. Dem. 25.52; Plato *Apology* 18bd; Aeschin. 1.157 and 130; Sîan Lewis, 'Barber's Shops and Perfume Shops: "Symposia without Wine"' in A. Powell, ed., *Greek World* (London, 1995), pp. 432–41.
7. Isoc. 21.5; J. G. Gager, *Curse Tablets and Binding Spells from the Ancient World* (New York, 1992), pp. 116–32, esp. 132.
8. J. Ober, *Mass and Elite in Democratic Athens* (Princeton, 1989), p. 206, adducing Dem. 48.81, 18.320, and 36.43, cf. W. Donlan, *The Aristocratic Ideal in Ancient Greece: Attitudes of Superiority from Homer to the End of the Fifth Century* (Lawrence, KS, 1980), pp. 160–1; O. Murray, 'The Symposion in History', in E. Gabba, ed., *Tria Corda. Scritti in onore di Arnaldo Momigliano* (Como, 1983), pp. 257–72.
9. R. Meiggs and D. Lewis, *Greek Historical Inscriptions* (Oxford, 1988), No. 79 B, 11.55ff; cf. Dem. 42.20; Ar. *Wasps* 78–80, 1208–15, O. Murray, 'The

Affair of the Mysteries: Democracy and the Drinking Group', in O. Murray, ed., *Sympotica. A Symposium on the Symposion* (Oxford, 1990), p. 149.

10. Ar. F 225 K-A; cf. 205.8, Hyp. *In Dem.* p. 24 (Jensen); Peter E. Corbett, 'Attic Pottery of the Later Fifth Century', *Hesperia* 18 (1949), nos. 78–81 and p. 333.

11. Dem. 54.7–8 and 14; Lycophron of Chalcis *ap.* Ath. 13.555a.

12. Xen. *Hell.* 5.4,4; Plautus *Poen.* 268; cf. *Pseudolus* 178; 214ff.; 229ff.

13. Ar. *Ecc.* 877ff.; Hyp. 177 (Kenyon); Plato, *Phaedr.* 227cd.

14. Timocles 11 K-A ll. 1–2; Ar. *Frogs* 1065ff.; Alexis 78 K-A; Diphilus 31 K-A; Antiphanes 188 K-A, l. 19; Ar. *Ecc.* 606. J. B. Salmon, *Wealthy Corinth* (Oxford, 1984), p. 200 suggests the Corinthian measure may go back to Periander. However, I think it must remain doubtful whether the measure ever existed at Corinth even in the fourth century. It is certainly of a kind quite different from other known archaic sumptuary laws.

15. There are some good surveys of the problem of Athenian class. Most thoughtful is S. Todd, '*Lady Chatterley's Lover* and the Attic Jurors: the Social Composition of the Athenian Jury', *JHS* 110 (1990), 146–73 esp. 158–63; cf. R. K. Sinclair, *Democracy and Participation in Athens* (Cambridge, 1988), pp. 119–127; J. Ober, *Mass and Elite*, sections V and VI and pp. 11ff; M. H. Hansen, *The Athenian Democracy*, pp. 106ff.

16. Thuc. 3.87,3; cf.3.16,1; Ar. *Wasps* 1071–101; And. fr. 4 (Blass.)

17. Dem. 23.206–7, 3.29, 21.158.

18. Plato *Protagoras* 315d; Matro *ap.* Ath. 4.135a and 136d. O. Murray, 'Histories of Pleasure', in id. and M. Tecuşan, eds, *In Vino Veritas* (London, 1995), pp. 7–9; Ch. Habicht, 'Die beiden Xenokles von Sphettos', *Hesperia* 57 (1988).

19. Dem. 57.30–36, 45.

20. *Ath Pol.* 56.2; cf. Dem 24.149; J. Ober, *Mass and Elite*, pp. 221–6; A. H. M. Jones, *Athenian Democracy* (Oxford, 1957), pp. 36–7.

21. Aeschin. 1.114–5; V. Hunter, *Policing Athens*, p. 52.

22. Dem. 25.88.

23. Ar. *Peace*, 439–40; Xen. *Mem.* 3.13,4; Theopompus 31 K-A. Even the manners of drinking need not split the population. A whole range of people had seen the inside of a *kapēleion* and even rather small and modest houses managed to find space for an *andrōn* in which vistors could be offered a drink, cf. M. Jameson, 'Private Space and the Greek City', in O. Murray and S. Price, eds, *The Greek City* (Oxford, 1990), p. 190.

24. Aeschin. 1.42; cf. Plato, *Gorgias* 493a-494e; K. J. Dover, *Greek Popular Morality*, pp. 125–6.

25. Dem. 8.70, 50.7; Lysias 21.1–9; cf. J. Trevett, *Apollodoros Son of Pasion* (Oxford 1992), ch. 1.

26. Isaeus 5.36–8.

27. Isaeus 7.38–9, 6.61 with Wyse ad loc.; and in general see K. J. Dover,

Greek Popular Morality (Oxford, 1974), pp. 175–7; S. Todd, *The Shape of Athenian Law*, pp. 106 and 108; A. R. W. Harrison, *The Law of Athens* (Oxford, 1968–71), i. 79–80; D. L. 1.55, cf. Lex. Rhet. Cant. 665.20; Dem. 57.32; Plu. Solon *c.* 22.

28. S. Todd, *The Shape of Athenian Law*, pp. 120–1.

29. Ar. *Wealth* 881–2; Isoc. 15.160.

30. Ar. *Ecc.* 601–2; *Wealth*, 237–41, A. R. W. Harrison, *The Law of Athens*, i. pp. 228–35; V. Gabrielsen, '*Phanera* and *aphanes ousia* in Classical Athens', *Class. et Med.* (1986); L. Gernet, 'Choses visibles et choses invisibles dans le droit grec', *Revue philosophique* 146 (1956), 79–86.

31. Lysias 19.48.

32. Dem. 40.58; Isaeus 5.43; cf. S. Todd, *The Shape of Athenian Law*, pp. 228ff.

33. Aeschin. 3.240; Isaeus fr. 35 [Thalheim 30]; cf. Dem. 38.26.

34. Aeschin. 1.97 and 101; [Dem.] 59.50; Dem. 38.27; Isaeus 7.39 cf. fr. 1, (22 Thalheim); R. Osborne, 'Vexatious Litigation in Classical Athens', in P. Cartledge, P. Millet and S. Todd, eds, *Nomos. Essays in Athenian Law, Politics and Society* (Cambridge, 1990), pp. 92–3.

35. Alexis 78 K-A; Diphilus 31 K-A; Ar. *Ecc.* 601–8. The fragments both of Diphilus and Alexis might be post-classical, but the reference to *sykophants* implies Diphilus is really thinking of Athens and an Athens with some democratic institutions intact, cf. K. J. Dover, *Greek Popular Morality*, pp. 109–10 on poverty leading to crime.

36. Her. 2.177 and 174.

37. Hegesander of Delphi *ap.* Ath. 4.167e.

CHAPTER VIII · POLITICS AND POLITICIANS

1. G. Adeleye, 'The Purpose of the *dokimasia*', *GRBS* 24 (1983); S. Todd, *The Shape of Athenian Law* (Oxford, 1993), p. 288.

2. M. H. Hansen, *Apagoge*, section III, esp. 72–4 and 92–3.

3. Aeschin. 1.31, 94, 116, 154, 194–5; cf. V. Hunter, *Policing Athens* (Princeton, 1994), pp. 104–5; S. Todd, *The Shape of Athenian Law*, p. 116.

4. D. Halperin, *One Hundred Years of Homosexuality* (New York, 1990), p. 97; M. Foucault, *The Use of Pleasure* (Paris, 1984), Eng. transl. (New York, 1985), p. 219.

5. Aeschin. 1.94; V. Hunter, *Policing Athens*, p. 105.

6. Aeschin. 1.42, 75–6.

7. Aeschin. 1.54.

8. Aeschin. 1.95–6, 106.

9. Aeschin. 1.107–8, 110, 113.

10. Timocles 4, 17 K-A; F. D. Harvey, 'Some Aspects of Bribery in Greek Politics' in P. A. Cartledge and F. D. Harvey, eds, *Crux, Essays in Greek History presented to G. E. M. de Ste Croix* (London, 1985), p. 94.

11. Gorgias DK 82 11a c.15; Isoc. 12.140, 3.170.

12. Aeschin. 3.173.

13. Isoc. 8.126; Thuc. 6.12,2.

14. Dem. 6.27, 8.66, 9.30–1; cf. 13.20.

15. Dem. 19.122, 286.

16. Aeschin. 1.56.

17. Phoenix of Colophon *PLG* fr. 3; Ar. *Ach.* 1085ff., 1125–6; O. Murray, 'Les règles du *symposion* ou comment problematiser le plaisir' in M. Aurell, O. Domoulin, F. Telamon, eds, *La Sociabilité à table: commensalité et convivialité à travers les âges*, (Rouen, 1992), pp. 65–8, cf. F. Dupont *Le Plaisir et la loi*, (Paris, 1977) p. 23.

18. Antiphanes 188 K-A; Alexis 198 K-A.

19. Ar. 205; cf. 206, 233 K-A; *Wasps* 1208ff. cf. Cratinus 342 K-A.

20. Dem. 24.212ff.; cf. R. L. Hunter on Eubulus 107 (Kock).

21. Aeschin. 1.119, 3.218.

22. Aeschin. 1.57, 58–9, 65.

23. Aeschin. 1.70, 110.

24. Aeschin. 1.61, 65; Dem. 19.128; Alexis 293 K-A; cf. Clearchus 1 K-A; Ar. *Lys.* 203 ff., 695 K-A, and in general for conspiratorial drinking cf. H. Schmitz, 'Heiliger Wein', *ZPE* 28 (1978), 288–94.

25. Ar. *Wasps* 1220 with MacDowell's note ad loc., 1301ff.; cf. Bob Dole in an interview with the *New York Times*: '. . . it's unfortunate that politics has reached a point . . . that were I to go out to dinner with you or somebody in the private sector, somebody out there, maybe somebody in the press, would try to put two and two together and say, "Oh, there's something happening out there. They're not just having dinner, they're making some kind of deal." And the cynicism has reached that level. It's pretty bad.' (*New York Times*, 16 August 1996, p. A28.)

26. Aeschin. 1.75; cf. Gow ad Machon 236; H.-G. Nesselrath, *Lukians Parasitendialog* (New York, 1983), pp. 98, 66 and note 178: one of the 'entscheidenden Erkennungsmerkmalen des Komödie parasiten'. For the services of parasites to their keepers, see Axionicus 6 K-A; Aristophon 5 K-A with editors' notes ad loc. For Amynias, Ar. *Wasps* 1267ff.; Cratinus 227 K-A; cf. schol. ad Ar. *Wasps* 74b, *Clouds* 109; cf. R. Osborne, 'Vexatious Litigation in Classical Athens', in P. Cartledge, P. Millet and S. Todd, eds, *Nomos. Essays in Athenian Law, Politics and Society* (Cambridge, 1990), p. 87. For Smicythion, *Wasps* 401; cf. MacDowell ad loc.; Pherecrates 37 K-A, ll. 2–3; Kaibel although seeing Smicythion as a parasite is not sure if the 'throat-man' is 'voracem' or 'vociferantem', cf. Kassel and Austin ad loc. Probably he is both.

27. Aeschin. 1.110–11, Kirchner *PA* 9077; Aris. *Rhet.* I. 7.1364a; Dem. 20.146; Aeschin. 3.139.

28. Ar. *Knights* 969; *Clouds* 690–2.

29. Ar. *Ecc.* 461; Eur. *IA* 749; Lynceus of Samos *ap.* Ath. 13.584b, 6.246b; Machon fr. 6 and 7 (Gow); Athenaeus 13.591de; J.-P. Vernant, 'At Man's Table', in M. Detienne et al, *The Cuisine of Sacrifice* (London, 1989), pp. 60, 68–73; cf. Theopompus 56 K-A where a household is said to get a four-obol income when a two-obol man takes a 'wife', possibly a reference to doubling the Assembly-pay by taking another citizen as a wife?

30. Aeschin. 1.68, 70. For the crucial importance of cohabitation in the Athenian concept of marriage, see [Dem.] 59.13, 16, 122, 124, 126; And. 1.124 and 129; H. J. Wolff, 'Marriage, Law and Family Organization in Ancient Athens', *Traditio* 2 (1943–4), 65–6 and; J. P. Vernant's comments in *Myth and Society in Ancient Greece* Eng. transl. (Brighton, 1980), p. 47; id., *Myth and Thought Among the Greeks* Eng. transl. (London, 1983), 134–6; cf. E. Fraenkel ad Aeschylus *Ag.* 1625f.

31. Ar. *Knights* 638–42, 877ff.; cf. Eupolis 104 K-A.

32. Aeschin. 1.29; cf. 188, 2.23; F. D. Harvey, 'Some Aspects of Bribery', pp. 84–6.

33. Theopompus *FGrHist* 115 F135; Ar. *Wasps* 682ff.; P. Schmitt Pantel, *La cité au banquet* (École Française de Rome, 1992), pp. 180–6 and 193–6; Sitta von Reden, *Exchange in Ancient Greece* (London, 1995) p. 92.

34. Plu. *Mor.* 806f.; Dem. 19.189–90.

CHAPTER IX · TYRANNY AND REVOLUTION

1. Ar. *Wasps* ll. 493–502.

2. Alexis 249.4 K-A.

3. Her. 5.49,4; 9.82.

4. Plu. *Cimon* 9, 10 and 13; *Pericles* 12.

5. Isoc. 2.2, 21, 29, 3.31–3, 9.45; Xen. *Poroi* 5.6; cf. J. Davidson, 'Isocrates Against Imperialism', *Historia* 39 (1990) pp. 20–36; esp. 29–32.

6. Ar. *Wasps*, 665–79; Theopompus *FGrHist* 115 F113; Thuc. 1.138,5; Her. 2.98,1, 7.118–20; Plu. *Them.* 29.11 cf. Xen. *Anab.* 1.4,9; [Plato] *Alcibiades I* 123bc; D.S. 1.52; D. M. Lewis, 'The King's Dinner', in Heleen Sancisi-Weerdenburg and Amélie Kuhrt, eds, *Achaemenid History II The Greek Sources* (Leiden, 1987), pp. 79–87; id., *Sparta and Persia* (Leiden, 1977), pp. 4–5, 53–5, 122; P. Schmitt Pantel, *La cité au banquet* (École Française de Rome, 1992), pp. 429–38; Alan B. Lloyd, *Herodotus Book II. A Commentary* (Leiden, 1976), Vol. II ad loc.

7. R. Meiggs, *Athenian Empire* (Oxford, 1972), pp. 292–4, 300–2; Thuc. 3.104; Diodorus 12.58,6.

8. Heraclides *ap.* Ath 4.145bc; Ar. *Ach.* 65ff.

9. Arrian 4.12,3–5; Plu. *Alex. c.* 23; Ath. 4.146c D.S. 17.108,4–5; cf. Hegesander *ap.* Ath. 12.544c; P. Schmitt Pantel, *La cité au banquet*, pp. 429–35, 458–9.

10. On Polycrates, Her. 3.42,1–2. On Syrians, Men. 754 (Koerte); Ath. 8.346de; Xanthus of Lydia *FGrHist* 765 F17. Cf. Xen. *Anab.* 1.4,9; Antipater of Tarsus F64 (*SVF* III, 257), Mnaseas of Patara *FHG* (Müller) iii, 155; Lucian *De dea Syria* 14 and 45–7. On Naxos, Arist. fr. 510 (Rose).

11. Plu. *Solon* 24–5; P. Schmitt Pantel, *La cité au banquet*, pp. 49–50, 97–9, 485; M. Detienne, 'Culinary Practices and the Spirit of Sacrifice', in M. Detienne et al, *The Cuisine of Sacrifice* (London, 1989), p. 13. Detienne and Svenbro, 'The Feast of the Wolves', ibid. pp. 150–2 note the similarities with one of the Fables of Aesop, a very difficult text to date, in which a wolf becomes leader of the wolf army and establishes laws by which all booty is to be pooled. The plan is spoiled by an ass who asks the wolf general if he will also be putting the booty he won the day before into the common pot. The wolf decides to repeal his laws. It is not really that the partition of food *symbolizes* the partition of political rights, but that the political extends all the way down to the level of feeding, or, as Pauline Schmitt Pantel has remarked, the political level of history and the level of 'manners and customs' are not separate.

12. Her. 3.142,3; Solon 33 (West).

13. Ar. *Knights* 313, 359ff., 1030–4; Antiphanes 188.19 K-A.

14. Satyrus *ap.* Ath. 534d; Plu. *Alc. c.* 12; P. Schmitt Pantel, *La cité au banquet*, pp. 196–201.

15. Thuc. 6.15,3–4.

16. Cf. Macdowell ad Ar. *Wasps* 1259.

17. R. Osborne, 'The Erection and Mutilation of the Hermai', *PCPhS* n.s. 31 (1985), 47–73, J. M. Camp, *The Athenian Agora* (London, 1986), pp. 74–77.

18. Thuc. 6.60,1–2; And. 1.36.

19. Thuc. 6.28 and 15,3–4; cf. R. Seager, 'Alcibiades and the Charge of Aiming at Tyranny', *Historia* 16 (1967), 6–18.

20. Thuc. 2.65; And. 1.36.

21. Plato *Rep.* 572e–575d.

22. Aeschin. 1.190–1.

23. Theopompus *FGrHist* 115 F224; cf. 225 *ap.* Ath. 6.260d–261a; Polybius 8.8–9.

24. W. Burkert, *Greek Religion* (Oxford, 1985), pp. 223–4.

25. Arrian, *Ind.* 34, 30, 29,9–15; Her. 3.23.

26. Aeschin. 1.182, 81–4; Plato, *Rep.* 577e.

Bibliography

Marianna Adler, 'From Symbolic Exchange to Commodity Consumption: Anthropological Notes on Drinking as a Symbolic Practice' in Susanna Barrows and Robin Room eds, *Drinking. Behaviour and Belief in Modern History* (Berkeley, 1991), pp. 376–98.

D. A. Amyx, 'The Attic Stelai III', *Hesperia* 27 (1958), 164–310.

Arjun Appadurai ed., *The Social Life of Things* (Cambridge, 1986)
—'Introduction: commodities and the politics of value', ibid.

W. G. Arnott, 'Towards an edition of the fragments of Alexis', *PCPhS* N.S. 16 (1970), 1–11.
—Review of R. L. Hunter, *Eubulus. The Fragments* in *CR* 34 (1984), 180–2.

Derek Attridge, 'Language as history/history as language: Saussure and the romance of etymology' in Derek Attridge, Geoff Bennington and Robert Young eds, *Post-structuralism and the Question of History* (Cambridge, 1987), pp. 183–211.

Susanna Barrows and Robin Room eds, *Drinking. Behavior and Belief in Modern History* (Berkeley, 1991).

Roland Barthes, 'Lecture de Brillat-Savarin', introduction to Brillat-Savarin: *Physiologie du goût* (Paris, 1975), transl. in M. Blonsky ed., *On Signs* (Oxford, 1985), pp. 61–75.

C. Baudelaire, *Du vin et du haschisch comparés comme moyens de multiplication de l'individualité*, reprinted in Claude Pichois' edition of *Les Paradis Artificiels* (Paris, 1961).

Friedrich Bechtel, *Lexilogus zu Homer* (Halle, 1914).

G. Berthiaume, *Les Rôles du Mageiros* (Leiden, 1982).

Janine Bertier, *Mnésithée et Dieuchès* = *Philosophia Antiqua, A Series of Monographs on Ancient Philosophy*, XX (Leiden, 1972).

Émile Boisacq, *Dictionnaire Étymologique de la Langue Grecque* (Paris, 1923).

A. B. Bosworth, *A Historical Commentary on Arrian's History of Alexander I* (Oxford, 1980).
—*From Arrian to Alexander* (Oxford, 1988).

Pierre Bourdieu, *The Logic of Practice* (Cambridge, 1990).

E. M. Bowie, 'Wine in Old Comedy' in Oswyn Murray and Manuela Tecuşan eds, *In Vino Veritas* (British School at Rome, 1995).

Fernand Braudel, *Capitalism and Material Life* (London, 1973).

Frank Brommer, 'Gefässformen bei Autoren des 5. Jhdts. v. Ch.', *Hermes* 115 (1987), 1–21.

P.G. McC. Brown, 'Plots and prostitutes in Greek New Comedy', *Papers of the Leeds International Latin Seminar, Sixth Volume* (Leeds, 1990), 241–66.

Alfred Brueckner, *Lebensregeln auf athenischen Hochzeitsgeschenken*, [Winckelmanns-programm der Archäologischen Gesellschaft zu Berlin 62 1907]

W. Burkert, *Greek Religion* (Oxford, 1985).

G. Busolt and H. Swodoba, *Griechische Staatskunde* (Third edn. Munich, 1926).

D. L. Cairns, '*Hybris*, dishonour, and thinking big', *JHS* 116 (1996), 1–32.

Averil Cameron and Amélie Kuhrt eds, *Images of Women in Antiquity* (Beckenham, Kent 1983).

Christopher Carey ed., *Apollodorus Against Neaira* (Warminster, 1992).

Anne Carson, 'Putting her in her place: Women, dirt and desire' in D. Halperin, J. J. Winkler and F. Zeitlin eds, *Before Sexuality* (Princeton, 1990), pp. 135–69.

Paul Cartledge, 'The Politics of Spartan Pederasty', *PCPhS* n.s.27 (1981), 17–36.

Paul Cartledge, Paul Millett and Stephen Todd eds, *Nomos: Essays in Athenian Law, Politics and Society* (Cambridge, 1990).

Isaac Casaubon, *Animadversiones in Athenaei Dipnosophistas* (Second edn. Lyons, 1621).

T. J. Clark, *The Painting of Modern Life* (London, 1985).

D. Cohen, 'The Athenian Law of Adultery', *RIDA* 31 (1984), 147–65.
—'Law, society, and homosexuality in Classical Athens', *P and P* 117 (1987), 3–21.
—'The Social Context of Adultery at Athens' in *Nomos: Essays in Athenian Law, Politics and Society*, Paul Cartledge, Paul Millett and Stephen Todd eds, (Cambridge, 1990), pp. 147–65.
—*Law, Sexuality and Society* (Cambridge, 1991).

S. G. Cole, 'Greek Sanctions Against Sexual Assault', *CPh* 79 (1984), 97–113.

A. B. Cook, *Zeus: A Study in Ancient Religion* (Cambridge, 1925).

Johann Friedrich Crome, 'Spinnende Hetairen?', *Gymnasium* 73 (1966), 245–7.

Alan Davidson, *Mediterranean Seafood* (Second edn. Harmondsworth, 1981).

James Davidson, 'Isocrates Against Imperialism: An Analysis of the *De Pace*', *Historia* 39 (1990), 20–36.
—'A Ban on Bars in Thasos?' *CQ* (forthcoming).
—'Gnesippus' in J. Wilkins and F. D. Harvey eds, *Aristophanes and his Rivals* (forthcoming).

J. K. Davies, *Athenian Propertied Families: 600–300 BC* (Oxford, 1971).
—*Wealth and the Power of Wealth in Classical Athens* (Salem NH, 1984).

M. Davies, 'Sailing, Rowing and Sporting in One's Cup on the Wine-Dark Sea' in *Athens Comes of Age: from Solon to Salamis* (Princeton, 1978), pp. 72–90.

M. Delcourt 'Le prix des esclaves dans les comédies Latines', *AntCl* 17 (1948), 123–32.

M. Detienne and J-P. Vernant, et al., *The Cuisine of Sacrifice Among the Greeks* (London, 1989).

E. R. Dodds, *Plato Gorgias: A Revised Text with Introduction and Commentary* (Oxford, 1959).

Mary Douglas, *Constructive Drinking: Perspectives on Drink from Anthropology* (Cambridge, 1987).

K. J. Dover, *Aristophanic Comedy* (Berkeley, 1972).
—*Greek Popular Morality* (Oxford, 1974).
—*Greek Homosexuality* (London, 1978).
—ed. Plato's *Symposium*, (Cambridge, 1980).
—review of Halperin, *One Hundred Years of Homosexuality*, *CR* 41 (1991).

Jean-Louis Durand, 'Ritual as Instrumentality' in M. Detienne and J-P. Vernant et al., *The Cuisine of Sacrifice Among the Greeks* (London, 1989), pp. 119–28.

E. Fantham, 'Sex, status and survival in Hellenistic Athens: A Study of Women in New Comedy', *Phoenix* 29 (1975), 44–74.

Michel Feyel, 'Nouvelles inscriptions d'Akraiphia', *BCH* 60 (1936), 11–36.

Liv Finstad and Cecilie Høigård, *Backstreets: Prostitution, Money and Love* (London, 1992).

N. R. E. Fisher, '*Hubris* and dishonour I', *G & R* 23 (1976), 177–93.
—'Drink, *Hubris* and the Promotion of Harmony' in Anton Powell ed., *Classical Sparta: Techniques Behind Her Success* (London, 1989), pp. 26–50.
—'The law of *hubris* in Athens' in Paul Cartledge, Paul Millett and Stephen Todd eds, *Nomos: Essays in Athenian Law, Politics and Society* (Cambridge, 1990), pp. 123–38.
—*Hybris: a study in the values of honour and shame in ancient Greece* (Warminster, 1992).

William W. Fortenbaugh et al. eds, *Theophrastus of Eresus, Sources for his Life Writings, Thought and Influence* (Leiden, 1992).

Michel Foucault, *Les mots et les choses* (Paris, 1966).

—*L'Usage des plaisirs* (Paris, 1984) Eng. trans. *The Uses of Pleasure* (New York, 1985).

E. Fraenkel, 'Neues Griechisch in Graffiti (I) Katapugaina', *Glotta* 34 (1955), 42–5.

J. G. Gager ed., *Curse Tablets and Binding Spells from the Ancient World* (New York, 1992).

T. W. Gallant, *A Fisherman's Tale* (Ghent, 1985).

Dwora Gilula, 'The concept of the *bona meretrix*. A study of Terence's courtesans', *RFIC* 108 (1980), 142–65.

A. W. Gomme and F. H. Sandbach, *Menander, A Commentary* (Oxford, 1973).

J. C. B. Gosling and C. C. W. Taylor, *The Greeks on Pleasure* (Oxford, 1982).

John Gould, 'Law, Custom and Myth: aspects of the social position of women in Classical Athens', *JHS* 100 (1980), 38–59.

A. S. F. Gow ed., *Machon The Fragments* (Cambridge, 1965).

A. S. F. Gow and D. L. Page eds, *The Greek Anthology, Hellenistic Epigrams* (Cambridge, 1965).

Virginia Grace, *Amphoras and the Ancient Wine Trade* (Athens, 1961).

Michel Gras, 'Canthare, société étrusque et monde grec', *Opus* 3 (1984), 325–39.

C. A. Gregory, *Gifts and Commodities* (London, 1982).

A. Greifenhagen, 'Fragmente eines rotfigurigen Pinax' in L. Bonafante and H. von Heintze eds, *In memoriam Otto J. Brendel. Essays in archaeology and the humanities* (Mainz 1976), pp. 43–8.

—'*Philopotès*', *Gymnasium* 82 (1975), 26–32.

E. Grzybek, 'Die griechische Konkubine und ihre Mitgift (P. Eleph. 3 and 4)', *ZPE* 76 (1989), 206–12.

David Halperin, 'Plato and Erotic Reciprocity', *Classical Antiquity* 5 (1986), 60–80.

—*One Hundred Years of Homosexuality* (New York, 1990).

D. Halperin, J. J. Winkler and F. Zeitlin eds, *Before Sexuality* (Princeton, 1990).

Richard Hamilton, *Choes and Anthesteria: Athenian Iconography and Ritual* (Ann Arbor, 1992).

E. W. Handley, 'Notes on the *Theophoroumene* of Menander', *B.I.C.S.* 16 (1969), 88–101.

M. H. Hansen, *Apagoge, Endeixis and Ephegesis against Kakourgoi, Atimoi and Pheugontes* (Odense, 1976).

—'Rhetores and Strategoi in fourth-century Athens', *GRBS* 24 (1983), 151–80.
—*Demography and Democracy: The Number of Athenian Citizens in the Fourth Century* (Herning, Denmark, 1985).

A. R. W. Harrison, *The Law of Athens I, The Family and Property* (Oxford, 1968).

François Hartog, *Le Miroir d'Hérodote: Essai sur la représentation de l'autre* (Paris, 1980), Eng. trans. *The Mirror of Herodotus* (Berkeley, 1988).

F. D. Harvey, '*Dona Ferentes*: Some aspects of bribery in Greek politics' in P. A. Cartledge and F. D. Harvey eds, *Crux Essays in Greek History presented to G. E. M. de Ste Croix* (London, 1985), pp. 76–117.

Dwight Heath, 'A critical review of ethnographic studies of alcohol use' in R. Gibbons, Y. Israel, H. Kalant, R. Popham, W. Schmidt, and R. Smart eds, *Research Advances in Alcohol and Drug Problems* (New York, 1975), 1–92.
—'A decade of development in the anthropological study of alcohol use: 1970–1980' in Mary Douglas ed., *Constructive Drinking* (Cambridge, 1987), 16–69.

Nick Heather and Ian Robertson, *Problem Drinking* (Second edn. Oxford, 1989).

Jeffery Henderson, *The Maculate Muse* (New Haven, 1975).
—ed., Aristophanes *Lysistrata* with introduction and commentary (Oxford, 1987).

Hans Herter, 'Die Soziologie der antiken Prostitution im Lichte des Heidnischen und Christlichen Schrifttums', *JbAC* 3 (1960), 70–111.
—'Dirne', *Reallexicon für Antike und Christentum III* (Stuttgart, 1957), 1149–1213.

Michael Hillgruber, *Die zehnte Rede des Lysias [= Untersuchungen zur antiken Literatur und Geschichte* Bd. 29] (Berlin/New York, 1988).

Rudolf Hirzel, *Der Name. Ein Beitrag zu seiner Geschichte im Altertum und Besonders bei den Griechen = Abhandlungen der Philologische-Historischen Klasse der Sächsischen Akademie der Wissenschaften* 36,2 (1918, second edn Amsterdam, 1962).

Arnold Hug, 'καπηλεῖον', *RE* X, 1988–9.

R. L. Hunter, *Eubulus: The Fragments* (Cambridge, 1983).

V. J. Hunter, *Policing Athens. Social Control in the Attic Lawsuits, 420–320* (Princeton, 1994).

Luce Irigaray, *Ce sexe qui n'est pas une* (Paris, 1977), English trans., *This sex which is not one* (Ithaca NY, 1985).

Felix Jacoby, *Die Fragmente der griechischen Historiker* (Leiden, 1954–57) [=*FGrHist*].

H. D. Jocelyn 'A Greek indecency and its students. *Laikazein*', *PCPhS* 26 (1980), 12–66.

Roger Just, *Women in Athenian Law and Life* (London, 1989).

Bert Kaeser, 'Griechischen Vasen-Trinkgeschirr' in B. Kaeser and Klaus Vierniesel eds, *Kunst der Schale: Kultur des Trinkens* (Munich, 1990), 186–93.

Johannes Kalitsunakis, ''Οψον und ὀψάριον' in *Festschrift für Paul W. Kretschmer Beiträge zur griechischen und lateinischen Sprachforschung* (Vienna etc., 1926), 96–106.

R. Kassel and C. Austin eds, *Poetae Comici Graeci* (Berlin/New York, 1983–) [=K-A].

Eva Keuls, *The Reign of the Phallus* (Second edn., Berkeley, 1993).

Ursula Knigge, *Der Kerameikos von Athen* (Deutsches Archäol. Inst. Athen, 1988).

T. Kock ed., *Comicorum Atticorum Fragmenta* (Leipzig, 1880–88) [=K].

A. Koerte ed., *Menander II Reliquiae apud veteres scriptores servatae* (Leipzig, 1953).

Igor Kopytoff, 'The cultural biography of things: commoditization as process' in Arjun Appadurai ed., *The Social Life of Things* (Cambridge, 1986), pp. 64–91.

W. K. Lacey, *The Family in Ancient Greece* (London, 1968).

S. I. Landau, *Dictionaries. The Art and Craft of Lexicography* (New York, 1984).

Mabel Lang, 'Numerical notation on Greek vases', *Hesperia* 25 (1956), 1–24.

H. G. Levine, 'The Discovery of Addiction. Changing Conceptions of Habitual Drunkenness in America', *Journal of Studies on Alcohol* 39.1 (1978), 143–74.

David Lewis, *Sparta and Persia* (Leiden, 1977).

—'The King's Dinner' in Heleen Sancisi-Weerdenburg and Amélie Kuhrt eds, *Achaemenid History Workshop II The Greek Sources* (Leiden, 1987), pp. 79–87.

Hans Licht, *Sittengeschichte Griechenlands* (Dresden/Zurich 1925), English trans., *Sexual Life in Ancient Greece* (London, 1932).

H. Lind, 'Ein Hetärenhaus am Heiligen Tor?', *Mus. Helv.* 45 (1988), 158–169.

A. W. Lintott, *Violence, Civil-strife, and Revolution in the Classical City* (London, 1982).

J. H. Lipsius, *Das Attische Recht und Rechtsverfahren* (Leipzig 1912).

François Lissarrague, *Un Flot d'Images: une esthétique du banquet grec* (Paris, 1987), English trans., *The Aesthetics of the Greek Banquet* (Princeton, 1990).

BIBLIOGRAPHY

—'Un Rituel du Vin: la Libation' in O. Murray and M.Tecuşan eds, *In Vino Veritas* (British School at Rome, 1995), pp. 126–144.

A. B. Lloyd, *Herodotus Book II. A Commentary* (Leiden, 1976).

Pierre Louis ed., Aristotle, *Problemata* (Paris, 1991).

D. M. MacDowell, '*Hubris* in Athens', *G & R* 23 (1976), 14–31.
—'Bastards as Athenian citizens', *CQ* 70 (1976), 87–91.

Paul Millett, 'Sale, credit and exchange in Athenian law and society' in Paul Cartledge, Paul Millett and Stephen Todd eds, *NOMOS. Essays in Athenian Law, Politics and Society* (Cambridge, 1990), pp. 167–94.
—*Lending and Borrowing in Ancient Athens* (Cambridge, 1991).

Oswyn Murray, 'The Symposion in History' in E. Gabba ed., *Tria Corda: Scritti in onore di Arnaldo Momigliano* (Como, 1983), pp. 257–72.
—ed., *Sympotica. A Symposium on the Symposion* (Oxford, 1990).
—'The Affair of the Mysteries: Democracy and the Drinking Group' in O. Murray ed., *Sympotica. A Symposium on the Symposion* (Oxford, 1990), pp. 149–61.
—'War and the Symposium' in William J. Slater ed., *Dining in a Classical Context* (Ann Arbor, 1991), pp. 83–104.
—'Greek Man and Forms of Sociality' in J-P. Vernant ed., *The Greeks* (Chicago, 1995), pp. 218–53.
—and M. Tecuşan eds, *In Vino Veritas* (British School at Rome, 1995).

H.-G. Nesselrath, *Die Attische Mittlere Komödie: Ihre Stellung in der antiken Literaturkritik und Literaturgeschichte* (Berlin, 1990).

M. P. Nilsson, 'Die Götter des Symposions' in *Opuscula Selecta* I (Lund, 1951), pp. 428–42.

J. Ober, *Mass and Elite in Democratic Athens* (Princeton, 1989).

D. Ogden, *Greek Bastardy* (Oxford, 1996).

Robin Osborne, 'The erection and mutilation of the *Hermai*', *PCPhS* 31 (1985), 47–73.
—*Classical Landscape with Figures* (London, 1987).

Pauline Schmitt Pantel, 'Les Repas au Prytanée et à la Tholos dans l'Athènes classique', *Annali, Istituto orientale di Napoli. Archeologia e storia antica.* 2 (1980), 55–68.
—*La cité au banquet* (École Française de Rome, 1992).

U. E. Paoli, 'Note giuridiche sul Δύσκολος di Menandro', *Mus. Helv.* 18 (1961).
—'Il reato di adulterio in diritto Attico' in *Altri Studi di Diritto Greco e Romano* (Milan, 1976) 253ff [=*SDHI* 16 (1950), 123ff].

H. W. Parke, *Festivals of the Athenians* (London, 1977).

H. N. Parker, 'Love's Body Anatomized: The Ancient Erotic Handbooks and the Rhetoric of Sexuality' in Amy Richlin ed, *Pornography and Representation in Greece and Rome* (Oxford, 1992), pp. 90–111.

Robert Parker, *Miasma* (Oxford, 1983).

Franz Passow, *Ueber Zweck, Anlage und Ergänzung griechischer Wörterbücher* (Berlin, 1812).

Cynthia Patterson, 'Those Athenian Bastards!', *Class. Antiq.* (1990), 39–73.

G. Ferrari Pinney, 'For the Heroes are at Hand', *JHS* 104 (1984), 181–2.

W. Pritchett, 'The Attic Stelai II', *Hesperia* 25 (1956), 178–317.

Sitta von Reden, *Exchange in Ancient Greece* (London, 1995).

Carola Reinsberg, *Ehe, Hetärentum und Knabenliebe im antiken Griechenland* (Munich, 1989)

P. J. Rhodes, 'Bastards as Athenian citizens', *CQ* 72 (1978), 89–92.
—*A Commentary on the Aristotelian Athenaion Politeia* (Oxford, 1981).

Amy Richlin ed., *Pornography and Representation in Greece and Rome* (Oxford, 1992).

Carl Robert, *Archaeologische Hermeneutik* (Berlin, 1919).

G. Rodenwaldt, 'Spinnende Hetären', *AA* 47 (1932), 7–22.

L. E. Rossi, 'Il simposio greco arcaico come spettacolo a se stesso', *Spettacoli conviviali dall'antichità classica alle corti italiane del' 400: Atti del VII convegno di studio* (Viterbo, 1983), pp. 41–50.

J. Rudhardt, *Notions fondamentales de la pensée religieuse et actes constitutifs du culte dans la Grèce classique* (second edn. Paris, 1992).

E. Ruschenbusch, *Solonos Nomoi: Die Fragmente des Solonischen Gesetzeswerkes mit einer Text- und Überlieferungsgeschichte [Historia Einzelschriften Bd. 9]* (Wiesbaden, 1966).

J. B. Salmon, *Wealthy Corinth* (Oxford, 1984).

François Salviat, 'Le vin de Thasos, amphores, vin et sources écrites' in J.-Y. Empéreur and Y. Garlan, eds, *Recherches sur les Amphores Grecques* (École Française d'Athènes, 1986), pp. 145–96.

F. Salviat and C. Vatin, *Inscriptions de Grèce Centrale* (Paris, 1971).

F. de Saussure, *Cours de linguistique génerale* (Second edn. Paris, 1922).

D. M. Schaps, *Economic Rights of Women in Ancient Greece* (Edinburgh 1979).
—'Comic inflation in the market-place', *Scripta Classica Israelica* 8–9 (1985–8), 66–73.

K. Schauenburg, '*Eurumedon eimi*', *AM* (1990), 107–22.

Wilhelm Schulze, *Quaestiones Epicae* (Gütesloh, 1892).

Robin Seager, 'Alcibiades and the charge of aiming at tyranny', *Historia* 16 (1967).

R. Sealey, *Women and Law in Classical Greece* (Chapel Hill, 1990).

Charles Seltman, *Women in Greek Society* (London, 1953).

T. Leslie Shear Jr., 'The Athenian Agora: Excavations of 1973–4', *Hesperia* 44 (1975), 331–74.

Georg Simmel, *Die Philosophie des Geldes* (Second edn. Berlin, 1907), English trans., *The Philosophy of Money* (London, 1978).

—'Die Koketterie' in *Philosophische Kultur: Gesammelte Essais* (Third edn. Potsdam, 1923), translated by Guy Oakes, in *Georg Simmel: On Women, Sexuality, and Love* (New Haven, 1984), pp. 133–52.

W. Slater, 'Symposion at Sea', *HSCP* 80 (1976), 161–70.

—ed., *Dining in a Classical Context* (Ann Arbor, 1991).

B. Sparkes, 'Illustrating Aristophanes', *JHS* 95 (1975), 133–52.

Stephen Todd, *The Shape of Athenian Law* (Oxford, 1993).

K. Tsantsanoglou, 'Memoirs of a Lady from Samos', *ZPE* 12 (1973), 183–95.

E. G. Turner, 'The lost beginning of Menander, *Misoumenos*', *Proceedings of the British Academy* 73 (1977), 315–31.

J. -P. Vernant, *Myth and Society in Ancient Greece* (London, 1980).

Paul Veyne, *Le pain et le cirque* (Paris, 1976).

G. Vlastos, 'Socratic Irony', *CQ* 37 (1987), 79–96.

Susan Walker, 'Women and Housing in Classical Greece' in A. Cameron and A. Kuhrt eds, *Images of Women in Antiquity* (Beckenham, Kent 1983), pp. 81–91.

T. B. L. Webster, *Studies in Later Greek Comedy* (Manchester, 1953).

—*An Introduction to Menander* (Manchester, 1974).

Fritz Wehrli, *Die Schule des Aristoteles* (Basel, 1944–74).

David Whitehead, *The Ideology of the Athenian Metic* (Cambridge, 1977).

Molly Whittaker, 'The Comic fragments in their relation to the structure of Old Attic Comedy', *CQ* 29 (1935), 181–91.

Dyfri Williams, 'Women on Athenian vases: problems of interpretation' in A. Cameron and A. Kuhrt eds, *Images of Women in Antiquity* (London, 1983), pp. 92–106.

John J. Winkler, *The Constraints of Desire* (New York, 1990).

—'The Ephebes' Song: *Tragoidia* and *Polis*' in John J. Winkler and Froma T. Zeitlin eds, *Nothing to Do with Dionysos? Athenian Drama in its Social Context* (Princeton, 1990), pp. 20–62.

H. J. Wolff, 'Marriage law and family organisation in ancient Athens', *Traditio* 2 (1944), 43–95.

R. E. Wycherley, *The Athenian Agora III Literary and Epigraphical Testimonia* (Princeton, 1957).

W. Wyse, *The Speeches of Isaeus* (Cambridge, 1904).

Netta Zagagi, *Tradition and Originality in Plautus* [=*Hypomnemata 62*] (Göttingen, 1980).

—'A note on *munus, munus fungi* in Early Latin', *Glotta* 60 (1982), 280–81.

—'Amatory Gifts and Payments: A Note on *munus, donum, data* in Plautus', *Glotta* 65 (1987), 121–32.

—'Obligations in Amatory Payments and Gift-giving', *Hermes* 115 (1987), 503–4.

Robert Zahn, 'Kleinigkeiten aus Alt-Athen', *Antike I* (1925), 273–85.

Index

Caesar

Christian Meier

'Meier's is a compulsively readable, scholarly, imaginative, and almost poetic account.' PETER JONES, *Sunday Telegraph*

James Boswell called him 'the greatest man of any age'. As politician and diplomat, writer and lover, but above all as a military genius, Julius Caesar is one of the most perennially fascinating figures in history. Christian Meier's biography is the definitive, modern account of Caesar's life and career, and places him within the wider context of the crisis of the Roman republic. Written specifically for a general readership, this authoritative, stimulating book serves, amongst other things, as a reminder to those who believe that men are mere servants of historical forces that the great individual still has an unarguably significant part to play.

'Meier's Caesar goes well beyond the confines of biography to present a radical analysis of a political system in decline, and the opportunities it afforded one of the most brilliant and unscrupulous individuals of all time.' JOAN SMITH, *Independent on Sunday*

ISBN 000 686349 3

FontanaPress
An Imprint of HarperCollins*Publishers*